Verwoerd
Architect of Apartheid

VERWOERD
ARCHITECT OF APARTHEID

HENRY KENNEY

New Introduction by David Welsh

JONATHAN BALL PUBLISHERS
Johannesburg & Cape Town

First published in hardback in South Africa by Jonathan Ball, 1980
This edition published in 2016 by
JONATHAN BALL PUBLISHERS
A division of Media24 Limited
PO Box 33977
Jeppestown
2043

ISBN 978-1-86842-716-1
ebook ISBN 978-1-86842-717-8

*Every effort has been made to trace the copyright holders and to obtain their permission
for the use of copyright material. The publishers apologise for any errors or omissions
and would be grateful to be notified of any corrections that should be incorporated in
future editions of this book.*

Twitter: www.twitter.com/JonathanBallPub
Facebook: www.facebook.com/JonathanBallPublishers
Blog: http://jonathanball.bookslive.co.za/

All photographs reproduced by kind permission of South African Associated
Newspapers, the Argus Group and the South African Broadcasting Corporation.

Cover photo by GREATSTOCK/Corbis
Cover by publicide
Design and typesetting by Pointset (Pty) Ltd, Randburg, and Purple Pocket Solutions,
    Cape Town
Printed and bound by CTP Printers, Cape Town
Set in 11 pt on 13 pt Times New Roman

Contents

Preface

This book is an appraisal of Hendrik Verwoerd's career in the context of his times. For a man who so dominated South Africa in his heyday, surprisingly little has been written about Verwoerd. There are two book-length studies, each highly unsatisfactory. One is by the former South African Labour M.P., now living in exile, Alex Hepple, and appeared the year after his death. It is readable, partisan, inaccurate and portrays Verwoerd as an authoritarian racist who could not change. At the other extreme is an effort which is so different from Hepple's that one wonders at times whether it is about the same man. Perhaps the flavour of G.D. Scholtz's two-volume, 600-page labour of love can best be conveyed by saying that it should have been subtitled *The Man Who was Never Wrong*.

Now, more than a decade after Verwoerd's death, there should be room for a relatively detached assessment of his contribution to our history. This is both a work of synthesis and analysis. It is a synthesis because it is based on the numerous secondary sources now available, contemporary newspapers and parliamentary debates. The pedants who may complain that this is not a work of "original research" will be correct – but irrelevant. This is not the kind of book I have tried to write, and I freely concede that the definitive work on Verwoerd still lies in the future. It is an analysis because I have tried to clarify, at least for myself, some of the main issues of South African history in this century. Sadly, some of the most widely cited and seriously considered interpretations of our recent past have been by "radical" writers, who have been treated with more respect than they deserve by historians at our English-speaking universities. Marxist jargon seems to have an endless capacity to confuse and intimidate. I have addressed myself to the issues raised by "class analysis"; I am sure I have left no doubt about what I think of this way of rewriting history.

I wish to thank my friends and former colleagues, Brian Kantor and David Rees, for commenting on parts of the manuscript, for frequent discussions, and for encouragement when the going was not too easy.

My father's encouragement was continuous and often strenuous. He contributed in other ways which can hardly be enumerated in a preface.

I also wish to thank Alison Lowry for her editorial work, in spite of the occasional act of censorship, for which I forgive her.

Finally, I was granted interviews by some prominent public figures concerning their impressions of Verwoerd. I do not know whether all of them would appreciate being mentioned in this preface. I have decided to take no chances, but am grateful to them all for their courtesy.

Introduction to the 2016 edition

Henry Kenney's appraisal of H.F. Verwoerd, originally published in 1980, has stood the test of time as one of the best books written about a South African politician. It is a far better book than the hagiographic two-volume biography by G.D. Scholtz or the tendentious account by Alex Hepple. The merit of Kenney's book is its balance and its accuracy. To this writer's knowledge, no reviewer or other critic has been able to find a serious fault or omission. The republication 50 years after Verwoerd's death comes at an appropriate time, enabling the reader to realise what apartheid meant, and how far South Africa has since changed. In his lifetime Verwoerd enjoyed a large cult following. By 2016 their numbers have dwindled into insignificance. Rather than "solving" the racial issue, Verwoerd compounded it, leaving later generations with the massive problem of repairing the damage.

The subtitle *Architect of Apartheid* needs qualification. Some years before Verwoerd's entry into politics, the design of apartheid had been sketched, and principles had been laid down. Verwoerd's role was more that of master-builder than architect. This is not to deny that Verwoerd added distinct touches to the design.

Dr Nico Smith, a Dutch Reformed Church clergyman, quoted Verwoerd as saying that he wanted to implant the concept of apartheid so deeply into society that no future government would be able to undo what had been done.[1] Smith did not provide details of when and where he heard this, but it may well have been at a meeting of the Afrikaner Broederbond, of which both he and Verwoerd were members. (Smith later resigned from the Broederbond and became a doughty opponent of apartheid.)

Whether Verwoerd's boast, as reported by Smith, will be realised, if only in part, remains to be seen.

* * * * *

Hendrik Frensch Verwoerd was born in the Netherlands in September 1901.[2] His parents were strong supporters of the Boer cause in the Anglo-Boer War, so much so that they decided to emigrate to South Africa, arriving in November 1903. The young Verwoerd grew up in a household that was fervently pro-Afrikaner. Verwoerd senior, a building contractor by profession, was a devout Christian, eager to undertake missionary work for the Nederduitse Gereformeerde Kerk (N.G.K.).

After some years in Cape Town, whose white population was predominantly English-speaking, the family moved to Rhodesia in 1914. Hendrik, who had spent over a year at Wynberg Boys' High School, was now enrolled at Milton High School, near Bulawayo. He shone as a pupil – and even played the quintessentially English game of cricket! But he disliked the imperial atmosphere of the school, and avoided singing the (British) national anthem.

His stellar performance resulted in the headmaster's offering him a bursary, which he declined, since the family had been called to the Orange Free State by the Church. The headmaster took a dim view of this, deeming the Free Staters to be "those rebels" and chasing Verwoerd out of his office. One asset derived from his years in English-medium schools was an ability to speak fluent English.

In the Orange Free State, the Verwoerds found themselves in a thoroughly Afrikaans environment, and Hendrik attended an Afrikaans school in which he flourished, passing the matriculation examination with the top marks in the province.

Verwoerd's intention was to study Theology at Stellenbosch University, where he enrolled in 1919. His progress was rapid: a BA degree in 1921 and an MA in 1922, both *cum laude*. By 1924 he had completed his doctoral dissertation entitled "The Blunting of the Emotions" (translation). By this time, his intellectual interest had switched to Psychology. Nevertheless he had applied to the N.G.K. authorities to enter the Theological Seminary. There are differing accounts of the fate of his application, both of which agree on Verwoerd's stubbornness in refusing to cooperate with his interlocutors. Piet Meiring recounts his father, P.G.J. Meiring, chairman of the examining board for aspirant candidates, asking Verwoerd the standard question of why he wanted to enter the ministry. Verwoerd responded that this was his business and no concern of the board. Meiring senior was infuriated, and sharply rebuked him, whereupon Verwoerd withdrew his application. Dominee Meiring was furious, subsequently describing Verwoerd as "cleverer than is good for him".[3]

In spite of this episode, Verwoerd seems to have remained within the Christian fold, although not a regular churchgoer, possibly because of pressure of work. He never, however, invoked supposedly biblical legitimations of apartheid in his speeches.

He was actively involved in student affairs, becoming chairman of the Student Council in 1923 and being active in the debating society. As the "cradle of Afrikaner nationalism", the student environment consolidated his political views. His strong opposition to white/black contact was evident. Moreover, his concern with the poor white problem had been sharply increased by his first-hand observation of poor white living conditions in slums near Cape Town. He was horrified to discover that white and Coloured families were living in the same houses. No wonder, he concluded, that young Afrikaners could see no objection to marrying their former playmates.[4]

In addition to these extramural interests, Verwoerd made rapid progress up the academic hierarchy: he was made a temporary assistant in Psychology in 1923, a lecturer in 1924, and professor at the end of 1927. It was an astounding ascent, which, without casting doubts on his ability, probably owed something to the university's eagerness to appoint bright young Afrikaners to senior positions. Remarkably, Verwoerd switched disciplines, becoming Professor of Sociology in 1932.

The publication, in 1932, of *The Poor White Problem in South Africa: Report of the Carnegie Commission* found that in 1929/30, conservatively over 300 000 whites, mostly Afrikaners, out of a total white population of some 1.8 million, were "very poor". The severe drought and economic depression of the early 1930s substantially increased the numbers of very poor people. Their lack of skills and low educational standards meant that they could hardly compete against poor blacks (whose numbers were even larger). The Carnegie Commission recommended that poor whites be protected against this competition, but "merely as a measure of transition" for a period in which the poor white could adapt himself to new conditions.[5]

The poor white problem, with which Verwoerd already had acquaintance, created the opportunity for him to launch himself on the national stage. This occurred in 1934 when the N.G.K. organised a *volkskongres* on the problem. Verwoerd was a dominant figure in the proceedings. The core of his paper read: "If someone has to be unemployed, a white man or a native, it is best in the current circumstances and with the existing differences in living standards more economical for the nation that the native should be unemployed."[6]

The justification for Verwoerd's proposal was hard to follow, but it chimed with popular white sentiment – and helped to boost his reputation as a rising star in Afrikaner nationalism. He was appointed deputy chairman of the Congress's continuation committee, and successfully pressed the United Party government to establish a Department of Social Welfare.

Another notable feature of Verwoerd's contribution was his repudiation of the popular nostrum that the solution of the problem was sending poor whites "back to the land": they should be rehabilitated where the greatest chance of success existed, namely, in the urban areas.[7]

* * * * *

By the mid-1930s it was becoming even clearer that Verwoerd saw his future as lying in *volksdiens* – service to the (Afrikaner) *volk* – and it was no giant leap to recognise, in South Africa's circumstances, that involvement in politics was the best strategy.

His opportunity arrived in a roundabout way.[8] It was apparent to the Nationalist leadership that Fusion in 1934 (the joining together of Smuts's South African Party and General J.B.M. Hertzog's National Party to form the United Party) had devastated the NP in the Transvaal. Indeed, in the 1938 election the NP won only a single seat, held by the redoubtable J.G. Strijdom. It was no less apparent to the NP leader, D.F. Malan, that the centre of political gravity in the country was shifting to the Transvaal. Without a sizeable contingent of Transvaal MPs, the NP had little hope of winning a general election.

A small group of Cape Nationalists (meeting on a train in 1935) concluded that without a pro-NP Afrikaans daily newspaper in the Transvaal the possibility of a breakthrough was slender. The solution? To establish such a newspaper, which was achieved in 1937 after a struggle to raise the capital necessary for such a venture. Much of the money derived from Cape sources.

Paul Sauer, a Nationalist MP and a confidant of Malan, suggested Verwoerd as the founding editor of *Die Transvaler*, as the newspaper was named. By 1936–37 Verwoerd was widely known in Nationalist circles: he had become a member of the Broederbond and was also a leading figure in anti-Semitic agitation.

Verwoerd did not require much persuasion to leave the relatively cloistered isolation of academia and ply his skills where he believed them to be most needed. Like D.F. Malan (founding editor of *De Burger* in 1915), Verwoerd had no journalistic experience. Sauer had suggested that he be appointed as assistant editor so that he could devote more time to party matters, but Verwoerd, self-confident as always, would not hear of this. He did, however, undertake to take a crash course in journalism at *Die Burger*'s offices in Cape Town. Essentially, however, Verwoerd never learned the journalist's craft; with the connivance of the NP, he saw his primary role as a polemicist for the party. Much of his time would be devoted to party activity.

Strijdom, the leading figure in the Transvaal NP, was at first hesitant about Verwoerd's appointment, fearing that he was one of those "liberal" Cape Nationalists who lacked the fiery republicanism that Strijdom himself displayed. The new editor soon showed that these apprehensions were misplaced. From the start of his editorship Verwoerd's republicanism rivalled Strijdom's – which caused some concern to Malan, who was anxious not to offend Afrikaners whose commitment to a republic was at best uncertain. Indeed, he had hoped that, as a Cape man, Verwoerd would do precisely what Strijdom feared.

Verwoerd's editorial in the first issue of *Die Transvaler*, on 1 October 1937, was unambiguous in laying out the role he envisaged for the newspaper: "*Die Transvaler* comes with a calling. It comes to serve the *volk*, to make the sound of true and exalted [*verhewe*] nationalism reverberate as far as its voice can reach. Its inspiration will flow from this calling; the struggle will determine its character [translation]."

In a further article in a supplement, Verwoerd addressed a topical theme among Transvaal Nationalists: the Jewish "question". Jews, he claimed, had established themselves as a separate group with indifferent, even hostile, attitudes to the national aspirations of Afrikaners. Their dominance in trade and industry made it difficult for Afrikaners to acquire their rightful share. It followed that Verwoerd was staunchly opposed to Jewish immigration from Nazi Germany. The reaction of the Jewish community was swift: Jewish advertisers boycotted *Die Transvaler*, thereby denying it much revenue that it desperately required.[9] For some time thereafter advertising contributed no more than 15 per cent to the newspaper's income – far less than a prospectively profitable newspaper should receive.

Undeterred, Verwoerd laid down political criteria for the acceptance of advertisements: no recruiting advertisements for the Union Defence Force would be accepted; and readers were urged not to patronise shops that did not advertise in *Die Transvaler*.[10]

The Second World War greatly exacerbated tensions between Afrikaners and English-speaking whites, but also among Afrikaners. Pro-Nazi groups such as the Greyshirts, New Order and others arose. Most important was the *Ossewabrandwag* (OB, or Oxwagon Guard), led by a self-confessed pro-Nazi, J.F.J. van Rensburg. The forces of Afrikaner nationalism were divided, and by 1941, when it appeared as if a German victory was probable, the divisions seemed unbridgeable. The attempted reunification of Hertzog's followers and the NP broke down amid acrimony, and when the OB, with which an uneasy coexistence had been brokered, cut loose and threatened the NP's political dominance of Afrikaner nationalism, the gloves came off.[11]

Vain attempts were made to create a unified Afrikanerdom throughout 1941–42. Verwoerd viewed these efforts with concern. He believed that real unity must be based squarely on NP principles: compromises would be fatal. To him it appeared that Malan, in his efforts to accommodate Hertzog, was watering down his (mild) republican convictions. The issue was resolved when the entire *hereniging* (reunification) was aborted. The disagreement with Malan, however, left its scars.

Initially Verwoerd welcomed the advent of the OB, seeing it as a channel for attracting young people to the cause, but he was adamant that the sole responsibility for political affairs resided with the NP. Unlike a number of senior NP figures, Verwoerd never joined the OB, although his wife did and attained the rank of *kommandant*.

During 1941, relations between the NP and the OB deteriorated steadily and eventually broke down altogether in September. In his editorials, Verwoerd made clear his rejection of the OB's tactics and the Nazi tendencies of some in the leadership, notably Van Rensburg: totalitarian dictatorship was unacceptable to Afrikaners. Equally deplorable were the attacks on individuals committed by the *Stormjaers*, a strong-arm unit associated with the OB. In response to Verwoerd's attacks, two attempts to kidnap – and either beat up or even kill him – were made, the first on 22 September 1941, and the second late in 1944.[12]

It was not only pro-Nazi ideologies that caused Verwoerd concern; he feared also that he might be interned under the wartime emergency regulations, and took steps to ensure his family's welfare.[13] It is doubtful, however, whether the Smuts government had any such intention. Verwoerd had made it clear, as had the NP, that political change could be achieved only by constitutional methods.

This view, however, did not prevent Verwoerd from an entanglement with the law, albeit on his own initiative. In an editorial on 31 October

1941, *The Star* (Johannesburg) accused *Die Transvaler* of "Speaking up for Hitler", claiming that Verwoerd was making propaganda for the "evil forces" of Nazism. Verwoerd took umbrage and decided, without consulting the proprietors of *Die Transvaler*, Voortrekkerpers, to sue *The Star* and its proprietors for libel. Judge P.A. Millin of the Supreme Court found that indeed Verwoerd had been a propagandist for Nazism, and that no libel had been committed. Costs were awarded against Verwoerd, and these were heavy, far beyond his ability to pay. Fortunately for him, both Voortrekkerpers and Nasionale Pers (proprietor of *Die Burger*), together with some admirers, put up the funds. Malan considered that Verwoerd had acted unwisely by not separating his editorship from his personal views, but he acknowledged that Judge Millin did not understand the Afrikaner struggle.[14]

It was noted at the time that Millin was Jewish, spoke no Afrikaans and was mildly liberal – a combination of attributes unlikely to have allowed Afrikaner nationalists to believe him capable of delivering a fair judgment against a leading Afrikaner nationalist in an essentially political case. Verwoerd's counsel wanted him to appeal, but after consultation, presumably with the directors of Voortrekkerpers, it was decided not to do so.

Years later, in 1948, by which time Verwoerd was in the Senate and opposition members taunted him with the judgment, Verwoerd responded by challenging his critics to page through *Die Transvaler*'s editorials, which showed how "we attacked National Socialism in the strongest and most unambiguous words" (translation).[15]

Far from damaging Verwoerd's standing in the ranks of Transvaal Nationalists, the case enhanced his and the newspaper's reputation as doughty fighters for Afrikaner interests; but more cautious Nationalists, like Malan and other leading Cape Nationalists, were no doubt confirmed in their view of his impetuousness. But his sheer intellectual ability and value as a propagandist trumped the doubts.

By the early 1940s, Verwoerd was well entrenched as a leading figure in the Transvaal Nationalist hierarchy. He and J.G. Strijdom, who was leader of the provincial party and chairman of Voortrekkerpers, formed a formidable combination. Much of Verwoerd's activity was political work. Moreover, he was active in the Broederbond, becoming a member of its *Uitvoerende Raad* (Executive Council) in 1940, and serving on it until 1950, when his appointment as Minister of Native Affairs required his resignation. He continued to participate in its ordinary activities.

Only a few glimpses of Verwoerd's activities in the Broederbond appear in its official history, written by E.L.P. Stals.[16] In December 1943, however, the state's intelligence service managed to bug a plenary meeting held in Bloemfontein, attended by some 300 members. According to E.G. Malherbe's account, Verwoerd is reputed to have said that "[T]he Afrikaner Broederbond must gain control of everything it can lay its hand on in every walk of life in South Africa. Members must help each other to gain promotion in the Civil Service or any other field of activity in which they work with a view to working themselves up into important administrative positions."[17]

Unsurprisingly, no confirmation of this and other speeches was forthcoming, least of all from the Broederbond itself. But the statement was never denied.

An abortive Broederbond initiative in which Verwoerd was involved was the Afrikaner *Eenheidskomitee* (Unity Committee), set up in 1940 in an attempt to coordinate the various factions of Afrikanerdom. During 1940 it produced a draft republican constitution, mostly the work of Professor L.J. du Plessis and Verwoerd.[18] The draft included a clause recommending that Afrikaans be made the official language, with English relegated to the second language. The draft was never accepted by the NP. Malan would almost certainly have rejected it, but his allowing it to be regarded as a basis for discussion gave the OB the opportunity to disseminate it. It was to cause the NP embarrassment, despite their disavowals.[19] Verwoerd's involvement in producing the draft was, to this writer's knowledge, never publicly revealed.

P.J. Meyer, a member of the Broederbond's Uitvoerende Raad from 1952 to 1972 (as chairman from 1960 to 1972) was a powerful figure in Transvaal Nationalist politics who knew Verwoerd well. His view was that Verwoerd regarded his membership of the Broederbond as a secondary interest, his primary focus being on the political struggle. According to Meyer, he never showed the slightest inclination to transform the Broederbond into a *stut-organisasie* (support organisation) of the NP. Other parties who sought to do so were similarly denied. Meyer claims that, in 1942, Verwoerd accused him, then assistant secretary of the Broederbond, of being too partial to the OB.[20]

The general election on 7 July 1943 was a "khaki" election, being contested during wartime. On the face of it, the Smuts government won a huge victory that contributed to the complacency of the United Party, which was to prove fatal in the 1948 election. The NP won only 43 seats, compared with 27 in 1938, but the number of votes it won increased from 247,582 in 1938 to 316,320 (35.8 per cent of the total vote). Moreover, it won 11 seats in the Transvaal, suggesting that Strijdom's and Verwoerd's efforts had borne some fruit.

Malan had regarded the election as an opportunity to establish the NP as the main political front of Afrikaner nationalism; and he had largely succeeded, having rejected offers of electoral pacts from the Afrikaner Party (the small residue of Hertzog's followers) and the OB. Several thousand OB followers opted to boycott the election, as did Oswald Pirow's New Order. It is impossible to estimate how many seats this cost the NP.

Malan, nevertheless, derived some comfort from the possibility that wartime governments frequently fell after the conclusion of war, and that he could henceforth attack the United Party government as *volksleier* (people's leader) of a unified Afrikaner nationalism. The Afrikaner Party had been comprehensively eliminated as a political force, and the OB, although still dangerous, was beginning its downward spiral.

By 1943 the tide of war was turning against Germany, and the possibility that a German victory would hasten the advent of the republic was fading. While Verwoerd had been convinced that the defeat of Britain would make attainment of a republic easier, he declined to link the two possibilities.[21]

The tenor of Verwoerd's republicanism can be gauged from an editorial in December 1943: "One fact must be very clearly understood. There can be no true republic inside the British Empire. That would only mean that the Governor-General would be renamed as President and that he would be elected rather than appointed. Regarding the nature of the state, its social and economic relationship with Britain, the relationship between population groups and to internal policy differences and the solution of the country's problem no difference would be made. The republican ideal's fulfilment cannot mean only the achievement of complete constitutional independence, but also requires radical economic reform in the interests of the ordinary person and the country as a whole. That is not possible within the capitalist British Empire [translation]."[22]

The comment reflected the rejection of what radical Nationalists termed the evils of "British-Jewish capitalist democracy".

Apart from the republican issue, Verwoerd found plenty of opportunities to flay the lacklustre Smuts government, which, apart from Smuts himself and a few others, was notable for its mediocrity. The cabinet, said Verwoerd, consisted of "imperialists and Anglicised Afrikaners".[23]

Much of *Die Transvaler*'s editorial comment targeted the racial issue, and every instance of racial "mixing" – in parks, on tennis courts, in universities, army units and elsewhere – was denounced as compromises that would lead to racial "equalisation" and, ultimately, to *verbastering* (miscegenation).

Verwoerd maintained his concern for poor whites, even as rising prosperity in the late 1930s and during the war years was reducing the scale of the problem. Urbanisation, however, was a "natural and un-avoidable process". The entry into commerce and industry could contri-bute to Afrikaner self-reliance. He pointed out that reluctance to accept urbanisation as permanent disadvantaged Afrikaners in entering urban occupations, and hindered the *verafrikaansing* (Afrikanerisation) of trade unions.[24]

Verwoerd's decision in 1947 not to report any news about the Royal tour was controversial. He ignored Strijdom's opposition. He believed, probably with some justice, that Smuts, who had invited the Royal Family, did so in the hope of gaining political advantage, but also to express his thanks to King George VI for his support during the war.[25] Whether Verwoerd's gesture resonated among diehard Nationalists, or whether Smuts gained any more votes, cannot be known.

* * * * *

By 1947 anticipation of the following year's election was mounting. Although few, including Malan, anticipated a victory, some of the omens were auspicious: the NP had won four by-elections between 1943 and 1948, and reduced United Party majorities in others. Moreover, it was evident that public discontent with shortages of food and housing was widespread. It was probable that the NP would make significant gains, though, it was believed, falling short of a majority.

Verwoerd had been urged by some Nationalists to contest a seat in the 1943 election but Strijdom had insisted that his role as editor of *Die Transvaler* was more valuable. No such consideration applied in 1948 and, with the permission of the newspaper's directors, Verwoerd was nominated as NP candidate for Alberton, one of Johannesburg's southern suburbs, with a sizeable working-class population. He lost narrowly, by 171 votes, against the United Party's S.J.M. Steyn. A victorious NP candidate offered to stand back and allow Verwoerd to take his place, but Verwoerd declined because, he said, he had neither been nominated nor elected by the voters of the constituency in question, Ventersdorp.[26]

He had to be content with a seat in the Senate, in which he served until 1958. His ambition to become a member of the House of Assembly, nevertheless, remained strong.

There had been serious divisions in the NP prior to the election. The issue was Malan's decision to offer to cooperate with the Afrikaner Party, led by Klasie Havenga. Strijdom, supported by Verwoerd, took immediate umbrage, arguing that many OB members had moved to the Afrikaner Party as the OB itself declined. How, Strijdom argued, could the NP enter a pact with a party that welcomed pro-Nazis who rejected the idea of democracy? Malan, however, remained adamant, believing that, small though its support base might be, the Afrikaner Party could just tip the scales in favour of the NP. (Some maintained that a stayaway by OB supporters actually cost Verwoerd victory, but it is impossible to confirm this.)

Further wrangling was caused by the issue of which seats the Afrikaner Party should be allocated to contest. Whether the pact with the Afrikaner Party gave the NP the electoral edge cannot be conclusively confirmed, but seasoned politicians like Ben Schoeman believed this to be so.[27]

One consequence of the disagreement over the pact was a further deterioration of relations between Malan and Strijdom – Strijdom even threatened resignation as Transvaal leader unless he got his way. For the radical Transvalers, Malan's advocacy of the republic was too tepid, and his insistence that the republic should remain within the Commonwealth was unacceptable. For his part, Malan had not forgotten the destructive role that they, as well as some Free Staters, had played in eliminating Hertzog as a significant political force in the early 1940s. Nor was Malan prepared to accept the exclusivist brand of Afrikaner nationalism that they, especially Verwoerd, had propagated. Eager to pick up some English-speakers' votes, Malan insisted that the policy of equality between Afrikaans and English be maintained, and that the issue of the republic be downplayed in the election campaign. Furthermore, the anti-Semitism propagated by Verwoerd and, especially, Eric Louw was to be toned down (much to Louw's displeasure).

Further serious wrangling was caused by the issue of appointments to the new cabinet. This was the prerogative of the Prime Minister, but a Nationalist Prime Minister had to reckon with provincial sensitivities in the party. Since the NP had won more seats in the Transvaal (32 plus four Afrikaner Party seats), it seemed right to the Transvaal Nationalist hierarchy that they should receive the lion's share of posts – five. But this was not to be. Strijdom had reckoned that he, Verwoerd and Ben Schoeman were obvious choices, with Tom Naudé and De Wet Nel as others. Nel had been a party organiser and was a reputed expert on "the native problem". He was close to both Strijdom and Verwoerd.

Malan had other ideas: the Transvaal would receive only three posts, one of which would go to E.G. Jansen, leader of the NP in Natal, but an MP for a Transvaal constituency. Strijdom was outraged, and Verwoerd was *erg omgekrap* (seriously annoyed) at his omission. Schoeman wanted Strijdom to refuse a cabinet post unless Verwoerd was also included; if he did so then he, Schoeman, would decline to accept a post. Strijdom, however, responded that it would not be in the interests of the party. In any case, Verwoerd would certainly get his opportunity later.[28]

The opportunity came sooner than expected. Jansen owed his position as Minister of Native Affairs to Malan's controversial distribution of portfolios and to his having served in that capacity between 1929 and 1933. The mild-mannered Jansen lacked the fire and decisiveness necessary for the portfolio in the crucial period South Africa was entering. Moreover, he appeared to have shown little interest in Native Affairs between 1933 and 1948.

By 1949 some of the hardliners, led by De Wet Nel, were critical of Jansen's performance. He had botched his reaction to the Fagan Report (the Native Laws Commission) of 1948, and, worse, it became known that he was contemplating property rights for urban Africans, which flew in the face of the apartheid dogma that urban Africans were "temporary sojourners". Nel and his group appealed to Malan to replace Jansen with Verwoerd.[29]

Schoeman denies that Nel's delegation made much impression on Malan, but, in 1950, when Jansen was appointed Governor-General, he thought of replacing him as Minister of Native Affairs with his trusted Cape colleague, Paul Sauer, who had chaired a party commission on racial policy in 1947. Sauer, however, let it be known that he would resign rather than accept the portfolio.

Malan was shocked by Sauer's refusal and its accompanying threat. Who, then, should get Native Affairs, Malan asked Schoeman. Schoeman made a strong pitch for Verwoerd, conceding that he knew little about Africans, but praising his exceptional capability and energy. Malan acknowledged that he was intending to elevate Verwoerd to cabinet status, but in another portfolio. But he agreed to consider Schoeman's suggestion.[30] Verwoerd was duly appointed Minister of Native Affairs in

October 1950, a position he held until he became Prime Minister in 1958.

Before he left office, Jansen had made three important decisions: first, the appointment of W.W.M. Eiselen, the son of German missionaries, as Secretary for Native Affairs in 1949; second, setting up the Commission on Native Education (1949–1951), of which Eiselen was chairman, and De Wet Nel and other senior Nationalists were members; and third, setting up the Commission for the Socio-Economic Development of the Bantu Areas within the Union of South Africa, with F.R. Tomlinson, an agronomist, as chairman, and (inevitably?) De Wet Nel among its members. It reported in 1954.

Eiselen's previous career had been as a professor and thereafter chief inspector of African education for the Transvaal. His appointment as Secretary for Native Affairs was part of a concerted move to shift holdovers from the previous government, and to replace them with people committed to carrying out the new policy. Of the 26 senior officials in the department, only two had Afrikaans surnames – and both of them had alleged liberal tendencies. The Public Service Commission had refused to recommend Eiselen's appointment, but pressure from Jansen himself and some Nationalist MPs enabled the commission to be overridden.[31]

Eiselen's appointment was important for Verwoerd, whose knowledge of Africans was slight. As an ethnographer, virtually all of Eiselen's research concerned traditional institutions.[32] His principal focus was cultural, rather than racial, and his respect for traditional cultures was genuine.[33] The focus on these traditional cultures was exactly what Nationalists wanted, as they strove to shore up chieftainship and the communal occupation of land, and to demarcate ethnic divisions among Africans. That Africans, whether urban or rural, must retain a sense of ethnic (so-called tribal) identity would be a hallmark of Verwoerd's policy.

It is evident that Eiselen mentored Verwoerd, who described him as his "right hand". They had, moreover, been colleagues at Stellenbosch in earlier times. Fred Barnard, Verwoerd's private secretary, describes their working relationship: "For me it was always sheer delight to see these two in action; Verwoerd always in highest gear in front; Dr Eiselen always in lowest gear, the thinker, in the background. Hour after hour, until late at night, they could puzzle over a problem, debate and reason until a solution was found. Better cooperation over the years between these two workhorses could hardly be imagined [translation]."[34]

The essence of Verwoerd's approach was that Africans should be culturally anchored in the reserves, subsequently called "homelands". Development should take place in a matrix formed by tradition, but not stultified by it. The linchpin of the administrative system for Africans should be the traditional chieftainship (nowadays termed "traditional leadership"). The Bantu Authorities Act of 1951 sought to reinstate the authority of chiefs. The same legislation abolished the Natives Representative Council, whose elected members were educated people, some of whom belonged to the African National Congress (A.N.C.). The NP deemed them unrepresentative of the various African groups.

The strategy behind Verwoerd's plan is apparent in a long speech delivered in Parliament shortly after his appointment as Minister of Native Affairs:

> Up to now the native policy of the Union ... operated on the basis of two concepts of policy: the one depending on the recognition of the tribal system, as a static system, which would sooner or later disappear together with the Bantu national character of which it is the vehicle, and the other resting on the acceptance of the proposition that socio-economic progress of the Bantu people is only possible in its being linked up with Western-oriented forms of control. From that we should have had the result of more and more demands for complete political equality with the whites. That in turn would have brought with it eventual non-European domination ... [I]t is clear that the key to the true progress of the Bantu community as a whole and to the avoidance of a struggle for equality in a joint territory or in common political living areas lies in the recognition of the tribal system as the springboard from which the Bantu in a natural way, by enlisting the help of the dynamic elements in it, can increasingly rise to a higher level of culture and self-government on a foundation suitable to his own inherent character.[35]

It is clear that Verwoerd's policy derived less from solicitude for Africans' supposed "inherent character" than from an effort to protect white rule. Some Nationalists, mindful of earlier, post-1902 attempts by the British to anglicise Afrikaners, invoked official solicitude for traditional African culture as a well-intentioned attempt to protect Africans from "denationalisation" – the word used by Afrikaner nationalists. But any analogy between the Afrikaner and African experiences breaks down: Afrikaners had acquired the vote.

The "dynamic elements", referred to above by Verwoerd, had for the most part departed from their rural communities and headed for the cities. Nelson Mandela and Oliver Tambo are classic cases in point. The further consequence was that the urban areas would be the site of the most acute contestation between black and white, as had been the case with urbanising Afrikaners. For the NP it was critical that this potentially volatile situation be defused, and Verwoerd was the man to do so.

The view that urban Africans were "temporary sojourners" had had a long history. Despite its repudiation by Smuts and, more emphatically, by the Fagan Report in 1948, it was resurrected by the NP in its programme for the 1948 election. The size of the urban African population had increased dramatically during the war years, growing from 1.14 million in 1936 to 1.79 million, or by over 57 per cent, in 1946, thereby slightly outnumbering the white urban population.[36]

Verwoerd accepted existing estimates that one-third of the African population resided in each of the following areas: in the reserves, on the platteland and on white-owned farms, and in the urban areas. Apartheid, he claimed, acknowledged that a section of the urban population was "detribalised". However, "many so-called urbanised natives still have their roots in the native areas and have their tribal ties, many more than is usually appreciated".[37]

* * * * *

Henry Kenney's analysis of the legislation initiated by Verwoerd is comprehensive and needs no repetition here. What follows are brief analyses of the ideological contexts within which policies were implemented.

Fundamental to Verwoerd's thinking was a particular view of the distribution of land in South Africa. In a letter to Robert Menzies, the Australian Prime Minister, written in August 1960, he wrote:

> It must be remembered that both the Bantu and the White are foreign to South Africa. Each settled portions of what was, fundamentally, empty land. It has been the policy of the White man throughout the centuries to preserve the black man's areas for him, and during the last fifty years to add to it at the White man's expense. It is true that in the White man's areas large numbers of Bantu have been allowed to enter, at first as refugees from black tyrants for protection, later to seek work and food in order to escape poverty through their own lack of knowledge and initiative. Their numbers were further increased in those areas by health and other services. It is against all sense of justice and would be a form of bloodless conquest if the White man should now have to give away the political control of his country to those at present in his midst as a result of his humane and Christian treatment.[38]

Many whites shared this blinkered, self-serving view of history, despite the work of historians such as W.M. Macmillan and C.W. de Kiewiet, who had described the large-scale alienation of African land. This Xhosa lament tells the African side of the story: "When the white man came he had the Bible and we had the land; now we have the Bible and he has the land." By tradition, the reserves had served the twofold function of reservoirs of labour and standing pretexts for the withholding of political rights from Africans. "They have their own areas" now became the mantra of the white supremacist claim to continuing domination.

A major concern for Verwoerd in his first years as a minister was the attempt to "freeze" the number of Africans who were permanently domiciled in "white" urban areas. The principal instrument for achieving this was the massive tightening of influx control and the extension of passes, now called reference books, to women (see Kenney, pp. 169–170). Urban Africans, moreover, were to be divided along ethnic lines; freehold property rights (acquired decades before) were terminated, and secondary schools and other training facilities would henceforth have to be located in the homelands. As far as possible, African labour must be migratised.[39]

Verwoerd went even further, shortly after his appointment, proposing that legislation should be enacted that imposed a complete ban on Africans in the Witwatersrand, and particularly in the municipal area of Johannesburg. Ben Schoeman, then Minister of Labour, did not mince his words, declaring that such a measure would have a deadly effect on economic growth. Hard words were exchanged with Verwoerd, and Malan had to make peace. Verwoerd had to be content with the imposition of extreme measures of influx control.[40]

Further skirmishes with Verwoerd occurred a few years later, when J.G. Strijdom was Prime Minister. At an informal meeting of cabinet members, Verwoerd said that while he recognised that total territorial separation of Africans was impracticable, it could be put to "our people" as an ideal to be striven for; it would encourage them to support government policy even more strongly. Schoeman lashed out vigorously, deeming the proposal to be "blatant fraud" to which he would not be party. Again, hard words were exchanged, and this time Strijdom had to make peace.[41]

Yet another dispute arose when Verwoerd proposed that no Africans were to be allowed to work in the western Cape, where Coloured labour was to be exclusively used. Schoeman considered this to be a "stupid proposal", and that as far as he was concerned, the Railways would continue to employ Africans. Verwoerd was furious and accused Schoeman of always stabbing him in the back. Yet again, Strijdom had to act as peacemaker.[42]

In future years Schoeman and Verwoerd managed to put aside their differences, to the extent that Verwoerd even retained him in his cabinet after 1958 when he became Prime Minister. This was surprising: Schoeman was certain that he would be omitted, but Verwoerd told him that he was irreplaceable and urged him to let bygones by bygones.[43]

African education was another major target of Verwoerd's plan (see Kenney, pp. 155–161). There was a long tradition among Nationalists of antipathy towards African education; educated Africans tended to be more resentful of white domination and, moreover, the expansion of educational opportunities would diminish the supply of farm labour. Even the introduction of school feeding schemes was opposed.

The new dispensation, introduced in 1953 as the Bantu Education Act, sought to realign African education in accordance with the wider programme of apartheid. Previously, most African school education had been in the hands of missionaries under the general control of provincial education departments. Much the same was true of Fort Hare University College, established in 1915 under missionary auspices, which admitted not only Africans but also Coloured and Indian students (plus a handful of whites).

The allegation against the existing system, levelled by many Nationalists, including Verwoerd, was that it produced "Black Englishmen". Not only were they being severed from their ethnic traditions, but they were also liable to be in the forefront of those demanding equal rights. Moreover, the overwhelming predominance of English as the medium of instruction tilted the cultural balance in the wider society against Afrikaans.

The legislation of 1953 sought to remedy all these evils: control of African education was to be removed from the missions, churches and the provinces and taken over by the central government. A separate Ministry of Bantu Education was established in 1958, headed by W.A. Maree, an ideological clone of Verwoerd.

In a major speech in Parliament in 1954, Verwoerd spelled out the aims of the new system.[44] No other speech of his was to cause more of an uproar. For decades afterwards, Africans were to cite extracts to demonstrate that apartheid meant the intensification of oppression. One sentence, in particular, was often quoted: "There is no place for [the

African] in the European community above the level of certain forms of labour." The following sentence, seldom quoted by his critics, read: "Within his own community, however, all doors are open." This was hardly a *quid pro quo*, since the reserves/homelands were backwaters, even rural slums, incapable, even on the most optimistic projections, of providing satisfying life-chances for educated people for years to come.

* * * * *

The report of the Tomlinson Commission, published in 1955 as *Socio-Economic Development of the Bantu Areas within the Union of South Africa* (UG 61/1955) was intended to be a milestone in the implementation of apartheid (see Kenney, pp. 142–154). Verwoerd himself was opposed to the Commission's very existence, believing that he and his officials were capable of providing all of the data that were necessary. Moreover, he considered that policy proposals – many of which were contained in the report – were exclusively his domain. Apart from rejecting its principal proposals, Verwoerd showed his vindictiveness by launching a series of personal attacks on the Commission's chair, F.R. Tomlinson, a scrupulously honest person. Verwoerd accused him of embezzling Commission funds, ordered him to refrain from public comment on the report, and blocked his career advancement in the public service. Moreover, Verwoerd put pressure on two departmental officials to retract their support for certain proposals and to sign a minority report (which Tomlinson believed to have been drafted by Verwoerd himself).[45]

Essentially, Verwoerd repudiated the Commission's key proposals: that white capital should be permitted to invest in the reserves/homelands; that individual tenure should replace communal tenure; and that £104 million should be spent on development over the following decade. (A former senior leader of the NP told this writer that implementation of these recommendations, while not "solving" the racial problem, might have mitigated it – and possibly also improved living conditions in the homelands.)

What Verwoerd could not repudiate, however, were the demographic projections contained in the report. Indeed, Verwoerd's underestimation of African population growth and his overestimation of the homelands' capacity to absorb a growing proportion would eventually destroy his grand vision. The Tomlinson Commission accepted a projection that by 2000 the population would be: 4.58 million whites, 21.36 million Africans, 3.9 million Coloureds and 1.38 million Asians. It over-optimistically projected that by 2000 the increased carrying capacity of the homelands would enable them to accommodate 70 per cent of the entire African population. This, however, was subject to the proviso that the Commission's reforms were implemented. It estimated that 6.5 million Africans would remain in the "white" areas, a figure that would exceed the projected white population – unless the unlikely event of mass immigration boosted it to 6.15 million.

Even before the Commission had reported, Verwoerd had in 1952 used projections calculated by the noted economist J.L. Sadie to argue that "white civilisation" would be better able to retain its position if the situation in 2000 were "six million against six million" than if African entry to the cities were to remain unchecked.[46]

Verwoerd advanced two (dubious) reasons why the substantial number of Africans in the "white" areas should not be a source of concern: first, of the 6.5 million, 4 million would be in the rural areas, mostly on white-owned farms, "where the problem of apartheid presents no difficulty to us and where apartheid is maintained locally". This meant that the strength of the colour bar was so rigidly enforced that there was no question of equality. Secondly, those Africans in the urban areas would as far as possible be migrant workers oscillating between the "white" areas and their homelands. All of the 6.5 million "will have their anchor in their homeland …". What could be wrong with a policy that resembled the *gastarbeiter* (guest worker) system, in which workers from the poorer parts of Europe worked for spells in the richer states without shedding ties to their homelands? He could not know that in time most of the *gastarbeiter*s settled permanently in the states where they worked.

It was a bogus argument on several levels, not least because Africans in the "white" areas were, in fact, South African citizens, whose labour over decades had contributed massively to the growth of white-owned enterprises. As Kenney aptly remarks, Verwoerd's policies were "an elaborate system of make-believe which delayed … the inevitable confrontation with reality" (p. 48).

Anton Rupert, the doyen of Afrikaner entrepreneurs, advocated a 50/50 partnership between white businessmen and blacks in the homelands. Verwoerd rejected the proposal out of hand. Coming after previous clashes with Rupert on policy issues, Verwoerd now cut all ties with Rupert, saying, according to Paul Sauer, that he "never again wanted to hear anything good about Rupert". He even refused Rupert's offer in 1961 to pay for an advertisement in the British press warning against the losses Britain would suffer if South Africa were expelled from the Commonwealth. The advertisement, nevertheless, appeared, to Verwoerd's fury.[47]

* * * * *

By 1958 Verwoerd had built up something of a cult following among whites – and not only Afrikaners. Here was a man, they reasoned, who had cut through all the waffle and implemented a programme that would "save the white man". He was redoubtable, brooked no opposition and offered a system that was ethically justifiable. So they said. These views were not shared by many Africans, other than chiefs whose status and power had been enhanced by the Bantu Authorities Act. A significant minority, including the important Zulu chief, Mangosuthu Buthelezi, dissented.

Among the more bizarre aspects of Verwoerd's make-believe vision was his projection that by 1978 (the *annus mirabilis*!) the flow of Africans to the "white" areas would reverse, and Africans would start returning to their respective homelands. By what kind of statistical legerdemain – or, perhaps, merely stargazing – he had arrived at this date is not known. Apparently it arose out of the demographic speculations that accompanied the report of the Tomlinson Commission.

1978? It seemed improbable as Africans continued to stream to the "white" areas. By the early 1960s, some Nationalists were expressing their doubts. Even De Wet Nel, the Minister of Bantu Administration and Development and a staunch supporter of Verwoerd, had become cynical, and let slip in a parliamentary debate that the 1978 fable should not be taken too literally. For this the unfortunate Nel was given a tongue-lashing by Verwoerd.[48] But the reinstatement of the *annus mirabilis* did not survive Verwoerd's death in 1966; his successors abandoned it completely.

Verwoerd as Prime Minister

J.G. Strijdom had succeeded Malan in 1954, but his health was poor, and by mid-1958 it was clear that he was a very sick man. He died on 24 August 1958, sparking a fierce struggle for the succession.

Earlier, in April, the NP had won the election, pushing its total of seats held to over 100, and, for the time, winning more votes overall than the United Party. Verwoerd now became MP for Heidelberg (Transvaal), having persuaded Strijdom that he should enter the House of Assembly. No doubt he felt that he could exert more influence in the House than in the decorous environment of the Senate.

But there was a far more powerful reason: Verwoerd realised that his chances of succeeding Strijdom would be slim since the NP caucus would hesitate before electing a Senator. Hence the imperative for becoming a member of the House of Assembly.[49] His ambitiousness had long been evident: even as a young student he had told a classmate that he had set his sights on someday becoming Prime Minister.[50]

Even as Strijdom lay on his deathbed, manoeuvres over the succession began. This may have been in poor taste, but the high stakes involved made it inevitable. There were three candidates: Dr. Eben Dönges, Cape leader of the NP; C.R. Swart, Orange Free State NP leader; and H.F. Verwoerd. Dönges and Swart were senior, both having been ministers since 1948, and Dönges an MP for 17 years, and Swart for a total of 33 years. Dönges had been responsible for piloting some of the most odious pieces of apartheid legislation through Parliament, including the Population Registration Act and Group Areas Act, both enacted in 1950.

By 1958 the political centre of gravity had moved to the Transvaal: it held 48 seats in the House of Assembly, compared with the Cape's 33. Moreover, a majority of the new Senators – appointed when the Senate was enlarged in 1955 to enable legislation removing Coloured voters from the common voters' roll – were Transvalers. It would be the NP caucus, comprising members of both Houses of Parliament, that would elect the new Prime Minister.

Of the party's 176 (including MPs and Senators), 74 were Transvalers. It would be the first time in the NP's history that its leader would be elected.

Provincialism had long been a factor in the internal politics of the NP. Partly, this was attributable to the federal structure of the party, which gave the provinces their own power bases, and partly it was attributable to their differing political histories. Ben Schoeman's insider account of the election provides interesting insights: Schoeman himself wanted to block Verwoerd's candidacy "at any price". Albert Hertzog, leader of the pro-Verwoerd camp, canvassed him for support, saying, according to Schoeman, that Verwoerd was a Transvaler, and that Transvalers should stand together. Schoeman gave him short shrift, saying that he deplored provincialism.[51]

In the first round of voting, Verwoerd received 80 votes, Dönges 52, and Swart 41, whereupon Swart dropped out. In the second round Verwoerd received 98 votes and Dönges 75. Verwoerd was aware that in the first round a majority had voted against him. He must also have known that only three cabinet ministers had supported him. The flood of rumours that had accompanied the election and its outcome heightened the tensions in the party.

According to Dönges's biography, the Broederbond, the N.G.K., Afrikaner business interests and party loyalists exerted their influence to assert that party unity was the most important consideration. They feared that the intensity of provincial rivalries was so strong that discontented Cape supporters could break away. There was even talk that if this were to occur Dönges might form a pact with the United Party. This was far-fetched, and Dönges, who had pledged his loyalty to Verwoerd immediately after his defeat, would never have agreed to anything of the kind.[52]

Verwoerd was fully aware of the internal tensions and realised that he had to tread with extreme care when it came to cabinet appointments. It required a balancing act between rewarding his own supporters and not further alienating those who had opposed him. He increased the size of the cabinet by two additional ministers and created eight deputy ministerial posts.

One of the beneficiaries of Verwoerd's gratitude was Albert Hertzog, an eccentric individual who had laboured hard among Afrikaner mineworkers, and whose support for the NP had been important in the 1948 election. He had also been a key organiser on behalf of Verwoerd in the prime ministerial election. Schoeman was shocked when he heard of Verwoerd's decision, remarking that Strijdom, who loathed Hertzog, would turn in his grave. Verwoerd reacted defensively to this outburst, saying that he was giving him the portfolios of Health and Posts and Telegraphs "where he could do no damage".[53]

Dönges, who had had a torrid time as Minister of the Interior, coveted the Finance portfolio. Verwoerd offered it to him on condition that he accepted Jan Haak as his deputy minister. Haak had been Verwoerd's strongest canvasser in the Cape in the prime ministerial election. Dönges was not biting: he offered Verwoerd a perfunctory excuse for refusing the arrangement, but his real reason was that he did not want a Verwoerd man continually looking over his shoulder – which presumably had been Verwoerd's intention. Stalemate had been reached, whereupon Verwoerd summoned Dönges to his official residence and gave him an ultimatum. Dönges was not fazed, and threatened to tell the press that he had been offered Finance but that Verwoerd had withdrawn the offer because Dönges had refused to accept a deputy.[54] Verwoerd backed down – a rare event.

If cabinet-making required some delicate footwork on Verwoerd's part, he was soon able to establish not only control, but also domination.

He kept a watchful eye on what was happening in each department. He was an assiduous reader of newspapers and clipped items to which he would draw the relevant minister's attention. The cabinet was welded into a tightly cohesive body in which few, if any, ministers dared challenge Verwoerd's authority.

* * * * *

Two visions had long animated Verwoerd: first, a republic outside the Commonwealth, and second, the implementation of measures that would make South Africa "safe for the white man".

By 1958 much of the preliminary spadework for "Bantu" policy had been achieved. Regarding other minority categories, Asian and Coloured people, uncertainties remained. At least the goal of repatriating Asians to India had been recognised as an impossibility and abandoned, although the "Indian problem" remained. Coloured voters had been removed from the common voters' roll in the Cape, but the problem of the political future of the Coloured people remained – and would cause headaches for the NP in future.

As far as Africans were concerned, however, their future, at least in Verwoerd's mind, was clear. The "negative" phase of apartheid was over; all manner of protective barricades to protect whites had been entrenched. Verwoerd's programme, now termed "separate development", would unfold.

In 1959 he introduced the Promotion of Bantu Self-Government Bill, which provided for the creation of eight "Bantu" ethno-national territorial units, and for the elimination of the (white) African representatives in Parliament and the Cape Provincial Council (see Kenney, pp. 197–200).

The Bill had not been discussed by the NP caucus prior to its introduction on the day before the Easter parliamentary recess – deliberately planned, according to Japie Basson, an NP backbencher. Basson was flabbergasted to hear from De Wet Nel, now Minister of Bantu Administration and Development, that the haste had been due to "pressure from Bantu leaders".[55] This was a highly improbable explanation.

More plausible is that Verwoerd knew that he was running the risk of alienating some of his own supporters. The possibility, which he acknowledged, that the Bantustans (as they became colloquially known) might eventually become independent was a startling idea for many Nationalists, while the abolition of the Native Representatives was considered by some to be premature. Basson, however, was the solitary

Nationalist openly to oppose the abolition, for which he was expelled from the party.

Verwoerd, however, was adamant: not only was the existence of the Native Representatives a symbolic denial of his grand vision of political separation, the individuals concerned represented for the most part "semi-educated" Africans. Moreover, he was profoundly irritated by the likes of Margaret Ballinger, an outstanding parliamentarian whose knowledge of African life and conditions, and of Africans' aspirations, was far greater than Verwoerd's or De Wet Nel's. She had entered Parliament in 1937 after a career as an academic historian. Twenty years of hostility from the Nationalists had made her impervious to their attacks and the many stories of how she allegedly stirred up African agitators. She observes in her memoirs that she was to Verwoerd "the tool – or the inspirer (the accusation varied with the occasion) – of a handful of agitators ..."[56]

Verwoerd was building yet another castle in the sky, even at a time when unrest was occurring in Sekhukuneland, Zeerust and Pondoland, much of it a reaction to the Bantu Authorities Act. Moreover, protests were incubating in urban areas, as the Sharpeville and Langa episodes in March 1960 would show. He told Parliament in 1959: "My belief is that the development of South Africa on the basis of the [Promotion of Bantu Self-Government] Bill will create so much friendship, so much gratitude, so many mutual interests in the process of the propulsive [sic] development that there will be no danger of hostile Bantu states, but that there will arise ... a commonwealth, founded on common interests ..."[57]

This was a severe case of self-delusion.

Always apprehensive of offending the extreme right-wingers in the NP, Verwoerd managed to get away with only minimal damage. As a bonus, the legislation split the already enfeebled United Party wide open, leading 12 of its ablest MPs to resign and form the liberal Progressive Party. These included the indomitable Helen Suzman, who admitted that Verwoerd was the only man who had ever scared her stiff.[58] She did not flinch, and continued, in and out of Parliament, to publicise the human misery that Verwoerd's policies caused. Surprisingly, Verwoerd respected her, praising her (privately) as an outstanding parliamentarian with well-considered views.[59] So far as this writer knows, she was the only opposition member ever to earn such praise from Verwoerd. She did not return the compliment.

The year 1960 was a traumatic one for South Africa, and for Verwoerd

32

in particular. It was clear to him that international hostility to his policies was growing. It was clearly expressed, albeit in genteel terms, by British Prime Minister Harold Macmillan in his "wind of change" speech in Cape Town on 3 February. Not even Verwoerd's off-the-cuff response – although praised as brilliant by his followers – could blunt the impact of Macmillan's message.

Worse was to come: the shootings at Sharpeville on 21 March, followed by the disturbances at Langa, and the huge march of township Africans to the centre of Cape Town. A mere three weeks after Sharpeville, Verwoerd was shot at point-blank range by a deranged farmer, David Pratt. Miraculously, Verwoerd survived.

While recuperating in hospital, he was visited by Sir De Villiers Graaff, leader of the parliamentary opposition. In an interview Graaff said that Verwoerd had referred to God over a dozen times, insisting that his survival was "proof of divine acceptance of Nationalist policy".[60] Verwoerd, in comparison with other Nationalist leaders, seldom invoked the Afrikaner civil religion. This was, no doubt, an exceptional circumstance. For many of his supporters his survival was proof of his divine appointment (see Kenney, pp. 219–231).

Having swatted down the protests, and rejected the plea for reforms advocated by Paul Sauer, the Minister of Lands, Forestry and Public Works, Verwoerd concluded that strong-arm action was required: a state of emergency was declared, and thousands were detained, and both the African National Congress and the Pan Africanist Congress were banned. In addition, with the appointment of B.J. Vorster as Minister of Justice in 1962, security laws were massively expanded, the security forces were strengthened and, in effect, given free rein to treat detainees however they wished.[61] Tough security legislation, including detention without trial, became part of "ordinary" law for the next three decades.

Verwoerd's appointment of Vorster to a key portfolio was ironic since he had bitterly opposed his candidacy in 1948, on the grounds that Vorster, a former "general" in the Ossewabrandwag, should have been excluded from the Afrikaner Party's candidates. Now, Vorster would become a symbol of the mailed fist, thereby propelling himself into pole position to succeed Verwoerd.

The events of 1960 and after, and Vorster's comment that South Africa was on the verge of revolution, contributed to the widespread feeling of unease among whites. Verwoerd's reassurances, delivered to a crowd at Meyerton, said to number 80 000, followed a familiar line: "These troubles are not troubles caused by the black masses. The black masses of South Africa – and I know that Bantu in all parts of the country – are orderly. They are faithful to the government ... The masses are beginning to realise that we are also thinking of their interests ... [translation]"[62]

Verwoerd's strategy, in the exacting circumstances of the time, was to ensure that the institutions of Afrikaner nationalism were coordinated as a single, solid bloc – with himself as the overall *volksleier*.

Arising out of Japie Basson's opposition to the removal of the Native Representatives, which he spelled out at a caucus meeting on 21 April 1959, Verwoerd responded angrily, saying that the caucus was not a policy-making body; rather, it was a body that had to fight. "It does not have the right of approval or disapproval. Its role is only for consultation on how to fight." It was a curious view of the role party caucuses were supposed to play in parliamentary systems. Surely, Basson wondered, caucus had the right to know beforehand what they should vote for and why, and to have the opportunity to oppose proposed legislation or suggest amendments. Verwoerd was not pleased.[63] The expulsion of Basson was clearly intended as a deterrent to other would-be dissenters (of whom there were very few), even in the caucus.

Few NP MPs were as independent-minded as Basson; hopes of promotion to ministerial rank ensured docile obedience to the *volksleier*'s wishes. Even ministers were aware that their activities were closely scrutinised by Verwoerd, and their shortcomings noted. The case of De Wet Nel's comment on the magic year 1978 has been mentioned. Another case in point comes from a functionary in the Verwoerd household who happened to overhear part of a cabinet discussion. The unfortunate minister got his figures mixed up, which the eagle-eyed Verwoerd spotted. The minister was roundly rebuked, in front of his colleagues: "Please ... when you come to the cabinet, please ensure that your facts are correct. You are wasting the cabinet's time, you are wasting the *volk*'s time, the country's time [translation]."[64]

Although Verwoerd rarely attended church and retained a certain distance from the N.G.K., of which he was a member, he was well aware of the Afrikaner churches' pivotal role in Afrikaner nationalism. They, after all, had provided the theological legitimation for apartheid. Splits were to be avoided at all costs. It was exactly this fear that concerned Verwoerd about delegates from the N.G.K. who had supported resolutions critical of apartheid at a consultation at Cottesloe (Johannesburg) organised by the World Council of Churches. The N.G.K. clergy in question had signed in their personal capacities so that no Synod was implicated. The most prominent was Beyers Naudé, who would subsequently be forced out of the N.G.K. He became an influential opponent of apartheid.

Since many of the clergy were also members of the Broederbond and strong supporters of apartheid, it was relatively easy to mobilise against the offending delegates – and to ensure that the Synods would repudiate their views. Verwoerd interpreted the dissidents' actions as a challenge to his authority, which could not be tolerated. He used his New Year Message on 31 December 1960 to add his weight to the Synods' likely repudiation, pointing out that it was mistaken to suppose that the views of the critics should be regarded as those of the Afrikaans churches, who had not yet spoken.[65]

Verwoerd was instrumental in destroying another Afrikaner institution that had arisen on the Broederbond's initiative: this was Sabra (*Suid-Afrikaanse Buro vir Rasse-aangeleenthede*, or South African Bureau of Racial Affairs), established in 1948 as a research/think-tank to promote apartheid. It was largely Cape-based, and its most prominent members were Stellenbosch professors, a fact that immediately raised the (provincialist) suspicions of Transvalers. Since the Broederbond contributed financially to Sabra, its leverage was considerable.

The kingpin in Sabra was N.J.J. Olivier, Professor of Native Administration. He was committed to apartheid, provided it was equitably and ethically implemented. But his disillusionment set in after Verwoerd's rejection of the Tomlinson Commission's recommendations. Pierre Hugo, a former student of Olivier's and author of the most authoritative account of the onslaught on Sabra, writes: "During his earlier period as Minister of Native Affairs ... Verwoerd had already bracketed those, and Olivier especially, who dared to influence policy in a manner which he construed as interfering with his prerogative as master of South Africa's political and racial destiny."[66]

Olivier and his colleagues soldiered on, but the rumblings of discontent among the conservatives in Sabra and in the Broederbond continued. It was the question of the Coloured people's status that brought the simmering tensions to a head in 1961. This was compounded by Sabra's research findings on the alienation and frustration of Africans and their mistrust of government.

This went completely against the grain of Verwoerd's soothing claims that the Bantu, apart from a few agitators, welcomed separate development. He responded with vigour: he gave instructions that, as long as Olivier and his supporters were in charge of Sabra, government officials were to withhold cooperation.[67]

The consequence of further machinations, engineered by Verwoerd, was that Olivier was forced out of the leadership. He and his supporters, including able academics, left the organisation, to be replaced by people, mainly extreme conservatives, several of whom were later associated with *verkrampte* (reactionary) bodies. Sabra was left largely bereft of talent, being reduced to little more than a low-grade propaganda organisation.

* * * * *

Verwoerd wanted to exercise control over the whole of Afrikanerdom, including the NP and Afrikaner civil society. It came as no surprise that he reacted ruthlessly to an article in *Die Burger* on 23 July 1960, written by the editor, Piet Cillié, in which he advocated that Coloured people should be directly represented in Parliament, and, if they so wished, by Coloured MPs. Verwoerd was infuriated by the article, as well as by D.P. Botha's book and its foreword, written by N.P. van Wyk Louw, which pleaded for the full integration of Coloured people, who were culturally part of a wider Afrikaner community. Having terminated Coloured common-roll voting rights, the NP now found their political future ideologically troublesome since there was no Coloured "homeland".

A fierce row began among Afrikaner nationalists when Verwoerd firmly rejected any thought of direct Coloured representation. Characteristically, Verwoerd took the view that any concession would start a chain reaction of further demands that would eventually include full integration and the elimination of all forms of discrimination. It could lead to "biological assimilation".[68] He said privately that granting any representation to Coloured people would spark heightened demands from Africans for political rights.

Cillié was subjected to considerable pressure, and even considered resigning his editorship. Verwoerd expected NP-supporting newspapers faithfully to toe the line and to avoid raising awkward issues. No concessions, no compromises and no exceptions would be tolerated.

In January 1961, at Verwoerd's instigation, the Federal Council of the NP issued an extraordinary statement, expressing its conviction that "the Government is better placed than outsiders to pass judgement on matters such as: who the leaders of the different racial groups are and how consultation with them is best conducted; what legislation is necessary to prevent mixed marriages; what forms of migrant labour are unavoidable and even necessary for various reasons, including consideration of the rights of others; how justified attacks on existing wages are ... what

36

necessity there is for job reservation to allow justice to be done to all ... how and where development of the Bantu areas could take place ... what the consequences of injustice and misery would be if theories of the voting rights for non-whites were implemented ... [translation]".

The list of issues on which outsiders should not pass judgement continued. Schalk Pienaar, Piet Cillié's colleague and friend, commented acidly that, since the government was better placed to judge, "lesser mortals should rather remain silent". If people wish to discuss the issues this should be done through existing party channels, and not in public. This was a clear message to Boland Nationalists.[69]

If Cillié tended to retreat in the face of such hostility, Schalk Pienaar remained undeterred. He was convinced that what Van Wyk Louw had termed the "*oop gesprek*" (free conversation) was vitally necessary. When Nasionale Pers decided in 1965 to establish a Sunday newspaper in Johannesburg, Pienaar was appointed editor. In spite of Verwoerd's opposition to *Die Beeld* on grounds that it would compete with *Dagbreek en Sondagnuus* (owned by a company of which Verwoerd was chairman), Nasionale Pers went ahead, recognising that it was in its own interest to break into the Transvaal market. The first issue appeared on 1 October 1965. Efforts by the Transvaal NP to organise a boycott got nowhere.[70]

To Verwoerd's continuing dismay, *Die Beeld* struck out in consistently *verligte* (enlightened) vein, ignoring the constraints that Verwoerd and the Transvaal NP would have liked to impose. In particular, what irked the establishment was the keen attention *Die Beeld* paid to intra-Afrikaner quarrels. As a broad generalisation it is true that Afrikaners are intensely interested in politics, far more so than their English-speaking counterparts. Stories about factions and intrigues within Afrikanerdom were eagerly read by, particularly, young, educated Afrikaners who were bored by the dull propaganda served up by the two existing Afrikaans dailies in the Transvaal.

Pienaar was at pains to expose the activities of Dr Albert Hertzog and the coterie of extreme conservatives around him, known as the Afrikaner Order. Hertzog was a believer in Afrikaner exclusivism (despite being married to an English-speaking woman), and a resolute opponent of television, believing that it would erode the Afrikaners' sense of morality. Close to him stood another eccentric, S.E.D. Brown, editor of the *SA Observer*, whose conspiracy theories were readily believed by Hertzog. The critical point is that this cluster of extreme right-wingers existed under Verwoerd's protection.[71]

In due course the Hertzogites were termed the *verkramptes*, who were sworn to defend Verwoerd and all his works. (From this lineage subsequently were born the Herstigte Nasionale Party and, later, the Conservative Party.)

Verwoerd appeared not to realise that by the 1960s Afrikaner society had changed: a new generation had grown up, urban, well-educated and upwardly mobile. In short, embourgeoisement was taking place, and the old pieties and intellectual straitjacketing of traditional Afrikaner nationalism were becoming increasingly unacceptable. The 1960s saw the arrival of the avant-garde writers whose themes were considered shocking by traditionalists. Moreover, a few young intellectuals braved potential hostility by criticising apartheid, or, at least, aspects of its implementation.

To Verwoerd's dismay, Pienaar encouraged this critical questioning. The unanointed patron of these developments was Van Wyk Louw, who was also the uncrowned poet laureate of South Africa. Louw, as noted above, had already incurred Verwoerd's wrath by his advocacy of Coloured rights. Moreover, he had participated in a protest march against the imposition of university apartheid organised by the University of the Witwatersrand. There could be no doubting Louw's credentials as an Afrikaner. His books, *Lojale Verset* (1939) and *Liberale Nasionalisme* (1952), both published by Tafelberg, provided plenty of stimulus for questioning, doubting and critical Afrikaners.[72] His famous comment: "I would rather go down than continue to exist through injustice" (translation) became a motto for critical journalists like Pienaar.

The differences between Louw and Verwoerd reached a climax in May 1966 when Verwoerd obliquely but unmistakeably attacked a play, *Die Pluimsaad Waai Ver*, which had been written to commemorate the fifth anniversary of the Republic.[73] Louw had drawn a picture of the Boer fighters in the Anglo-Boer War, with all their strengths and weaknesses, bravery and cowardice, and the treachery of some. Towering above them was Louw's particular hero, President Marthinus Steyn (last President of the Orange Free State), whose stout heart could not completely conceal the occasional doubt.

It is a magnificent play, but it fell short of Verwoerd's criteria for "patriotic" writing: *volksdigters* (*volk* poets) who would uncritically sing the praises of the nation.[74]

* * * * *

The coming of the Republic in 1961 would no doubt have been regarded by Verwoerd as the greatest achievement of his career in public life. From his earliest days he had been an ardent republican. It was a supreme irony that he had been selected by a group of Cape Nationalists to edit *Die Transvaler*, with the hope that he would calm the raging republican tempest in the north. If anything, from the start Verwoerd proceeded to do the exact opposite, to the consternation of D.F. Malan.

Malan had played down the republic issue in the 1948 election. Strijdom, although a dedicated republican, did little to advance the cause, probably because his health was poor. Verwoerd may have modified his earlier views, but his republican ardour remained undiminished. On becoming Prime Minister in 1958, he was determined to press ahead.

A significant step was taken in 1958 when the voting age was reduced from 21 to 18. This could have been defended on other grounds since the same reduction was occurring elsewhere in the world, but the real reason for the move was the Nationalists' expectation of a demographic dividend: the Afrikaans-speaking section of the white population was increasing faster than that of the English-speakers. Moreover, many of the newly enfranchised voters would have emerged from Afrikaans-medium schools and universities where a strong nationalist ethos prevailed.

According to Verwoerd's account, he and his associates realised in the last few years before Strijdom's death that if the Republic were not achieved in the following five-year period, the opportunity might be lost forever.[75] There was extensive debate within Nationalist and Broederbond circles about strategy: some argued that it would be more prudent to await a closer relationship between Afrikaners and English-speakers, and greater progress on racial issues. Both Strijdom and Verwoerd believed the opposite, namely, that a republic would accelerate progress on both issues.

There were intense discussions on how the republic should be achieved, whether any major changes should be incorporated in a new constitution, and whether it should be a republic inside or outside the Commonwealth.

Verwoerd was adamant that even a majority of one, either by parliamentary vote or a referendum, would suffice. Many in the Orange Free State and Transvaal felt strongly that the head of state should be vested with executive power, but Verwoerd counselled against this, believing that to win sufficient support countrywide the constitutional principle with which people were familiar should be retained, that is, that the Prime Minister and his cabinet would be responsible for governing the country.

In earlier unpublished thoughts Verwoerd had concluded that a republic outside the Commonwealth might be in the best interests of maintaining British-South African relationships since South Africa would no longer be a source of discord in an increasingly multiracial Commonwealth. Furthermore, if there were to be any hope of attaining a majority, including significant support from English-speakers, then debate about whether to remain inside the Commonwealth or to withdraw would be counter-productive.

In comments to a Broederbond delegation during 1959, Verwoerd acknowledged that, according to statistical data available to him, a majority of voters would not, at any stage, favour a republic. Thousands of voters had strong bonds with other Commonwealth states, and those who feared greater world hostility to South Africa would vote against a republic, especially if it were not to be a member of the Commonwealth. It would be sensible to be pragmatic: "Let us first try to achieve the Republic inside the Commonwealth, and address further development in the light of prevailing circumstances" (translation).[76]

Ben Schoeman revealed figures that Verwoerd had cited: according to all the party offices (and probably with a certain amount of guesswork), a majority of between 60 000 and 70 000 were opposed to the republic – this in spite of the NP's having, for the first time, won a majority (55 per cent) of the votes cast in the 1958 election. Subsequent estimates in June 1960 by party offices showed that pro-republican voters were 18 000 votes short of victory, but approximately 100 000 were "doubtfuls".[77]

Verwoerd decided to run the risk. On 20 January 1960 he announced that a referendum would be held, and, later, he announced the date as 5 October 1960. He promised that retention of Commonwealth membership would be sought if a majority voted for a republic: the government, he continued, was convinced that the Commonwealth would give its consent, "as has always been customary when such constitutional changes have taken place …".[78]

Only white voters would be permitted to vote, and, in addition, after pressure from the six MPs representing them, voters in South West Africa would also be eligible to participate. In the uncertain times regarding the territory, their inclusion was viewed as a further means of strengthening the tie to South Africa.

As anticipated, the referendum was close-run. A poll of 90 per cent was recorded, and the pro-republican vote won by over 74 000 votes.

Considering that over 1.8 million people voted, this was a narrow margin. But it was enough to satisfy Verwoerd and his followers. The Transvaal and Orange Free State had voted overwhelmingly for a republic; the Cape vote was evenly balanced; and in Natal (commonly known as "the last outpost of the British Empire") rejection of the republic was decisive. It is impossible to provide a breakdown of how Afrikaner and English votes were distributed, but it is apparent that few English-speakers voted for a republic. Threats of secession and mayhem emanated from Natal, but it was no more than hot air.

In his earlier days as an editor, Verwoerd had been a strong proponent of an exclusivist Afrikaner nationalism. In the post-referendum republican days he seemed to have mellowed. Whether this was a genuine change of heart or a tactical shift aimed at shoring up the whites as a bloc is not known. Probably both factors played a part. In his message to the people after the referendum, Verwoerd made a pitch for English-speaking support: "Naturally I would prefer them to join my party on the basis of the principles which I have enunciated so often. Should English-speaking people find this difficult at present, I hope that they will at least form a conservative party on their own with similar colour policies so that we can co-operate and I can find real active English political leaders who agree with our policies."[79]

Not long thereafter he appointed two (undistinguished) English-speakers, A.E. Trollip and F.W. Waring, both former United Party MPs, to the cabinet.

The coming of the Republic elevated him to the pinnacle of his power. Developments elsewhere in Africa, notably in the former Belgian Congo and Rhodesia's U.D.I. in 1965, strengthened white resistance to local African political mobilisation: the formation of Umkhonto we Sizwe, the terrorist organisation Poqo and the Rivonia trial in 1963 all contributed to a growing sense of siege among whites. And who better to defend them against this onslaught than Verwoerd and his strong-arm Minister of Justice, B.J. Vorster? That the rule of law was left in tatters was of no account.

Increasing numbers of English-speakers now jettisoned their old anti-Afrikaner prejudices and supported the NP. In the election held on 30 March 1966 the NP won its highest number of seats yet: 126, with the United Party being reduced to a paltry 39. Some estimates suggested that as many as 25 per cent of the English-speaking section had voted for the NP. An indication of the change is that, in Natal, compared with the 1961 election, the vote for the NP in 1966 had more than doubled. Moreover, sympathy for white Rhodesians as Britain imposed sanctions, and general agreement with Verwoerd's statement that black government over whites in Rhodesia would lead to "destruction and chaos", had strengthened support for apartheid.

On 6 September 1966 Verwoerd was assassinated by a deranged parliamentary messenger, Demetrio Tsafendas.[80] Conspiracy theories sprouted, but none was ever confirmed. There was also speculation about what Verwoerd had been going to say in what promised to be an important speech on that very afternoon.

An intriguing possibility is cited by Ebbe Dommisse in his biography of Anton Rupert: in 1995 Koos Potgieter, a former chief whip of the NP for 27 years, invited Rupert to an interview in Pretoria. First, he apologised to Rupert for an attack he had made on his company, Rembrandt, in 1957. The attack was made at the request of Verwoerd. Second, he had been summoned to Verwoerd's office two days before his death; to Potgieter's amazement Verwoerd told him that apartheid was incapable of being implemented. Why don't you change it? asked Potgieter. Verwoerd replied that it was not politically feasible at that stage: "You can't turn the car around too sharply, it will capsize." Rupert, knowing Potgieter to be an honest man, believed him.[81] Alf Ries, political editor of *Die Burger*, had heard the same story, and believed that Verwoerd was intending to say, on that fateful afternoon, that apartheid was failing.[82]

The shocking circumstances of Verwoerd's death brought grief and uncertainty to his many admirers, but among his critics another emotion was evident: relief. It was poor taste to express this, but Schalk Pienaar recounts how the wife of a friend, also good friends of the Verwoerds, remarked: "We all feel now as we feel. But tell me, for how long could South Africa still bear Verwoerd? [translation]"[83]

Conclusion

Henry Kenney has provided an excellent overview of Verwoerd's policies and his character. Little more needs to be added, other than some additional material about his personality.

Verwoerd was always sensitive about not being South African by birth. Although he was completely assimilated to Afrikaner culture and spoke Afrikaans without a trace of a Dutch accent, he played down, and even tried to erase, public knowledge of his origins. Indeed, he gave the impression of trying to "out-Afrikaner the Afrikaners". Several commentators have drawn analogies between Verwoerd and Napoleon (born in Corsica), Stalin (born in Georgia) and Hitler (born in Austria). The analogy, however, is far-fetched since Verwoerd resembled none of the three except in that he became leader of a country other than his country of origin.

In most accounts, Verwoerd is presented as an arch-racist. The spate of discriminatory legislation and practices for which he was largely or wholly responsible makes it hard to gainsay this view. There is, however, no conclusive evidence in Verwoerd's speeches to suggest that he believed in the racial inferiority of black people. It is likely that he agreed with the finding of the Commission on Native Education (1949–1951) that there was no conclusive evidence to show that as a group Africans "could not benefit from education or that their intelligence and aptitudes were of so special and peculiar nature as to demand … a special type of education".[84]

Hermann Giliomee observes that Verwoerd "rejected the notion of different innate abilities", attributing what appeared to be differences in skills to "simply differences in culture due to historical experience".[85] He told a senior official in his department that African culture was not inferior: "Their culture is worth just as much to them as ours is to us; it is just different."[86] Their indigenous culture was the essential foundation for their development. It was "engraved on their souls".

If culture was the critical difference between peoples, or *volke*, how then could the enforcement of apartheid on Coloured people be justified? Most were Afrikaans-speaking and members of the Dutch Reformed Church. Moreover, having been a stalwart proponent of Afrikaner exclusivity in earlier times, how could he support the rapprochement of Afrikaners and English-speakers in 1960 and after, especially after warnings in earlier days of the dire threat that the overwhelming power of English culture posed to Afrikaner culture?

The obvious difference between the cases of the Coloured people and the English is colour (despite the considerable variation in the actual hue of Coloured people themselves). The recourse to culture differences cannot acquit Verwoerd of the charge of racism. Moreover, the pressure of white public opinion had the effect of hardening his racial views. He told his son Wilhelm that there was no middle road between "separation" and "integration": "If separation was the choice, as most voters have decided, we cannot permit slackening by making exceptions under pressure from the opposition."[87]

Verwoerd's racism extended also to Jews. He was in the forefront of anti-Jewish protest in the 1930s, opposing alleged "Jewish domination in business and the professions, the unassimilability of Jews, Jewish alienation from the Afrikaners, questionable Jewish commercial morality, and the use of money by Jews to influence government through the English-language press".[88]

He insisted that he did not hate Jews; he opposed their immigration because they posed a threat to Afrikaner welfare.[89]

Racism has another dimension: behaviour targeting stigmatised groups. On this count Verwoerd's obsessive concern with discriminatory rules prohibiting racial mixing on an equal basis marks him as guilty. His career both as Minister and Prime Minister is pockmarked with incidents demonstrating the point: forbidding a touring New Zealand rugby team from including Maori players; debarring people of colour from attending a performance of *Messiah* in Pietermaritzburg; forbidding African American sailors from coming ashore when their ship docked in Cape Town; and, most foolish of all, banning the film in which Laurence Olivier played Othello with his face blackened!

Many opponents accused Verwoerd of supporting Nazism during the Second World War. There is no evidence to suggest that Nazi ideas had rubbed off on Verwoerd during his time in Germany as a student. Homegrown racism was sufficiently sturdy not to require assistance from Nazism. Moreover, Verwoerd was quite clear in his rejection of Nazi ideology, declaring it to be incompatible with the principles of the NP, which were "*in murg en been*" (in marrow and bone) democratic. He believed that Hitler was a psychopath. After the breakdown of the NP-Ossewabrandwag agreement, he attacked the neo-Nazi OB with vigour. He also condemned the German invasion of the Netherlands as "dreadful and a blot on civilisation that a powerful state could play with the peace, freedom and lifeblood of the inhabitants of smaller countries".[90] He pleaded for assistance for the Netherlands, and started a fund that the F.A.K. administered.[91]

Opposition to the Nazis and Fascists did not mean that Verwoerd's insistence on neutrality was being abandoned. After the war ended, he pleaded for aid to Germany, recalling the assistance that Germany had provided to the Boers in the Anglo-Boer War.[92]

* * * * *

Verwoerd's legacy was twofold: severe repression and control galvanised opposition among blacks, ensuring that the Bantustan fantasy could never succeed, But it also left scars on society, both physical and mental, that have not been fully eradicated, despite apartheid's castles-in-the-sky having been demolished. The National Development Plan observed in 2013: "Eighteen years into democracy, South Africa remains a highly unequal society where too many people live in poverty and too few work. The quality of school education for most black learners is poor. The apartheid spatial divide continues to dominate the landscape. A large proportion of young people feel that the odds are stacked against them. And the legacy of apartheid continues to determine the life opportunities for the vast majority."

Verwoerd cannot be exclusively blamed for this state of affairs. Structural racial inequality existed long before he came to power. Nevertheless he exacerbated and entrenched inequality more than any of his predecessors, and bequeathed to the country hundreds of thousands of diehard racists who revered his memory.

Professor David Welsh
Cape Town
April 2016

Introduction

The remarkable career of Hendrik Frensch Verwoerd affords an object lesson in the enduring realities of South African history. To an extreme degree he embodied the Afrikaner's will to survive, and dominate; for a short time it seemed that he was in fact shaping history according to his own ends, that he had genuinely managed to impose a framework on South African politics that was entirely new, indeed revolutionary. Of all South Africa's rulers since 1945, or, for that matter, in this century, none so dominated his time as this foreign-born son of immigrants. If anyone appeared to be making events conform to his own will it was Verwoerd, with his dominating personality, his dynamism and his formidable intelligence. Yet, strangely, he is almost a forgotten man in the South Africa of today, although he died only just over a decade ago.

Nationalists seldom invoke his authority for present policies. When his name is mentioned it is with that reverence appropriate to remote father figures who are fortunately no longer around to stultify the present. Much of it is probably due to plain, old-fashioned embarrassment: when Verwoerd was bestriding South Africa like a colossus he did not brook dissent from fellow Nationalists (the Opposition he simply ignored). He imposed an intellectual straitjacket on the Afrikaners which most accepted with extreme docility, even when it meant tolerating policies which seemed only designed to cater to anyone's sense of the absurd. There were few in the land prepared to say him nay. The recollection of such spinelessness must be unpleasant today, when so many of the grossest absurdities have been ditched, with no detriment to white supremacy.

But could there be another reason for the present obscurity of Verwoerd's memory? Could it be that his policies are dead and gone, with no further relevance to the present? Superficially, this is not so. His vision of "separate freedoms" still provides the official rationale for Nationalist policy today. South Africa is still, in theory, what Verwoerd made it: political separation between white and black remains now, as it did then, the cardinal principle informing the ordering of relations between the races. But human events are rarely so simple. By now it is evident that "Verwoerdism" has collapsed. There are more blacks in the "white" areas than ever before, and they show no signs of going back to the ethnic fate Verwoerd had in store for them. Of the "homelands", three have become "independent" (recognised by South Africa alone), while the other six are in varying degrees of preparation for their separate constitutional destinies. Scarcely viable, as nearly all of them are, it is clear that they are no solutions to South Africa's racial problems. No amount of metaphysical theorising will conjure away the blacks who form a majority of the population of "white" South Africa.

In the final analysis, Verwoerd's policy of "separate freedoms" stood or fell by its ability to undo what economic forces had shaped. 1978 was to be the year when the flow of blacks into the white areas would be reversed, and they would start going back to their homelands. They have done nothing of the sort and it is clear that the policy has failed. White South Africa has no alternative; it continues from day to day, waiting and hoping, like Mr. Micawber, for something to turn up. Like him, it will be disappointed but by then it would be too late. Dr. Verwoerd, in spite of his enormous ability to impress friend and foe, left a legacy which is curiously insubstantial. Had he never been, the course of South African history would have changed very little. His one considerable contribution was to provide white South Africans with an elaborate system of make-believe which delayed, and still delays, the inevitable confrontation with reality. But this is not to deny Verwoerd's importance. He has un-doubtedly been the most important white politician in South Africa since the Second World War. He did not invent the term or the policy, but he fully deserves to be called the architect of apartheid. It was Verwoerd who transformed it into a system, and gave it a form and content which had previously been absent. Ultimately, his failure reflects the hopelessness of any attempt to maintain a white-ruled state in a country, and on a continent, where the overwhelming majority of inhabitants are black.

If Verwoerd's policies are defunct, we may well ask: How long will South Africa survive? This question, the title of a recent book (its answer: until about the 1990s), had been bothering white South Africans to an ever-increasing extent during the troubled decade of the 70s, which contrasted so remarkably with the euphoric and booming days of the 1960s, the day of the post-Sharpeville Verwoerd and the early, golf-playing Vorster. The question is of course wrongly phrased; it actually refers to a South Africa which will still be ruled by white people.

It is a question which has frequently been asked but never satisfactorily answered. The stock Nationalist reply, "For ever", appears more and more ludicrous as the end of the 20th century approaches. Few things seem more certain than that white rule in South Africa cannot, and will not, endure. Yet the predictions for the demise of white supremacy have consistently proved wrong. South Africa has been a graveyard for scenarios of the future. Faced with the obvious injustices of apartheid, of which the contrast between white luxury and black poverty is commonly supposed to be the most glaring manifestation, and the huge disparity in numbers between white and black, not to mention white and non-white, the liberal and humane observer is tempted to cast analysis to the winds. Surely such a monstrous situation cannot last? Surely, sooner or later, the white oppressors will be swept away in a vast revolutionary upsurge of frustrated and impoverished blacks, driven past the point of endurance by the harshness of white domination? Well, perhaps. It has not happened yet, in spite of the frequent and increasingly disturbing expressions of black protest during South Africa's history since 1910, but it does not follow that it cannot happen. Certainly, it can readily be predicted that, as long as white rule lasts, black unrest will continue, finding periodic expression in outbursts that will be as ruthlessly suppressed as they will be upsetting to white hopes for a tranquil future.

But revolution? The violent overthrow of white supremacy? These are different propositions entirely, and it is not easy to see how they are likely to come to South Africa in any foreseeable future. The truth is that white rule in the southern part of Africa has been extraordinarily resilient. Rhodesia, with a white population which is only 5 per cent of the total (compared with 20 per cent in South Africa), managed to survive for 14 years under U.D.I., in spite of Harold Wilson's confident prediction at the time that it would all be over within weeks rather than months. More than twenty years ago a South African left-wing academic (now an exile) wrote an article, "No Revolution Round the Corner", which title speaks for itself, where he argued that the conditions for a successful revolution did not exist in South Africa, no matter how many similarities the country had with England, America, France and Russia when they had their revolutions. In all these countries the revolutionaries could rely on significant support from the armed forces. In South Africa this was the very last thing any black rebels against the status quo could rely upon. Up-to-date military equipment and efficient organisation can go immensely far to counteract any numerical imbalance between rulers and oppressed and in South Africa they have done just that. Accompany this with the

Government's well-known rigour in suppressing internal black dissent, and it seems that white rule still has many years of thriving life ahead of it. What reason then for South Africa's blacks to expect "freedom" in our time?

The answer is simply that it is likely to come through a combination of internal and external factors. Within there are forces for change, but by themselves they can do little except give an occasional shake to the structure of supremacy, which, however disturbed it may temporarily be, soon returns to equilibrium. Within the dominant white group the resolve to "move away from discrimination" is more a matter of pious words than of any genuine intent. Indeed, this resolve seems to be fairly minimal. The Government's new *troika*-type constitutional system of separate (but supposedly equal) parliaments for whites, Coloureds, and Indians respectively, with a president (who can in principle come from any of these groups, but will in practice be an Afrikaner nationalist) wielding autocratic powers, is merely an elaborate piece of window-dressing that will entrench ultimate control as securely in the hands of the Afrikaner minority as it has ever done before. (It goes without saying that for the 4–5 million urban blacks there is no provision at all, except for some form of local government, mere exported labour units from the homelands that they are.) What is P.W. Botha's "constellation of states" but Verwoerdism revamped for slightly more sophisticated tastes? But even in minor fields the readiness to abandon outrageous forms of discrimination admits of conspicuous, and officially sanctioned, exceptions. What is one to make of the kind of debased Christianity that refuses a homeland Minister admission to the funeral service of a former Commissioner-General of his homeland, and this after he had been invited by the son of the deceased? And what can one say about the "whiteness" which continues to be the decisive criterion for access to Pretoria's Breytenbach Theatre?

The ruling Afrikaners are so clearly unwilling to overcome these forms of infantilism, so adamant in regarding South Africa as peculiarly *their* country, in which all other groups, including the English-speaking whites, can only have a minor say, that they will evidently not yield except under the most extreme forms of pressure. They will hold what they have, irrespective of the injustice to others, because their present way of life is exceedingly comfortable and human beings only change when they must. Also, to be quite fair, the monstrous proliferation of tyranny and corruption in independent Africa must make even the most *verligte* Afrikaner pause to think more than twice about the merits of "majority rule". But the Afrikaners will only accept the inevitable when it is almost certainly too late, when the only choice will be between getting out of Africa fast or submitting to a black government as unjust and iniquitous as blacks found the white supremacy.

As for their reluctant junior partners, the English-speaking whites, how will they respond to the need for change? They will do as the Afrikaners do, if not by inclination, then because they have hardly any choice. Supporting the Government, as they now do in massive numbers, it may seem that Verwoerd's ideal of a white South African nation, united in its resistance to Communism, liberalism and, above all, black domination, is swiftly being forged in the searing conditions of a post-colonial world. But it is probably more an alliance of necessity than of choice. It is difficult to see how it could be otherwise. The Afrikaners are no doubt sincere in their profession of belief in white unity, but in the final analysis they trust only themselves to have the necessary will and determination to ensure white control. As they like to say, they can go nowhere else, but the English can always return to Britain. The Afrikaners have thus, to a remarkable degree, maintained their cohesiveness as an exclusive and self-reliant group. The English, with a few token exceptions, like the Minister of Finance, Senator Horwood, which only confirm the rule, have not been admitted to South Africa's top governing circles; it is Afrikaner hands which will remain on the most important levers of power. Repelled as they inevitably must be by this exclusiveness, which only helps to confirm many of their standard anti-Afrikaner prejudices, the English have had no option but to submit. Whether they like it or not, the Afrikaner's struggle is also their struggle. They share in the privileges of being white South Africans and they are just as reluctant to relinquish them.

Politically, the English-speaking are an appendage of the Afrikaners, but economically, in spite of the post-war rise of Afrikaner capitalism, it is still they who dominate the private sector. It is they who have led South Africa's industrialisation over the last thirty to forty years. And here, it is frequently argued, is where the "real" dynamic for change resides, which will peacefully transform the Republic's archaic social structure into one more akin to the demands of a civilised way of life. Apartheid, it is held, is ultimately incompatible with an advanced industrial economy. Economic imperatives must eventually destroy it. There can be little doubt, as the experiences of the leading economic powers have suggested, that industrialism is a universal solvent, that it has a corrosive effect on traditional ways of life. But the relationship between economic development and political change is no simple one; entrepreneurs have flourished in many seemingly unpromising environments, including South Africa. This has led many to think that the relationship between capitalist industrialisation and apartheid is, far from being antagonistic, actually one of mutual support. The argument is fallacious. It ignores the many obvious constraints, such as higher labour costs through influx control, which Government policies have imposed on profit-maximisation. Yet, if continued industrialisation does tend to subvert the racial status quo, it takes time to do so. Conceivably there may be a day when the trade-off is far more acute than it is now, and then it is the economy which could suffer, not apartheid. But this is no immediate prospect, while South Africa's relatively poor hopes for such rapid growth as that of the 60s further reduces the possibility of white supremacy being undermined by industrial development.

From the whites there will be no strong impulse to "move away from discrimination". But none of those with apocalyptic visions of revolutionary upheaval in South Africa ever thought this possible. They have no doubt that it is the blacks who will have to liberate themselves, and by the only means possible under the Nationalist racial autocracy, namely, bloodshed and violence. Here industrialisation may well have sowed the seeds of white supremacy's future ruin, not by its supposed structural requirements, but by concentrating a huge, impoverished and severely repressed black proletariat in South Africa's main urban centres. Sharpeville in 1960 and Soweto in 1976 were urban disturbances, the outcome of the grievances of urban blacks. The Nationalists have themselves been only too well aware of the fateful implications for apartheid of the concentration of so many blacks in a relatively few urban complexes. They have been powerless to turn back the thousands of blacks who converge on South Africa's "white" towns and cities every year. All the tough talk (or perhaps whistling in the dark) by Verwoerd in the 50s and 60s about the reversal of the black flow to the cities by 1978 has come to nothing. Reading such statements today, one has the impression that they come from some bygone era, so distant that it can only be understood by dint of much arduous study of obscure documents and learned volumes. The truth is that apartheid is a total failure, that virtually nothing remains of "separate development" except a name. The Government has implicitly accepted this, for it has no serious interest in living up to long-forgotten and embarrassing predictions about "turning points" in the flow of black labour to the urban areas. Rather, it is mainly concerned with keeping to an absolute minimum those "permanent" blacks in town who have relatively secure residential rights, while the proportion of migrants in the black labour force is to be enlarged as far as possible. In theory, of course, all blacks in the white areas are temporary, impermanent, but some are less impermanent than others. It is the blacks in this category who must be reduced at all costs. Under Vorster it appeared that the number of migrants had been increasing more rapidly than the economically active black population as a whole. This is in striking contrast with the situation under Verwoerd, where the exact opposite happened. In this respect, at least, apartheid can claim to be successful, for one of the subtler points of the theory has always been that blacks in the white areas were really not all that important; it was their degree of "permanence" that mattered. But it is a hollow triumph. Juggling with words cannot conceal the economy's dependence on the presence of 4–5 million blacks in white South Africa, of whom an undetermined, but certainly very large, number cannot ever be plausibly seen as inhabitants and citizens of their respective homelands.

What revolutionary potential is there in the urban black working class? The first temptation is to reply that it is truly frightening, that a repetition of the events of 1976 could precipitate the Republic into chaos. Undoubtedly the spectacle of rampaging blacks a few years ago, was sufficiently terrifying to send many whites hurrying to the safer, if probably less comfortable, shores of countries like the United States and Australia. Not that emigration was such a poor decision. Considering white supremacy's long-term prospects, it was an eminently sensible choice. But the feeling of urgency was misplaced. Soweto in 1976 was the outcome of a combination of circumstances unlikely to be repeated in the near future. It is a classic illustration of the so-called inverted J-curve which some academics have professed to find in certain revolutionary situations. It refers to a period of prolonged growth, suddenly followed by a sharp downturn in the economy. The heightened expectations aroused and, to a large measure, satisfied during the time of prosperity, are suddenly frustrated. The resultant bitterness and resentment are infallible generators of violence and upheaval. The rebels, not yet having realistically lowered their expectations to suit a period of reduced opportunities and bargaining power, believe that something can still be salvaged if they act with sufficient force and vigour. They do act – and invariably fail to achieve their objectives, but in doing so unleash a far-reaching chain of violence that can precipitate profound changes in the structure of society. Soweto did not have this effect, but its occurrence can most plausibly be seen in terms such as these.

During the 1960s growth was sufficiently rapid to ensure Africans in the modern sector of the economy of significant increases in average real incomes. At the same time, the Government effectively used its formidable apparatus of repression and control to ensure that black political expectations were kept at an appropriately low level. But it is well known that rapid growth and the rising incomes to which it gives rise do not so easily reconcile the victims of an oppressive system to their fate. It did not do so in South Africa. By the early 70s a new generation of Africans had arisen, forgetful of the repression of the post-Sharpeville years, and led by the collapse of Portuguese authority in Angola and Mozambique to believe that a similar crisis was in store for white rule in the Republic. Growth was still proceeding at a respectable rate, which made for a relatively tight labour market for blacks and increased their bargaining power. Also, a high and rising rate of inflation was eroding the purchasing power of African wages. Rising money incomes did not necessarily mean rising real incomes. The wave of strikes by black workers which began in 1972 took white South Africa by surprise but in retrospect it is all too understandable, for all of the above reasons. The strikes were successful, within limits. They led to considerable wage increases which, for a time, meant increases in black purchasing power as well, before these gains, too, were nullified by inflation.

But by 1976 the economy had lost its buoyancy. The growth rate had declined to a mere 2 per cent, and the prospects of economic revival were poor and remote. Growth was certainly not rapid enough to provide employment for the thousands of blacks who were coming onto the labour market every year. From this point of view the wage increases won by the strikes had not done African employment any good. Higher black wages had induced greater investment in labour-saving machinery; the amount of black labour demanded, particularly unskilled, was correspondingly reduced. Soweto was the outcome of this new situation. It was the result of the sudden frustration of expectations which the previous momentum of the economy had maintained at a relatively high level. A rate of inflation of more than 10 per cent was sharply reducing the real incomes of black wage-earners. The numbers of unemployed in the urban areas were swelling every day in spite of influx control, which had proved incapable of stemming the black invasion of the cities, and black school-leavers could only look with trepidation to an immediate future that threatened joblessness, poverty and unending discrimination. Soweto, in short, was the result of a suddenly widened gap between rising expectations and an uncooperative reality.

It is unlikely that there will be other Sowetos soon. The economy shows no signs of recapturing the dynamism of old. The best that can probably be hoped for is steady growth at a fairly low rate, which will not be nearly adequate to absorb the soaring number of unemployed blacks. Faced with these dismal prospects, the urban black working class is certain to be discontented, but probably singularly deficient in militancy. Low growth and massive unemployment are bound to demoralise. Those with jobs are unlikely to hazard them in futile displays of anti-status quo aggression and protest. They will be glad to settle for the little they can get. There may, probably will, be acts of urban terrorism, but experience elsewhere suggests that such methods are unlikely to topple any moderately powerful regime.

The great threat to social stability, as Vorster had himself acknowledged, is indeed massive black unemployment. There are no official statistics on Africans without jobs, but their number is undoubtedly very high. According to one estimate, made in 1973, blacks without work were increasing by 100,000 a year. The inability of the South African economy to provide a decent living for these people will be reflected in the usual indices of social decay, such as rising crime rates, and a high incidence of alcoholism and disease. But, and this is the important consideration for white South Africans, while black unemployment may heighten social instability and make life less secure for the ruling caste, it will not imbue Africans with those hopes for the future that are seemingly a prerequisite for revolutionary fervour.

The Government's transparent willingness to use extreme methods in maintaining internal control makes it hardly conceivable that white supremacy will be overthrown by any massive black uprising within the country. The costs of revolt will be entirely certain, and virtually prohibitive; the gains will be huge, in principle, for they will bring "freedom" but the chances of success will be so remote that only the foolhardy will embark on so dubious a venture. What then are the dangers to white rule? Can it really not survive when the domestic circumstances are actually not all that unpromising?

Literally and metaphorically, South Africa is not an island. It is this basic truth which makes the future of white rule so bleak. South Africa's diplomatic isolation, its ostracism by its "friends" in the West, has never been so complete. Western expressions of moral repugnance at white supremacy have become as frequent and predictable as death and taxes. But, for the foreseeable future, these ritual hypocrisies need not be taken too seriously. Threats of economic boycott will remain empty, partly because exchange relationships with South Africa benefit the Western countries themselves, and partly because the collapse of the Republic's economy will initiate a period of anarchy in the subcontinent which will be all too susceptible to Communist exploitation. It is rather in the disappearance of white-ruled buffer states of South Africa's borders that the real threat to apartheid resides. The unforeseen takeover of Angola and Mozambique by Marxist but, fortunately (for South Africa's whites), ramshackle regimes was a bad blow to the white sense of security. At the time of writing the prospects for Rhodesia and South West Africa were still uncertain but, for the former at least, the future offered little room for optimism. Should a "revolutionary" government emerge in Rhodesia too, there would be the prospect of continuous warfare against guerrillas, or terrorists (depending on one's political obsessions), on South Africa's borders. For a long time South Africa will be able to repel these onslaughts, but the cost of doing so will be an immense and inescapable burden on an economy which has not been performing impressively for some years. More whites will flee the country, raising the cost of domination for those who remain. Within South Africa the effect of such protracted warfare on the frontiers will be to heighten black expectations at a time when the whole apparatus of repression and control will be stretched to its limits. In these entirely changed circumstances, new, and perhaps bigger, Sowetos will be a strong probability. Faced with the prospect of South Africa being "liberated" under Communist auspices, for the "freedom fighters" will undoubtedly rely heavily on Russian financial and military aid, the West will at last feel compelled to act. In return for acceptance of majority rule, it may offer South Africa's whites a package deal which will "secure" them certain basic rights. Quite likely, in view of the inherently high risk of any such arrangement, the offer will be rejected, but the consequences will probably be, for the first time, vigorous action by the West to end white supremacy, first by economic boycott and, if that fails, by direct military intervention.

This, at least, is one scenario for the future. Whatever happens, it seems certain that South Africa's whites will in years to come have to make more and more sacrifices for their privileged way of living. Life will become more difficult, although still far from unbearable. Eventually, it seems just as certain that numbers must prevail, that it will not be possible to maintain white rule in the face of widespread internal unrest and a never-ending military commitment on the Republic's frontiers.

How did events come to their present pass? Was there ever a time when it was possible to take a different course, which would have avoided all the destruction and upheaval which now seem so unavoidable? Looking back on the past, it is tempting to find turning points. If only "this" had not happened or "that", then things would have been so different and everyone (or nearly everyone) would have been so much happier. Of course, there are some decisive events, which could quite easily not have happened, but which did, and changed the course of history. Had Lenin never arrived at the Finland Station, is it likely that there would have been a Russian Revolution? Yet, as one looks back on recent South African history, it is difficult to find such a decisive turning point, some "avoidable" event, that altered the very nature of things to come. The Nationalist victory in 1948 is a tempting candidate, and in many ways it was a crucial watershed. But had Malan not won in 1948, South Africa would still have had a white supremacist government, as little prepared to accept black rule as the Nationalists ever were. One must indeed go back to 1910, when the Union of South Africa was born, for a year that perhaps qualifies as such an historical turning point. The emergence of a unified South Africa under white rule, under a constitution which made it possible to subject the black majority to permanent inferiority with the full sanction of the law, had within itself the seeds of racial confrontation which would only be settled by force.

If the South African past placed such fundamental constraints on the ability to choose, if the country's future was predestined, as it were, since at least 1910, then it follows that the post-war politicians who have loomed so large on the South African stage have perhaps not played roles as decisive as they once appeared. It is in this context that Verwoerd must be seen. If he was not the heroic shaper of the Afrikaner destiny, as his followers were only too ready to believe, then neither was he quite the villain so remorselessly leading South Africa to destruction, as his opponents so adamantly maintained. His role was more limited, although it was not for want of trying. Verwoerd really did his best to act upon events and transform them in profound ways. But, like all the other South Africans of his time, he was truly a victim of history. It was a history which consisted in the interaction of diverse races in an intricate counterpoint of conflict and cooperation. These aspects were inseparably linked; it was Verwoerd's error to believe that the past could be undone, that his way of political separation would abolish the conflict, while retaining the cooperation. He was wrong. History is not so easily restructured, continuity is more important than social engineers like to think. Yet it remains true that any understanding of Verwoerd's failure must cast a powerful light on the South Africa he left behind him, on the permanent and the merely transient in what has aptly been called a very strange society.

1 Formation of a Nationalist

Verwoerd was an outsider, a man who could never wear his Afrikaner nationalism lightly. The Afrikaners have had their fair share of strong leaders, dedicated, frequently humourless, invariably God-fearing but none with quite as intense a sense of mission as this immigrant from the Netherlands. His parents came to South Africa when he was still a very young child. He grew up as an Afrikaner, to all intents and purposes he was an Afrikaner, but one thing was lacking: he was not born an Afrikaner. It would not have mattered so much if Verwoerd had an ordinary, humdrum career, but he became a politician, partly because he genuinely wanted to further the interest of the Afrikaner people, partly because he simply wanted to reach what Disraeli called the "top of the greasy pole". In the white-hot atmosphere of Afrikaner nationalism, with its frequent invocations of the glorious past of the Voortrekkers and of Paul Kruger, origins became important. It was at the very least reassuring to know that one's forefathers had participated, however modestly, in building the Afrikaner heritage. Verwoerd could make no such claim. Not one of his ancestors was an Afrikaner. In his chosen career he could not but be acutely aware of his liability. He took the way typical of a convert: he set himself to be an Afrikaner of Afrikaners. When he entered public life Verwoerd soon became known as an unrelenting exponent of Afrikaner isolationism, the enemy of all those willing to think of a broader South African white nation. One of his associates of those days wrote: "He was nearly fanatical about Afrikaans institutions and delighted in proving his loyalty to them."[1]

But being a foreigner in such a situation can be a paradoxical advantage, for reasons which go to the very heart of nationalism. Certain objective characteristics are supposed to define a nation, such as language, race or religion, but in practice, as Kedourie has written in his classic study of the nationalist phenomenon, "there is no convincing reason why the fact that people speak the same language or belong to the same race should, by itself, entitle them to enjoy a government exclusively their own. For such a claim to be convincing, it must also be proved that similarity in one respect absolutely overrides differences in other respects." Kedourie concludes therefore that, "Even if the existence of nations can be deduced from the principle of diversity, it still cannot be deduced what particular nations exist and what their precise limits are. What remains is to fall back on the will of the individual who, in pursuit of self-determination, wills himself as the member of a nation."[2] In other words, the element of consciousness is decisive. The subjective aspect has primacy. The nation is something that must be willed.

It is here that the foreigner who identifies with a "nation" has an advantage. He does so by deliberate choice; he does not take his membership for granted as if he were born to it. He wills his nationalism. In this conscious act of willing the foreign-born nationalist becomes superior to the indigenous type. He can be a more articulate and passionate exponent of his adopted faith than those who are to their nationalism born.

Verwoerd never spoke about it, but he must have known that he was an Afrikaner with a difference. His ancestors had not suffered in the cause of Afrikaner freedom as he had no doubt those of his fellow-nationalists had done. In this respect his nationalism was an artificial growth, which had to be constantly willed if it were to endure. And Verwoerd, as South Africans of all varieties were to learn, had a most formidable will. Paradoxically, his foreign birth qualified him in a unique way to become the most stubborn and unyielding Afrikaner leader of his time.

He came to South Africa with his parents when he was only two years old. The Netherlands at the turn of the century, odd as it seems today, fully shared in the general European sympathy for the Boers then undergoing final defeat at the hands of the British in what seemed a classic example of an imperialist war. Verwoerd's parents identified particularly intensely with the sufferings of the Afrikaners. Their emotional involvement with the Boer cause was heightened when Paul Kruger visited Amsterdam in December 1900 at the start of his exile, to unprecedented public acclaim. The elder Verwoerd, Wilhelm Johannes, had another reason for coming to South Africa. For a long time he had cherished a frustrated desire to be a missionary; now, in the closing phases of the Boer War, he finally decided to realise his ambition.

He arrived with his wife and two sons at the Cape in November 1903. The younger child had been born on 8 September 1901 in Amsterdam and had been baptised Hendrik Frensch Verwoerd. They settled in the Cape Town suburb of Wynberg, where Wilhelm Verwoerd soon succeeded as a building contractor and was able to provide for his family in reasonable comfort. In his spare time he also did missionary work amongst the large Coloured community of the Cape, thus partially satisfying his religious aspirations. In 1910 he qualified as a lay missionary. But if the Verwoerds wished to identify themselves with the Afrikaner people, they must have been disappointed during these early years. Few Afrikaners with strong nationalist views and sympathies were to be found in Cape Town, while English was the language spoken by most whites, including the descendants of many of the old Dutch patrician families. In the aftermath of the Boer War the Afrikaners appeared to be both defeated and demoralised. There were signs of recovery, which at the Cape manifested themselves in cultural rather than in political terms, centring especially around the growth of Afrikaans instead of Dutch as the medium of expression. But in the very English Wynberg these indications of revival could not have been very noticeable.

Inevitably therefore the early education of the youngest Verwoerd was wholly in English. Apparently it did not handicap him in any way. At Wynberg High School for Boys, to which he went in 1913 after completing junior school, his results were outstanding. During the one year he was there, he was placed second in the three examinations he wrote, yielding first place to the only other Afrikaans boy in his class, I.D. du Plessis, later the well-known Afrikaans poet and writer.

Outside school he was known for his energy, which seemed inexhaustible. This super-abundance of energy was to remain an outstanding feature of his whole life, leaving its distinctive mark on all his activities as a politician.

Although he had prospered materially, Wilhelm Verwoerd had still not satisfied his missionary yearnings. So when he received a call from the Dutch Reformed congregation in Bulawayo to assist in missionary work, he closed his business and left with his family for Rhodesia. In this British colony Afrikaners lived in an environment even less congenial for their national aspirations than that at the Cape. English was the only legal language and was spoken by the vast majority of whites, whose attachment to the imperial connection was intense. Not doubt the small number of Afrikaners felt themselves an embattled minority; some took the easy way out by assimilating with the dominant English. Not so the Verwoerds, whose identification with the Afrikaners remained unshaken. It was certainly strengthened by their close association with the Dutch Reformed Church, which has traditionally played a vital role in heightening the Afrikaner's sense of belonging to a distinct community with its own God-given purposes.

60

If anything it appears that the Verwoerds' consciousness of involvement with the Afrikaner destiny was sharpened by their Rhodesian experience, despite, or perhaps partly due to, the fact that their arrival coincided with the outbreak of the First World War, when pro-imperial and pro-British sentiments were at their most ardent.

Hendrik Verwoerd inevitably went to another English-language school, Milton Boys' High in Bulawayo. The contrast between his own sentiments and those of his fellow pupils and the teachers was marked and led to many unpleasant experiences. His biographer, G.D. Scholtz, records that at Milton he acquired a lifelong aversion to the playing or singing of the British national anthem, an ordeal to which he was subjected every day at school.[3] In spite of the depressing environment Verwoerd once again proved a brilliant pupil, easily overcoming the considerable problems of adapting to a new and different syllabus. The Verwoerds were in Rhodesia for only a few years. In 1917 they left for the Orange Free State where the elder Verwoerd was to sell Bibles and religious texts.

For the future Prime Minister his Rhodesian experience seems to have been mainly significant for having strengthened his existing beliefs. To the imperial-minded white Rhodesians he had been an Afrikaner like other Afrikaners, to be treated accordingly. His foreign birth cut no ice with them. What mattered was that he differed from them on the things that mattered: language, religious affiliation and love of the home country, Britain. Many factors went into the making of Verwoerd the hardline nationalist, but it is reasonably certain that his years in Rhodesia contributed much to his adult conviction that Afrikaners and English did not and should not mix, that the Afrikaners had a unique identity which could only be saved from dilution by insistence on strict limits to contact with other groups.

In the Free State town of Brandfort the Verwoerds for the first time lived in a mainly Afrikaans environment, where memories of the Boer War and of the 1914 rebellion against Louis Botha's pro-British government were still fresh. All the evidence tells us that Hendrik Verwoerd thrived in these new surroundings. He was a good sportsman and was popular at school. Once again there is the by now familiar story of his scholastic brilliance despite the necessity yet again to adapt to a different syllabus. Although he too became ill during the 1918 influenza epidemic, he wrote his matriculation examination the following January. This he passed not merely with distinction, but top of the list in the Free Sate.

Verwoerd decided to study Theology at Stellenbosch University. There were at the time only 600 students at this new university, which had only recently developed out of the old Victoria College, but Stellenbosch had for many years been the intellectual centre of the Afrikaners. In the late nineteenth century it had been one of the principal nurseries of the *taal* or language movement. It was logical that the university should become one of the main intellectual strongholds of Afrikaner nationalism. But as yet, in 1919, this nationalism was largely still an upper-class pheno- menon, so much so that when Dr. D.F. Malan in 1921 pleaded at Stellen- bosch for the use of Afrikaans, he had to do so in High Dutch.

When Verwoerd arrived at Stellenbosch, nationalism had taken root, but its growth had been slow, with few signs of the vigour that was later to be so impressive. The Afrikaners had already by the 1880s acquired the consciousness of being a distinct people, but they still lacked those decisive experiences which were to transform their nationalism into a movement intent on political power. These experiences only came with the Boer War* and the 1914 rebellion against South African participation in the Great War. Nationalist feeling was immeasurably strengthened by defeat in the Boer War and the subsequent attempts by the British, as the Afrikaners thought, to deprive them of their identity as a distinct people. The humiliation of defeat gave the Afrikaners throughout South Africa, and not merely those in the former Boer republics, a sense of cohesion, as well as a strong incentive to find symbols affirming their national worth. The main focus of this revived nationalism was the Afrikaans language. Its status was in fact ambiguous, as Afrikaans was the spoken language, while Dutch continued to be language of education. Yet it hardly mattered which language was preferred by individual Afrikaners, for the primacy of English was affirmed by the reconstruction regimes in the former republics after 1902.

The post-Boer War sense of grievance was accentuated by the insistence of Generals Botha and Smuts on participating in "Britain's War" in 1914, as well as by their refusal to use the opportunity now offered them to

* The Boer War did not only affect the Afrikaners, as the following entry in Beatrice Webb's diary on 31 January 1901 shows: "The last six months, and especially the last month at Plymouth, have been darkened by the nightmare of war. The horrible con- sciousness that we have, as a nation, shown ourselves to be unscrupulous in methods, vulgar in manners as well as inefficient, is an unpleasant background to one's personal life ... The Boers are, man for man, our superiors in dignity, devotion and capacity – yes *in capacity*. That, to a ruling race, is the hardest hit of all. It may be that war was inevi- table: I am inclined to think it was: but that it should come through muddy intrigues and capitalist pressure and that we should have proved so incapable alike in statesmanship and generalship is humiliating."

re-establish republican independence. The Rebellion of that year, and its failure, became a potent symbol in the mythology essential to every nationalism. At the time it powerfully stimulated the growth of General Hertzog's newly formed National Party, as was reflected by its showing in the general election in 1915.

At the same time Afrikaner nationalism was acquiring a more marked racial connotation because of the Poor White problem. Black poverty had always been an accepted feature of the South African way of life, but white indigence was a different proposition altogether. Shockingly, since the late nineteenth century, it had been on the increase. By the end of the Great War so many whites, of whom most were Afrikaners, could be described as Poor Whites that the phenomenon could no longer be ignored. Wide income differences had begun to emerge among Afrikaners as more and more found it virtually impossible to make a living from the land. It was due to many causes, such as unproductive farming methods on a soil unable to support a dense population, and the Afrikaner's traditional law of succession, which led to the sub-division of the soil amongst all the heirs, no matter how uneconomical the resulting farming lots may then be. Whatever the causes, the results were disturbing to all right-minded Afrikaners. What was originally a rural problem now became an urban one as well. Thousands of unskilled Afrikaners streamed to the towns and cities in mostly futile attempts to better themselves. They faced one immense obstacle: the competition of even cheaper labour, that of still poorer blacks willing to accept wages which undercut theirs. So there was no solution to the Poor White problem in South Africa's urban areas, while each day Afrikaner poverty was becoming more visible. It was now that Afrikaner nationalism began to acquire a distinct racial dimension which had previously not been overt. Afrikaner leaders began to see with new urgency the need to save white people from having to do "kaffir work".

This was the background against which Verwoerd went to Stellenbosch University. His years at this institution, both as student and teacher, were to be decisive in shaping his intellectual outlook. It was at Stellenbosch that there were close and intimate relationships with students whose parents and grandparents had been injured, in reality or in the imagination, by the British. It was at Stellenbosch that he first became aware of white poverty when, as a theology student, he went with other students to hold religious services for whites living in Cape Town's slums. It was also at Stellenbosch that the fate of the Poor Whites was indivisibly linked with the fate of the Afrikaner people.

As was only to be expected, Verwoerd was prominent in student affairs. He was a brilliant student with a powerful personality. He became chairman of the Students' Representative Council in 1923, and was a conspicuous performer in the University's debating societies. At this early stage Verwoerd was already involved with the stock in trade of nationalism. As S.R.C. chairman he tried unsuccessfully to have Afrikaans used, along with Dutch, at church services in Stellenbosch. But he had more success when he persuaded the Cape Town Municipal Orchestra to cease playing "God Save the King" at the end of each of its performances in Stellenbosch.

Student politics did not interfere with his studies. Verwoerd's academic achievements were outstanding. In 1912 he obtained his B.A. degree with distinction, with Psychology as one of his major subjects. A year later obtained an M.A. degree in Psychology, again with distinction. All this was supposed to be a prelude to his theological studies, but he abandoned those at the beginning of 1923 to concentrate on a Ph.D. in Psychology. He obtained his doctorate at the end of 1924 with a thesis on "Die Afstomping van die Gemoedsaandoeninge" (The Blunting of the Emotions), an experimental study in thinking processes.

By now Verwoerd had been appointed a lecturer in Psychology. He had also been awarded the Abe Bailey bursary of £400 a year for study at Oxford. It was a rich bursary at the time and it was a coveted award, but Verwoerd the incipient nationalist was made of stern stuff. He disapproved of Sir Abe Bailey, a man known for his strong imperial sentiments. He refused the scholarship and accepted another but lesser award which enabled him to study in Germany. He duly attended the Universities of Hamburg, Leipzig and Berlin, at each of which he studied for a term.

It was also in Germany that he married, in January 1927, Elizabeth Schoombee, a farmer's daughter from the Cape Province whom he had met at Stellenbosch. They spent their honeymoon travelling through Europe, subsequently visiting Britain and the United States. To Verwoerd domesticity was important, offering him a refuge from the vigorous and often strenuous activities of public life. The marriage produced seven children, five boys and two daughters, and was by all accounts extremely happy. In addition to rearing the children, his wife Betsie took a keen interest in his work, and later provided him with that encouragement in his political activities which he undoubtedly found an immense comfort.

In December 1927, while Verwoerd was still in the United States, he was offered the chair of Applied Psychology at Stellenbosch. He and his wife returned the following year, when he embarked upon an academic career which proved to be only temporary, but which laid the foundation on which his later public career was built.

Hendrik Verwoerd was quite definitely a competent academic. He was known as an excellent lecturer, who expounded his thoughts clearly and with a minimal reliance on notes. His photographic memory served him well when he gave the opening address, a considerable honour for so young an academic, at the beginning of the 1929 academic year. Without notes he spoke for an hour on the "The University of Life". It was a speech which expressed a basic dissatisfaction with academic life, however hard Verwoerd tried to convince himself that universities could be vigorous community-oriented institutions. He rejected the popular belief that academics were impractical dreamers and that a university training was no equipment for life's harsh realities. The main purpose of study was "to teach people to think for themselves in every conceivable situation". But more – he believed that universities could and should play a role in solving social problems, a belief to which he later gave practical expression in his intense preoccupation with the Poor Whites. For Verwoerd the university was an instrument of nation-building. It could only be rooted in the *volk* (people), whose spiritual life was its main concern. "The university of the past created giants; the university of the future must nurture the entire people."[4]

This was the same Verwoerd who, years before as a student, had been so strongly affected by the appalling poverty of the Poor Whites in the hovels of Cape Town. It was also the same Verwoerd who, five years later, was to be so active at the *Volkskongres* (People's Congress) convened to discuss the problem of white poverty. From the outset it seems that Verwoerd was dissatisfied with merely being an academic. Universities are inherently sheltered communities. Their members, with rare exceptions, do not participate actively in public life. For Verwoerd this was intolerable. An academic existence could never satisfy his urge to be up and doing, to make his own special contribution toward solving the many problems now afflicting the Afrikaners. Outstanding academic as he was, he did not have the temperament to remain one. Basically, he was an activist who wanted to give positive expression to his ideals for the Afrikaner people.

Gradually Verwoerd himself realised that he would not remain an academic. The first step to closer contact with the *volk* came in 1932 when he transferred to the new chair of Sociology which had been created because it was felt that the University had to do something positive about the Poor Whites. In 1928 a commission had been appointed, with the aid of the Carnegie Foundation, with the task of exploring in depth the problem of white poverty. As its own contribution the University of Stellenbosch decided the following year that a B.A. course be introduced for the training of social workers. It was later decided that sociology should be the basis for the course, and Verwoerd was asked to undertake the teaching of the new subject. His concern with the problem of white or, in effect, Afrikaner poverty was to involve him increasingly in public life, until he finally decided that it could only be solved within a more satisfactory political framework than the one which existed at the time. His conversion from psychologist to sociologist was a decisive watershed in his life.

The problem of the Poor Whites had until then caused much concern but little effective action. Conferences had been held in 1916 and 1923, but the abundant rhetoric at those gatherings had done nothing to improve white prosperity. It is true that the Nationalist-Labour Government which came into power in 1924 had followed a "Civilised Labour" policy, which attempted to give whites preferential access to jobs, especially in the public sector, such as on the railways. But the Poor Whites showed no sign of going away. By 1929 there were 220,000 of them. Most of them being Afrikaners, about one-fifth of the Afrikaans people consisted of these marginal men, too poor, too uneducated and too unskilled to hope for an improvement in their lot. Between 1929 and 1934 the situation was aggravated by the great drought and the depression of those years. Particularly disastrous for true Afrikaners like Verwoerd was the prospect that economic degradation would lead to social degradation. As the Carnegie Commission reported in 1932: "Long continued economic equality of poor whites and the great mass of non-Europeans, and propinquity of their dwellings, tend to bring them to social equality. This impairs the tradition which counteracts miscegenation, and the social line of colour division is noticeable weakening."[5] By 1934 the problem had worsened and Verwoerd himself estimated that more than 300,000 whites were impoverished.[6] One quarter of the Afrikaner people were now Poor Whites.

The five-volume report of the Carnegie Commission, which had been favourably received by the public, led to a press campaign for a congress to consider the commission's proposals, and then to formulate a plan of action. In October 1934 the *Volkskongres* on the Poor Whites finally met in Kimberley. Verwoerd had been one of the main organisers of this congress, which was supposed to be so different from the futile conferences of previous years. These high hopes were disappointed. The contribution of the congress to the alleviation of white poverty was negligible. Its proposals for action could only be a palliative and not a cure for a problem which required rapid economic growth for its solution. The Government in any event largely ignored its inadequate proposals. But for the student of Verwoerd's career the congress was memorable for two reasons: it was here that he first rose to national prominence as a spokesman for Afrikaner interests, while it was the Government's negative response to the proposals made which persuaded him that power had to be in proper Afrikaner hands before anything satisfactory would ever be done about the Poor Whites.

Verwoerd had been asked to deliver his first paper, which was concerned with the fight against poverty and the reorganisation of welfare work. It was a highly significant document. Here was the most complete formulation yet of how his mind worked on national (and nationalist) issues. He was already thinking along certain lines from which he was not to deviate for the rest of his life.

His whole approach was unashamedly sectional. For him one of the most unfortunate aspects of the situation was that "by far the most voluntary organisations which concern themselves with the impoverished are English-orientated". Afrikaner problems required Afrikaner solutions. The Afrikaans-speaking poor had a right to be uplifted by their own people. The risk of anglicisation was immense. On the more basic issue of what to do about the Poor Whites, Verwoerd believed that the state could do much to alleviate poverty. He proposed a "practicable minimum plan" in which regulation played a major role. But here he had to face "the connection between white poverty and the presence of Coloureds and Natives in the country". Verwoerd was nothing if not consistent: "It is impossible to make proposals for the increased economic welfare of the impoverished whites without in one way or another affecting these other groups. Our dilemma is that in the interests of the country increased welfare *must* be obtained for the white poor, and that, also in the national interest, it must not be obtained in such a way as to make the economic aspect of the Coloured and Native questions insoluble. This must be frankly admitted."[7]

It was the old nationalist dilemma in any heterogeneous country. How can one further the interests of one's own group or "nation" without harming those of others? His answer revealed Verwoerd the young professor as the father of Verwoerd the Nationalist politician. He identified the national interest with the preferential treatment of the Afrikaner. It could even be argued that it was in the interests of the less privileged groups themselves that they should be discriminated against. He did not put it in such blunt terms, but it was clearly implied by his argument. In his own words: "Accordingly, when some of the economic proposals contain a discrimination in favour of the white worker it must be realised that it was not only what was beneficial to our problem group – the white poor – that was considered, but to the country! Where, for instance, a certain privilege for the white poor causes a difficulty – but a removable one – for the non-whites, then it was chosen without hesitation." This was why protected industries and public bodies had to give some form of preference to "civilised labour". If someone, a white or a black man, had to be unemployed, "then in our present society, with existing differences in the standard of living, it is more economical for the country that the Native should be unemployed".[8]

Verwoerd's second argument for discrimination favouring whites foreshadowed the politician who was the great exponent and pursuer of apartheid. Urban poverty in places like Cape Town was aggravated because Coloureds were being ousted from their jobs by still cheaper black labour, as in the building industry. In turn, whites were forced out of their jobs by Coloureds. If work could be found for them elsewhere then there was no problem, but otherwise the Coloureds and whites had to be restored to their old jobs. Yet this was only feasible if blacks could find work elsewhere. Verwoerd suggested that the black worker, "although this is less attractive for him", should find alternative employment by increasingly taking the place of African miners imported from neighbouring territories, while the more rapid economic development of the native reserves could also provide him with work. He went on: "Then the reversal of the process whereby white and Coloured poverty partly originated or became aggravated in the cities, by a temporary discrimination in their favour, would be the wise course to choose in the interests of the country. It is a policy declaration, if you will, which takes sympathetic account of the rights and interests of whites and non-whites, and then decisively decides in favour of the community as a whole, even if it should superficially resemble favouritism."[9]

Thus, right at the start of his career as a public figure, Verwoerd was to display a talent for ingenious sophistry which was to serve him superbly well as a politician and as a minister of state. For him, throughout his public life, what was good for the Afrikaner was good for South Africa. It was an approach which logically led to authoritarian solutions to the problems he faced. If the unrestricted play of economic forces did not produce results favourable to Afrikaner interests, as Verwoerd conceived them, then the answer was to regulate. If black competition in the towns meant that whites were ousted from certain jobs, then send the blacks back to where they came from, even if there was no work for them there, and give back to the whites what was rightfully theirs. Later, as newspaper editor, faced with Afrikaner inability to compete with the Jews already well-established in the professions, he was to support a quota system according to which each white group share in the main professions "according to its percentage of the white population". In fairness to Verwoerd it must be stated that when he was Prime Minister he made no attempt to implement this astounding proposal, but by then times had changed. Not only do his views on competition by black and Jew testify to that economic illiteracy which was to stay with him all his life, but they bear witness to a markedly authoritarian temper. Verwoerd was never to lose his faith in controls as the best means of creating his ideal South Africa. Given his ends, he probably had little alternative, but Verwoerd never gave any sign that resorting to strong-arm methods ever caused him much soul-searching. The price in terms of economic inefficiency and loss of civil liberties was regarded by many as excessive, but it was a price Verwoerd was always prepared to pay.

It was the *Volkskongres* which impressed upon Verwoerd the need, as he saw it, for political solutions to economic problems. As he later wrote in the Cape Town Nationalist daily, *Die Burger*, on ways of alleviating white poverty: "A study of the resolutions will show that in a very large number of cases it will be government bodies that will have to be approached. In this respect the accusation has already been made that the congress is just like the poor people – it expects everything from the Government!" He continued: "The only organisation in the country which has the power to deal really effectively with the problem is un-doubtedly the Government."[10]

This approach was reflected in the resolutions, strongly influenced by Verwoerd, which were adopted by the congress. The emphasis was on prevention and rehabilitation, and on the vital role which could and should be played by the Government. But Verwoerd and the other participants in the congress were to be bitterly disappointed by the Government's failure to act. Early in 1935 the Government decided to convert the existing Department of Labour into the Department of Labour and National Welfare, but Verwoerd was not especially pleased, for it was an independent department that he wanted. In any event, it was weak on action. In June 1936 Verwoerd expressed his great regret, in an address to the *Afrikaanse Nasionale Studentebond* (Afrikaans National

Students' Union), that the converted department, in spite of all its resources, had "done virtually nothing to remove our social need".[11] It is doubtful whether it could indeed have done much, but what Verwoerd saw as its pathetic inadequacy drove him still further towards politics, a course on which his natural instincts were already urging him.

Up till now his impression of the politicians in power had been poor. Generals Hertzog and Smuts had in 1934 formed a Fusion Government that seemed to flout all the ideals of Afrikaner nationalism, or certainly at least the ideals of those to whom the Afrikaner identity was a precious thing, constantly endangered by contact with non-Afrikaners. The failure of the new Department of Labour and National Welfare was only another example of what could be expected when power came into the wrong hands. The ruling politicians simply did not behave as Verwoerd thought they should.

There was another issue which aroused Verwoerd's bitter hostility to the United Party Government of Hertzog and Smuts. This was Jewish immigration to South Africa. During 1936 many Jewish refugees from Nazi Germany entered the country, to the very considerable concern of Afrikaner nationalists. Hitherto anti-Semitism had not been an important factor in South African life. It was rather to be found in the exclusive clubs of the English-speaking than among the Afrikaners. Jews were in any event a very small percentage of the total white population, but they were highly visible as business and professional men in Cape Town and Johannesburg.

A new situation arose when the thousands of Poor White Afrikaners fled from the rural areas to find better employment in the cities. The prevailing Afrikaner stereotype of the Jew was of an avaricious capitalist who employed the cheapest possible labour, even if it was black, rather than help poor but deserving Afrikaners by paying them "civilised wages". To the more enthusiastic Afrikaner nationalists they were a *volksvreemde* (outlandish) element, and hostile, even if only unwittingly, to the preservation of the Afrikaner identity. Thus, although the rapid and sudden inflow of Jewish immigrants into South Africa could only marginally raise the Jewish proportion of the white population, their visibility was ominously increased.

The protests were quick and vociferous. *Die Burger*, the leading newspaper of the National Party, wrote: "The inflow is abnormal and is a danger to the country."[12] Even academics joined in the protest. One of the most prominent and outspoken was Verwoerd. He felt so strongly about Jewish refugees entering the Union that, together with four other

70

Stellenbosch professors he led a deputation to the Government. As at the *Volkskongres* he claimed the national interest as the sole reason for his concern. He was not anti-Jewish, he alleged, but simply interested in a fair share for all. As he put it: "The cardinal point of this Jewish colonisation is the fact that the Afrikaner's hope lies in taking over the influential positions in commerce and industry in accordance with his proportion of the population."[13]

His argument was perfectly consistent with that expounded at the *Volkskongres*. Verwoerd claimed not to be opposed to the advancement of any group, as long as it was not inimical to Afrikaner interest, which he regarded as identical with the national interest. Unlike many of his fellow-nationalists he accepted the urbanisation of the Afrikaner, but deplored the fact that it came too late: "Strangers with urban tendencies have acquired our industries. Their beginnings were small, but they grew with industry. For the Afrikaner it has become virtually impossible to rise to high position in the English atmosphere of the business world."[14] He thus claimed, with all the other more intellectually respectable opponents of Jewish immigration, that he was not anti-Semitic but pro-Afrikaner. For him, in his ignorance of economics, it seemed that the economic process, as long as jobs were scarce and the unemployed many, was a zero-sum game: a job for a Jew, an African, or a Coloured was a job less for an Afrikaner. Their gain constituted his loss.

In principle there was a clear distinction between Verwoerd's attitude and anti-Semitism. It could be argued that his attitude was based on a misunderstanding of economic principles, that his real crime was in being dangerously ill-informed and in his eagerness to act on the basis of that ignorance, but that he was not guilty of anything as crude and uncivilised as anti-Semitism. In practice it was not always easy to make this distinction. There was, for instance, the *Stuttgart* incident. The agitation against Jewish immigration had been so intense that the Government had drafted an Aliens Bill during 1936, and had imposed regulations with effect from 1 November 1936 in order to stop the Jewish inflow. A refugee organisation then chartered a ship, the S.S. *Stuttgart*, to bring 500 refugees to South Africa before that date.

There were immediate protests by the avowedly Nazi Greyshirt movement as well as by the National Party, which was the official Opposition and represented those Afrikaners who liked their nationalism undiluted with contact with English-speakers. The Greyshirts staged large protest rallies, while the Nationalists held a meeting at which Verwoerd was one of the main speakers. He made a point of informing his listeners that he and his Stellenbosch colleagues had pressed their opposition to Jewish immigration long before the *Stuttgart*. The resolution adopted at the meeting pointedly disclaimed any racial prejudice, but asked the Government to stop Jewish immigration as it would harm the established population and only aggravate anti-Semitism.

Superficially, there was a difference between the attitudes of the Greyshirts and those of the Nationalists. Yet the best that can be said for the Nationalists is that they, and especially intellectuals like Verwoerd, showed remarkable insensitivity in protesting against the *Stuttgart* refugees, when they knew that they were doing so at the same time as the enthusiastically pro-Nazi and anti-Semitic Greyshirts, as well as being perfectly aware that there would in any event be no further refugees after 1 November. Not to be pre-empted by the Greyshirts, the Nationalists were quite willing to stage protests which at the very least dangerously resembled anti-Semitism.

This is the best that can be said for Verwoerd and it is really not good enough. He gave the game away less than a year later in one of his first leading articles as editor of *Die Transvaler*. He wrote that there was a close resemblance between the views of the Greyshirts and the Nationalists with respect to "the seriousness of the Jewish question". It was in their attitude to democracy that they differed, the Nationalists after all being well-known enthusiasts for democracy and parliamentary methods.[15] These remarks are extremely significant. During the war years Verwoerd consistently rejected Nazism, but he did so because it represented a form of government he found incompatible with what he saw as the democratic principles of the National Party, not because of its persecution of the Jews. Anyone who sympathised with the Greyshirts' views on Jews, as Verwoerd explicitly did, can justifiably be regarded as an anti-Semite himself. In the first issue of *Die Transvaler* he displayed his strong feelings about Jews by choosing to write a 6,000-word article on "The Jewish Question from the Nationalist Point of View", complete with pictures of himself and his four fellow-professors who had protested to the Government about the Jewish influx, as well as pictures of the *Stuttgart* and the crowds awaiting it on the quayside. Nor was this Verwoerd's last word on the subject. He came back to it repeatedly in his editorials, which were replete with expressions such as "British-Jewish sham democracy", one of his favourite terms of abuse for the form of government under which South Africa was then suffering.

It is difficult to avoid the impression that when he left Stellenbosch

University for an active career in politics, Verwoerd had strong anti-Semitic sentiments, no matter how civilised the language in which he chose to express them. Even his admirers appear to be embarrassed by this aspect of his personality. Nobody could have wished for a more devoted biographer than Dr. G.D. Scholtz, yet in his lengthy two-volume life of Verwoerd, Scholtz does not refer to the deputation of which Verwoerd was so proud to have been a member, nor to the *Stuttgart* incident. Perhaps Dr. Scholtz did not regard these events as important, in contrast to many other apparently trivial ones which he recorded with loving care. Or perhaps he thought the less said about so distasteful a subject the better. Certainly, these omissions create a more favourable impression of Verwoerd than one would otherwise have had.

Verwoerd was to remain at the University of Stellenbosch only until the end of 1936, for he had accepted the chief editorship of a new Nationalist daily newspaper in Johannesburg, *Die Transvaler*. It was to be his first step toward active and full-time involvement in the shaping of the Afrikaner destiny. It had been his ambition to be so involved, but it was impossible while he continued his secluded academic existence.

Already the Verwoerd who was to have so powerful an impact on South African life could be discerned. He had a dominating personality, and those who came under his influence found him irresistible. This seems to have been one of those cases where that much-abused word "charismatic" is applicable. Verwoerd's intellectual powers were clearly formidable. Supremely self-confident, he never doubted the correctness of his views. It was an outstanding characteristic of Verwoerd the politician that, once having made up his mind, it was virtually impossible to make him change it. In the circumstances it would have been surprising had he not displayed autocratic tendencies. His admirers, such as Scholtz, deny that he was an autocrat at all. They maintain that he was friendly, cooperative and charming. These are admirable qualities, but they are not incompatible with plenty of domineering tendencies, and there is much evidence, particularly from his later life, that Verwoerd was a man determined to have his own way. Even as a young professor the signs were there. Piet Meiring, an early student of his who later became South Africa's Secretary for Information, tells us in his book about the country's first six Prime Ministers the highly revealing story of a student who so irritated Verwoerd with his never-ending questions, not all of them relevant, that he excluded him from his lectures, to which he was only readmitted after an appeal to the University Senate.[16]

Verwoerd's political views amounted to a total identification with the Afrikaner nationalist outlook on life, as most adequately represented by the Purified National Party (*Gesuiwerde Nasionale Party*) of Dr. D.F. Malan. As we have seen his Afrikanership did not come lightly. During his early life it required constant affirmation, particularly in the unsympathetic environment of Cape Town after the Boer War, and then in Rhodesia during the First World War. That he succeeded can be ascribed to his own strong personality, to his parents' determination to identify with the Afrikaner people, and to the family's close links with the Dutch Reformed Church, always a powerful means of binding Afrikaners together. His awareness of the condition of the Poor Whites, most of them Afrikaners, seems to have given his commitment to Afrikanerdom an emotional edge it was never to lose. The Afrikaners were his people. They had suffered much and were still suffering. It was a wretchedness which could only be removed, or at least alleviated, if the Afrikaners had a government responsive to their interests. However, in 1934 Hertzog did what few nationalists would ever forgive him for: he formed an alliance with the archenemy, Smuts. Once again Afrikaner interests were sacrificed for the English-speaking in South Africa, a group whose primary allegiance had always been to Britain.

It was the English-speaking whites who were seen as the biggest threat to the survival of the Afrikaners as a nation. Race was not yet as decisive in Afrikaner nationalist feeling as it was later to become, even if poor blacks were the most formidable danger to impoverished Afrikaners in the cities. It did play an important role, as in the 1929 Black Manifesto general election in which the Nationalists for the first time gained an overall electoral majority by blatantly playing on the racial fears and prejudices of the Afrikaners. Nevertheless, it was still the English-speaking section with its pro-British sentiments, its rich cultural heritage and its world language which was seen as the main enemy by the Afrikaner nationalists. Fusion in 1934 was thus an unforgivable betrayal. Hertzog, the Boer general who had led the National Party to electoral triumph, overnight became a traitor to his people. For reasons such as these Afrikaner nationalists knew it was essential to recapture the state. Only political power would secure for the Afrikaners justice in their own country and give them that sense of self-confidence they were prone to lack in relation to the English-speaking. Also, only an Afrikaner government would have genuine concern for the Poor Whites. We have seen that Verwoerd was convinced that only state action could solve the problem of white poverty. Is it surprising that if Verwoerd, with all his academic sophistication, could have such exaggerated expectations about the efficacy of state action then less well-educated Afrikaners should have been equally deluded?

But if Afrikaner nationalists undoubtedly exaggerated the power of the state to wipe out poverty, yet in a wider sense their priorities were logical and realistic. As nationalists they did not accept current Western political notions about the supremacy of the individual whose rights were guaranteed by the state. For them their own group was an object of supreme worth, to which the individual inevitably had to subordinate his rights. Verwoerd the nationalist felt about Afrikanerdom as Pericles was supposed to have felt about Athens, and as Maynard Keynes said Clemenceau felt about France: "Unique value in her, nothing else mattering. Nations are real things, of whom you love one and feel indifference for the rest, or hatred. The glory of the nation you love is a desirable end, but generally to be obtained at your neighbour's expense."[17] If "safety" is substituted for "glory" then these were exactly Verwoerd's views, as his attitude toward the economic advancement of blacks and Jews showed so clearly – their gain was the Afrikaner's loss. Once such views were accepted, it was only logical to aim at supreme political power, but in a heterogeneous society it was difficult to see how such power, once achieved, could result in anything but the oppression of other groups. What was remarkable, and puzzling, about Verwoerd was that anyone as intellectually sophisticated as he could so un-questioningly accept ideas which were not merely naive but obscurantist as well. Yet he did so, apparently without qualms, most strikingly in his acceptance and propagation of the anti-Semitism current amongst a large and growing number of Afrikaners in the 1930s. What set him aside was the sophisticated veneer he gave to arguments which ultimately were no more than the xenophobia of a group which felt itself threatened. For Verwoerd emotional commitment to the Afrikaners came first. This commitment was intense and complete, and never faltered; it was not primarily a matter of intellectual conviction. But if nationalism had been simply the product of rational argument, it would probably never have existed at all.

2 The Years in Journalism

The decision to publish a Nationalist daily newspaper in the Transvaal arose from the divisions amongst the Afrikaners which followed the establishment of the Hertzog-Smuts Fusion Government of 1934. It has often been said that South Africa's political history since 1910 can be written in terms of the Afrikaner's attempts to use his natural electoral majority as a means of capturing and maintaining control over the government. It is a familiar story which began in 1912 and which need not be repeated at length. The main theme of Afrikaner history since 1910, when the Union of South Africa under the British Crown was born, has been the sense of being threatened, at first by the English-speaking community with its loyalties to the Afrikaner's historic enemy, Britain, then increasingly after 1948 by the black majority in a world which was changing rapidly and disturbingly. Conflict between Afrikaners has largely been due to different assessments of the nature of the threat confronting the community at any one time. From the outset there were always Afrikaner leaders who proclaimed the need for a broad South Africanism (naturally confined to whites alone) in which the Afrikaner could nevertheless retain his identity. But always there were other Afrikaner leaders who claimed that it was still too early for such broad visions and larger loyalties, that the Afrikaner for the time being at least should cling to his own. In the struggle for political power, till Verwoerd became Prime Minister, it was invariably the latter who triumphed in the end.

Already in 1910 these divisions were reflected in the Union's first cabinet. The Prime Minister, General Louis Botha, believed in one South African white nation. His policy, commonly described as one of "conciliation", was designed to bring the two language groups closer to one another. One member of his cabinet, another Boer War general, J.B.M. Hertzog, could not agree. He believed that conciliation would inevitably be at the expense of the Afrikaner. For historical reasons, the English language and culture were so well established in South Africa that any call for concessions in the interests of a broader nationhood would in practice mean concessions by the Afrikaners alone. He had no objection to a common South African nationalism; in fact he supported it, but its realisation was still a prospect for the not so immediate future. Botha's "conciliation" was not the answer. Hertzogism, as it came to be known, was a "two-stream policy", in terms of which the two white language groups retained their cultural identities as well as a common South African loyalty. One day the two streams might merge – but not just yet.

Divisions such as these could not persist indefinitely in the same cabinet. In 1912 Hertzog was forced out after a particularly outspoken public statement of his views. Two years later the National Party was formed, with Hertzog as leader, to propagate his ideas and principles. It came immediately before the outbreak of the Great War, and the 1914 rebellion by about 12,000 Afrikaners against South Africa's participation. The rebels demanded as well the proclamation of a republic. They were easily suppressed, but their revolt gave a sharp stimulus to the revival of Afrikaner nationalism. In the general election the following year the National Party won 28 per cent of the votes. Clearly it represented the aspirations of a considerable body of Afrikaners.

Nationalist support grew so quickly that within a decade, in 1924, General Smuts, who had succeeded Botha, was defeated at the polls. Hertzog became head of the Pact Government, based on a coalition between the National Party and the Labour Party, which largely represented English-speaking white workers. The South African Party of Smuts still had substantial support, but the majority now backed Hertzog. In 1929 the Nationalists gained an absolute majority, which meant that they no longer needed the support of the Labour Party. They could do so, in spite of having only 40 per cent of the votes cast, because of the peculiarities of the country's delimitation system, which loaded the vote in favour of the rural areas where most Afrikaners still lived. It was estimated that four out of five Afrikaners had voted for the Nationalists.[1]

Hertzog's government was to remain in power till 1933. During this period, 1924 to 1933, many Afrikaner nationalist ideals were realised, to such a degree that by 1934 Hertzog had come to believe that the time for the old Afrikaner exclusiveness was past and that the country was ready for a government of national unity without compromising any Nationalist principles.

Hertzog's policies had been largely intended to allay the Afrikaner's sense of inferiority to the British world, both inside and outside South

Africa. Thus, in 1925 Afrikaans replaced Dutch as an official language, and bilingualism was encouraged in the civil service. In 1928, after a particularly bitter struggle, a South African flag was adopted, which enjoyed the same status as the Union Jack. South Africa's constitutional position was clarified by the Statute of Westminster in 1931, itself largely a product of Hertzog's persistence, which gave independence and equal status with the United Kingdom to the self-governing dominions in the Commonwealth.

The Hertzog government also tried to help the Poor Whites. It adopted a policy of providing them with employment at "civilised wages" in the public sector. Employers were given incentives to offer them jobs. It was not spectacularly effective in reducing the number of Poor Whites, but at least it could be said that Hertzog had visibly tried, whereas Smuts had done very little.

By 1930 Hertzog had decided that the time had come for a new approach to the question of nationhood. In the words of Roberts and Trollip: "The task of South African statesmanship now lay in the fostering of a really united national feeling to match that legal nation-hood which was to be conferred in the following year by the Statute of Westminster."[2] As Hertzog himself put it that same year: "What I have been feeling for a long time, and also been working for, is that the time has come for us South Africans, Dutch-speaking and English-speaking, to realise and to recognise the fact that as long as we remain separate and try to reach our goal along different roads, we must expect that most of what we as a nation wish to attain will not be attained."[3] In other words, Hertzog had decided that the psychological prerequisites for a common white nationhood now existed at last. After the legislative changes of the preceding years, the Afrikaner need no longer feel that he was a second-class citizen in his own country. Also, the flourishing of Afrikaans literature during the 1920s reduced, if it did not eliminate, the risk of large numbers of Afrikaners becoming anglicised. The affirmation of South Africa's equal status within the Commonwealth meant that the English-speakers would no longer give their main allegiance to Britain, and that they would think of themselves as South Africans first. These were Hertzog's hopes and expectations. For him a new era of South African history had begun.

It coincided with the worldwide economic depression, precipitated by Wall Street's great crash in 1929. In South Africa it inevitably aggravated the Poor White problem, leading to a further inflow of unskilled Afrikaners to the towns from the countryside, where existing difficulties were compounded by one of the severest droughts in the country's history. Industries which, far from expanding, were struggling to survive, could not absorb the thousands of poor and untrained whites who suddenly appeared in the urban areas. The Government seemed helpless in the face of the crisis, and made matters worse by regarding continued adherence to the gold standard not only as sound economic sense, but also as proof of South Africa's sovereign independence from Britain, which had left gold in 1931. The overvalued exchange rate, with its accompanying outflow of vast amounts of capital, only deepened South Africa's economic stagnation. By-elections showed that Smuts's South African Party was gaining votes from the Nationalists.

South Africa was eventually forced off gold in December 1932. By then there were strong pressures from inside both major parties for a coalition government. Not only political expediency, but also Hertzog's new ideas about white nationhood made it a highly congenial prospect. In February 1933 a basis for cooperation was reached. The terms of the agreement are important for they were the proximate cause of a major breach amongst the Afrikaners, one which Nationalists like Verwoerd believed would nullify all the gains that had been made since 1924.

The main points of the agreement were that South Africa's independent status and the unitary nature of its constitution were confirmed, while the equality of English and Afrikaans was recognised. It was agreed that the question of black political rights would be settled by removing them from the country's political system so that, optimistically, it would become a non-political issue.

Both parties found it easy to agree on most of these issues, but the rub came with the first, namely, the question of South Africa's sovereign independence. A considerable minority of Nationalists refused to accept an agreement which, they held, only papered over substantial cracks, and once more placed at risk the survival of the Afrikaners as a distinct people with its own traditions and culture.

At first such differences did not appear insuperable. The agreement between Smuts and Hertzog enjoyed popular support. At a general election in May 1933, coinciding as it did with the return of better times, the coalition was returned with an overwhelming majority, with 136 M.Ps out of 150 in the newly elected House of Assembly. Eventually, in December 1934, the two parties fused into the United South African National Party, generally known as the United Party, with Hertzog as Prime Minister and Smuts as his deputy. But by now the sharp differences within the National Party about the desirability of any form of coalition and, worse, fusion with the party of Smuts came to a head. The resistance was led by the Cape Nationalist leader, Dr. D.F. Malan. He had from the outset been opposed to the coalition and had refused to join the new ministry formed in February 1933. Subsequently he secured the condemnation of the new course by a large majority at the Nationalist congress in the Cape. Malan and the minority of M.Ps who supported him stood as coalition candidates in May, as otherwise most of them would certainly have lost their seats, but once safely re-elected, their hostility to Hertzog's new policy became more outspoken than ever. Attempts to settle differences failed. When the new Parliament met in January 1935, Malan with 18 other M.Ps constituted themselves the Purified National Party to become the official Opposition.

Ostensibly negotiations broke down because Hertzog and Malan could not agree on South African independence. Hertzog claimed that the Statute of Westminster had given the Afrikaners all they could wish for, and that South Africa was now a truly sovereign independent state. Malan rejected this argument, referring to such issues as the divisibility of the Crown and South Africa's right to remain neutral in a war which involved Britain, as well as its right to secede from the Commonwealth. It was indeed an issue on which consensus was impossible, not only between Hertzog and Malan, but also between Hertzog and Smuts, and their respective followers before Fusion. Afrikaners had a strong antipathy to becoming involved in any of "Britain's wars", but many, if not most, English-speaking whites thought it not only a moral, but also a constitutional, obligation. South Africa was independent, but not that independent.

The only agreement that could be reached between Hertzog and Smuts was that the whole insoluble issue should be ignored, for, hopefully in the course of time, Fusion would so strengthen common loyalties and habits of cooperation that it would ultimately become a non-issue. Malan could not see it this way. To him Fusion meant compromises on fundamental issues that could bring no benefit to the Afrikaner nation. The Nationalist split arose out of the issue of South Africa's independence, but in the final analysis it was based on different appraisals of the nature of the Afrikaner people, their stage of development and their readiness to embrace wider loyalties than those that had hitherto inspired them. Malan could not agree with Hertzog that the Afrikaners were now ready to transfer their allegiance to a common white South African nation. In principle he did not reject the ideal, but he was convinced that the English-speaker's belief in "Britain First and

South Africa Second" still made him an alien creature in the country of his birth, that, in short, it was too early to hope for the new nation which Hertzog so optimistically thought was now in being. The English-speaker would have to change his entire outlook on the world, his values and beliefs, if this were to be possible. In effect, Malan and his followers believed that the Afrikaner was the only true South African because of his roots in the country, and his willingness always to place South Africa first. They were prepared to accept the English-speaking community but it had to be on their terms. Anything less would be a betrayal of the Afrikaner people, who would once more be faced with the prospect of domination by an alien culture. In the long run it would make impossible the development of a common nationhood. Paradoxically, Afrikaner isolationism was the best guarantee that one day a South African nation would yet exist.

For the Purified Nationalists, then, the essence of the matter was inner conviction. The Afrikaner had South African inner convictions; his English-speaking counterpart had not and was a South African in name only. The task for Malan after 1934 was to re-establish the Afrikaner unity which Hertzog had so foolishly destroyed. It was a formidable endeavour, for most Afrikaners at first supported Fusion. Only in the Cape Province did a majority of Nationalist M.Ps reject it. In the Free State Malan had a considerable following, but had to contend with the widespread personal popularity of Hertzog, who was a Free Stater. Only about a quarter of the M.Ps in the province supported Malan, while in the Transvaal, the richest province where a rapidly growing number of Afrikaners was becoming urbanised, only one M.P. out of 32 was a follower of Malan. Needless to say, in the very English Natal there was none.

At first the Purified National Party was not a national body at all, but a regional, strongly Cape-centred party. It was in the Cape too that the Nationalists had vigorous press support, for the newspaper formerly edited by Dr. Malan, *Die Burger*, vigorously opposed Hertzog's new approach to the national issue. In the Free State there was a certain hard core of support for Malan, including the backing of a newspaper, but in the Transvaal the prospects were bleak. Funds were limited and party organisation was virtually non-existent. The only M.P., J.G. Strijdom, had strong and outspoken views, but had been relatively unknown till 1934. In particular, the Nationalists felt an urgent need for press support in the Transvaal, but its lack of funds made this impossible.

In spite of its unpromising beginnings, the new party proved itself a virile opposition. The one big drum it enthusiastically beat was of course that of nationhood. What did it mean and how should it be promoted? Was the Afrikaner destined for ever to be betrayed by leaders who had sold out to the enemy?

Malan had predicted that Fusion could not last, based as it was on an artificial unity which had brought together the irreconcilable. In retrospect, in view of the later course of South African history, it is a prediction which impresses because of its apparent harsh realism and its total refusal to be taken in by sham. Malan seems to have been so obviously right: it was far too early to start thinking in terms of one white nation. Yet, to some extent at least, his prophecy was self-fulfilling. Even if wider loyalties and unities were emerging, the Nationalists would do their best to destroy them. Their whole approach, understandably, was to emphasise the evident differences which existed between the white language groups and, when possible, to exacerbate them. In Parliament they pleaded the cause of impoverished Afrikaners, neglected when not ignored by a capitalist and British-oriented government. But economic recovery was under way by the mid-thirties, and so such propaganda began to sound more and more implausible. The Nationalists then reverted to their original great emotional issue: was South Africa really a sovereign independent state? Thus, in 1938, the national anthem became a question of heat and moment. Just what was the position of "*Die Stem van Suid-Afrika*" in relation to "God Save the King"? Hertzog, in his attempts to explain, compromised, tried to please both sides and predictably ended by giving pleasure to few.

But it was on the issues of neutrality and secession that the Nationalists were most vehement. The United Party included such polar elements that the only feasible policy was to let sleeping dogs lie and hope that they would not be woken by Nationalist propaganda. Hertzog's own position was close to that of the Nationalists, but they accused him of pursuing policies that were in fact incompatible with these views. Inevitably, therefore, South Africa would find itself once again involved in wars of others' making.

The logic of their position and the impetus of their propaganda drove the Nationalists to adopt republicanism as official party policy. Most Nationalists had been republicans before 1933, but cooperation with the largely English-speaking Labour Party held them back from actively propagating the ideal. After 1934 such restraints no longer held. In 1936 the establishment of a republic became the Party's official policy, to be attained "on the broad basis of the people's will", as expressed through a special referendum. It would be a republic Afrikaner in orientation, founded on the Calvinist principles of Christian Nationalism, which accepted the nation as the basic political entity continually subject to God's will, which alone gave it meaning and purpose. As Dr. Malan put it in his farewell sermon in 1915 before forsaking the pulpit to become first editor of *Die Burger*: "Is there behind the existence of our nation an eternal idea of God which gives a national life destiny and a vocation, or is it all purposeless, blind fate? ... Ask the nation to lose its identity in another existing nation or one that does not yet exist, and it will answer in the name of God, definitely not."[4]

Developments elsewhere paralleled those on the political front. Afrikaans-speaking organisations and institutions had existed before 1930, notably the Dutch Reformed churches and the *Suid-Afrikaanse Akademie vir Wetenskap en Kuns* (South African Academy for Arts and Science). But toward the end of the 1920s there was a concerted drive toward Afrikaner self-sufficiency in the cultural, social and economic fields. In 1929 the *Federasie van Afrikaanse Kultuurverenigings* (Federation of Afrikaans Cultural Associations) was established, followed in 1931 by the Afrikaans counterpart of the Boy Scouts. In 1933 the Afrikaans universities withdrew from the National Union of South African Students, which they regarded as much too liberal, to establish the *Afrikaanse Nasionale Studentebond* (Afrikaans National Students' Union). To break the iron grip of the two London-based commercial banks, Barclays and the Standard Banks, Volkskas was established. This accorded with the then popular Afrikaner belief that capitalism was an alien exploitative system, typically British and Jewish, which could not be allowed to flourish unchecked.

This sudden burgeoning of Afrikaner organisations in so many fields was more than coincidence. In fact a secret organising society did exist. This was the Afrikaner Broederbond, founded in 1918, with the aim of promoting the achievement of a republic, as well as of improving the social position of the Afrikaners and the status of their language. The Broederbond has acquired such a sinister reputation as a body of clandestine plotters, aiming at securing and maintaining Afrikaner domination in all spheres and at all costs, that objectivity is hardly possible. But some facts about the Broederbond are generally agreed upon. In its heyday during the 1930s and 1940s, it consisted of a small number of Afrikaners known for their commitment to nationalist causes. There were about 2,500 of them, mostly professional men, civil servants, clergymen and teachers. They aimed at infiltrating vital institutions such as schools and universities in order to promote the triumph of Afrikaner nationalist ideals. To promote and perpetuate Afrikaner exclusiveness the Broederbond, it appears, played the dominant role in furthering the growth of so many distinctly Afrikaner organisations and institutions after 1930, although it is still not clear just why it came then.

The links between the Broederbond and Malan's Nationalists were undeniably close. General Hertzog, not the most objective source, even alleged that the two organisations were identical, respectively the underground and aboveground sides of the same Afrikaner racialist coin. It is probably incorrect to think of either body controlling the other. Members of the Broederbond were virtually all Nationalists who were prominent in the party anyway. Among them was Verwoerd, who was both an active and important member of this secret organisation. He became a Broeder in February 1937 and was elected to its Executive Council in October 1940, on which he remained for ten years, only exchanging, in his own words, "the Cabinet of the Afrikaner Broederbond for the Cabinet of the nation". The Broederbond embodies in an extreme form the dominant trends within Afrikaner nationalism during the 1930s. Here was a body totally dedicated to promoting Afrikaner chauvinism. Its ambition was to further the growth of Afrikaner organisations in so many fields that Afrikaners would be sufficient unto themselves, that their sense of group identity would be fostered and reinforced by membership of wholly Afrikaans bodies. In the jargon of the political scientists, there were to be no crosscutting allegiances for Afrikaners through membership of open organisations with "alien" elements which could so easily dilute their loyalty to their "own". Complete success was obviously impossible, but the evidence suggests that the Broederbond's achievements in accentuating the cleavages between Afrikaners and the less genuinely "South African" members of society were significant and enduring.

It was against this background that Verwoerd became the editor of the new Nationalist daily in Johannesburg, *Die Transvaler*. For the Nationalists the need for such a newspaper could not be overestimated. The Transvaal was both South Africa's economic heart and the province which sent the largest number of M.Ps to Parliament, yet here Fusion enjoyed overwhelming support, making the National Party a very poor orphan, without the essential party workers and the money to employ them. Many thousands of Afrikaners were now becoming urbanised. To Nationalists their anglicisation seemed certain in the absence of adequate *volkseie* (wholly national) organisations and an ideologically sound newspaper.

Even if all the many difficulties in establishing a newspaper could be overcome, there was still the main problem of attracting enough readers.

84

Already the Transvaal had two Afrikaans dailies, four English-language ones and two Sunday newspapers in English, all of them supporting the Government. The Nationalist daily would not only have to sell the Party's point of view, but also provide an adequate news service if it were to stay in business. Yet Malan and his supporters saw the need for such a paper as so great that, despite all the sound arguments against its likely success, they decided to press on. Their appeal to Nationalists for money met with such an encouraging response from wealthy supporters that they established a company with a nominal capital of £150,000 (R300,000), a sizeable sum in those days. The company was the *Voortrekkerpers* and the newspaper was to be called *Die Transvaler*.

Early in 1936 Verwoerd was asked to become the editor-in-chief. Clearly acceptance could be hazardous. He was already a prominent academic with security of tenure. His prospects in university life were bright, whereas editing a new Nationalist daily in the peculiarly adverse situation then existing in the Transvaal held the prospects of an interesting but insecure future. Verwoerd's family was growing in numbers, while his father was strongly opposed to his son accepting the post. It tells us much about his strong Nationalist convictions that he hesitated not at all in deciding on a new career. In spite of all the potential dangers, the insecurity, it offered him the prospect of leaving the academic ivory tower in which life for him with his activist temperament was so frustrating. It also meant that he could henceforth participate wholeheartedly in the political struggle he regarded as so crucial for the future of the Afrikaner people.

Verwoerd stayed at Stellenbosch until the end of the academic year. Then, in January 1937, he worked on *Die Burger* for a period to familiarise himself with journalism. When he left for the Transvaal his experience of newspapers was still minimal. This was not necessarily a disadvantage if we think of other editors of Nationalist newspapers before and after Verwoerd. The first and classic example is of course Dr. Malan, who was a minister of the Dutch Reformed Church before he became the first editor of *Die Burger* in 1915. Subsequently there were other editors who were first prominent in non-journalistic fields. Verwoerd's biographer, G.D. Scholtz, himself a former editor of *Die Transvaler*, explains the phenomenon: "The editor-in-chief of such a newspaper must be someone who has already achieved prominence in another sphere of national life (*die volkslewe*) and who has acquired some reputation with the public. Nationalist newspapers must not simply be purveyors of news; they must also enlighten their readers about the great and vital problems which have confronted the Afrikaner people. However outstanding the man who chose journalism as a career, it was indisputable that he could rarely speak with as much authority as someone who already had considerable esteem among the Afrikaners. Even if such a man did not have the slightest journalistic knowledge or experience, he could still be far more effective than an ordinary journalist."[5] In effect, the Nationalist public liked editors whose previous experience showed that they could pontificate with authority on *volksvraagstukke* (Afrikaner problems). Here Verwoerd had a definite advantage. A born pontificator, it was to stand him in good stead in becoming the successful editor of a Party mouthpiece.

At first Verwoerd was faced by a potential obstacle in the person of the one Nationalist M.P. in the Transvaal, J.G. Strijdom, who was the Party's provincial leader. Strijdom differed greatly from Verwoerd both in temperament and style. He did not have the latter's intellectual power and inclinations. On the other hand, he was a born orator with that common touch and emotional appeal to ordinary Afrikaners which Verwoerd was never to possess. Strijdom had strong republican convictions which he insisted on making much of in public, not always to the satisfaction of the Cape Nationalists, who thought that more attention should be given to more immediately relevant subjects with a larger vote-catching potential. Verwoerd as a man of the Cape, so it was thought, would exercise a moderating influence on Strijdom's republican outspokenness. It was for precisely this reason that Strijdom opposed Verwoerd's appointment as editor, as he later told him. He suspected that Verwoerd as a southerner would be lukewarm about the republic. In any event, he was a novice to journalism.

Strijdom was to be agreeably surprised. He soon discovered that Verwoerd was as ardent a republican as he. And it was not only on the republic that they shared common ground. They found in one another virtually complete agreement on basic principles. Each believed in the republican destiny of the Afrikaner. Each had no doubt that a true South Africanism could only evolve on the bedrock of Afrikaner isolationism and exclusivism. Neither was prepared to yield on what he regarded as issues of basic principle, an approach which had already gained for Strijdom, and was to gain for Verwoerd, the reputation of extremist. In spite therefore of Strijdom's initial distrust, they were to become close allies and friends. It was a partnership of some significance in South African history.

The first issue of *Die Transvaler* appeared on 1 October 1937. It set the tone for what was to come under Verwoerd's editorship. The main editorial announced: "*Die Transvaler* comes with a mission – it comes to serve a people by making the voice of true and sublime nationalism resound wherever that voice can reach." A second contribution rang the changes on what was by then and would continue to be a well-worn theme with Verwoerd, and to which he would return with tedious frequency in his leading articles, "The Jewish Question from the Nationalist Point of View". The main burden of the article was that Jews played a disproportionate role in certain professions and kept deserving Afrikaners out, a deplorable state of affairs best remedied "by applying a quota system and resorting to such measures as the refusal of additional trade licences".

There can be little doubt that Verwoerd was a convinced anti-Semite, but his attacks on Jews and other race groups which competed economically with the Afrikaner reflect a more basic concern, namely, that the thousands of poor and unskilled Afrikaners who had streamed to the Witwatersrand from the rural areas should not go under in a new and alien environment. This was to be one of Verwoerd's main themes as editor of *Die Transvaler*. He took to his heart the cause of the Afrikaner worker on the Rand and became one of his great champions. As a dedicated nationalist it was of little concern to him how adversely other groups may be affected by attempts to uplift the Afrikaner poor.

But for Verwoerd, important as the social and economic rehabilitation of the Poor White Afrikaner was, it was only an aspect of a still more inspiring cause, the republic. As he summed up the Nationalist attitude over the years: "A republic which will only mean a change of government will be meaningless for us Afrikaners. We are only republicans because the achievement of that republic will have to be accompanied by the most drastic social and economic changes, that will make South Africa more habitable for everyone, as well as spreading its wealth more equitably among all its citizens. The republican ideal naturally includes for us too the ideal of far-reaching reform in all walks of life."[6]

The republic was to be Verwoerd's great overriding cause. This, more than anything else, was to give distinctiveness to his eleven years as editor. Other Nationalist editors may have been republicans too, but not with his total commitment, even when it affronted the Party leadership outside the Transvaal. Verwoerd believed in a republic because for him it was rooted in Afrikaner history. It was the Afrikaner's natural form of government, the only one which could satisfy his democratic beliefs and his aspirations for full and unqualified independence. The formal trappings of sovereignty conferred by the Statute of Westminster cut no ice with committed republicans like Strijdom and Verwoerd.

Verwoerd was a republican for another reason. It was the only basis for that white unity which Hertzog so mistakenly thought could be realised by Fusion. For Verwoerd the conditions for such a unity did not exist as long as English-speaking whites retained their dual allegiance, which made them place the interests of Britain above those of South Africa. His strategy was directed toward the unification of the Afrikaners on the basis of the republican ideal. Thereafter the English would have no choice but to become genuine, dyed-in-the-wool republicans themselves. The difference between his version of white unity and that of Hertzog was that under the former the Afrikaner would not lose his identity. Unity would be on his terms; it was the English who would be assimilated by the Afrikaners.

Republicanism, in Verwoerd's thinking, was a comprehensive strategy for social change and national renewal. But almost at once he had to face a very considerable obstacle. Dr. Malan was not much taken by Verwoerd's ardour for a republic. He himself was only a lukewarm republican, preferring to concentrate on those immediate issues which he was quite sure had more electoral appeal. This led to the first serious difference between the two.

As Verwoerd was to record years later, after the coming of the republic: "To my surprise Dr. Malan and the other directors rebuked me, and said that they had specifically thought that I would help dampen the Transvaal ardour for a republic."[7] Verwoerd took a stance that was to be among the most familiar and characteristic of his public career: he refused to budge. Instead, he offered his resignation. Fortunately for him, it was not accepted, largely, by his account, because the chairman of the board decided to defend him. It was typical of Verwoerd that he would not allow Dr. Malan's admonition to deter him in the slightest from continuing his outspoken propaganda for a republic cast in Voortrekker mould. He had certain principles and would not deviate from them at all. To him agreement meant adherence to common principles.

This approach was to make him one of the most vigorous and outspoken opponents during the Second World War of cooperation between the National Party and other opposition groups, such as the New Order and the *Ossewabrandwag* (Oxwagon Guard). They believed in Nazism and rejected democracy. For Verwoerd this was the end of the matter. Their beliefs and policies were alien to the Afrikaner, rooted as he was in a past where the will of the people was always regarded as sacred. This was Verwoerd's reading of history; he was not prepared to give aid and comfort to those who repudiated the Afrikaner past.

Afrikaner unity was important to him. It was indeed his long-term goal, but a unity achieved through compromise on principle was spurious and ultimately worthless. In the final analysis the unity of the Afrikaner people could only be achieved on the basis of the principles of the National Party. As editor Verwoerd was to be quite uncompromising in expressing this point of view.

Verwoerd went to the Transvaal not merely to be a journalist but to help rebuild the National Party. He undertook the task with his customary energy. He travelled widely to address Party meetings and soon became a member of the Party's controlling bodies in the Transvaal. He was elected to the Witwatersrand Council and appointed to the Transvaal Provincial Executive and the Federal National Council. Also, Verwoerd continued to concern himself with the situation of the Afrikaner worker on the Rand, threatened as he was by perpetual poverty and continuous exposure to alien ideological influences. To combat the first he established *Die Transvaler*'s Christmas Fund in 1939. It was to aid the jobless, thousands of whom were in fact given financial help.

On a wider stage, Verwoerd helped to organise another *Volkskongres*, which met in October 1939. At this congress Verwoerd delivered a paper in which he argued at length the need for the Afrikaners to organise their growing purchasing power. Consumer organisations were a vital necessity as a countervailing power to organised retail and producer interests. It was another Verwoerdian exercise in dualism. Exploited Afrikaners were engaged in deadly battle against the powerful forces of organised capitalism. He was proud of his role in convening this congress but it is doubtful whether it made any serious contribution to the Afrikaner's deliverance from poverty. Ultimately, however, such activities were, so to speak, extra-curricular. Verwoerd will be remembered for his role during these years as a writer of leading articles in which Nationalist principles were clearly and uncompromisingly stated in a part of the country where the United Party had hitherto won by default.

As editor-in-chief Verwoerd could rely on some impressive qualities. He was exceptionally industrious and could inspire by example. Sometimes he arrived in his office late in the evening to write his leading article, which had to be ready within a few hours. One of his colleagues of those years, J.J.J. Scholtz (not to be confused with G.D. Scholtz), has written: "After the tremendous effort of a long day I was surprised time and again to see him once more vigorous, cheerful and gay the next morning. 'I am not afraid of work,' he once said."[8] Verwoerd was extremely popular with his staff, some of whom even referred to him admiringly as "Baas Henk". He had a remarkable capacity for persuading others of the correctness of his views. The force of his personality was universally acknowledged. There was never any doubt as to who was in charge of the new daily. His former news editor, Piet Meiring, has said that under Verwoerd *Die Transvaler* was run as a "benevolent despotism".[9]

Verwoerd avoided personality conflicts. He saw them as a wasteful diversion from the real struggle against the enemies of Afrikanerdom. For Verwoerd agreement on basic principle was decisive, which could excuse many personal faults.

Verwoerd was not, however, the perfect editor. J.J.J. Scholtz doubted whether he had it in him to give of his best simply as a newspaperman: "Some of his most valuable qualities left him as soon as he started writing."[10] Frequently he wanted to say too much. He would keep on correcting and expanding his leading articles, writing long sentences between the lines which had already been typed. His editorials were generally lengthy and turgid, as if he was determined to cover every possible aspect of the issue being dealt with. Prolixity was one of his worst faults as writer of leading articles, just as it was to be of his performance as speaker on public platforms.

For the Nationalists, when *Die Transvaler* first appeared, prospects were truly bleak despite the obligatory expressions of faith in ultimate victory. The Fusion Government had a huge majority which it seemed destined to retain for a depressingly long time. It was an impression confirmed by the results of the general election of May 1938. The election came at a bad time for the Nationalists. Fusion had hitherto been a success, which really meant that economic revival had been impressive, with the Government naturally quick to claim credit for better times. In particular, an average annual growth rate of nearly nine per cent during the preceding five years had gone far toward alleviating the Poor White problem, and there had been a rapid increase in white employment in the expanding manufacturing sector. The Nationalists had perforce to concentrate on constitutional issues, loudly affirming South Africa's right to remain neutral in a possible war, while also attempting with some implausibility to convince the voters that the Government's race policies were too liberal.

They were to be bitterly disappointed. Nationalist representation in Parliament increased from 20 to 27 members, but the United Party returned with an unassailable majority of 111. Support for the Nationalists outside the Free State and the rural areas of the Cape Province was small, and in any event seemed correlated with extreme poverty. In the

Transvaal their performance was especially depressing. Once more Strijdom was the only Nationalist M.P. within the entire province, but with a reduced majority. Their only consolation was that a majority of Afrikaans voters, an estimated 60 per cent, had supported them.[11] Even so the gaining of enough Afrikaner votes to oust the Government seemed a very long-term prospect. And in the meantime there was the strong possibility, even probability, that Fusion, merely by surviving with success feeding upon success, would attract increasing support from Afrikaners. If it was the poorer Afrikaner who voted for the Nationalists, what would continued prosperity not do to their prospects? And would the passing of time not make the Afrikaners forgetful of all that they had fought for and suffered in the past? In spite of all their attempts to keep alive old divisions, even intensify them, the Nationalists must have been uncomfortably aware that this scenario was not at all implausible.

But if Verwoerd thought along these lines, he took care not to say so. He even drew comfort from their Transvaal performance by comparing the 75,000 votes cast for them in the general election with the mere 30,000 they had received in the Provincial Council elections two years before. He was determined to see light: "This is the turning point. Nationalism cannot die, cannot bend. We accept the task which lies ahead with fresh courage, and next time our opponents will not find us so poorly armed financially and organisationally."[12]

Yet even Verwoerd would have admitted that there was a long haul ahead. It was not appreciably shortened by the Voortrekker Centenary celebrations in Pretoria later that year. Nationalist sentiments received a temporary stimulus in the euphoria of reliving the heroic past. It did the Party a power of good, but did not lead to a new alignment in politics. As long as the existing one lasted such events were only straws in the wind. The trend toward the consolidation of Fusion and the erosion of traditional Afrikaner loyalties could only be reversed by a decisive outside event.

Fortunately for the Nationalists, it came very soon. On 1 September 1939 Hitler invaded Poland. Just as fortuitously, the South African Parliament had reconvened at that time to extend the life of the Senate. Now at last the latent tensions within the United Party came to the surface. The cabinet was split on the question of neutrality, as was the House of Assembly when it met to debate the issue. The pro-war group under Smuts defeated the supporters of neutrality under Hertzog by a small majority, 80 votes to 67. Hertzog resigned and was succeeded by Smuts as Prime Minister after the Governor-General, Sir Patrick Duncan, had refused Hertzog's request for a dissolution of the House to be followed by a general election. Duncan did so on the grounds that Smuts could command a majority in the House, but it was a controversial decision, for political commentators, then and later, have agreed that a general election at that time on South Africa's participation in the war would probably have resulted in a majority for Hertzog.

But for the Nationalists it was their long overdue opportunity. They made the most of it. Of the 104 United Party M.Ps, 38 had favoured neutrality. With the 29 Nationalist M.Ps, the Opposition was transformed. Hertzog and Malan began negotiations and, in spite of ominous differences from the outset, a new party was formed in March 1940 to embrace both old and new dissidents, the Reunited National or People's Party (*Herenigde Nasionale of Volksparty*). Hertzog was to be the leader, with Malan as his deputy.

Seemingly Afrikaner unity had been restored, yet Verwoerd was not pleased. For both him and Strijdom the struggle for unity had only begun. They wanted unity to be achieved their way, on the basis of fixed and irreducible principles which would not be sacrificed merely because of the general eagerness for Afrikaners to be together again. Such enthusiasm, they thought, was understandable, but dangerous. It would only divert Afrikaners from the one true way, the republican way. Malan's agreement with Hertzog was precisely the kind of unity despised by Verwoerd. It derived from a determination to gloss over basic differences in political principle. The new party, it was true, did declare itself in favour of a republic as the best form of government of South Africa, but interpretation of exactly what this meant was imprecise and elastic. Hertzog did not regard republicanism as an essential condition of membership. Reunited Nationalists could, if they so wished, propagate a republic but there was to be room for those who were not republicans. Malan, who differed from Verwoerd in temperament, political style and republican fervour, may have accepted this tolerant approach in the interests of unity, but he was never allowed to do so.

By now Afrikaner nationalism had become virtually synonymous with republicanism. If credit is to be awarded for this, much of it must go to Verwoerd who completely rejected the views of Hertzog, for whom, in any event, he had no great personal admiration. Had he not betrayed the nationalist cause by allying himself for so long with Smuts? Uncompromisingly he stated that membership of the National Party was incompatible with "non-republicanism" (5 January 1940). So he wrote even before the formation of the new party. But he and Strijdom were still to lose a battle before going on to win the war. The final agreement between

Malan and Hertzog affirmed the republic as "the most suitable form of government", but membership would not "be denied or refused to any national-minded Afrikaner willing to subject himself to the party obligations, but not convinced of the desirability of establishing a republic in existing circumstances." In a long, tortuous editorial (29 January 1940), Verwoerd did his best to explain why this agreement did not really violate his insistence upon republicanism as an essential element of membership. Of course it did, however much he chose to split hairs about "active" and "non-active" republicanism. All he could do was make the best of it for the time being, while awaiting the inevitable outcome of any such agreement not based on the acceptance of common principles.

The split came gratifyingly soon. Apart from the ideological cracks which had been papered over, conflicts of personality could not be avoided. After all the hard unkind things they had said about one another during the five years of Fusion, it was now difficult for many Hertzogites and former Purified Nationalists to accept one another as true Afrikaners after all. The memories were still too fresh, the wounds they had inflicted on one another were still too painful. Hertzog, in particular, had difficulty in cooperating with his former enemies, men whom he had once denounced as racialists because of their belligerent nationalism. He could not honestly believe that he had been wrong. His impressions were finally confirmed in November of that same year at the Free State congress of the new National Party. The congress was required to adopt a programme of principles. Hertzog had issued a draft programme, but so also had the Party's Federal Council. They were significant differences. The Federal Council's draft was far more insistent than Hertzog's on the early establishment of a republic, but the split came because the Federal Council was not as solicitous over the rights of the English-speaking as Hertzog considered it should have been. The Federal Council's programme guaranteed only language and cultural equality, but not equality of status and of political rights. Hertzog found this totally unacceptable. When the congress adopted the Council's draft by an overwhelming majority, he walked out of the meeting, after resigning his leadership and membership of the Party in the Free State.

The break had come over a specific issue, whether the English-speaking should have full equality with the Afrikaners, but there is no reason to believe that, had agreement been reached, Hertzog would have remained for long in the same party as Strijdom and Verwoerd. The differences in approach to what constituted the South African nation were basic and irreconcilable.

These differences were only reflected in the issue which led to Hertzog's dramatic exit. Hertzog did not resign over the republican question, but his views were all of a piece. The "rights of the English" were hardly likely to be respected in the kind of Voortrekker republic Strijdom and Verwoerd so passionately believed in. For him, as for his opponents, it was perfectly clear that no party could indefinitely contain such deep divisions as had been apparent from the start. His walkout was the prelude to his final departure from the political scene. A few weeks later he resigned his seat in Parliament to withdraw from public life completely. His followers, under the leadership of his close friend and one-time Minister of Finance, N.C. Havenga, formed the Afrikaner Party to propagate his policies. Without Hertzog's personal magnetism it could not survive in the climate of growing political polarisation and it was wiped out as a Parliamentary party in the general election of 1943. Its influence on Afrikaner politics during the war years was negligible.

The drastic elimination of Hertzogism from the H.N.P. was a foretaste of things to come within Afrikaner ranks. The story of the South African opposition during the Second World War is essentially that of the triumph of the National Party over all other groups and organisations which claimed to speak for the Afrikaner in politics. By 1945 Malan had become undisputed *volksleier* (leader of the people) and his party the sole authoritative voice of the nationalist Afrikaner. It also meant the triumph of the republican ideal amongst Afrikaners. From now on, to be an Afrikaner nationalist meant being a republican.

What kind of republic was envisaged by the Nationalists? Without any doubt republicanism was highly coloured by the circumstances of the time. Politicians in opposition are natural extremists. They take delight in stating in unyielding terms principles they would usually be highly cautious to implement once in power. In South Africa there were additional reasons for extremism.

The country's participation in the war meant the breakdown of the kind of consensus politics which had prevailed within the basically divided United Party. The Parliamentary opposition, which had formerly represented a relatively small percentage of the electorate, had a dismal future to look forward to. Now it was much enlarged, if itself divided, and opposing the Government in terms which left no doubt that nationalist Afrikaners if ever returned to power, in whatever form, intended to restructure South African society in a drastic way. Before 1939 such talk could be dismissed as the vapourings of a frustrated minority; now it represented the overwhelming majority of Afrikaners.

Resentment and frustration at being forced into yet another of "England's wars" drove many Afrikaners into ways of expressing their bitterness which went far beyond those advocated by such "extremists" as Strijdom and Verwoerd. This was the essential background to the formulation of the republican ideal after 1939.

Of the republicans Verwoerd was the most articulate and, with Strijdom, the most insistent. Tirelessly, week after week, his leading articles proclaimed the inevitability of a republic as the Afrikaner's natural constitutional destiny. He saw the republic as "rooted in the nature of the Afrikaans people" (23 January 1942). But for Verwoerd, as for other republicans, the constitutional change to a republic would also mean the transformation of South Africa. Their republic was to bring real democracy as against the "sham democracy" of the "British-Jewish system", which had till then prevailed in South Africa, but under which the Afrikaner worker still existed in a state of "slavery" (16 January 1941). Verwoerd's basic approach is expressed in one of his more succinct statements: "The Afrikaner has his own political approach, born of a history of suffering and oppression. This is his *Christian republican nationalism*. This political faith encompasses the whole broad circle of the radical desires for reform with which he desires to rebuild his country. In this most nationally conscious Afrikaners agree – even if they belong to different camps. This is so not just because of the content of a programme, but owing to *deep-rooted inner conviction*" (8 August 1941).

Verwoerd therefore had no doubts about his best of all possible Afrikaner republics. It was to be an "independent Boer republic", modelled on the South African Republic of Paul Kruger and the Free State of M.T. Steyn, "but adapted to modern circumstances" (8 June 1941).

What such adaptation meant became clear in January 1942, when *Die Transvaler* published a draft constitution for a future South African republic. It was the outcome of an enterprise initiated in Verwoerd's office in November 1939, when a number of prominent Afrikaner academics, as well as Verwoerd, met to discuss the drawing up of a republican draft constitution. The task was entrusted to three of those present, of whom Verwoerd was one, so there can be no doubt that the final document represented his own thinking at the time. This must be emphasised because in 1958, shortly after becoming Prime Minister, he felt sufficiently embarrassed about the document to minimise his own role in framing it. He denied that the National Party was in any way connected with it: "This is something that a young group of intellectuals drew up as a reflection of their ideas. I was connected with these people and I knew of the work they were doing. I do not hesitate to say so, but this had nothing to do with the Party. The National Party is not and was not in any way connected with it."[13] Verwoerd was right of course. The Party was not responsible for the document and it was never approved by any Party congress. It was, however, sufficiently representative of Nationalist thinking for Dr. Malan himself eventually to hand it to the press for publication with the statement that the Party accepted its main principles and broad outline: "It can therefore be taken as an indication of the course already taken by the National Party."[14]

This draft constitution for a republic has acquired a sinister reputation amongst English-speaking whites and opponents of the Nationalists in general, for good reason. The document stood in the sign of the times. It reflected a good deal of the rancour felt by nationalist Afrikaners towards Britain and the English-speaking in South Africa. The future republic would be Christian National and would break all constitutional ties with Britain. Its flag would be the *Vierkleur* of the old Transvaal Republic. Most notoriously, and thrown at the Nationalists with monotonous regularity by the Opposition after 1948, the constitution provided for Afrikaans, "the language of the original white inhabitants of the country", as "the first official language". English was to be tolerated as "a second or supplementary official language which will be treated on an equal footing and will enjoy equal rights, freedom and privileges with the first official language, everywhere and whenever such treatment is judged by the State authority to be in the best interests of the State and its inhabitants."[15]

It would be a presidential system, with a democratically chosen president who would have the right to suspend the constitution and rule by proclamation. Social and economic policy was vague, but predictably anti-capitalist in sentiment. The highest level of production would be the aim, but it would not be the "privilege of a specific group". Most frighteningly, in the Christian National republic, "The propagation of any state policy and the existence of any political organisation which is in strife with the fulfilment of this Christian National vocation of the life of the people is forbidden."

Apart from its authoritarian aspects, one feature of the constitution is especially striking today: Africans hardly figure in it at all. It emphatically provided for segregation between the races but said little else. It was simply unthinkable that blacks could have claims to political equality with whites, let alone with Afrikaners. They were part of the scenery but not actors in their own right. The real struggle, which so obsessed the drafters of this constitution, was against "the English". For Verwoerd what had been good enough for Andries Pretorius and Paul Kruger would certainly be good enough for the refurbished Boer republic to come. It was only much later that second thoughts began to intrude.

There is another aspect of the constitution which is not quite so obvious but which is nevertheless undeniably "there". In a perverse and highly qualified way, it is democratic. Afrikaners would be privileged compared with the English-speaking whites; the President would be accountable only to God, but he would still be chosen by all white citizens. In this respect it was not to differ so very much from the republic which finally was established by Verwoerd. Both were "pigmentocracies", based on the divine right of white skin. The exclusion of non-whites from the electoral process was in itself enough to exclude the envisaged republic from being a democracy in any acceptable sense of the word, but it was no mere blueprint for Afrikaner dictatorship. This is especially significant when considered against the background of the triumph of Nazism and Fascism in Europe. There were plenty of Afrikaners who were irresistibly attracted by the apparent order and discipline of Hitler's Germany and Mussolini's Italy. But the draft constitution, authoritarian as it was, refused to have any truck with these ideas. This was quite consistent with the Afrikaner political tradition, which has had its own authoritarian aspects but in which the elective principle for whites at least was always accepted.

In spite of Malan's (perhaps only diplomatic) favourable reception of the draft constitution, it was never considered or accepted by any congress of the National Party. It does, however, tell us how some influential Afrikaner intellectuals were thinking at the time, and for students of Verwoerd's career it is invaluable. The more extreme authoritarian aspects of the draft can plausibly be explained in terms of the very trying circumstances in which most Afrikaners found themselves after 1939, of being involved, much against their will, in another of "Britain's wars". They were rather expressions of frustration and bitterness than of fundamental political outlook. This at least was the usual Nationalist explanation, even apology, after 1948, and it has a certain cogency.

It is tempting to explain Verwoerd's own wartime views in the same terms, that he really believed in democracy for all whites, but, like so many other Afrikaners, succumbed to authoritarian temptations because of the policies of the Smuts Government. Perhaps – but he was a man who rarely changed his mind, a man with an autocratic temperament that made him impatient with those who thought differently. Meiring remarks on the "fair but domineering" way in which he ran *Die Transvaler*. He was not a man who "believed in losing an argument".[16] Yet his editorials so frequently condemned both Nazism and its South African followers, that it is impossible to believe that he was entirely insincere. His political philosophy will become clearer from an examination of his role in the National Party's struggle to eliminate the Afrikaner supporters of National Socialism as a political threat.

South Africa's continued participation in the war was of course vigorously, even stridently, opposed by the Nationalists. But at no time did the Party reject the Parliamentary system as such or democratic forms of government. The republic would bring sweeping changes in the structure of South African society but they would take place within a democratic framework. Nevertheless, for many Afrikaners the Parliamentary system with its never-ending conflict between parties had been tried and found wanting. They found Nazi Germany an especially glamorous and inspiring model. The overthrow of democracy and the establishment of totalitarian rule had apparently given the German people a new sense of purpose and a vigour in pursuing that purpose which made the bickering of politicians seem an expensive luxury. There was a further appeal, once the war had started, that Germany was the enemy of Britain, traditional enemy of the Afrikaner. It was quite natural and logical that Germany should be a friend, an impression strengthened by German successes in the early years of the war.

Nazi sympathy amongst the Afrikaners found its most conspicuous expression in two organisations, the Ossewabrandwag and the New Order, of which the first was by far the more dynamic and important. The O.B., as it was generally known, originated in the enthusiasm generated by the centenary celebrations of the Great Trek in 1938. Its aim was to maintain the spirit of Afrikaner unity which had been aroused by the celebrations. Founded in 1939, it was dedicated to the ideals of the Voortrekkers and was organised on paramilitary lines, complete with uniforms and a hierarchy of command culminating in a Commandant-General. Seeking to draw in the Afrikaner masses, it wished to imbue them with a proper appreciation of their heritage and a sense of that discipline essential for high national endeavour. It might have confined its activities to cultural discussions and semi-military parades, but for two factors. These were South Africa's entry into the war and the accession in January 1941 of Dr. J.F.J. van Rensburg as the new Commandant-General.

Van Rensburg had been Administrator of the Free State before resigning to take up his new post. He was an ardent admirer of both General Hertzog and Hitler. As a convinced Nazi, it was largely through his influence that the O.B. committed itself to National Socialism as

South Africa's future way of life. Van Rensburg believed that the country needed a man of destiny; it required little imagination to see whom he had in mind for the role.

At first the emergence of a mass-based Afrikaner organisation which stood outside politics appeared as a welcome complement to the National Party's function of expressing the political aspirations of the Afrikaner. Its mass base was genuine, with a membership, estimated by Dr. Malan, of between 300,000 and 400,000 at the beginning of 1941. But the O.B. soon began to play a far more activist role in its opposition to South Africa's war effort. Most ominously, in the Transvaal the O.B. had organised a body of shock troops, the *Stormjaers* (Storm Riders), clearly modelled on Hitler's *Sturmabteilung*. Ostensibly it was the duty of the *Stormjaers* to protect O.B. meetings from disruption, but it soon became evident that they had violent inclinations that were not always suppressed.

The New Order was a far more ephemeral organisation headed by the former Minister of Defence and current H.N.P. member, Oswald Pirow. Even as a Minister in the Fusion Government Pirow had been an enthusiastic admirer of the Third Reich. Having decided that elections and party politics had now become obsolete, he formed the New Order as a pressure group for National Socialism within the National Party, a development displeasing to Malan whose strategy was entirely geared to victory through the ballot box.

It was initially against Pirow that the anti-Nazi campaign of the Nationalist leaders was directed, later to broaden into an offensive against the O.B. as well. Pirow began to propagate National Socialism most actively at the beginning of 1941, to the evident disquiet of the Party leadership. After the Transvaal Provincial Executive of the Party had affirmed its faith in a Boer republic with a democratic basis, Verwoerd wrote, with all his usual emphasis that for Afrikaners "it would not be possible to accept the National Socialist system of Germany, which is founded on the principle of dictatorship".[17]

Gradually the H.N.P. was also drawn into conflict with the O.B. The basic dispute was over their respective spheres of authority. Malan was quite happy to tolerate the O.B. as long as it confined itself to "cultural" activities. In fact it had been formally agreed at a meeting in October 1940 that the two organisations would cooperate on the basis of a clear division of labour, with the political field reserved for the Party. But this was before Van Rensburg became Commandant-General of the O.B. He had far more grandiose ideas about the role of the O.B., and of himself, in the new South Africa that was struggling to be born than the

Nationalist leaders were prepared to tolerate. As he saw it, the Party should confine itself to "party politics", which would soon be on history's scrapheap anyway. More and more, the O.B. under Van Rensburg's leadership began to propagate the merits of Nazism as the foundation of the South African republic to come. Democracy and political parties were openly rejected; the authoritarian state and Hitler's ideas about race were willingly embraced in their place.

Un-Afrikaans sentiments such as these caused plenty of concern to the Nationalist leadership, but Van Rensburg went even further than political theory, if that is the appropriate description. He aspired to Afrikaner leadership, in place of Malan. In a speech in August 1941 he staked a claim to a more inclusive leadership than the National Party could offer: "We are not going to allow ourselves to be tied to sections that want to split ... The O.B. for the whole nation – it covers the whole front." Earlier, the O.B. had widely distributed a circular containing details of the proposed republican constitution Verwoerd had helped to frame. This was a clear encroachment on the National Party's prerogative. From now on cooperation ceased. In October Malan called on all Party members who also belonged to the O.B. to resign from that body. It was a declaration of war, fully supported by Verwoerd, who now attacked Van Rensburg personally for seeking to undermine the National Party's authority, for it was only through the Party that the republic could ever be established. He went further: the Nazi ideas of the O.B. and of the New Order were alien to the Afrikaner. Perhaps they were good for Germany but the Afrikaners were a distinct people with their own heritage and traditions, firmly rooted in those model Boer republics of the last century. Had not Hitler himself stated that National Socialism was not for export?

This was merely a reiteration of Verwoerd's original point of view, stated as early as November 1937, which was never to change: "The National Socialist system can have great value for Germany, but we cannot conceivably help to transfer it, or any related system, to our country."[18] The Afrikaner political tradition, Verwoerd never tired of saying, was a democratic one and so it would remain under the republic.

Several attempts were made to restore cooperation between the H.N.P. and the O.B. They all failed – the contrary viewpoints on the Parliamentary system and political parties of the two organisations were simply irreconcilable. The O.B. was still to survive for a number of years, but its days as a significant political force were over. It lost all claim to speak for the Afrikaner after the 1943 general election in which the National Party emerged as the sole voice of nationalist Afrikaners in Parliament. The Party had consolidated its position with the disappearance of the Afrikaner Party and the New Order (which by then had seceded from the H.N.P.) from the House of Assembly. Its authority was unassailable and that of the O.B. correspondingly diminished, whatever it might care to say about not bothering with elections. It was no longer a force; its membership declined rapidly, a living (but barely so) testimony to Verwoerd's claim that National Socialism was alien to the Afrikaans *volksaard* (national character).

In spite of Verwoerd's emphatic rejection of National Socialism as a way of life for the Afrikaner, there has been a widespread belief that he was little better than a Nazi himself, that in fact he was an active propagandist for a German victory. This impression is largely based on the court action in which Verwoerd sued the Johannesburg evening newspaper, *The Star*, for defamation. It is certainly true that *Die Transvaler*'s leading articles and its reporting of the war were not especially favourable to the British. Verwoerd's attitude was that neutrality was the best policy: "A plague on both British and German imperialism" probably best sums up his feelings. This ostensibly impartial aversion to both sides meant that he was not particularly outraged by German crimes against the conquered peoples of Europe. After all, he well knew that British imperialism had enough sins to its own account.

The Star found such "neutrality" so offensive that in an editorial on 31 October 1941 it accused Verwoerd of deliberately falsifying the news so as to promote the German cause. What had happened was that the State Bureau of Information had released to South African newspapers the script of some of the broadcasts on the Union by the German radio station, Zeesen. The Bureau had added its own comments to this script, but Verwoerd ordered that only the latter and not the Bureau's commentary should be published. In an outraged editorial entitled "Speaking up for Hitler" *The Star* wrote: "*Die Transvaler*, which is published in Johannesburg though its spiritual home lies somewhere between Keerom Street (*Die Burger's address is Keerom Street*) and the Munich Beer Hall, has this week given a rather better example than usual of the process of falsification which it applies to current news in support of Nazi propaganda ... Not only did it omit the Information Bureau's comments, but it made Zeesen's profession of benevolent intentions towards this country the occasion for a full dress article on the theme that Germany 'would not deny the Afrikaners their republic,' and the unwisdom of criticising national socialism as practised within Germany." *The Star* went on: "Its dishonesty is too easy to expose, and it identifies *Die Transvaler* so closely with Nazi propaganda that it must assist in opening the eyes of those who read the paper in question as to the extent to which it is a tool of malignant forces from which this country has everything to fear."[19]

Verwoerd now made, as he later described it, an error of judgement. He sued the editor and the proprietor of *The Star* for defamation, claiming £15,000 damages. He did this, typically, without consulting his board, to his detriment, for it is unlikely that his directors would have advised him to sue. In the hearings before Justice Millin *The Star* claimed in its defence that its allegations were true, submitting many articles from *Die Transvaler* which allegedly had falsified the news in favour of the German cause.

Verwoerd's counsel denied that *Die Transvaler* had falsified the news, claiming that it was instead a question of the right of free speech and of free press. If Verwoerd, who had in fact often sharply criticised the Nazis, were compelled to consider whether anything he published furthered the German cause, he would be silenced altogether. The case lasted a long time but the judge was not convinced by the argument of Verwoerd's counsel. He dismissed Verwoerd's claim with costs. Justice Millin said that "it was immaterial whether *Die Transvaler* inspired Zeesen, whether Zeesen inspired *Die Transvaler*, or whether the same idea occurred independently in both organisations. The point is that, in fact, Zeesen propaganda and *Die Transvaler*'s propaganda had much in common, and each may be said to have supported the other ... Dr. Verwoerd caused to be published a large body of matter which was on the same general lines as that coming to the Union in the Afrikaans transmission from Zeesen, and which was calculated to make the Germans look on *Die Transvaler* as a most useful adjunct to this propaganda service." He concluded with the words so frequently cited after Verwoerd became a Minister in 1950: "He did support Nazi propaganda, he did make his paper a tool of the Nazis in South Africa, and he knew it."[20]

Was this enough to make Verwoerd pro-Nazi? In spite of Mr. Millin's judgement, the answer is almost certainly "No". In his biography of Verwoerd Scholtz makes some remarks that are to the point. Firstly, the judge largely failed to appreciate the attitude of the Afrikaner nationalist: "That the Afrikaner, because he was not pro-British was not therefore pro-German, is a fact that the judge simply could not accept." He delivered his judgement at a time when war fever was running high. As a unilingual South African he had not succeeded in insulating himself from it. Secondly, his remark that *Die Transvaler* had been "a tool of the

Nazis" was not tenable, for it implied that all newspapers which criticised the British Government, in whichever country, were tools of the Nazis.[21] Even judges find it difficult at times to rise above the most emotional issues of public life. This seems to have been so with Justice Millin, an opinion confirmed by his alleged subsequent remark to Verwoerd's counsel that his judgement in this case was the worst of his career.[22]

Yet if Verwoerd was not pro-Nazi, neither was he anti-Nazi. Despite his frequent criticisms of "German imperialism", there is little evidence that he was morally outraged by Nazism as such. As a system he rejected it not because of its crimes against humanity, but because it was un-Afrikaans. It was a dictatorship and thus foreign to the democratic character of the Afrikaners. But while it was not suited to the Afrikaner people there was no reason why it should not be excellent for the Germans. Verwoerd was in fact given to appreciative remarks about all the Nazis had done for Germany. In the final analysis, it boiled down to national character; each nation had its own special traditions and characteristics which could by definition not be transferred elsewhere. What was good for one nation was not necessarily good for another.

Indisputably a man of autocratic temperament, Verwoerd nevertheless often asserted, perfectly sincerely, his belief in democracy. Still, reading his leading articles, it is not easy to avoid the impression that he claimed to be a democrat, not because of profound inner conviction, but because he saw democracy as a heritage of those Voortrekker republics which he admired so much and which were for him a model of the future South African republic. It is indeed tempting to speculate that if Nazism had been part of the Afrikaner tradition then Verwoerd would have had no difficulties in accepting it. To repeat Piet Meiring's remark about the man with whom he worked so closely for years: Verwoerd was "in heart and soul an Afrikaner. He was nearly fanatical about Afrikaans institutions and delighted in proving his loyalty to them."[23] For him, in short, the supreme moral imperative was loyalty to and identification with the Afrikaner people. This is the ultimate logic of nationalism, that the claims of the nation override all other claims, even those of humanity. Verwoerd, as a logician of some ability, arrived at the only possible conclusion once his assumptions were accepted.

During these early years *Die Transvaler* suffered from acute growing pains. It made no pretence of competing with the pro-Government newspapers on the basis of its quality of its reporting, by providing better news than they did. *Die Transvaler* was avowedly a propaganda organ first and a newspaper only second. In this respect, Verwoerd, with his missionary fervour for the Afrikaner cause and his lack of journalistic experience, was the ideal man for the job. But it also meant that its appeal to the Afrikaners of the Rand was primarily an emotional one. They were expected to read it because they were good Afrikaners, not because they wanted objective and well-informed reporting. As could be expected, not all Afrikaners on the Witwatersrand were willing to do so. *Die Transvaler's* circulation increased slowly and after a year it was barely 10,000. Moreover, only about 1,000 copies were sold in Johannesburg itself, the remainder being purchased in the surrounding country districts. There was little cooperation between *Die Transvaler* and the other Nationalist newspapers, *Die Burger* in Cape Town and *Die Vaderland* in Bloemfontein, which did have old-fashioned ideas about being reporters of news and looked down upon it with frank scorn as a propaganda sheet. The burden of debt was considerable and could not easily be alleviated. Verwoerd was, then, very much on his own in the Transvaal; he had to rely on himself or sink. He was always at his best when facing a challenge. He was doing so now. On *Die Transvaler* a strong *esprit de corps* developed, stimulated by its very isolation and Verwoerd's forceful leadership. Gradually it extended its influence and won over a growing number of Afrikaners to the Nationalist cause, as the 1943 general election helped to show.

The election was a triumph for the Government. General Smuts had reason to be pleased for the United Party increased its representation from 71 to 89, while the Nationalist M.Ps only went up by two, from 41 to 43. With the support of the other members of the coalition, the Government now had an overwhelming overall majority of 64, compared with 20 before the election, not counting the three Native Representatives. But Malan too had cause for satisfaction. The National Party had now emerged as the sole political voice of Afrikanerdom. Henceforth dissent within Afrikaner ranks about the destiny of the nation could be taken less seriously. From now on it would merely have nuisance value. For the foreseeable future the Afrikaner fate was to be firmly tied to the ballot box, together with the other manifestations of the "British-Jewish sham democracy".

The war and its successful prosecution was the main issue of the election. The Nationalists were convinced that had an election been held after Hertzog's resignation in 1939 they would have won. Now, belatedly, the electorate was asked to approve South Africa's participation. But since 1939 the anti-war faction had shrunk considerably. The Allies had recovered from their early failures and were now on the offensive. The country was experiencing a mood of confidence that did not favour any political party wanting to take South Africa out of the war.

The many divisions amongst Afrikaner nationalists suggested that it was still too early for the H.N.P. to think of forming a new government. Malan saw that his rivals had first to be destroyed, making the Nationalists the only effective opposition. Only then could he think in terms of an electoral victory. Moreover, the uncompromising sectionalism of the National Party, and its commitment to what promised to be an authoritarian republic outside the Commonwealth, could have had little appeal to those Afrikaners who still retained some Hertzogite ideas about a South Africa which was the heritage of the entire white population and not merely of Afrikaners.

For a number of reasons, then, it was unlikely that Malan would win the election, but he had every right to be pleased. Malan had gone into the election to prove that his party was the only alternative government and he had done just that. Pirow's 16 New Order M.Ps, not believing in the electoral process and doubtless anticipating defeat, did not stand for re-election. The New Order thus ceased to exist as a Parliamentary party and in most other senses as well. The Afrikaner Party was similarly wiped out but not for lack of trying. It contested 23 seats, concentrating primarily on the Free State where, as the party of Hertzog, it could have expected some support. Its failure could scarcely have been more complete. Ten of the Afrikaner Party candidates lost their deposits, not having gained the minimum number of votes prescribed in the Electoral Act. In only two constituencies did the Party receive more than a thousand votes. On average its candidates obtained only ten per cent of the votes cast in those constituencies contested by them.

The election had also been a defeat for the O.B. They too did not contest any seats, agreeing with the New Order that elections were a waste of time, but now it seemed that something could be said for parliaments and votes after all. As Roberts and Trollip put it: "The success of Malan was a blow to their contention that elections were futile and outmoded."[24]

They are equally apt in summarising the election gains for the Nationalists: "Meanwhile, Malan's long-term policy had obtained its goal. The Hertzogites, the Pirowites, the O.B. had all challenged the claim of himself and the H.N.P. to be the sole representatives of Afrikanerdom. The challenge had been met, and from the electoral battle the H.N.P. had emerged the victor. It had made good its boasted monopoly. It stood now, the sole effective organ of Afrikanerdom, compact, purified, and beyond the reach of revenge."[25]

For Malan there were other grounds for optimism. While the Government had considerably increased its representation, it had done so largely at the expense of the Afrikaner Party and the New Order. It gained only eight seats from the H.N.P., which in turn won two seats from the Government. Even in this election, at the worst possible time, the Nationalists had retained their hard-core support.

Another encouraging sign was that they had considerably increased their share of the vote on the Witwatersrand. Of the 23 Rand seats, the Nationalists gained only one but they had enlarged their share of the votes to 32 per cent, compared with 24 per cent in 1938. The Party needed another 34 seats for an overall majority, of which 21 could be expected to come from the Transvaal. Five of these seats were on the Witwatersrand for in each of them the Nationalist candidate was defeated by less than 840 votes.

This was a general feature of the election. The Government had achieved huge but pointless majorities in many constituencies, but at the other extreme it won 28 seats by majorities of less than a thousand. A comparatively small swing in the number of votes could therefore bring about a disproportionate change in the relative Parliamentary standing of the main parties.

Verwoerd himself was jubilant. He calculated that on the basis of the 318,000 Nationalist votes, three out of every four Afrikaners supported the H.N.P. His conclusion brimmed with confidence: "No other leader has ever had such a mighty phalanx of Afrikaners behind him as Dr. Malan. And this Reunited National Party which thus already represents Afrikanerdom will, together with those who stand by it on the basis of its republican and other policies, rule the country in the future."[26]

He had at least one other reason for delight. Whatever other causes were responsible for the impressive Nationalist performance, the decision to establish a Nationalist daily on the Rand had clearly produced dividends. Verwoerd had every reason to be proud of his own contribution to the H.N.P.'s success.

For the United Party the election was both a climax and a turning point. From now on little went right. In the Transvaal Provincial Council elections later that year 19 Nationalists were elected compared with the 11 chosen for Parliament earlier that year. In 1944 the H.N.P. gained the Wakkerstroom seat in a Parliamentary by-election, while two additional seats were won by Nationalists before the next election. In other by-elections Government majorities showed a marked decline. These results suggested that the anti-Nationalist tide had turned and that Afrikaner solidarity was growing.

The coming of peace in 1945 deprived the Government of its main *raison d'être*. At the same time it was compelled to deal with a number of grievances which could no longer be shelved because the country was at war. Housing was an outstanding grievance for the imperatives of war had left few resources for the provision of homes, particularly for the lower-income groups. The Government offered little except promises plus bureaucratic inefficiency. Food shortages persisted, and even if this was not largely the Government's fault, blame was laid at its door with a resultant loss of popularity. White unemployment had increased, especially on the Witwatersrand, and although not considerable, could not be ignored.

There were also racial issues which have traditionally been given great importance in explanations of the Nationalist election victory in 1948. It has been convincingly argued by Newell Stultz in his book on Afrikaner politics between 1934 and 1948 that apartheid was not after all the decisive issue in that election, and that the seeds of future Nationalist triumph had already been sown in 1939 when South Africa entered the war. The result was to restore earlier partisan alignments based on language and culture. The 1943 general election, taking place in such special circumstances, obscured this effect, but afterwards it was to reassert itself. "The cost for South Africa of the Union's deciding for war in 1939 was nearly all of the electoral margin of safety that sheltered the experiment of Fusion in the middle of the 1930s. Ultimately this cost, when coupled with a mild turn of the political tide against Smuts, meant the return of Afrikaner nationalists to power."[27]

Previous elections, including that of 1933, had also made much of the race issue, so "the primary effect of Nationalist agitation on the issue of race after World War II was not that of realigning partisan preferences but rather that of reinforcing and mobilizing existing Nationalist support, although this is not to suggest that no voter shifted his vote to the H.N.P. for this reason."[28]

Race was thus an important issue in 1948 but probably not the all-inclusive explanation later commentators have managed to find. Nevertheless, Nationalist propagandists, including Verwoerd, got as much mileage as they could out of the traditional racial fears and obsessions of the white population. They made virulent propaganda against Smuts's proposal to give the perpetually victimised Indians of Natal representation in Parliament by whites, on a separate roll, supposedly as compensation for restrictions on the sale and purchase of land by Asians. The Nationalists completely approved of the restrictions, but were bitterly opposed to any form of franchise for the Indians, whom they regarded as an alien community which should be repatriated. For the white voters of Natal they conjured up the awful prospect of eventual domination by the numerically superior Indians. Verwoerd was no mean hand at this game and wanted to know: "Must Natal become an advance post of India in which there is no room for whites?"[29]

But it was naturally black South Africans who provided the fullest opportunity for the exploitation of racial fears. The urban black population had increased by 47 per cent in the decade before the 1946 census. Provision of amenities for them did not keep pace with the inflow, so that thousands of blacks lived in makeshift shanties in squatter camps around South Africa's urban centres. Living conditions were appalling and were reflected in the very high crime rate among the Africans so swiftly being absorbed into the modern sector of the economy.

Most dramatically, the racial issue was kept alive by the black mineworkers' strike of 1946 in which 60,000 to 70,000 Africans were involved. It was finally suppressed by the police and was followed by the voluntary suspension of the Natives Representative Council in protest against the Government's action. All this kept the race issue firmly in the public mind, which was grist to the Nationalist mill.

Die Transvaler had its fair share in keeping alive what promised to be a very effective political issue. On the strike Verwoerd commented: "The Smuts regime with its *laissez faire* policy will one day be smothered by the weeds it has sown on South African soil. Those who do not wish to share in such a downfall must now help with the cleaning-up. It is late, but not yet too late."[30] Above all he was concerned with the urbanisation of the African and its disastrous implications, about which he had no doubt, of eventual social and political equality with the white man. For the poorer Afrikaner the threat of social degradation seemed imminent: "The Afrikaner is proud of his white origins, and one of his most important aspirations is to maintain the race barrier. Must poor Afrikaners, who are often of the noblest origins, now be forced as a result of their financial position to live in suburbs where such a race barrier is not maintained and where violence is done every day to their feeling as Afrikaners?"[31]

Verwoerd first acquired immense fame and notoriety, both at home and abroad, as the man of apartheid, the great architect and theoretician of race policy. To what extent was the apartheid to come, in particular the policy of independent black homelands, foreshadowed by his editorials in *Die Transvaler*? The answer is hardly at all, that Verwoerd's views were still of a very conventional segregationist variety. For example: "This segregation policy, which also means protection of and care for the Native in the land of the Afrikaner, but decisively rejects any attempts at equality, gives the Native an opportunity to develop what is his own, so that he can have pride and self-respect as a Native, instead of being continually humiliated as a failed and imitation white" (September 1943).

"The Afrikaner's attitude is one of trusteeship, which also brings obligations of care, and of segregation, whereby the Native can be allowed to develop in his own manner" (23 July 1941).

"One of the basic principles is that the Native may not be withdrawn from his tribal bond and the influence of healthy ancestral practices" (24 July 1941).

There is plenty here of Verwoerd the Minister of Native Affairs, but not quite so much of Verwoerd the Prime Minister. There is nothing that is really new or original. Verwoerd was simply echoing what the more sophisticated Nationalist thought about the African, when he thought about him at all. The black man was a simple creature, basically a tribal animal, who would only be corrupted by exposure to alien Western practices. It was in his own interests to be kept apart from the white man as far as was humanly possible. He had the right to develop, but it was to be strictly in his own areas. Above all, racial equality was to be avoided. Apart from these horrific consequences to the Afrikaner, which so exercised Verwoerd, it harmed the black man too by uprooting him from his tribal community, the ultimate source of his self-respect, and by providing a camouflage for exploitation by white capitalists.

It was a paternal view of the African. In reality he was still a child who would take a long time to grow up – if he ever did. In the meantime he needed white trusteeship, which would as far as possible prevent the decay of tribal solidarity and authority.

Obviously self-serving as these views were, they were also an expression of Verwoerd's profoundest convictions about nationalism. A people had institutions peculiarly suited to itself, not readily transferable to others. Just as Nazism may well have suited the Germans, and Voortrekker democracy definitely suited the Afrikaners, so the black man's destiny was a tribal one. If he rejected the tribe he could never be anything but "an imitation Englishman".

How did these ideas, unoriginal and the common coin of Afrikaner thought on the racial issue at the time, differ from the apartheid which Verwoerd was to enforce so strenuously after he became Minister? Very little, in fact, until 1959, when, as Prime Minister, he announced the homelands policy. Apartheid, to anticipate, was hardly different from the old segregation, which so many Nationalists had professed to find wanting. The emphasis in both was on separation between the races, except that after 1948 its enforcement, when feasible, was far more doctrinaire and thoroughgoing than it had been before.

By 1948 "apartheid" was a word that had acquired wide currency. It was one of the Nationalists' chief election slogans, but it was hardly more than that, a slogan. Few were sure what it meant, in spite of the appointment of a committee headed by one of the Party's most senior politicians, Paul Sauer, to formulate the basic policy of apartheid. The report, when presented shortly before the election, appeared to recommend a stricter enforcement of segregation, with racial separation in all walks of life. But in spite of its lack of originality, "apartheid" was a word that had come to stay.

Race thus seems to have been a vital issue in the 1948 election but not of such supreme importance as the later conventional wisdom has suggested. It was not the first time that race was a substantive issue in a South African election, and it was not to be the last. For Verwoerd it had been a decidedly less important issue during the years on *Die Transvaler* than the passionately coveted republic. It helps to explain his exceedingly conventional, if forcefully stated, views on the race question.

Apart from those issues on which it was good politics to concentrate, the Nationalists took further steps to consolidate Afrikaner unity. They were now also at pains to present themselves in a more moderate light to the English-speaking voters, as well as to that less extreme minority of Afrikaners with Hertzogite views on nationhood. Neither of these developments appealed to Verwoerd's uncompromising brand of nationalism, but at this late stage he was not prepared to jeopardise Party prospects by open protest. It was not, after all, a compromise on principle and the H.N.P. still remained a republican party.

The first development was formal cooperation between the National Party and the Afrikaner Party, which had been so badly mauled in the previous election. It was an attempt by Malan to attract the support of those Afrikaners who were not yet willing to subscribe unreservedly to those Nationalist policies which they regarded as too extreme. Verwoerd was not at all pleased, but approved of the agreement as a basis for the eventual absorption of the Afrikaner Party by the Nationalists, though he preferred to call it "a joining together" (*samevoeging*).[32] Even so, his doubts were strong, for he regarded the Afrikaner Party as so inherently weak that it had no long-term viability. The agreement in his view gave the Afrikaner Party Parliamentary seats that could easily have been won by the Nationalists. His friend and colleague, Strijdom, shared these doubts. In fact, he expressed them so forcibly to Malan that an estrangement arose between the two men which lasted for the rest of their political careers. But Verwoerd and Strijdom, despite their opposition, did not have their way and had to accept the agreement in the interests of Party unity.

In presenting themselves as really moderate men who had suffered much from being misunderstood, prominent Nationalists dissociated themselves from some of the wilder statements of the war years. The Party too began to express itself cautiously about the republic. It remained the ultimate goal, but the National Party would certainly not declare a republic as soon as it came to power. Instead, a republic could only be established through a favourable result at a special election or a referendum. The Party also rejected the now famous (or notorious) draft constitution for a republic published in 1942. It was emphasised that the rights of the English-speaking population would be safeguarded; English would in all respects enjoy equality with Afrikaans as an official language. Amusingly, Verwoerd made it clear in an editorial (17 July 1947) that the Party had in no way been involved in the drawing up of the document. This was indeed an authoritative statement, considering that Verwoerd himself had been one of the three men responsible for the draft constitution.

Verwoerd could not have enjoyed this soft-pedalling of the republic, but it was another sacrifice demanded by the greater good of the Party. That his republican convictions remained as strong as ever is shown by the curious episode of the Royal visit. The British Royal Family had been invited by Smuts to visit South Africa in 1947, but Verwoerd decided to ignore it completely. He saw it as an election ploy by Smuts which deserved no publicity. Also, it could benefit the republican cause in no way. So *Die Transvaler*, over a period of two months, carried no reports of the Royal visit. It had its comical aspects, as when the newspaper was forced to refer to traffic disruptions, without specifying their cause. Verwoerd's policy was in sharp contrast to that of the other Nationalist newspapers which all carried reports on the Royal procession through South Africa. His decision earned the disapproval of Strijdom, who believed that a newspaper should carry at least some news and not simply be a propaganda sheet. Verwoerd, characteristically, did not budge. At least no one could blame him for being inconsistent. As a newspaper-man he was a propagandist for the Afrikaner cause: good journalism only came second.

For a number of reasons, then, the National Party won its narrow victory in May 1948. So narrow was it that the person said to be most surprised by the result was Malan himself. The Nationalists won 70 seats and the Afrikaner Party 9, as against the 65 of the United Party and the 6 of the Labour Party. Adding the three Native Representatives to the opposition, Malan had an overall majority of five. It was a minority government in every sense, except where it counted, in Parliament. The Nationalists represented only the white minority of the total South African population, as had all governments before them. But they only represented a minority of whites, having attracted merely 42 per cent of the votes cast. The United Party was to make much of this situation, which was to endure until at least the 1958 general election. This peculiar outcome was the result of a decision taken at the National Convention in 1909 to ensure that the rural voters would not be submerged by the growing urban population. A delimitation system was adopted which permitted a variation in the numerical value of constituencies of either 15 per cent above or below the average.

A phenomenon of the 1943 general election also repeated itself, without being offset by the special factors which previously gave Smuts his huge majority. The United Party gained overwhelming victories in many urban seats which, however impressive, were effectively useless from the electoral point of view. By contrast, the Nationalists won a number of very close victories, 11 seats being gained with majorities of under 400 votes.

The most dramatic breakthrough had been in the Transvaal. The H.N.P. retained all 15 seats it already held and gained 17 new ones, while the Afrikaner Party won 4. Of the 21 gains, 6 were on the Witwatersrand, a reflection both of the urbanisation of the Afrikaner and of the Nationalist success in winning his support.

Verwoerd himself stood for the Rand seat of Alberton. It was his first political appearance as a candidate, though he had been asked in 1943 to contest a seat. He had then refused as Strijdom felt that his services as a newspaper editor were too valuable to be lost to the H.N.P. But now the time had come for a participation in politics more congenial to his activist temperament. He did not expect to win for the seat included a number of Johannesburg's southern suburbs where few Afrikaners lived. But he very nearly did win, and only lost by 117 votes to the United Party candidate, Marais Steyn, then at the beginning of his extraordinary political career.

It was nevertheless the end of Verwoerd's career as a journalist. He had expected to be appointed to the Cabinet, and was extremely upset when he was not. However, when offered a Senatorship, he accepted, which meant that he had to resign as editor of *Die Transvaler*, although he was reluctant to do so, for he was quite prepared to combine the two offices.

As editor-in-chief of *Die Transvaler* Verwoerd was one of the men responsible for the Nationalist resurgence in the Transvaal after 1938. And it was a particular kind of nationalism, an uncompromising brand which proclaimed Afrikaner unity based on the republican ideal. It was a nationalism which had little time for conciliating fellow-Afrikaners outside the National Party, even though they too opposed the United Party Government. The only possible way was that of the Reunited National Party; outside it there was no political salvation. This approach could not triumph completely as long as Malan was the leader of the Party, as his conciliation of the Afrikaner Party showed, but after his departure its victory was total. Verwoerd's contribution to this triumph was immense. His will, his unremitting dedication, played a powerful role in making the Transvaal National Party what it was, the embodiment of an Afrikaner exclusivism that has shaped the whole course of South African history. *Die Transvaler* was primarily a propaganda organ for this cause, but it nonetheless managed to maintain certain journalistic standards. Two non-Nationalist historians, Roberts and Trollip, have even described it as a "first-class newspaper".[33]

From the point of view of his later career, Verwoerd's years as a newspaperman saw his emergence as one of the most powerful Nationalists in the Transvaal. He had established a power base in that province which was eventually to dominate the National Party. It was to be a decisive factor in his accession to the Premiership.

3 The Unfolding of a Pattern

For Verwoerd his first two years as Senator were a time of frustration. This is understandable. The staid unexciting atmosphere of the upper chamber clearly did not suit an energetic and dynamic man with a sense of mission. He was also far removed from the House of Assembly, where all the important decisions were taken, even if only formally. He who was a glutton for work suddenly found that he had virtually nothing to do. After *Die Transvaler* it was, so it seemed to him, a change for the worse, aggravated by his lower salary as Senator, as well as by his absence for part of the year from his family, for they remained in the north while he attended the Parliamentary session in Cape Town.

Nevertheless, these years were not a total loss, for he acquired a valuable knowledge of Parliamentary procedure. He also had plenty of time to prepare well-researched speeches. His first speech as Senator was indeed on that policy with which his name was to be so closely linked, apartheid. It was an attempt to give meaning to what the Opposition plausibly suggested was merely an election catchphrase, largely devoid of content, something, in the words of General Smuts, "wrapped in a mass of misrepresentations such as we have never had in our political life before".[1]

In the Senate one of the Native Representatives had asked the Government to explain its policy with respect to the acquisition of land for blacks. He also wanted to know what opportunities there would be for blacks to serve their communities in administrative and professional capacities. Senator Verwoerd's first speech came in response to this request. It deserves detailed consideration, not because of its originality, which was not conspicuous, but as a comprehensive outline of the principles which would inform his behaviour as Minister of Native Affairs.

Verwoerd's point of departure was to deny the oft-heard allegation that the Nationalists had propagated a policy of total segregation, which they well knew to be impracticable. By extensive quotations from the Party's programme of principles he could show that total segregation was only an ideal, which the Nationalists were quite aware was impossible. In fact, the

114

Government's policy envisaged various forms of territorial segregation. Blacks would not be allowed to own land among white people. Instead, their right to land ownership "would be confined to the various Native reserves". Blacks and Coloureds would not be allowed to live in white residential areas, but would respectively have separate residential areas of their own. Not only would whites and non-whites be separated at places of work but also certain jobs would be reserved for whites alone.

Verwoerd proceeded to one of the cardinal points of Nationalist race policy. The programme of principles stated that the main black ethnic groups would, as far as possible, be concentrated "in their own separate territories, where each group will be able to develop into a self-sufficient unit". Verwoerd provided his own gloss on this statement: "As the nations of the world each in its own territory accomplishes its own national development, so also will the opportunity be given here to the various Native groups each to accomplish its own development in its own territory. To each of them, from the tribal chief to the ordinary Native, the chance is being given to accomplish a fair and reasonable development within his own national group. That has come from those who are stigmatised by the other side as oppressors of the Natives."[2]

The reserves would be developed economically, enabling large numbers of blacks to live there. In town Africans would only be "visitors" in a white man's land; they would never be entitled to "any political rights or equal social rights with the Europeans in the European areas". Verwoerd drew the logical conclusion that this would only be possible if there were strict control over the influx of blacks into the urban areas from the reserves and the white-owned farms. The Party programme stated that "the number of detribalised Natives must be frozen ... All surplus Natives in the towns will have to be sent back to the country districts or to the Native Reserves, or wherever they came from." Verwoerd elaborated: "What will happen is that in a sense the numbers in the cities will be frozen to such an extent that no more Natives will be allowed to come in from outside other than the Natives who have the full residential right to stay there: let only those who are there retain the right to stay ... Freezing therefore means that we are not going to permit any new influx as happened under the previous Government, and indeed, to such an extent that Johannesburg and the Witwatersrand, and the whole of that neighbourhood has become one vast breeding place of injustice and crime, of unemployment and all sorts of misery, of poverty, and of mutual oppression."[3]

Black self-government would always be limited. In the urban areas they would never have more than local government: "If they have ambitions in the direction of full citizenship, then they have to go back to the areas that are theirs; but if for their own selfish interests and their own economic gain they want to stay in the Native residential areas within the European areas, then the greatest share in government which they can achieve will be local government." In "the areas that are theirs", the reserves, the Party programme favoured "an individual system of local government ... in which the Native chiefs will be completely incorporated, and which will at the same time present the educated Native with an opportunity of enlisting himself in the service of his own people. Such a council will be brought into being for every reserve, and they will be able to develop into separate central groups for the various ethnic and sub-groups."[4]

Till then the Natives Representative Council had provided some limited expression for the views of Africans. Established in 1937 and consisting of a majority of elected members, it was supposed to act as an advisory body to the Government, to which it was meant to convey the views of their constituents on those non-political issues which affected them. But it was no surprise when the elected members soon insisted on discussing political matters too, also making political demands which the Government invariably rejected. Well before 1948 relations between the Government and the Natives Representative Council had broken down.

The Nationalists had no intention of trying to get on with the Council; on the contrary, they were determined to abolish it. For them it was a body dominated by educated black upstarts who did not know their place, suffering from delusions of grandeur instilled in them by interfering white liberals. Or as Verwoerd put it in more civilised terms, the Natives Representative Council was a body designed "to function within the integration policy of some of the members on the other side of the House. There we have a body by which all dividing lines between various groups of Natives are broken down." He envisaged the Council developing into "a sort of parliament". General Smuts himself had spoken of the Council possibly acquiring its own civil service. For Verwoerd the possibilities of conflict inherent in the situation were immense: "Gradually we should have spread over a single country what would virtually be two parliaments and two public services."[5] Conflict and strife were inevitable; in the new Nationalist scheme of things there could be no place for the Natives Representative Council.

Verwoerd saw the existing state of race relations in terms of total, unvarnished horror: "Europeans and non-Europeans scattered and mixed up about the whole of South Africa; Europeans and non-Europeans travelling mixed up in the trams and the trains; Europeans and non-Europeans are already mixing in hotels and places where meals are served; engaged more and more in taking possession of the theatres and the streets; engaged in devastating the reserves; engaged in seeking learning which they do not use in the service of their own people, but which they use in order to cross the borderline of European life, to become traitors to their own people."[6] He was absolutely convinced this was only the beginning. J.H. Hofmeyr, the United Party's most prominent liberal and favourite Nationalist bogeyman, had already spoken of the end of the colour bar. The extension of limited political rights would merely lead to pressure for more, always "in the direction of complete equality", with black domination as the inevitable outcome. But this could never be allowed, for as he put it "unequivocally", South Africa was "a white man's country ... In the reserves we are prepared to allow the Natives to be the masters, we are not masters there. But within the European areas, we, the white people in South Africa, are and shall remain the masters."[7]

This was the essential Verwoerd. Over the years he was to devote all of his abundant energy, and unquestionable ability, to carrying out this vision of the future, of a South Africa which belonged, and always would belong, to the white man, or more accurately, to the Afrikaner. His exposition had not been original. It was all there in the Party programme of principles. Whatever originality Verwoerd was to bring to the policy of apartheid was to come much later, when he was already Prime Minister. Before 1959 his distinctive contribution was not to the theory but to the practice of apartheid. With a dedication already apparent in this first Senatorial speech, he was to draw sharp lines of division between white and black wherever it was possible, in all walks of life. Only thus could the future of the whites be assured. The overwhelming danger was not injustice to the African but to the white man: "Indeed, it is not the Native whose future is being threatened, it is that of the Europeans; the European is really the person who should say: 'My rights must be protected.'"[8] Verwoerd would have gone to any lengths to prevent "injustice" to the whites of South Africa.

He was soon able to translate purpose into action. Although only a junior Senator, his obvious superiority to most of his colleagues, both in intellect and force of character, could not be ignored indefinitely. The man who had in 1948 been appointed to the vital Ministry of Native Affairs, E.G. Jansen, had not been a success, at least as far as many

Nationalist M.Ps who interested themselves in race relations were concerned. Known as one of the most moderate men in the Party, he was notably lacking in ideological fervour and had indeed little stomach for the partisanship of party politics. Jansen was not the person to give life and purpose to the hitherto quite nebulous concept of "apartheid". During his two years as Minister his approach to "the Native problem" had been piecemeal, dealing with such immediately pressing administrative problems as black housing in the towns. The overall vision and the drive informing it were absent. But Jansen was elevated to Governor-General late in 1950. On 19 October 1950 Verwoerd took office as Minister of Native Affairs, at the same time becoming leader of the Senate. Malan had intended offering Verwoerd another post in the Cabinet, but, when Paul Sauer refused to become Jansen's successor, took that decision which was to have such far-reaching consequences.

It was his task to implement apartheid but, despite his own lengthy exposition on the subject in his first speech as Senator, it somehow remained a vague concept. After all, Verwoerd's own explanation did not have the blinding clarity which he thought it had. What, for instance, had Verwoerd meant when he said: "In the reserves we are prepared to allow the Natives to be the masters, we are not masters there." How could this be reconciled with the fact that the black areas were integral parts of South Africa and thus subject to the ultimate authority of an exclusively Afrikaner government? Was local government all they could ever hope for? In practice apartheid simply amounted, so it seemed, to more systematic and rigorous discrimination than ever before against blacks, as well as the other non-white groups. Verwoerd, more than anyone else, was to give coherence to what before 1950 had simply been a set of *ad hoc* practices not too closely related to one another. For years still there would be no answer to the question of just how the blacks were masters in the reserves, but Verwoerd undeniably gave a purpose and direction to "Native policy" which had previously been absent. As he was to put it less than two years after he became Minister: "The main criticism which has been justly brought against the Native policy of the Union during the past 40 years is that it was not built up into an organically related system. The aim of the present Government, however, is to plan and to act according to definite principles, so that matters and problems may not simply arise uncontrolled, and perhaps be controlled in a wrong direction."[9]

Whatever the differences between the Nationalists and their predecessors, they had one thing in common: all South African governments since 1910 have agreed on the need for white supremacy, whether they

118

chose to call it "segregation", "trusteeship" or "apartheid". At first, after Union, the "Native problem" did not have the urgency for the whites it was to acquire later. The colonial empires were still intact, the Pax Britannica still prevailed and the world was not even remotely inclined to question the right of a white minority to rule over a black majority. The process of economic integration had not yet developed its later momentum, for the economy was still primarily based on agriculture and mining. Manufacturing industry was in its infancy and black urbanisation was therefore limited. All this was to change during the course of economic growth, based as it increasingly was on the absorption of unskilled black workers into an economy exclusively controlled by white men. If the labour these blacks provided was of a low level of productivity it was exceedingly cheap. As the economy became more diversified and complex, dependent as it was on black labour, the problem of political relations became even more intractable than before.

The Union of South Africa only became a reality because blacks were refused the franchise, except in a qualified form in the Cape, which was the only province that before Union gave limited political rights to the blacks. Now even such restricted political power seemed a threat. As the economy became racially integrated the whites looked to their political power as a defence against black demands for more rights. This tension between political and economic factors lay behind the Hertzog Government's 1936 legislation, which removed the Cape Africans from the common roll. Instead, seven white representatives for all the country's blacks were now to be elected to Parliament on a separate roll. This constant interplay between economic facts and political solutions was to be the backdrop to the evolution of apartheid after 1948.

The economic interdependence between white and black, long a feature of South African history, received its first considerable stimulus with the mineral revolution of the late 19th century, based on the development of gold and diamond mining. The process continued during the 20th century, but its second marked acceleration had to wait till the 1930s and the Second World War. South Africa's departure from the gold standard in 1932 coincided with a new phase of rapid growth, especially of the hitherto insignificant manufacturing sector. Freed from the burden of an overvalued currency, and subsequently stimulated by a rise in the price of gold, the economy grew at a rate of more than 7 per cent a year between 1934 and 1940. It was the major reason for the end of the Poor White problem, so little amenable to direct state intervention. Not only did the increase in the demand for labour largely eliminate white unemployment, but it also accelerated the absorption of blacks into the modern economy. In the manufacturing sector the number of white workers grew by more than 60 per cent, but the supply of black labour increased by nearly 90 per cent.

The transformation of the South African economy during these years was real but limited. The most impressive structural changes were still to come, during the Second World War, and even more so afterwards.

After the outbreak of war in 1939, South Africa was deprived of many goods normally available from abroad. South African entrepreneurs fully responded to the consumers' demands; industry expanded rapidly. By the end of the war manufacturing had become both the largest single sector of the economy and far more diversified than before. This industrialisation was accompanied by still more dependence on black labour. While employment of all races grew, non-white employees in the manufacturing sector, mainly black, increased far more rapidly than white workers, respectively by 74 per cent and 20 per cent.

The end of the war seemed to confirm the words of only a few years before of one of South Africa's outstanding historians, C.W. de Kiewiet: "... it is clear that the leading theme of South African history is the growth of a new society in which white and black are bound together in the closest dependence upon each other."[10] Yet the political policies of this new society, under whatever name they went, had always been committed to some form of separation between the races. It was one of the ironies of history that the political party most adamant and uncompromising in its dedication to racial separation, came to power at a time when such a purpose seemed least capable of fulfilment.

Apart from the increased need of the modern sector for black labour, there was another good reason for the unstoppable inflow of Africans from the rural areas. Black agriculture has not been one of the flourishing sectors of the South African economy during this century. The reasons have been both political and economic. Of the political causes the most important has been the Natives' Land Act of 1913, which defined and delimited the area of black occupation, thus imposing severe restrictions on black ownership of land. It is true that some very fertile areas were included in the black-occupied parts of South Africa, but Africans were now confined to much-restricted regions when their numbers were growing rapidly. The predictable outcome was both overpopulation and overstocking of cattle, of which the acquisition had long been one of the few forms of investment open to blacks. While it may have been profitable for the individual owner of cattle, the social consequences were deplorable. Access of blacks to capital was relatively limited, hence there was little scope for investment in land, machinery, buildings etc. This was in marked contrast to white agriculture, on which state expenditure has traditionally been considerable, a difference which can be directly related to the enormous disparity in political power between white and black.

Black farmers also had far greater problems than whites in marketing their products. Transport facilities in the white areas were excellent, those in the black areas far less so, with obviously adverse effects on the competitive ability of black farmers.

For a number of reasons, then, black agriculture was less prosperous than its white counterpart. Potential cultivators were forced to seek a more profitable return for their labour in the "white" areas.

For any government intent on halting the process of economic integration, it did not suffice to control the influx of blacks to the cities. They only left their homes and families in the reserves because there were better opportunities elsewhere. Sending Africans back to stagnate in a backward agriculture was no answer at all. The reserves clearly had to be made economically viable so that they could sustain a larger population. This required, *inter alia*, greater availability of capital and better transport facilities. But policies directed to these ends could only yield their fruits over a relatively long term, while in the short run there was the problem of the increasing flow of blacks to the towns and cities of white South Africa. Such were the racial problems as they related to blacks which confronted all South Africa's governments during this century. How did they attempt to cope with them?

After Union in 1910 "Native policy" was still a piecemeal and haphazard affair, a reflection of the compromise on which the unification of South Africa had been built. At the National Convention in 1908–9 the conflict between the so-called northern and Cape points of view on race relations could only be unsatisfactorily resolved by an agreement to differ. The Cape would retain its qualified non-racial franchise, while the northern provinces would keep their exclusively white electoral systems, with a Parliament consisting only of white members. These diverse and ultimately irreconcilable points of view were both reflected in the first South African cabinets of Botha and of Smuts, which meant that no systematic race policy was possible.

Some laws were adopted, such as the Natives' Land Act, mentioned above, which wrote the principle of racial differentiation into the statute book. Yet, while black urbanisation was growing apace, the South

African Party Government did virtually nothing to allay the fears of those whites disturbed at the prospect of the towns becoming blacker by the day. Only in 1923 did Parliament adopt one of the crucial measures underpinning the whole South African system of race relations, the Natives (Urban Areas) Act, which not only provided for residential segregation as well as influx control to urban areas, but explicitly described Africans so treated as "visitors" to white man's territory.

The long-awaited "systematic" approach, reflecting the northern point of view, came with Hertzog's advent to power in 1924. Although his was a coalition government, the Labour members felt as strongly about the black threat as their Nationalist colleagues. Initially the alliance attempted to provide sheltered employment for whites through a Civilised Labour policy, and to impose segregation wherever whites and blacks met. But Hertzog's search for system and coherence could only be satisfied in 1936 when his huge Parliamentary representation gave him the two-thirds majority required to abolish the Cape franchise for blacks. In the same year the Natives' Trust and Land Act gave further expression to territorial segregation by providing for additional land for Africans. Hertzog's scheme of racial separation was given its final legal form with the Native Laws Amendment Act of 1937 which, in response to the black urbanisation of those years, provided for further residential segregation and enlarged control over the movement of blacks within and to the towns.

Yet these measures did not slow down economic integration. White South Africans, including those especially ardent for "segregation", have rarely been willing to accept the economic implications of their beliefs. Black urbanisation has been an inevitable by-product of South Africa's economic development. At the same time it has heightened white insecurity, the sense of being submerged by an advancing black tide. The result has been a policy which has desired the best of both possible worlds: do not cut off the supply of black labour so essential to white affluence, but regulate it at every turn, and make it clear to the black worker that he is only temporary, a "visitor" in those areas which belong by right to the white man.

Segregation has thus proved compatible with economic integration, with blacks continuing to stream into the white areas at an impressive rate. During the Second World War hardly any effort was made to apply a strict policy of influx control, both because it would have interfered with the war effort and Smuts and his cabinet had none of Hertzog's ideological fervour for racial separation. After the war white South Africans suddenly realised that they were now outnumbered by blacks in the urban areas. The official census of 1946 showed that while there were 1,740,000 whites, the urban black population amounted to 1,810,000. Between 1921 and 1946 the white proportion of the total urban population declined from 49 to 41 per cent, while the black share rose from 34 to 42 per cent. For the whites such changes were most alarmingly manifested in the thousands of black squatters in camps surrounding the main cities, as well as in the soaring black crime rate.

Such was the background to Smuts's now famous speech to the Institute of Race Relations in 1942, when he said, "I am afraid segregation has fallen on evil days ... You have this urbanisation and the phenomenon of detribalisation. What is taking place in our midst is as great a revolution as has ever happened on this continent."[11] For Smuts there was evidently little point in resisting economic forces. He accepted that economic integration between white and black had come to stay. It had to be accepted for the irrevocable fact that it was.

Smuts represented an attitude the Nationalists found anathema. They could not agree that the needs of the economy were decisive, that their political implications could be left to look after themselves. During the 1940s a growing number of Afrikaner politicians and intellectuals were becoming dissatisfied with segregation as a solution to the race problem. They sought a more satisfactory alternative and found apartheid. Before the end of the war Dr. Malan was quoted as saying: "(I) do not use the word segregation, because it has been interpreted as fencing off, but rather 'apartheid' which will give the various races the opportunity of uplifting themselves on the basis of what is their own."[12] The Cape Nationalist newspaper, *Die Burger*, also took up the cause of apartheid as the alternative to segregation, frequently publishing articles on the latest state of apartheid theory. The seriousness of it all was further confirmed in 1944 and 1947 when *Volkskongresse* on, respectively, the race policy and the urbanisation of the Afrikaner called for an "extensive policy of racial apartheid in every sphere of life".

Before 1948 the vision of eventually autonomous and independent black nations had already been given currency in various works by Professor Geoff Cronjé, with titles like *Regverdige Rasse-apartheid* (*Fair Racial Apartheid*). In this work published in 1947, Cronjé wrote: "... the destiny of every non-white community in this country is to become equal in value with the white community ... each community in its own fatherland, with its own socio-economic system and political structure."[13] As everyone was to learn after 1948, the difference between theoretical and practical apartheid was substantial, to put it only mildly. Even as a theory, the concept of independent black nations had to wait till 1959 for official acceptance and, in spite of all that has happened since, it has never quite ceased to resemble some escapee from a professional ivory tower who, having made good his escape, has imposed himself on the surrounding world, with consequences truly surprising to all. In 1948, however, it was still leading a rarefied existence, paid lip-service to by some deep thinkers, but totally unfamiliar to the Nationalist in the street.

When Malan ousted Smuts apartheid had been accepted as official Party policy. The Sauer Committee had laid down a general framework which was to serve as a guide in the formulation of policy, but as yet apartheid was hardly more than a word, distinctly lacking in content. Only after 1950, with Verwoerd's entry into the cabinet, did it begin to acquire an outline, which to many was disturbingly sharp. Verwoerd himself disclaimed all originality. In that memorable first speech as Senator he had even denied that apartheid differed from segregation: "… there is nothing new in what we are propagating, nor have we made any claim that there is anything new in it. The claim that we have made is that we are propagating the traditional policy of Afrikanerdom, the traditional policy of South Africa and of all those who have made South Africa their home … whether it is called segregation or by the clear Afrikaans name 'apartheid'."[14]

It was still a policy in which the negative aspects were dominant, to the virtual total exclusion of those more positive features which had been so widely proclaimed. It was poor comfort to an African to be told by Verwoerd that he would be given the chance "to accomplish a fair and reasonable development within his own national group".[15] What mattered to him was that the apartheid regime exercised increasing control over his right to move from one job to another, that it progressively eliminated his rights of domicile in the "white" areas, and that his bargaining power in the labour market was reduced. For the black man the losses, which were immediate, inevitably far outweighed the gains, which lay in the not so foreseeable future.

This was perfectly understandable, for apartheid was a policy formulated by white men to preserve the supremacy of white men. It was a policy born out of their fear of being "swamped" by the many thousands of blacks now entering the modern economy. White security seemed only possible through heightened insecurity for blacks.

During the early years of Nationalist rule, the holders of political power used it to an extreme extent to impose disabilities on those who had no political power at all. Even Oswald Pirow, Minister of Justice under Hertzog and Nazi enthusiast during the war, was to write in 1949: "We know about the things that the non-European may not do, but what about the things he may well do, and which we shall help him to carry out? Or is apartheid advantageous only for the white man? ... The Government may have a positive and not merely a negative apartheid policy, but if that is so, we – and with us the mass of the Union's population – are entirely ignorant of its character."[16]

It was against this background that Verwoerd became Minister of Native Affairs. His predecessor, Dr. E.G. Jansen, in addition to lacking Verwoerd's drive and enthusiasm, had had too little time in which to leave his stamp on the Department. Verwoerd was in the fortunate position of being able to start with a virtually clean slate, except in one respect, which he frequently regretted. Before leaving office, Jansen had appointed a commission of inquiry to investigate the condition of the reserves and to make recommendations for their development. This was to be the famous Tomlinson Commission, whose findings were later to be so widely quoted and discussed by Nationalists and their opponents alike. But Verwoerd was not enthusiastic. He usually had his own very definite ideas about what to do and did not now propose to be told by a commission of inquiry, however competent, about the best way of developing the reserves. The commission had already been appointed, there was little he could do about that, but he would still be free to disregard its recommendations in a most definite manner.

After his frustrating inactivity as just another member of that staid body, the Senate, Verwoerd was now able once more to display his tremendous capacity for work. He seemed obsessed with a sense of the urgency of the race problem. Since 1948 the threat of anglicisation had receded, now that the Afrikaner could once more look after his own, but black urbanisation had not slowed down at all. The maintenance of the Afrikaner's racial identity did not depend simply on victory at the polls. Africans, through the Native Representatives in Parliament, had only slight political influence, but their growing importance as workers in a fast industrialising economy had political implications as serious as those of any multiracial Parliamentary system. Barriers between black and white had to be erected before it was too late. Those broken down before 1948 had to be restored, with stronger foundations, while many new ones had to arise.

Verwoerd did not hesitate to work long and strenuous hours for the sake of an Afrikaner posterity. His one-time private secretary, Fred Barnard, records that Verwoerd regularly arrived at his office early in the morning to work till eight and even ten o'clock at night. "It was Dr. Verwoerd's practice to remain at his desk until the last possible second. He believed in making the most of every moment of his time, utilising every minute judiciously and profitably. His lunch time was supposed to start at one, but he rarely left his office until well after that, and when he was driven home for lunch, he usually took some official document to study on the way."[17]

Verwoerd was singularly fortunate in having Dr. Werner Eiselen as his Secretary for Native Affairs. Eiselen, who had been a colleague at Stellenbosch, was an anthropologist with a wide-ranging knowledge of the Bantu-speaking peoples of South Africa. He imparted much of this knowledge to Verwoerd, who, at this early stage, was still quite ignorant of the "Bantu way of life", although he proved "a fast learner".[18] Ideologically, both were on the same wavelength. As an anthropologist who had acquired his training when the functionalist approach was dominant, Eiselen believed that societies were organic wholes of which the parts were functionally interdependent. A change in one part of the system would inevitably have repercussions elsewhere and, if this were significant enough, could threaten the integrity of the whole. Also implicit in this approach was the notion of cultural relativism. Societies were not superior or inferior to one another, but different. Each society had its own distinct character. It was thus futile to attempt to impose one's own way of life on people who had grown up with a completely different set of values. The result would only be an unpalatable mish-mash, combining the worst of the societies thus brought together. For Verwoerd the fear and revulsion conveyed by the product of one society doing his pathetic and ineffectual best to ape the ways of another was best expressed by one of his more cherished phrases, "a black Englishman".

Eiselen saw black urbanisation as dangerous, for continued exposure to an alien way of life threatened the stability of the tribal system, the organic whole which had traditionally given meaning to the life of the African. The system had to be saved before it decayed completely. Change was possible, but it had to be within the tribal framework, with tribal institutions and tribal authority remaining intact. Eiselen's disapproval of "Westernisation" was expressed as early as 1929 in a talk at Stellenbosch University, when he said that "Native policy … must … no longer regard the Bantu as merely part of our South African environment, but as people who are entitled to a form of existence of their own, which includes the freedom to develop their own culture."[19] Referring to the emerging black intelligentsia, Eiselen said, "We can certainly not go wrong by emphatically pointing out to them that their first duty is not to become black Europeans, but by raising their people to a higher Bantu culture."[20] He was

126

to retain this belief in the supreme value of the tribal connection for the rest of his life. In 1959, when Secretary for Bantu Administration and Development (as the Native Affairs Department had been renamed), Eiselen wrote in a frequently quoted article: "The present system of having an unattached mass of Bantu individuals living in cities not subject to any traditional authority or sanctions has proved a dismal failure. It is therefore well worthwhile to establish lines of social, cultural, and educational communication between the city Bantu and the homeland Bantu."[21]

It could be expected that Verwoerd the believer in nations as fundamental human entities would find Eiselen's views highly congenial. Intellectual conviction and Afrikaner expediency went hand-in-hand to form a potent combination that would give apartheid a coherence and purpose which had previously been absent. The belief that there was one emerging black nation in South Africa was now conveniently disposed of. In fact, there were many, such as the Xhosa, the Zulu and the Tswana, so that for propaganda purposes it could be claimed that the whites (not merely the Afrikaners) were, after the Xhosa, the largest nation in South Africa. As the first clause of the Bantu Self-Government Bill of 1959 was to put it, "The Bantu peoples do not constitute a homogeneous people, but form separate national units on the basis of language and culture."

But the Verwoerd system was not simply a classic example of the old colonial stratagem, Divide and Rule. It was informed by genuine intellectual conviction, for the anthropologist's concept of societies as organic wholes automatically accorded with Verwoerd's view of a nation as an organism with a culture, traditions and history so peculiarly its own as to set it quite apart from all other nations. For the blacks in South Africa the only basis for development was the tribe. As Verwoerd asserted in one of his earliest statements as Minister of Native Affairs: "It is clear that the key to the true progress of the Bantu community as a whole, and to the avoidance of a struggle for equality in a joint territory or in common political living areas, lies in the recognition of the tribal system as the springboard from which the Bantu in a natural way, enlisting the help of dynamic elements in it, can increasingly rise to a higher level of culture and self-government on a foundation suitable to his own inherent character."[22] It did not quite follow that blacks were incapable of making a success of Parliamentary democracy, but it would be a gradual process, evolving from tribal roots. Nation-building was a slow, evolutionary development. It was so with the Afrikaner; it would inevitably be so with the incipient black nations of South Africa.

All this talk about tribalism and the inevitability of gradualism would not cost Verwoerd any votes. Conservative Afrikaner audiences could be relied upon not to become too disturbed by the idealistic prospect of developing black nations, as long as the developing was not too fast. Verwoerd also saw tribalism as a guarantor of the status quo. The stronger the tribal system, he believed, the less the appeal of that small unrepresentative body of "agitators" with a Western education who believed in black rule in one multiracial South Africa. Speaking in the House of Assembly on the Mau Mau revolt in Kenya, Verwoerd found support for his belief in tradition: "There we saw that generally it was the chiefs with their authorities who took sides with forces of law and order and who assisted European authority. In other words, the tribal authority is the natural ally of the government of the country against such rebellious movements."[23]

Here of course Verwoerd was trying to give respectability to that ancient colonial device, indirect rule. What he did not consider was that in most parts of Africa where indirect rule had been imposed, tribal authority had been so irremediably weakened by its subservience to the colonial authorities that the system had in fact simply been a relatively inexpensive camouflage for direct rule. If Verwoerd was aware of this, he probably regarded it as yet another of the priceless advantages of building on a tribal base.

The new Minister of Native Affairs went to great pains to explain his views and to make them acceptable to the people, a majority of the South African population, over whom he had been given authority. During the next eight years he was to travel extensively throughout the country on visits to African kraals. There he was received with traditional pageantry and participated in elaborate exchanges of gifts with the chiefs and headmen. He would listen to them, for he regarded them as the true representatives of the "Bantu", as they made representations and stated their grievances. Verwoerd as the wise and sympathetic father would attend patiently for hours during these sessions. All this play-acting was important to him, for the traditional rulers were the decisive element in his plans to bolster the tribal system. He was prepared to go to considerable lengths to gain their support.

According to his private secretary, Fred Barnard, in a personal communication to G.D. Scholtz, Verwoerd's behaviour on these occasions was always marked by two features. He fully recognised the human dignity of the African, as he showed in his willingness to listen endlessly to the problems of the tribal leaders. The second feature became apparent once the listening had ended. Verwoerd was always open and forthright. He never made vain promises. If he was not prepared to grant a request, he said so, but if he did say yes, his word was his bond. This, Scholtz is sure, inspired Africans with great respect for Verwoerd.[24]

Quite possibly Scholtz is correct, but there were aspects of Verwoerd's dealings with blacks which did not make him the ideal man for understanding and getting on with that growing number of Africans who had some education. According to Barnard, Verwoerd told the tribal spokesman to speak to him "as a child to his father". And when he could not grant a request he told them that he was "the father who can judge on the desirability of what is good for my children and what is not". Verwoerd, in short, was a paternalist. He thought of blacks as children who would take a long time to grow up. During this protracted infancy and adolescence they had to submit to a benevolent discipline, in practice, Verwoerd's. Educated Africans who did not look forward to the tribal future he had planned for them were to him just "agitators". He may have recognised their "human dignity" too, but his paternalistic attitudes must have made it difficult for him to treat them as equals. Verwoerd was not unique; paternalism has been a feature of colonial administrations everywhere. However, they have generally had difficulties in coming to terms with Westernised Africans and Asians and in regarding them as spokesmen for anyone except themselves. The problem was incomparably more difficult in South Africa, for here the "colonialists" were also permanent inhabitants of the country. In South Africa there was no prospect of a colonial withdrawal in favour of an educated indigenous elite which would become the new ruling class. Given the quite different aspirations of Afrikaner and African nationalists, a satisfactory *modus vivendi* between them was highly unlikely. Yet the problem was made even more intractable because the new Minister of Native Affairs was, by background and temperament, ill-qualified, even if he had been willing, to understand the African outside his tribal environment. Many would have said inside as well.

Nowhere was this better shown than in Verwoerd's brief relationship with the Natives Representative Council. Although the programme of the National Party had promised to abolish the Council, and Verwoerd himself had condemned it as "a body by which all dividing lines between various groups of Natives are broken down",[25] he decided to address the Council in December 1950, shortly after becoming Minister. The Council had previously shown its profound dissatisfaction with the powers granted to it by Hertzog in 1936. During the war tensions between the Council and the

Smuts Government had been becoming increasingly overt. Finally, in 1946, it went into voluntary recess as a protest against the Government's failure to consult it over the suppression of the miners' strike on the Rand. The Council had been addressed immediately before its decision by the famous liberal, J.H. Hofmeyr, but its members had failed to be impressed by his account of how fortunate Africans were to be living under so beneficent a government. The Council had condemned Hofmeyr's speech in words which clearly reflected changing times and moods: "To us it seemed to be merely an apology for the status quo, apparently oblivious of the progressive forces at work not only in the world in general but even in South Africa itself. The statement makes no attempt to deal with some of the burning questions of the day such as the pass laws, the colour bar in industry, the political rights of the non-Europeans in the Union, etc. and in effect it raises no hope for the future as far as the African people are concerned."[26]

Why Verwoerd decided to convene the Council is not clear. According to Scholtz, it was to determine whether cooperation was not after all possible.[27] Perhaps, but his declared views on the Council and that body's own record make it difficult to understand why he should have been so optimistic. Possibly he only convened it so as to prove once again that the Council was not a viable institution within the framework of apartheid. As it turned out, this was correct.

Verwoerd's message to the Council was simple. Apartheid was necessary, for the alternative of a racially mixed society meant "competition and conflict everywhere". Yet apartheid was no policy of oppression, for it believed "in the supremacy (*baasskap*) of the Bantu in his own sphere". Separate societies would have to arise. The Government would increase the absorptive capacity of the reserves "through soil reclamation and conservation methods", to be accompanied by "an urban development founded on industrial growth". In the white towns and cities blacks would have "as much self-government as is practicable under the guardianship of the town councils ..."

For the educated African there was the attractive prospect of serving his own people, whether as shopkeeper, clerk or preacher. "The mistake that many leaders of the Bantu make is to think only in terms of the highest superstructure of politics. Within this sphere they seek their own personal ambition, and forget that 99 per cent of the people do not have these ambitions." Africans actually needed a very special kind of education: "We are not against education which makes a man a worker in the service of his own nation, and we believe that what the Bantu needs

130

more than anything else today is a vocational training in many directions. There is one very clear proviso and that is that when he is educated he may not use his education to slip out of the company of his fellow Bantu and try to go among the white man and use the knowledge there."[28]

There was little here that could appeal to the members of the Council. They were simply being told that in return for restrictions on their advancement in the most economically advanced part of the country, they would one day be allowed to practise a nebulous *baasskap* of their own in areas that would for a long time still be economic backwaters. Verwoerd had instructed them that the Council could not discuss "matters of political policy". They now insisted on doing so. The first spokesman, Professor Z.K. Matthews of Fort Hare, was still relatively restrained: "The Minister believes and his supporters are entitled to believe that apartheid is the answer to our problem in this country. I do not quarrel with anyone believing that, but I say that as long as a policy is a unilateral policy, conceived, worked out and applied by one section of the population, it will not meet the needs of all sections of the population." Other responses were more strident. One member described the reserves as zoos in which he could not agree that the inhabitants should live like animals.[29]

The Council adjourned at a point of complete deadlock. It never met again, and in 1952 ceased to exist in terms of the Bantu Authorities Act. Verwoerd must have found the whole exercise eminently worthwhile. It proved to him beyond any doubt that he had been right all along about the Natives Representative Council. As he said in the House of Assembly the following year: "It is a body which has no meaning apart from being agitational, because an advisory body can only complain and ask. It has no responsibility towards anyone whom it represents or towards the whole community."[30] Now he could proceed with his plans. Nobody could say that he had not given the Natives Representative Council a fair chance.

The Council had been one attempt to shape African political development on Western lines. Verwoerd did not reject the aim in principle, but it could only succeed if it built on a tribal base. This had been ignored in the establishment of the Council, hence its failure. To Verwoerd it reflected a cultural egocentrism which by-passed the African's own past and traditions by foisting on him institutions with which he was completely unfamiliar. There had been previous attempts to do so, with no greater success. They had their origins in the old Cape Colony, with its liberal policies derived from a Victorian optimism about the universal superiority of British institutions and practices. In the Transkei in the Eastern Cape a system of local government had developed, which still existed, that virtually ignored the tribal system. The district councils that were established had a majority of elected members, while the territorial body, the United Transkeian Territories General Council or, less officially, the Bunga, consisted of representatives of these councils. It did not matter that the Bunga had only strictly limited functions in a limited context. It was important that the whole system of local government in the Transkei, the most politically advanced and the most populous of the Union's black territories, was, like the Natives Representative Council, founded on bad principle. The black man's traditional system of government had been disregarded as if it were an embarrassing relic from the past, destined for the rubbish heap of history.

Verwoerd's first important measure as Minister of Native Affairs was designed to undo the previous hundred years, and to refurbish those traditional institutions which had such enduring value. It would also, incidentally, make the Nationalists' task of governing far simpler. The Bantu Authorities Bill which he introduced in 1951 proposed to do away with the Natives Representative Council, that classic example of how not to give political responsibilities to developing peoples. A body divorced from tradition, it had no grass-roots support because it started at the top instead of evolving from below. "Only a limited number of people were selected as members of a body by a method of election which was not in fact based on the principle of self-government. That small group assembled on behalf of the Natives without having been elected by existing self-governing bodies, and without any experience of self-government on a lower level." Without any governing responsibilities, purely an advisory body, it was free with irresponsible demands and inevitably became "an organisation of agitators".[31]

Verwoerd was being less than fair to the Council, as the leading Native Representative, Margaret Ballinger, pointed out.[32] Many of its members had had experience of local government in the rural areas, while the Council's urban members were familiar with the partly elected Advisory Boards which had been established in the cities and towns to assist in the running of black residential areas. The objection was sound, but rather beside the point. Nor would it have been pertinent to observe that if black representative bodies made irresponsible demands because they only had advisory powers, the obvious answer was to give them real governing responsibilities. Such considerations could not have counted for much with Verwoerd: it was to ignore the tribal foundation of all genuine black self-government.

His remedy was to restore "the natural Native democracy".[33] Previously chiefs and headmen had exercised authority on their own, but this was really a perversion, "an unnatural autocracy ... foreign to the natural Bantu system". Tribal leaders would henceforth exercise their authority with the advice and assistance of their council, as it had been before the imposition of that white rule which had led to the decline of the traditional system.

It was now to be restored in the form of a three-tier hierarchical system of authority. At the lowest level, so crucial to Verwoerd's approach, would be the tribal authority, consisting of the chief or headman and his councillors. The next tier would be the regional authority, consisting of two or more tribal authorities which would administer a wider area with common interests. Finally, and eventually, a territorial authority for the ethnic group concerned would be formed out of two or more regional authorities. These bodies would not simply have advisory powers, but administrative, executive and judicial powers too. All their members would be black, including the chairman of each council. Their authority would "be exercised according to Native law and Native custom".

There was one snag. At first, "and certainly for some time afterwards", the traditional authorities would receive the "assistance" of white Native Commissioners, who would supervise and advise, but would not themselves be members of any of the councils. Helpful officials would ensure, in effect, that white control, for the foreseeable future, would be the reality behind "the natural Bantu system". It was emphatically to be a guided democracy.

A distinguishing feature of Verwoerd's new political dispensation for blacks was its gradualism. He may have been obsessed with the urgency of maintaining the white racial identity, but he felt no similar urgency in developing adequate political outlets for the African. The main immediate aim was to erect rigid barriers between black and white. Blacks, particularly if they were educated, had to know that there could be no future for them in the "white" areas. There they were merely guests, staying on sufferance, always with the prospect of being returned to their respective ethnic homelands. The deliberate strengthening of tribalism was part of this process of erecting barriers. Western-type political institutions were not as yet for Africans. Their only salvation lay in the development of their own institutions, in their own areas.

Verwoerd's system of Bantu Authorities was the assertion of a principle, that black and white were different, with different destinies in store for them. But, the principle once asserted, Verwoerd felt no powerful compulsion to hasten the political evolution of the African. There is no evidence that he wished to do so and, even if he had, the opposition of his colleagues in the cabinet to "radical" measures from a very junior Minister would most likely have been too strong. Ideas about black self-rule and independence soon were no part of the intellectual climate of South Africa at this time, which was understandable, for Western colonial control over Africa still seemed assured for many years, with no inkling yet of the hasty retreat which began toward the end of the decade. For the moment, the Government simply wanted the natives kept as quiet as possible with the minimum of bother.

The new tribalism seemed admirably suited to this end. One of the main attractions of the traditional system of government was indeed its freedom from Western-type controls through the ballot box. The Department of Native Affairs admitted as much in a pamphlet published in 1958 on "Bantu Authorities and Tribal Administration", which found much to admire in the fact that the councillors of the tribal authority "will perform their task without fear or prejudice, because they are not elected by the majority of votes ..."[34] To make assurance doubly sure, not only were tribal leaders largely insulated from popular pressures, they were highly subject to Government controls and influence. Chiefs who were not prepared to cooperate could be, and as events proved often were, deposed by the Minister of Native Affairs. In the years 1955 and 1958 inclusive, 34 chiefs and headmen were removed. For the time being at least the development of political institutions in the reserves was to be firmly under white control.

Unpromising as it was, the Bantu Authorities Act of 1951 contained within itself, difficult to discern, the seeds of change. The ability of governments to shape events according to their own purposes has always been limited; it was so in South Africa as well. When change came it was reluctant, belated and slow, and hedged about with Government controls. Bantu authorities began as a system of black political tutelage, designed to continue indefinitely, but under the pressure of events in a decolonising world, it began to give blacks in South Africa a degree of political leverage they had never had before. This is perhaps not saying much and it was still some years away, but the Bantu Authorities Act was withal a significant landmark in South African history.

Apartheid would remain for some time still largely a negative phenomenon. For those who were discriminated against the positive benefits were few, and consisted mainly of promises which might one day be fulfilled. Pirow's question of 1949 did not cease to be relevant: "... is apartheid advantageous only for the white man?" In these early stages, apartheid with a positive face seems more to have been a conscience salver for uneasy Nationalists than a serious attempt to provide blacks with equal opportunities in "their own areas". In view of the decayed state of the reserves, with the limited economic opportunities they provided, this was really a contradiction in terms. Genuine prospects of advancement, to a growing number of blacks, were in the great urban complexes of the Union, but here they would always be "guests", but with a difference, for the normal rules of hospitality did not apply.

The system of Bantu authorities was therefore only one side of the apartheid coin, and certainly not the most important. The race question was becoming more and more an urban question. The ultimate success of the Government's policy would stand or fall by its ability to deal with the problem of African urbanisation. From the Nationalist point of view there was only one feasible long-term policy – to reverse the flow of blacks into the towns and cities. But the emphasis was on the long term. No one suggested that this was immediately feasible. During the 1940s blacks had been streaming into the urban areas at the alarming rate of more than 4 per cent a year. The Smuts Government had apparently accepted it as an irresistible fact of life. It was an impression only confirmed by the famous Fagan Report, the report of the Native Laws Commission, appointed in 1946 under the chairmanship of a former Minister of Native Affairs, Henry Fagan. Submitted in 1948, just before Malan's victory, the Fagan Report explicitly accepted the urban African as a permanent feature of South Africa's population. The Commission found that black immigration from the rural to the urban areas was due to economic imperatives: "It should be clear, firstly, that the idea of total segregation is utterly impracticable; secondly, that the movement from country to town has a background of economic necessity – that it may, so one hopes, be guided and regulated, and may perhaps also be limited, but that it cannot be stopped or turned in the other direction; and thirdly, that in our urban areas there are not only Native migrant labourers, but there is also a settled, permanent Native population."

The Commission maintained that since the 1920s legislation relating to urban blacks had been based on an "untenable proposition", namely, that they were "all temporarily migrant". A "new formula" was needed, one that would "serve as a guide in respect of our suggestions for revision of the existing legislation".[35]

It was an argument and a conclusion that the new Government could not accept. The Nationalists too believed in a new formula, but a formula that would not accept economic forces as decisive in the shaping of South African history. This was what apartheid was supposed to be about: it was not opposed to temporary migrancy, but claimed instead that of the too numerous blacks entering town too many were becoming permanent residents. Eventually, in a future that would not bear too close examination, the trend would be reversed, but what should be done in the mean time to prevent South Africa's urban areas from being submerged by a black flood?

The Government was faced with a dilemma which it never managed to resolve, then or later. The country's economic development, particularly its industrialisation, had been intricately bound up with the employment of blacks in ever-growing numbers in the modern white-controlled sector of the economy. Large-scale repatriation of blacks to the reserves would seriously harm economic growth. The electoral implications of a reduced growth rate could not appeal to the ruling party, but the unchecked influx of blacks into the towns, Nationalists unquestioningly believed, was a most serious menace to the apparently always fragile Afrikaner identity. The self-preservation of the Afrikaners and of the National Party demanded that something be done, even if the efforts impressed more by their visibility than by their efficacy. The Government opted then, as it has done ever since, to have its cake and eat it. Total territorial segregation had in any event never been its policy, as it had so often emphasised. The decision was that nothing would be done to impede economic growth, but, at the same time, the Government would give convincing proof that the old-time religion was not dead. Blacks would continue to be temporary workers in the urban areas, but now they would be even more temporary than before.

Verwoerd and his colleagues refused to distinguish between urban and rural Africans, although various distinct groups could in fact be discerned amongst them. At the one extreme were those fully urbanised blacks who had been born in the cities or who had resided there a long time. At the other extreme were the migrant workers who came to the urban areas for a specified time before returning to the reserves. There was also an intermediate group which depended mainly on urban wage labour, but retained their links with the reserves, to which they returned periodically. These differences did not exist for Verwoerd. For him the fully urbanised black belonged as much to the reserves as the rural African who had never been outside them in all his life.

In his very first speech as a Parliamentarian, Verwoerd had stressed that the urban African was only a visitor. Ten years later, just after he became Prime Minister, his views had not changed in the least: "The Bantu in the cities are not distinct from the Bantu in the Native Reserves. They belong to one another and, as I have often said, the urban Bantu are visitors in the white areas who are there for their own economic benefit. Their roots are in the Native Reserves. The opportunities for them to enjoy rights, whether they be social or political rights, are available in their home areas."[36]

The Government's policy was to accept total segregation as an ideal, so long-term as to be practically meaningless, but to do nothing that would disrupt the working of an economy that had come to depend on black labour as a vital necessity. Instead, it set about increasing the range of controls over blacks in the urban areas, as well as steadily eliminating their nights of domicile outside the reserves. Thus, in 1952 the Native Laws Amendment Act sought to channel the movement of black workers in town through labour bureaus. To a degree, the Act was what Verwoerd claimed it to be, an attempt to allocate labour more efficiently by providing work-seekers with information about job opportunities. As he explained, it sought to deal with the problem of blacks who arrived in town and were unable to find work. The permission of the nearest labour bureau was now required by an African if he wanted to move from a "nonprescribed" (mainly rural) area to one which was "prescribed" (mainly urban) because job opportunities there were limited.[37]

But the Native Laws Amendment Act was a little more than this. Margaret Ballinger went to the heart of the matter when she stated that the Bill, when introduced by Verwoerd, was an attempt to strengthen "the original character of the Urban Areas Act in exactly the opposite direction from that recommended by the Fagan Commission". In other words, this was another step toward rejecting the permanent nature of urban black settlement. In fairness to Verwoerd she added, "I know that he inherited this drive. It has been my continuing criticism of the Native Affairs Department for the last seven or eight or nine or ten years that they have driven solidly for this type of legislation." And she went on to blame the United Party which, during the war, "began this system of extending the area subject to permits".[38] This emphasis on continuity is in striking contrast with that of her book, *From Union to Apartheid*, which appeared seventeen years later. Here she argued, presumably with the benefit of a longer perspective, that the Nationalist victory in 1948 was the prelude to what was in fact a revolution in South African life. That 1948 was a watershed in South Africa's history there can be little doubt, but it is salutary to remember, in the light of her own later argument, that Mrs. Ballinger at this stage was not inclined to distinguish too sharply between the United and the National Parties.

Whether strongly rooted in the past or not, Verwoerd's policy was based on the premise that the African in town was just a temporary worker. Labour bureaus may well have been designed to provide information to black work-seekers, but they were also a means of directing the flow of African labour. A prospective employee who now required the permission of a labour bureau to enter a "prescribed area" had his freedom of movement restricted and his competitive ability reduced in a way which had not been so before. There was indeed reason to fear that the labour bureaus would not be used to promote labour mobility, but to provide the politically influential farmers with black workers at artificially low rates of pay. As Verwoerd said in the debate on the Bill in the Senate, "Emigration control must be established to prevent manpower leaving the platteland to become or to create loafers in the cities."[39] This sort of statement was vintage Verwoerd. He had no doubt that he knew better than others what was good for them, and was therefore entitled to impose controls on them for their own benefit. If blacks, in pursuit of their economic self-interest, found that opportunities in the cities were even fewer than those in the rural areas, it was after all logical to conclude that the outflow from the platteland would eventually have reversed itself, without any need for controls. Verwoerd could not see this. His grasp of economics had never been good, and in any event his belief in controls, as long as he did the controlling, was a basic feature of his whole approach to public affairs. And there was also that strong incentive to further the interests of the farmers with their perpetual complaints about labour shortages, which in practice meant that they found it difficult to obtain black workers at the relatively low rates of pay they were prepared to offer.

Controls were further extended that same year by the Natives (Abolition of Passes and Coordination of Documents) Act. Administratively this was a considerable improvement on the prevailing system. Instead of carrying a variety of passes as before, Africans over the age of sixteen now had to have a reference book which they had to produce on demand. It contained the holder's identity card plus a number of other documents such as his employment contract, poll tax receipts, and so on. For the first time African women had to carry a pass, a provision which produced widespread protest. It was a more efficient system and, as Scholtz truthfully observed, "made it much easier for the police and the authorities to control the movement of the Bantu to the urban areas".[40]

4 Tomlinson and Bantu Education

The laws which increased state control over blacks outside the reserves were part of the whole pattern of early Nationalist legislation. However small their majority in Parliament, the Nationalists wasted no time in introducing apartheid wherever they could, as well as enlarging their powers to deal effectively with opposition to their policies. There was, for instance, the Native Building Workers' Act of 1951, which made it possible for blacks to be trained as building workers in "Native areas", but at the same time stipulated that no African could be a skilled worker outside his own area. The Group Areas Act of 1950 divided the whole country, but especially the urban areas, into separate areas for the different races. In a group area for any one race, no member of another race could own or occupy property. Impartial in principle, in practice it discriminated against the politically powerless. Indians and Coloureds were liable to be moved from areas where they had always lived to areas which were smaller and where alternative accommodation was scarce.

As this pattern of legislation unfolded there were frequent protests by groups and individuals, not yet fully aware of the nature of the new era South Africa was entering. The Government's response was prompt and uncompromising: in 1950 Parliament passed the Suppression of Communism Act and in 1953 the Public Safety and the Criminal Law Amendment Acts. The first-named was a far-reaching measure which enabled the Government to ban any organisation, or person, it chose to describe as Communist. The latter two measures provided respectively for the declaration of a state of emergency when security was endangered and for harsh punishment for incitement to break a law.

Even more extraordinary were the Government's attempts to remove the Coloured voters in the Cape Province from the common roll. To succeed it needed, in terms of the South African constitution, a two-thirds majority of both Houses of Parliament in a joint sitting. This was no deterrent, and in 1951 the Government introduced a bill providing for the removal of the Coloured voters. It was passed by a simple majority both in the House of Assembly and in the Senate. The new "Act" was thereupon challenged in the courts, which ruled it invalid. The Government responded with the High Court of Parliament Act, which set up a new constitutional court consisting of all the members of both Houses of Parliament sitting together, which could by a simple majority vote act as the final court of appeal in all constitutional cases. This High Court of Parliament thereupon proceeded to uphold the Government's appeal against the Appeal Court's judgement. But the High Court of Parliament Act was then itself declared invalid by a court judgement.

There the matter rested temporarily, but it was clear that this was a new style of politics. The Nationalists were decidedly not to be shaken in the pursuit of their aims by a slight Parliamentary majority, or by what they chose to regard as constitutional niceties. Setbacks were to them only temporary; they went ahead with their programme despite not only their thin majority in Parliament, but also their minority support among the electorate. They managed to enlarge their Parliamentary majority by giving representation in the House of Assembly to the mandated territory of South West Africa, which duly obliged by electing six Nationalist M.Ps in 1950. More fundamentally, the Government must have realised that once it had the support of the great majority of Afrikaners, which constituted 60 per cent of the white population, there was little prospect of being defeated at the polls and every prospect of increasing their majority at the next election. Not only were the Afrikaners a majority of the whites, but they were also growing more rapidly than the English-speakers. Politically they were far more dedicated, while the National Party had better organisation than the United Party, which enjoyed the support of the vast number of English-speaking voters. Thus, for a number of reasons, the Government was entitled to feel confident about its political future. It could proceed with impunity in implementing a programme which, to old-time liberals like Margaret Ballinger, nostalgic for the days of Smuts, seemed to amount to a qualitative change in the nature of South African society.

The five years between 1948 and 1953, when the next election took place, turned out to be a time of confrontation. Many Opposition supporters saw the Nationalist victory in 1948 as a mere flash in the pan, an unfortunate aberration which would be undone at the next general election when the voters would have returned to their senses. It is safe to say that during its first term of office the Government appeared to its opponents more vulnerable than it was, partly because of its very small majority in Parliament, partly because its ruthlessness and sense of purpose were not yet plain for all to see. Before its anticipated defeat in 1953 it seemed very likely that the Government could be deterred by protests, if they were widespread enough.

It was in 1952, timed to coincide with the tercentenary celebrations of the Dutch arrival in 1652, that the Defiance Campaign took place. In many parts of the country Africans and Indians deliberately courted imprisonment by defying the segregation laws. Thousands were imprisoned, but the campaign was not a success. It soon lost momentum and fizzled out with little, if any, positive results. Its main effects were two. It exposed the weakness of the black nationalist movement when faced with the Government's determination to make no concessions at all. Secondly, it led to the passing of the Public Safety Act and the Criminal Law Amendment Act, laws which would make similar protests in the future far more hazardous than before.

These were also the years of the Torch Commando, a body of war veterans organised to resist the Government's attempts to have its way with the constitution. But after a spectacular march on Cape Town in May 1951, which culminated with a parade through the streets with lighted torches and ended with baton charges by the police, this movement too fizzled out. It consisted of too many diverse elements, of members who only wanted to prevent the Nationalists from violating the constitution, and others who wanted to use the Torch Commando as an instrument for social change. There was no unity of purpose, an asset abundantly possessed by the Government.

The irrevocable nature of Nationalist rule first became apparent in the 1953 general election, when the Government was returned with a much-enlarged majority, with 94 seats as against the combined Opposition total of 64. In what, with the benefit of hindsight, looks like sheer blind optimism, the United Party had high hopes of reversing the 1948 result. It waged an energetic campaign, and its disappointment was all the more bitter. The single most decisive cause of the Nationalist victory was probably the growing importance of the racial issue, especially as reflected in cities and towns which were becoming blacker every year. Inevitably, it intensified the Afrikaner's sense of being threatened by millions of primitive blacks.

The Government was now secure, with little prospect of ever being turned out at a future general election. But it was no closer to achieving greater territorial segregation between black and white. Apartheid was still the negative affair it had always been. Segregation laws proliferated to separate the races in all conceivable walks of life, whether in trade unions, the nursing profession, or the facilities of railway stations. Yet continuing industrialisation was making the races more interdependent every day. Ideals of territorial separation were coming to resemble the figments of a utopian imagination, destined never to be realised. It was in this context that the Tomlinson Report appeared. Under its chairman, the well-known agricultural economist, F.R. Tomlinson, the Commission had spent years investigating the social and economic conditions of the reserves. Finally, in 1954, it submitted to the Cabinet an enormous report of 3,755 mimeographed pages, later summarised in over 200 printed pages. Verwoerd, it will be recalled, had not been pleased about the appointment of the Commission by his predecessor. While the investigation was under way, he frequently remarked in private conversation that had he been Minister of Native Affairs at the time he would have opposed its appointment. He was confident that with the assistance of his officials, and with the knowledge he had gained on visits to the reserves, he himself would have been perfectly capable of deciding what ought to be done about the development of the black areas. So, when the Tomlinson Report was ready at last, Verwoerd was in no hurry to act. The Cabinet sat on it for more than a year; it was eventually only published in March 1956. The impression that the Government did not quite know what to do with this report which had been so long in the making and had been so costly an enterprise, was confirmed a few months later when it welcomed the Report's conclusions, but rejected some of its main recommendations.

The Commission had been required "to conduct an exhaustive inquiry into and to report on a comprehensive scheme for the rehabilitation of the Native Areas with a view to developing within them a social structure in keeping with the culture of the Native and based on effective socio-economic planning". These terms of reference were widely interpreted, "because the Commission very soon realised that the problems relative to the development of the Bantu Areas, could only be thoroughly analysed and studied in the light of the wider economic, social and political framework on the Union of South Africa".[1]

The basic premise of the inquiry was that separate development (as apartheid was euphemistically referred to) was the only way to a viable future for South Africa. The Commission knew that the existing tendency towards integration meant that black and white were "becoming interwoven to an increasing extent". But this created a "dilemma" for the people of South Africa. The whites had "the unbreakable will to maintain their identity in the national and biological sense", while the blacks were becoming more and more convinced that they were "entitled to enjoy the

142

fruits of integration, *inter alia*, by demanding progressively an increased say in the administration of the country as a whole". It was a dilemma that had to be resolved by a policy of separate development "as the only direction in which racial conflict may possibly be eliminated and racial harmony possibly be maintained". This required the "sustained development of the Bantu areas on a large scale".[2]

The problem was that developing the reserves would be an immense task, for they were the most backward areas of South Africa. Life in the reserves, for the overwhelming majority of their inhabitants, meant a poverty so pervasive as to appear virtually irremediable. Population density here was far higher than in the rest of the country: in 1951 there were on average 63 persons per square mile in the black areas, compared with 27 for South Africa as a whole.[3] And this density was to increase substantially over the years, throughout the Verwoerd era: in 1965 the respective figures were 79 and 38.[4]

The reserves comprised a relatively small part of South Africa, about 12 per cent of the surface area, although this did not reflect the quality of the soil, the availability of natural resources, proximity to markets, and so on. But neither in these respects were the reserves especially favoured. The Commission found that the soils of the black areas were generally "a fair reflection of the soils of the Union as a whole",[5] although they were relatively well situated with respect to power, coal and electricity. But the most important minerals, gold and diamonds, were in white South Africa, and the reserves were bypassed by the transport network, largely designed to serve the expanding market economy which had emerged after the mineral revolution.

The reserves were mainly rural, suffering from acute soil erosion and overstocking. Scratching a bare living from the soil with primitive techniques could not sustain the whole population, so that a large proportion of the able-bodied males left each year to work in the modern sector. It was remittances from these migrant workers which played a vital role in maintaining living standards in the reserves, low as they were. The reserves were actually supporting a declining proportion of the total black population of the country. This was yet another trend which was to continue throughout the Verwoerd years. Between 1951 and 1965 this proportion declined from about 43 per cent to 40 per cent.[6]

Inevitably, what production there was in the reserves was largely of a subsistence nature. The Commission's estimate was that agriculture contributed at least 62 per cent of the income of the reserves, but that only 25 per cent of the agricultural product was marketed.[7]

For all these reasons, then, per capita production in the reserves in 1951 was extremely low, a mere £12.9 (R25.8) compared with £99.4 (R198.8) for the country as a whole. Since 1936 it seemed that per capita incomes had "even fallen", while the contribution of the black areas to South Africa's total geographic income was insignificant, less than 4 per cent in 1950–1.[8] These proportions were to become even more unfavourable in future. It appears there was a marked fall in the ratio of reserve to non-reserve outputs between 1951 and 1965.[9]

The Commission stressed the necessity for developing other income-earning activities, estimating that "efficient agricultural development of the Bantu Areas" required the removal of about half the existing population from the land.[10] Those so removed would have to find a living outside agriculture. A transition from communal tenure to individual tenure was desirable, as a prelude to those greatly improved farming practices by means of which food supplies would have to be made available to the non-farming population.

There is reason to believe that the Commission exaggerated the inefficiency of black farmers, and that it was not simply a matter of persuading Africans of the superiority of more advanced techniques. It is quite likely that they had little incentive to adopt more advanced methods, which would have involved greater outlays of capital, of which there was a chronic shortage in the reserves. Combined with poor marketing facilities for their produce and the enormous difficulty of competing with the heavily subsidised white agricultural sector, it is understandable why blacks should have thought the investment in more advanced methods too costly, and why so many should have sought more remunerative employment in the white areas.

But it was industrialisation which was the Commission's one great hope for ending the economic stagnation of the reserves. It estimated that if the carrying capacity of the land were to be raised, 50,000 new jobs outside agriculture would have to be created annually for the next 25 years. Secondary industry would have to provide the initial impetus by giving annual employment to 20,000 workers; this would stimulate tertiary activities, which would provide jobs for the remaining 30,000.[11] Here the Commission was being hopelessly optimistic, for, in its own words, "as far as industries are concerned, the Bantu areas are in fact a desert ..."[12]

Whatever industrialisation there was to be could take two forms, not necessarily incompatible. The Commission distinguished between "border areas" development and industrial development within the reserves. It was a vital distinction, going to the very heart of "separate development". A border area was defined as "one where development takes place in a European area situated so closely to the Bantu Areas, that families of Bantu employees engaged in that development can be established in the Bantu Area in such a way that the employees can lead a full family life". The advantages of border areas industrialisation were that development in the reserves themselves would be stimulated, especially in the tertiary sector, and that the employment it would provide would have multiplier effects in the black areas proper. It would relieve population pressure on agricultural resources and raise the capacity of the reserves to sustain their existing population. But the main objection to such a strategy for development was that it would "only partially remove the 'ceiling' for the Bantu". In other words, the industrial colour bar, applicable in the other white areas, would be in force in the border areas too. This would make it "particularly difficult to create a class of skilled workers and entrepreneurs among the Bantu".[13]

The Commission therefore saw border areas development as a less satisfactory alternative than the internal development of the reserves themselves. "Industrial development inside the Bantu Areas is necessary because it is an integral part of an economic structure which wishes to achieve the maximum socio-economic development for the people, to provide the largest possible Bantu population in these areas with a lasting livelihood, and to remove the 'ceiling' over its head in all spheres of social life. The development of border areas will undoubtedly increase the carrying capacity of the Bantu Areas, but inside development will increase it the maximum extent."[14] Purely in economic terms there were, in fact, strong reasons for concentrating on the development of border areas. The latter had more advanced social overhead capital facilities, such as communications and transport, than the reserves, and were also more urbanised. The initial capital investment to stimulate a given degree of development would therefore probably have been much smaller. It would have been easier to attract entrepreneurs and technicians to border areas. In short, their prospects for economic development would at first have been rather better than those of the reserves.[15] But, in the long run, it seemed to the Commission that it would be preferable to concentrate on the internal growth of the reserves, which would otherwise simply become economic dependencies of the white areas. Whatever strategy was adopted, it would be extremely costly. The Commission believed very strongly in white capital investment in the black areas, but even then the Government would have to make a very substantial contribution of its own. It recommended that the Government should make available at least

£25 (R50) million over a period of five years for the purpose of industrial development "irrespective of whether other sources of capital can be found or not".[16] The estimated cost of its programme for diversifying the economy of the reserves during the first ten years would be £104,000. If these proposals were implemented the reserves would "accommodate about 60 per cent of the Bantu population by 1981, and about 60 per cent by the close of the century ... The ideal should be that the non-Bantu areas house a swiftly shrinking portion of the total Bantu population."[17] However, even if the desired tempo were realised it was still clear that blacks would outnumber whites in the "white" areas by the end of the century. It was no exhilarating prospect, but the alternative was incomparably worse. If the Commission's programme were rejected and existing trends continued, then the increase in the black population would only spill over into the rest of the country; by the end of the century the reserves would accommodate a mere quarter of the black population.

Although Verwoerd disliked the Report, he could not ignore it. He was however determined to be influenced only by those recommendations that he found politically acceptable or intellectually congenial. The way was prepared for his negative response in Parliament by the Government's White Paper which welcomed the Commission's endorsement of apartheid, but poured cold water over its suggested choice of methods as being not "a matter of scientific proof but of individual judgement".[18]

Verwoerd had accepted Margaret Ballinger's argument that more productive agricultural practices required the consolidation of holdings into economic units, and had appointed committees to investigate the appropriate size of such units in the various areas.[19] He also agreed that an improved agriculture required the removal of large numbers from the land. This he proposed to do by gathering into villages those landless families which depended upon wage earning for a living. The consolidation of holdings could be expected to increase the numbers of these village inhabitants.

But how would this "surplus" population be gainfully employed? Would it involve an economic diversification of the reserves themselves? Nearly a year before the publication of the Report, Verwoerd had already given his answer. He told the Senate that the "establishment of a number of potential towns in Bantu areas" was intended "to begin with strategic well-placed localities from which existing or potential European industrial towns can be served, in the vicinity, and which at the same time will bring a fuller life for the Bantu areas concerned".[20] In other words, he was thinking in terms of the border areas strategy; the industrial development of the reserves was a secondary consideration. The economic diversification of these areas would be a by-product of the development of the "white" areas, on which they would be dependent.

Verwoerd's rejection of the main recommendations of the Tomlinson Commission in the House of Assembly was couched in that intricate blend of political expediency and apartheid ideology at which he has never been equalled. Once again there was that obsessive concern with gradualism as far as the African was concerned. But gradualism simple and by itself was undesirable. As Verwoerd profoundly pointed out, it had to be understood "that you can apply gradualness on a wrong course, or gradualness on a correct course, and if you are engaged in working in the direction of increasing apartheid step by step, then gradualism is sensible and not a danger. That is quite distinct from a gradual swamping of European civilisation and the process of integration." The policy of apartheid was one of "slow development, by means of mother tongue, and by means of environmental education to make literate and useful people of them within their own circle. By stabilising the land for the best use thereof; by site-and-service schemes for good economic accommodation for all; from traditional tribe through tribal authority to area authority and to territorial authority; by elementary education for all to the creation of a broader basis upon which progress is possible for the foremost and the strong personalities amongst the Bantu, through community service to constructive leadership."[21]

Verwoerd certainly believed all this on intellectual grounds, but it is easy to see how politically convenient it was to have such convictions. Making haste slowly with the development of the black peoples, and the relatively low expenditure it involved, would be unlikely to cost the Government any votes with a conservative electorate still accustomed to master-servant relationships. Throughout the 1950s the Government, in spite of the urgings of some Afrikaner intellectuals, went about "decolonising" at a deliberate pace which suggested that time was not of the essence. Nor was it surprising, for the Western colonial powers themselves were still talking about leaving their African colonies in terms soon to be made absurd by the sudden acceleration of change after Ghana's independence in 1957.

Given the Tomlinson Commission's sense of urgency and the Government's own lack of it, the outcome was predictable. Verwoerd completely rejected white capitalist enterprise in the reserves in terms that perhaps do credit to his sentiments, but none at all to his intellectual depth. Such enterprise would lead to "a gradual penetration of Whites into the Bantu areas instead of the present gradual withdrawal". It was incompatible with separate development because "the Whites would pocket everything economically", while blacks could not logically be denied similar rights in the white areas. "That would mean following the path of integration, an even more serious integration within the Bantu areas than we have within the White areas." Nor would the white presence be merely temporary, as the Commission thought in its innocence: "When established rights of this nature are created, it is wishful thinking to believe that after ten or twenty years the industries will pass from the hands of the Whites into the hands of the Bantu."[22]

Verwoerd gave these reasons for public consumption, but there was more to his rejection of white capital in the reserves than his uncritical rehash of some very old anti-capitalist clichés. He had at least one other reason, but he could never stand up in public and say it. Since he had left *Die Transvaler* Verwoerd had not flaunted the anti-Semitism which had been so pronounced in his academic and editorial days, but there is no reason to believe that he had abandoned it. Its survival is attested by the remark he made, according to the former Nationalist M.P., Japie Basson,[23] at a caucus of the National Party which he addressed as Minister of Native Affairs. White capital had to be kept out of the reserves, Verwoerd allegedly said, because, *inter alia*, "it would keep the Jews out". In view of his entire previous record on this issue, it sounds only too plausible as coming from Verwoerd.

Economic partnership in the reserves between black and white would thus lead to the far worse evil of political partnership. This was the thin-end-of-the-wedge argument, quite devoid of logic but much cherished by Verwoerd, and often used by him later to justify his refusal to soften the apartheid laws in even minor ways. Would one concession not lead to another, and so to ultimate black majority rule? In this context, the "whole country and not only the Bantu area would in due course become one area of competition and one ownership area".

From the African's viewpoint, there was even less justification for opening the reserves to white capitalist enterprise. His inability to compete with whites would deprive him "of his only opportunity of economic self-development". In his own interests he had to be protected against an inflow of white capital. It was his only guarantee for eventual self-development, even if it could mean that growth in the reserves would temporarily be slow.

Verwoerd provided an even more elaborate rationalisation for doing as little as possible about the backwardness of the black areas. For the

African development had "to start on a small scale. Psychologically, he is not adapted to industrial life and certainly not to private enterprise, to be able to start on a big scale. Nor would he be in a position in ten or twenty years' time to take over big industries which have been developed there, if his relationship towards industry has been simply that of the recipient and the outsider."[24] The African had to start modestly and he had to help himself. Thus he would avoid the evils of "spoon-feeding" and of the Smuts Government's bad mistakes in its own attempts at rural rehabilitation.

The Minister of Native Affairs clearly did not believe in the industrialisation of the reserves if it had to come through white capital investment or through pampering the Africans. It was a conviction that saved the taxpayer a considerable amount of money. The Commission had recommended that the Government make £25 million available over five years for industrial development in the reserves. Verwoerd interpreted this as being "intended for White industrial development" in the black areas; the amount was now no longer necessary. But he ignored what the Commission really did say, namely that "this amount should be provided by the Government, irrespective of whether other sources of capital can be found or not." Similarly, he could dismiss the £34 million the Commission had suggested for agricultural development. This amount, he alleged, had been "based on the system in vogue then, before 1952–3, viz. the old system which this Government inherited of doing everything for the Native, the system of spoon-feeding".[25] As spoon-feeding was out, so also were the millions for agricultural development. The Government's complete lack of any sense of urgency about separate development could not have been more strongly emphasised. The Tomlinson Commission had explicitly said, "Half-hearted efforts will make no impression."[26] There was plenty of reason to believe that the Commission's estimates had been too low, but even these had been too high for Verwoerd. It was just such a half-hearted effort that the Government had been making before 1956. It now proposed to continue in exactly the same way.

If the industrial development of the reserves was out of the question, and if Africans were to be kept as far as possible out of the urban areas, then a border areas policy was the only alternative. The evidence suggests that Verwoerd had decided on such a course long before. As early as 1952 he had informed the Senate that an inter-departmental committee had been appointed to investigate "how white industrial undertakings in white areas can be brought to, or close to, such concentrations of population, so that the invasion by a steady increase of

Natives of our cities, which are not in the least organised to receive them, may be prevented in an effective and positive way."[27] It was, presumably the findings of this committee that Verwoerd now put to the House of Assembly, as he informed M.Ps just how a community was "really constituted".

It appeared that figures for other countries showed that for every one person employed in primary or secondary industry services had to be provided for five people, as constituting the average size of the family. For Verwoerd it meant that there would be such a considerable "superstructure" of people employed in tertiary activities that "for 100,000 persons to whom employment can be given in the course of the next 50 years with the growing industries in the vicinity of Native areas, it will be possible on this broad basis, within Native areas, where they perform all their services for themselves, to make provision for 2,500,000 persons."[28]

This of course was total nonsense, as subsequent events were to show, for the very limited industrial development in the border areas was not to be accompanied by anything like the predicted expansion of employment in the tertiary sector. It was only to be expected, for the 1 to 5 correlation between the growth of employment in the primary and secondary sectors on the one hand, and that in the tertiary sector on the other, was largely a figment of Verwoerd's tendentious imagination, based on a misreading of the experience of a number of unmentioned other countries. The tertiary sector is simply too ill-defined, especially in conditions of economic backwardness, to be subject to the kind of universal "law" Verwoerd professed to find. The human capacity for self-deception being infinite, Verwoerd simply saw in the "evidence" what he wanted to. On these flimsy grounds was the border areas policy rationalised.

After 1956 the concept of border industries came to be justified on more sophisticated grounds, but there was never any doubt that while there may have been a strong case for economic decentralisation in South Africa, as in other countries, the overriding aims of the policy were political. Essentially, it was a compromise between allowing an increasing flow of blacks into the urban areas, and the Tomlinson Commission's proposal that the industrial development of the reserves be stimulated. The only difficulty was that it was not really separate development. The industries established just outside the reserves would still be in the white areas. Labour migrancy would continue. The difference was that if the policy proved successful fewer migrants would be drawn to South Africa's main urban areas, and more would move back and forth across the borders of the reserves every day. As an economist was to write eight years after

Verwoerd's declaration: "Border development cannot be reconciled with separate development. The policy is more consistent with economic integration combined with residential segregation than with the independent development of the reserves as separate areas."[29]

At this early stage it was clear that the development of the reserves as viable economic entities was not one of the Government's overriding priorities. What was important was that the flow of black urbanisation should at least be slowed down, if not actually halted. Border development seemed admirably suited to this purpose.

The decisive consideration was apparently not the number of blacks working in the white areas, but their permanence. Total territorial apartheid may still have been the ultimate ideal, but it was never taken too seriously. It was rather one of those comforting beliefs that help to give legitimacy to an ideology. This is suggested by Verwoerd's attempt to explain why apartheid was entirely compatible with the 6,000,000 blacks who would still be in South Africa's "white" areas by the end of the century, as the Tomlinson Commission had predicted, on the false assumption that the Government would accept its proposals for developing the reserves. Verwoerd's first point was that this did not mean that the same persons would "always be domiciled here permanently. I foresee an interaction between the White area and the Bantu area, that those who acquire knowledge and training within the White area will use it in their own areas where there are further opportunities for using their knowledge and skill. In other words, this interaction between the White and the Bantu area is of great importance in considering the question whether we are dealing here with 6,000,000 permanent inhabitants." It was permanent Africans in the white areas who were the problem, but the mere fact of working for the white man was not the decisive criterion. By itself this did not, to the Government, amount to "economic integration". But once in the city, there was always the risk of permanence. This is what Verwoerd seemed to have in mind when he stated that "of the 6,500,000 or thereabouts, 4,000,000 will in all likelihood be on the platteland; in other words, in a place where the problem of apartheid presents no difficulty to us and where apartheid is maintained locally. These problems present themselves to the cities and this is of great importance."[30] Apparently, "permanent" blacks in the white areas were mainly an urban problem. In the platteland they were indeed "no difficulty", for there the traditional master-servant relationship could still be upheld. Even if permanent in practice, in theory blacks could still be regarded as temporary, without rights of domicile. It was not economic integration as far as Verwoerd was concerned. As he was to put it in Parliament, in his first speech as Prime Minister: "Economic integration assumes the simple intermingling of racial groups that cannot later be separated. This is the important point. We say that when a Native drives a tractor on a farm, he is not economically integrated. Merely because he helps the farmer to produce, is such a Native who operates a tractor integrated into the farmer's life and community? Of course he is not, because the concept of integration relates to people, and here we do not have people whose activities are becoming interwoven. They will only become interwoven in this way if the other forms of integration, namely equal social and political rights, result from these activities."[31]

For Verwoerd, then, the crux of the matter was whether black labour could, in changing economic circumstances, be removed from the economic life of the white areas. He did not say it in so many words, but he seems to have thought that industrial employment was more likely to lead to black labour becoming interwoven "into the whole of the communal life in such a way that it can never be removed". As an example he cited the African industrial worker who becomes a member of a trade union along with whites and because he "has acquired a share in the industrial and capital assets of the country, he cannot easily be removed at a later stage from the economic industrial entity".[32] If the blacks in the cities were increasing, this did not necessarily mean economic integration in Verwoerd's sense. But the risk was always there, far greater than in the countryside. Cities were places of ferment and change; the difficulty of maintaining traditional social relations was much more an urban than a rural problem. As far as possible therefore blacks had to be kept out of the cities. When they were allowed in they could not be permitted to become permanent residents. From this point of view, border industries must have been a perfect solution. They would, ideally, divert the flow of African labour from the main industrial areas, but their labour would not be lost to white South Africa, for border industries would not actually be in the reserves.

There was another advantage. Workers in the border areas would be similar to the predicted 6,000,000 blacks still in the white areas by the year 2000. These latter with "their anchor in the homelands" would be comparable, he believed, with that of Italians who worked in France for a limited period: "They remain Italians and they remain anchored in their homeland; that is where they seek their rights; they do not expect and ask for rights in the other place."[33] This was to become a popular argument with Nationalists in later years, once Verwoerd had spoken, for reasons which are transparent. It had a specious plausibility which must have been comforting to Government M.Ps as economic integration (in the non-Verwoerdian sense) was proceeding apace during the boom of the 1960s. It did not really matter all that much if the towns and cities were becoming blacker every day. If these workers were foreigners, what was there to be afraid of? The analogy was not wholly appropriate, to say the least, but it reflected the lack of urgency with which the development of the reserves was treated during the 1950s, and helped to perpetuate this complacent mood even afterwards. As long as blacks employed in the white areas were suitably "anchored in their homelands", it was not important if they worked for the white man and there was not really room for them in the reserves. As with too many other aspects of race policy in South Africa, it was the fiction which mattered, not the reality.

Verwoerd had rejected the main recommendations of the Tomlinson Commission. On reading his speech one wonders with amazement that this mish-mash of half-truths and specious arguments could have been allowed to decide so important an issue, till one realises that it really was not all that decisive. Expenditure on the scale proposed by the Commission, modest as it was in terms of the objective of "separate development", was scarcely practical politics at the time. It was Verwoerd's job to provide an elaborate rationale for turning down the Tomlinson proposals. He did so with that blend of complete self-confidence and sophistry at which he was a master, and which so mightily impressed his fellow-Nationalists. Never had they come across his like before, at no time at a loss for an answer, and with so single-minded a dedication to his purpose. As for Verwoerd, however absurd or far-fetched his arguments, he believed in them with absolute faith and sincerity. But for him the ultimate purpose remained the greater good of Afrikanerdom; he would always manage to find arguments which would serve this end. The welfare of blacks was no great concern of his: they were not his people and he was not elected by them. If eventually he was to pursue policies that, in principle, held out the prospect of a better future for Africans, it was because he was driven by the trend of world events to pursue a new course that would still serve the traditional goal of Afrikaner security. But in 1956 it still seemed possible to continue along some very old ways, with more lip-service paid than before to the ideal of blacks being given opportunities of their own in their own areas, with very little actually being done about it. The announcement by the Government that £36 million would be earmarked for the development of the reserves, and not the proposed £104 million, was a perfect reflection of this attitude.

While the economic development of the reserves was not an urgent priority, neither was their political advance. The Tomlinson Commission had expressed no opinions on this subject, which was outside its terms of reference. It might, however, have been expected that the Government would hold out prospects to the black areas of more rapid political development as a financially inexpensive sop for the rejection of the Commission's main recommendations. As yet there were no prospects of eventual independence for the respective ethnic "homelands". In 1951 Verwoerd had emphatically denied that the black areas could ever hope for more than enlarged local government within the boundaries of a unitary, white-controlled state.[34] Overall white supremacy or, more bluntly, *baasskap*, was then the Government's policy and now, after Tomlinson, it continued to be.

Both economically and politically, then, the tempo of advance was expected to be slow. As times changed, however, so at least did the rate of political change, but throughout Verwoerd's 16 years as a member of the cabinet, both as Minister of Native Affairs and as Prime Minister, the economic development of the reserves was hardly noticeable. "Positive" apartheid was to be largely a political phenomenon during Verwoerd's lifetime. It was only after his death that the Government took a more constructive approach to the economic development of the homelands.

Verwoerd's policies did not merely amount to changing as little as possible and hoping for the best. He was not an old-time conservative simply attempting to preserve traditional master-servant relationships, although he had no aversion at all to the ways of the Afrikaner past. But, unlike any of his predecessors, he had a passion for system, for finding a framework which could contain all the measures he introduced as Minister of Native Affairs. It was a pedantic approach to race relations; once the framework had been found it was hardly necessary to think: everything followed automatically from the simplicities imposed upon a complex world. As early as 1952 he had tried to show the Senate "how the various Acts, Bills, and also public statements which I have made, all fit into a pattern and together form a single constructive plan".[35] The pattern that had begun to emerge by then and as it was to unfold was truly simple. The black man was different from the white man in a way in which the Coloured and the Asian apparently were not. What was special about Africans was that there was no one distinct black identity, but a number of black identities, corresponding respectively to the different black ethnic groups in South Africa. Essentially the African's identity was conferred upon him by the tribe to which he belonged.

Hence it became imperative to strengthen his tribal links through the Bantu Authorities system, the control over the flow of black migrants to town and the establishment of the reserves as areas of domicile for workers in border industries. Even so, there was always the risk of psychological lag, that blacks would have been so exposed to the "wrong" kind of education in mission and church schools unsympathetic to Government policy that they simply became "black Englishmen" with unrealistic aspirations for advancement in white society, which had no hope of being realised. Education would have to find its place in the pattern of apartheid. It would have to be an education specially designed for blacks, which would teach them above all that there was no future for them in the white areas, that their ambitions could only be satisfied as members of their respective ethnic communities.

Before 1948 black education was under the jurisdiction of the provinces, with the majority of schools being controlled by English-speaking missions of a variety of denominations. The primary school syllabus in each province was specially devised for blacks, but the secondary syllabus was largely the same as for white pupils. The main obstacle to the expansion of black education had been financial, for contributions by the State had, until 1945, been meagre, while voluntary contributions by the missions and the Africans themselves were only enough to provide tuition for a relatively small number of children. The guiding principle had been that African education should be financed out of taxes paid by the blacks themselves. A change came only in 1945, when the Native Education Act made black education a direct charge on the Consolidated Revenue Fund. Now education for blacks no longer had to rely on taxes solely paid by Africans.

In spite of such obvious shortcomings as overcrowding and a shortage of teachers, particularly at the primary level, due again to a lack of funds, real advances had been made. By 1953, 41 per cent of children in the 7 to 16 age group were attending school, compared with a mere 4.1 per cent in 1935. But the average school life of those black children who did attend school was only four years in 1951, while the proportion which went beyond the primary level was minute and had scarcely risen over more than 20 years. Nevertheless, those secondary and teacher-training esta-blishments that did exist were generally efficient and produced well-educated pupils.

Verwoerd and his Government had no objection to more and more blacks becoming educated. After 1948 they themselves were to hasten the process, which even became a source of pride to them, proof of the beneficence of separate development. What they disliked was the kind of education they thought black children were receiving. One of the new Government's first actions was to appoint a Native Education Commission in 1949, headed by Dr. Werner Eiselen, which was charged to formulate "the principles and aims of education for Natives as an independent race, in which their past and present, their inherent social qualities, their distinctive characteristics and aptitudes, and their needs under ever-changing social conditions were taken into consideration". It included the restructuring of the existing system of black education "in order to conform to the proposed principles and aims, and *to prepare Natives more effectively for their future occupations*" (added).[36]

Under Eiselen's chairmanship and with such terms of reference it was inevitable that the Commission would recommend radical changes in the nature of black education. Its report, submitted in 1951, argued for the centralisation of African education under the Department of Native Affairs. This would entail a separate educational system for blacks, as the Department of Education administered the schooling of the other races. The proposal was logical enough within the framework of apartheid, which set blacks aside as being so specially "different". It meant too that they required an education rather substantially different from that of the whites. Such specious reasoning naturally applied in principle to Coloureds and Asians as well, but apartheid has never been very consistent in its treatment of these groups. Their "differentness" was acknowledged in the form of separate schools and, later, separate universities for Coloureds and Asians, but no serious claims were ever made that they should have an education different in kind from that of the whites, something more suited to their respective ethnic peculiarities. While all races were undoubtedly different, the "Bantu" were clearly a lot more different than any of the others. The era of Bantu Education had begun.

In Parliament Verwoerd was quite frank about his aims. Education for blacks "must not clash with Government policy" and should "not create wrong expectations on the part of the Native himself".[37] He blamed the English-speaking missions and their belief in equality for creating such misguided expectations and the frustration which followed their inevitable disappointment. As he later phrased it in the Senate: "By simply blindly producing pupils who were trained in European ideas the idle hope was created that they could occupy positions in the European community in spite of the country's policy. This is what is meant by the unhealthy creation of white-collar ideals and the creation of widespread frustration among the so-called educated Natives."[38] The task of education was not to inculcate ideas about individualist striving, but to teach everyone that he could only advance if his community did so as well. It would be one of the chief aims of Bantu Education to ensure that this ideal of community service always had priority. In white South Africa the prospects for blacks would always be limited. They would never rise above a certain level in white society, but in their own areas, as Nationalist spokesmen liked to phrase it when the Verwoerd pattern began to unfold, the sky was the limit.

The new approach meant a stronger emphasis on the vernacular in the teaching of black children. Even in the past mother-tongue instruction had been the official policy, but this vital principle had been disregarded by black teachers, hostile to what they regarded as relics of tribalism, and also by school inspectors who were frequently ignorant of any Bantu language. Under Verwoerd the three R's would be taught in all primary schools through the vernacular. The syllabus would in fact be the same as before but the discrepancy between theory and practice would now disappear: Nevertheless, admirable as it was to be educated to be a worthy member of one's own community, it could not be ignored that many thousands of blacks would still have to enter white society in search of jobs: "For that reason it is essential that Bantu students should receive instruction in both official languages from the beginning so that they can already in the lower primary school develop an ability to speak and understand them."[39] It involved, in particular, greater attention to the teaching of Afrikaans.

It may be doubted how important a knowledge of Afrikaans would be in qualifying most blacks to work for white capitalists, but it was quite in keeping with the basic assumptions of Bantu Education. If the Eiselen and Verwoerd approach meant that black education had to conform more closely with Government policy, then it was only consistent that Nationalist values should at least be partly inculcated through the language of virtually all Nationalists. Or so it must have seemed at the time. As events were to show much later, the approach was not wholly successful. Essentially, however, the Government's policy was a realistic acceptance of the fact that blacks would continue to work in the modern sector and that it would be easier for them to do so if they possessed certain basic skills.

It could be argued, and of course it was, that this simply amounted to an education for inferiority, that it was designed to provide Africans only with that minimum level of competence which would enable them to provide efficient manual work for white employers. There is some evidence for such an interpretation. The most striking is undoubtedly the very large difference in per capita annual expenditure by the State on, respectively, white and black education. In 1953 such expenditure for white pupils was about R128 compared with R18 for blacks. Even more remarkable, while the State's per capita spending on white education was to increase, the corresponding amount devoted to black education actually declined, and ten years later amounted to less than R12. To some extent this reflected the far more rapid growth in the number of black children who were attending school, but even so these differences are extraordinary. Verwoerd justified the low level of State expenditure on black schooling on the familiar and expedient grounds that blacks should themselves be largely responsible for financing their own education. Was it not well known that "spoon-feeding" was not appreciated? The best results would be achieved if blacks helped themselves by looking after their own. Such was the ideal, but even Verwoerd accepted that at that time (1953) blacks were still unable to finance their education entirely on their own. The Government would therefore continue to provide an annual amount of £6,500,000 (R13,000,000) for this purpose, but more funds would in future have to come from the Africans themselves, which would presumably be made possible by higher direct taxation of the black community (which indeed came in 1956).

The Government would evidently not exert itself to provide more education for blacks, especially as increased financing from general revenue would be politically unpopular. Nevertheless, it is still doubtful whether sharply increased per capita expenditure on black education would have greatly raised black incomes or much reduced the so-called black-white wage gap. The South African economy during the 1950s did not grow particularly rapidly, especially when compared with the boom of the following decade. The performance was respectable, 4.6 per cent a year, but as population was growing at the high annual rate of 3 per cent, per capita incomes did not rise very markedly. It was the black population which increased most rapidly. Substantial unemployment had been a feature of the homelands for many years. As job opportunities were limited and black unemployment was high, it is likely that the result of more State expenditure on black education, at least to begin with, would have been to raise the educational qualifications both of those who were doing menial work and, no doubt, of many unemployed. But probably there would have been no such striking result as higher average black incomes. More black workers would have been educated, but they would have done much the same work in the absence of a corresponding increase of demand. This argument is reinforced by the fact that formal educational qualifications are less important on many jobs than learning-by-doing. It is plausible that the policy of migrant labour, which insisted on regarding blacks as visitors to the white areas, tended to prevent them from acquiring on-the-job training, which in turn would explain many of the differences in productivity between white and black workers. The consideration that blacks themselves were ardent believers in better educational facilities does not disprove this argument but merely underlines that they realised that those with more formal education had relatively easier access to the better jobs. In other words, education tended to be a screening device, separating the educated men from the uneducated boys. More and better education would have led to some Africans moving up the job ladder, but the structure of the South African economy being what it was, it is doubtful whether average black incomes would have risen much, if at all. Developments during the 1960s confirm these conclusions, for the economy grew rapidly, as did black incomes, in spite of low, if eventually rising, per capita expenditure on black education.

This must be seen in a wider context. A purveyor of the standard left-wing orthodoxy, Alex Hepple, accuses Verwoerd as Minister of Native Affairs of having achieved "something of a miracle – he had pegged the African people to poverty in the midst of the greatest economic boom in the country's history. His tight administration, aided by ferocious police power and harsh labour and apartheid laws, had successfully prevented Africans from getting higher wages, or from attaining their aim of participation in the social and cultural benefits of an industrial civilisation."[40]

The rhetoric impresses, as well as the sins Verwoerd is credited with, but Hepple is wrong on two counts. The 1950s was not a time of rapid growth, let alone "of the greatest economic boom in the country's history". Secondly, Hepple must explain why Verwoerd's even tighter administration, even more ferocious police power *et al* after Sharpeville did not prevent blacks from getting higher wages during the undoubted boom of the 60s. If he cannot then it is very likely that these factors were not so important in preventing black wage increases during the previous decade. The correct explanation seems to be quite simple. In any functioning market economy, South Africa included, in spite of all the numerous bureaucratic controls over free enterprise, there are severe constraints on the ability of politicians and civil servants to "peg people to poverty" even if they wanted to do so. Discrimination is generally most effective in the public, sector, where political norms, such as the advancement of the white race, may be imposed at the expense of productivity. In the private sector employers are concerned with profits above all. They only injure themselves if they indulge any obscurantist prejudices by employing on grounds of race instead of competence. In South Africa the Government has interfered extensively with the operation of the labour market, but it has not been able to prevent capitalists, within these constraints, from pursuing their self-interest.

In practice this has meant more economic opportunities for blacks. The failure of real black wages to rise in the 50s can be explained in terms of rapid black population increase over a period of years and the relatively slow growth of the economy. In the 60s on the other hand growth was so fast that not even population increase could prevent black wages from rising.

Bantu Education, then, was not so much an attempt to keep blacks economically backward by providing them with an inferior education, but more an effort to indoctrinate black children about the blessings of apartheid. Financial pressures were put on missions to hand over their schools to the Government, which then placed them in charge of black school boards. A differential syllabus was imposed, geared to the Nationalist conception of what was good for Africans.

The new system began operating in April 1955. It was greeted with an attempted boycott organised by some of the younger leaders of the African National Congress. It was partially successful on the Witwatersrand and in the Eastern Cape. But Verwoerd was the last man to be intimidated. He announced that pupils who had not returned by a certain date would be excluded from school altogether. When the time limit expired, most children had gone back to school but 7,000 on the Rand had not done so. Verwoerd was as good as his word: the names of those who could not give a valid excuse for their absence were removed from the rolls.

Later he agreed to meet a deputation from the school boards in the areas affected. He was presented with signed undertakings by hundreds of parents, who undertook not to support any more boycotts by keeping their children at home. Verwoerd was sufficiently influenced by these signs of submission to give an assurance that he would have the undertakings investigated and, if genuine, allow the children to be re-admitted in batches in 1956 and 1957.

In later years there were sporadic disturbances at black schools but not on a large scale until ten years after Verwoerd's death, in 1976. It is inherently difficult, if not impossible, to say how much of this discontent can be ascribed to the system of Bantu Education, and how much was due to the African's resentment of his inferior status in South Africa. What is clear is that blacks regarded Bantu Education as better than no education at all. In years to come the number of children educated under this system grew very considerably, but if the Government expected them to emerge as enthusiasts for separate development then it must have been disappointed. After more than 20 years of Bantu Education the unrest and discontent within urban black society showed, even when all due allowance has been made for the ubiquitous "agitators" of Nationalist propaganda, that the system of differential education had done little to convince blacks that separate freedoms had been devised for their own good. It seemed rather that more education for more Africans, coupled with rising living standards, only made them increasingly aware of and impatient with the disabilities under which they still had to live. This has been a frequently observed phenomenon in societies where large numbers of underprivileged find that their material conditions are improving. It was first discerned by Tocqueville in his study of French society before the revolution and his insight has been confirmed by historians who have studied other countries. The general point has been well made by Eric Hoffer in his book on mass movements: "Discontent is likely to be highest when misery is bearable, when conditions have so improved that an ideal state seems almost within reach. A grievance is most poignant when almost redressed ... It is not actual suffering but the taste of better things which excites people to revolt."[41]

Actions often have unforeseen consequences and, for the Nationalists, one of the most unforeseen results of their policies must have been the widespread discontent after so many years of an educational system designed to convince blacks that separate development was the only way.

5 Control and Response

Black unrest in South Africa during the present century has not been an exclusively urban phenomenon. There has been plenty of rural violence, as in Pondoland between 1957 and 1960, when it took the form of protest against the Bantu Authorities system and agricultural betterment schemes. Nevertheless, the potential for unrest has generally been greater in the urban areas. It has been here that social and economic change has gone furthest and Africans are most advanced. It has been in the urban areas that the real improvements in black standards of living have helped to heighten an awareness both of existing deprivations and of the sharp contrast between white affluence and black poverty. Nor has black urban violence stayed away. The years 1946, 1960, 1973 and 1976 stand as landmarks in the history of post-war unrest among urban blacks in South Africa. If only for this reason, that the potential for violence has always been present, the success of apartheid must largely be measured by its ability to deal with Africans in the city.

The Nationalist view that the urban black was merely a "visitor" to the white areas was not original. It was simply the old Stallard Doctrine, named after the chairman of the Transvaal Local Government Commission of 1922, which argued that blacks had no business in town except to cater for white needs: "The Native should only be allowed to enter urban areas, which are essentially the white man's creation, when he is willing to enter and administer to the needs of the white man and should depart there from when he ceases so to minister."[1]

The first law to embody the Stallard approach was the Natives (Urban Areas) Act of 1923. This Act, which laid the basis for urban segregation, was frequently amended as the structure of control became more complex and encompassing. The dominant idea was that the African should not be allowed to acquire a stake in urban society for property rights would make it difficult to deny other, including political, rights for ever. Blacks could thus acquire no freehold rights in town, except for the

162

later introduction of thirty-year leases. For this reason too there was strong resistance to the expansion of African trading in urban locations, the separate residential areas provided for blacks in town. The original Act gave local authorities the right to grant trading licences to black residents in the locations but the objection by many whites to the subsequent growth of black businesses led to an amendment of the Act in 1930, which conferred powers on the Minister of Native Affairs to curb this trend. These powers were never fully enforced and black trade in the locations continued to expand up to and during the Nationalist era. It remained Government policy to discourage such trading in the hope that African businessmen would eventually pack up and depart for the homelands, but it was only in 1963 that harsher measures were taken to penalise these undesired activities.

Such policies all assumed residential segregation. One of the main objectives of the 1923 Act had been to eliminate those multiracial residential areas which had emerged in some of the larger towns, especially Johannesburg. These areas soon degenerated into slums, for the housing provided for the many blacks who entered them was wretched. The intention had been to re-house Africans in locations but this was often impossible as locations were further from the amenities of city life than the mixed areas the planners were trying to get rid of. So slums, and their attendant problem of squatting, continued to flourish. They proliferated on a massive scale during the Second World War as thousands of blacks entered the cities.

We have noted that this was one of the problems which most exercised Verwoerd as editor of *Die Transvaler*, perceiving, as he thought he did, the incipient social degradation of poor but worthy Afrikaners, com-pelled by circumstances to live in close proximity to black slums and the crime and violence they engendered.

In theory there was a wide variety of controls over the movements of blacks within the borders of South Africa. They had to carry a complex number of documents relating *inter alia* to travel, labour and residence. In spite of proposals to simplify the system, the pass laws, in all their complexity, had remained unmodified. The number of blacks arrested for failure to produce the relevant documents had always been high. During the Second World War arrests on the Witwatersrand were so numerous that application of the pass laws was temporarily relaxed. The number of arrests fell sharply, but the strict enforcement of these laws was resumed when it was found that many Africans were now entering the area without registering at the labour exchanges. Nevertheless, so long as the

Smuts Government remained in power, there was always some prospect that the pass laws would be less rigidly applied.

In 1942 the Secretary for Native Affairs, Douglas Smit, had actually recommended that the pass system be abolished altogether. The Fagan Commission, which reported early in 1948, did not go so far, but believed that the laws should be more leniently enforced. Smuts endorsed this recommendation, although by then he had forfeited most of his support among educated blacks. But it was also too late, for a few months later a new government came to power, with totally different ideas about the treatment of blacks in urban areas.

The Nationalists, we know, violently disapproved of the ever-increasing numbers of Africans in the cities. They had made of it a major election issue, condemning as iniquitous what they regarded as the United Party's *laissez faire* approach, which they had no doubt was endangering South Africa's future as a country for white people. As an academic apologist for apartheid has written: "The Party's viewpoint was that Afrikaner nationalism and the unregulated economic integration of the Black man were two incompatible forces, and that only separate development would be able to create a pattern of race relations that would prevent White South Africa from succumbing to revolutionary Africanisation."[2]

Unfortunately, or perhaps fortunately, political catch-phrases and economic trends are only distantly related. It was the new Government's misfortune (although not in electoral terms) to preside over a process of economic integration which was as rapid as it was discouraging of ideas of preserving "the survival of white civilisation in South Africa". Not only had the black population been increasing faster than the white throughout the century but, even more disturbingly, black urbanisation had been much more rapid than that of the whites. Between 1921 and 1946 the number of blacks in the urban areas grew by 182 per cent, compared with a mere 108 per cent for whites. In this respect 1948 was no turning point, however distinctive a landmark it may be for other aspects of South African history. The trend continued unchecked by the Nationalist advent to power. Between 1946 and 1960 the increases were even less favourable from the white point of view, namely, 87 per cent and 46 per cent respectively.[3]

Black urbanisation was partly the result of rapid industrialisation, but it stimulated the process as well. The growing employment of blacks in the modern sector meant that large numbers who had before been engaged in subsistence activity in the reserves now formed part of the market. Considerable pent-up demand had also developed during the war and it was now released, making its own contribution to a rapid industrial upsurge. In the decade after the war, the volume of industrial output increased at a rate of 7 per cent annually, compared with a growth rate for the economy as a whole of just over 5 per cent.

A discouraging feature for the Nationalists of all this industrial development was its highly centralised form. It was mainly concentrated in the four great urban complexes of the Western Cape, Durban-Pinetown, Port Elizabeth-Uitenhage and, above all, the Southern Transvaal. New industries were usually established here, for industrialists naturally wished to benefit from existing and developed infrastructures, as well as from rapidly growing markets. For them these advantages far outweighed those disadvantages arising from huge urban conglomerations, such as pollution and congestion, which have been so prominent a feature of the post-war world. The adverse implications for apartheid were obvious. Verwoerd and his colleagues were to become committed believers in industrial decentralisation in the form of border industries, but for entrepreneurs who were solely interested in profits and who left questions of white survival to the politicians, the incentives to establish themselves in such backward areas were minimal. The Nationalist dilemma therefore was serious. Any attempt to implement their policies would involve them in far-reaching intervention in the market process, which could harm the country's economic development and, in turn, their own continued success at the polls.

Yet, if apartheid was to be more than a successful political slogan, something had to be done about the black influx into the urban areas. Not only were more Africans entering towns than ever before, but growing numbers were also becoming permanent urban residents, of whom many had no meaningful tribal affiliations at all. Detribalisation went hand in hand with urbanisation. For Verwoerd and those who thought like him it was an ultimate evil, to be resisted at virtually any price. A black man who had lost his tribal identity was a man without a country, a rootless individual who would contribute immeasurably to social unrest. For it remained an axiom that he could not be given roots by being accepted as a permanent inhabitant of the "white" part of the country. Here the Stallard Doctrine still had all the force of an unquestioned faith. No matter how permanent an African may have been in terms of the obvious criteria of length of work service and of residence, he remained a "visitor" to the white areas, but subject to more than the usual number of disabilities visitors anywhere can normally expect. But such permanent visitors were increasing alarmingly. It was reflected in the number of black women who were entering town. Previously, the ratio of black men to black women had been exceptionally large, of the order of 23 to 1 in Johannesburg in 1910. But in 1927 it had become 5 to 1 while in 1960 it was only 1.09 to 1.[4] As settled black families in the urban areas grew, so there was a corresponding decline in the migrant labour system, that all too visible embodiment of the transient nature of black residence in white South Africa.

Verwoerd knew that a permanent black population in town had disagreeable political implications. In theory, apartheid was not oppression at all. Blacks could have no political rights in the white areas but, as Verwoerd never tired of repeating, they would eventually enjoy them in their own areas, however nebulous such rights still were at this stage. But the larger the number of Africans who were becoming detribalised in the urban areas, which was in Verwoerdian terms the same as becoming denationalised, the more difficult it would be to give even theoretical credibility to the policy. An African who lost his links with his ethnic group existed in some state of limbo, belonging neither to the white community nor, in any meaningful sense, to a black community. This was the logical conclusion from Verwoerd's assumptions, once it was accepted that there were urban blacks who had lost their tribal affiliations. Verwoerd's answer in this event was to insist on the continued supremacy of ethnicity, that in some ultimate, metaphysical sense such rootless individuals had roots after all and that they did, willy-nilly, belong to a tribal community. Still, this was not very satisfactory. It would obviously be for the best if the number of detribalised blacks could be kept to a minimum. Ideally, it meant reversing the flow of black labour to the urban areas, but this was only an ideal. No Nationalist would seriously suggest its realisation in the foreseeable future. In his more optimistic and unguarded moments Verwoerd liked to mention 1978 as the turning point, when at last the trend would be reversed, but in the 1950s this was still a reassuringly long time away. Meanwhile, before utopia, the only policy was to strengthen the migrant labour system in order to ensure that as few blacks as possible acquired the right to permanent residence in an urban area and that of those who came to serve the economic needs of the white man, as many as possible be allowed in for only a limited period.

We have seen that, faced with the indefinite certainty of a majority of blacks in the white areas, Verwoerd reacted by denying that this was "economic integration" as long as the activities of black workers were not becoming "interwoven" with those of whites. This simply meant that it was all right if blacks only worked for whites, but that social and political rights would in no way be allowed to follow from a mere relationship for mutual gain. Instead, Verwoerd liked to believe, it would be enough if the

166

living conditions of urban Africans were satisfactory. "As a first principle," he argued in 1952, "it must be laid down that in every town and particularly in every industrial area, a potentially comprehensive location site, virtually a Native group area for their occupation must be found. It will have to be large enough to house the whole of the Native working population, so that peri-urban squatting, the overcrowding of Native residential areas and unlawful lodging in backyards may be stopped."[5]

As a condition for the siting of locations, Verwoerd specified that they should be at a suitable distance from the white township, from which they should be separated "by an area of industrial sites where industries exist or are being planned". For adequate housing, Verwoerd proposed his site-and-service scheme. Slums could no longer be tolerated, but neither could the white taxpayer be expected to bear the cost of suitable houses for the thousands of urban blacks. The answer was "economic housing", which meant that adequate sites for all Africans would be provided, with essential services, such as water and housing, by the local authority, to be financed by a levy imposed on employers of black labour. On these sites the local authority would build as many economic houses as possible, while Africans, varying with their ability to pay, would also be allowed to build houses on them. "Such houses," Verwoerd envisaged, "could from a small start ... be enlarged from year to year into complete family homes, as the ability of the family to pay for them improves." Homes built in this way would belong to their occupants, although the latter, as visitors only, could never acquire ownership of the sites on which they stood. The white local authorities would continue to control these, but for Verwoerd this was no problem, for it "was in keeping with Native custom where the tribe and not the individual owns the land".[6]

All this was expected to contribute to "an orderly communal life" among urban Africans, which in turn would "bring great relief for the European community". In further pursuit of this aim, blacks were to be given a limited form of self-government. The partially elected Advisory Boards established under the Urban Areas Act had been unsatisfactory and indeed powerless, a fact which Verwoerd ascribed to their being "foreign to the Natives' own traditional form of government", but which can more plausibly be seen as due to the ultimate control of locations by white officials.

He now proposed, consistently enough, to form Bantu Authorities for urban blacks. As far as possible, they would be divided "into their natural ethnic groups", as this would mean that "certain social sanctions of their own can be applied better for the benefit of all". On this ethnic basis, they would systematically be trained to look after their own affairs within limits ..." Verwoerd saw this as "an educational process". Within this paternalist framework, they would only acquire "greater rights and responsibilities" as they showed themselves able "to deal dutifully with smaller matters".[7] His purpose here was twofold. Strict limitations on the political rights of the urban African to the local government level would ensure that economic dependence did not lead to black political power in the white areas. This goal was to be reinforced by splitting the urban blacks into their respective ethnic groups. If they were detribalised, so much the worse for them: Verwoerd refused to recognise that such animals existed, and they would still be tied to their homelands. It was also consistent with his conviction that there were a number of separate black nationalisms in South Africa, each corresponding to a distinct ethnic community. An African nationalism which claimed to override such differences was to him a spurious entity with no identifiable counterpart in reality. He took no official cognizance of it. At the same time his scheme was also designed as an attempt to prevent the emergence of such a nationalism.

Such was the theory, but it was an aspect of Verwoerd's policy about which nothing much was ever done. It was only in 1961 that the Government, of which he was now the head, began to replace the Advisory Boards by Urban Bantu Councils with blacks as chairmen. But their powers never became as extensive as those originally envisaged by Verwoerd. They were to remain in the "small matters" stage, largely because the policy of Bantu homelands had then changed so drastically that the Government revised its original ideas about local government for urban blacks. Yet this statement of Verwoerd's early intentions remains important, revealing as it does aspects of his, and Nationalist, thinking which were not to change. Whatever self-government urban Africans would ever have would be tightly circumscribed, hedged in by restrictions and controls, permanent proof of their temporary status in white man's land. Further, blacks in town remained ethnic creatures, whose tribal identities continued intact in spite of exposure to an urban environment remote from their "traditional way of life". In fact, the persistent weakness of the Nationalist approach to urban blacks was nowhere more clearly exposed than in this speech by Verwoerd. It was comforting to assume that the influences of urban life had done little to change the African's identification with the ethnic group to which he belonged, and that his presence in the white areas was only transient, but it was also patently inadequate. They were assumptions which were at the root of the Nationalists' failure to devise a satisfactory policy for the urban black man.

In the final analysis, it was a policy which relied overwhelmingly on controls. They were of two kinds: there were controls over the black inflow to and outflow from the white areas, and there were controls over the allocation of black labour to particular spheres of work. Some of these measures have already been discussed and there is no need to deal with them at length.

The Native Laws Amendment Act of 1952 limited Africans with a right to live permanently in an urban area to those who had been born there, those who had lived there continuously for 15 years, and those who had worked continuously for the same employer for 10 years. The labour bureaus established under the Act provided information to African work-seekers, but also helped to channel them into appropriate directions. In the same year the pass system, in the form of reference books, was extended to black women, while labour service contracts now had to be entered in the simplified documents Africans had to carry on them at all times. In 1955 the Natives (Urban Areas) Act was amended, so that "locations in the sky", large numbers of blacks living on the top storeys of buildings in the white areas where they worked, could be eliminated. The maximum number which could stay in an urban block of flats was now five. The same law also extended bureaucratic control over the movement of black workers by providing for permits which enabled them to do only particular kinds of work, depending on the economic needs of the moment.

Also in 1955, Verwoerd spoke about the removal of Africans from the Western Cape, traditionally the preserve of the Coloured people. But this was one of those times when he had to accept disappointment. Many farmers in the area depended upon black labourers. They were perturbed at the prospect of doing without them. Responsive as it traditionally was to the disproportionately powerful rural vote, the Government never made any serious attempt to remove blacks from the Western Cape. The episode was illuminating: It shows the Government hamstrung by special interests from enforcing its policy as sweepingly as it would have liked. Even Verwoerd, uncompromising as he was in his intellectual formulations, had to be prepared to go slowly when he would have preferred to have proceeded much faster. The limited evidence suggests that Verwoerd was extremely sensitive to opposition from within, especially when it came from the right wing of the Party. As yet the political and economic development of the reserves, where Verwoerd seemed to think that he had plenty of time, was no prominent cause of internal dissent. The prevailing snail's pace was unlikely to upset very many Nationalist susceptibilities. But while it was easy to subscribe to general notions about reducing the number of blacks in the white areas, it was less simple to acquiesce when faced with the prospect of losing one's own African workers. Verwoerd, it appears certain, would have liked to have reduced the number of blacks in the white areas to a much larger extent – but it was never politically feasible.

Still, if he could not remove black workers, he had at least been given extensive powers to control their movements outside the reserves. If the number of blacks increased in the cities and the towns, as it did during the 1950s, both absolutely and relatively to the whites, at least he could ensure that the "permanent" blacks did not grow compared to those who were only temporary. Numbers in themselves were not decisive in the success of apartheid. It was how they were constituted. Migrant workers would not become "interwoven" with the economic life of the whites in the same sense that non-migrants could – if given the chance. For Verwoerd this was what economic integration was all about, not the mere fact of economic interdependence between black and white.

It is difficult to judge how successful apartheid was in this esoteric sense. Many black workers were largely but not exclusively dependent on urban wage labour, and they could not always be distinguished from permanent workers on the one hand and migrants on the other. There were certainly all too many deterrents to permanent settlement, even when it was possible. Blacks in town lived in a traditionally insecure environment, made more so by the laws, old and new, controlling their movements and restricting their right to own property. There must have been a strong incentive, even if only on psychological grounds, to retain a holding in the reserves, to which it was possible to return if evicted from town. Yet, except in the very special Verwoerdian sense, it seems that urban apartheid during his sixteen years of power was a decisive failure. The evidence, although not conclusive, suggests that permanent migration grew more rapidly than the number of temporary migrants during the years between 1951 and 1965. In this period the population of the reserves increased by only 28 per cent, compared with an increase of 41.5 per cent of the country's black population as a whole. In other words, the number of blacks outside the reserves grew rather more rapidly than those inside. At the same time, the available evidence reveals that the number of temporary migrants grew relatively slowly. For instance, the more settled character of the black urban population in

Johannesburg, South Africa's largest city, is revealed in the previously mentioned decline in the ratio of men to women since 1910. A study of the city of Pretoria also showed that the age and sex distribution of its black population suggested that in 1946 less than 60 per cent was "settled", defined as being "more or less permanently committed to an existence based on wage-earning", compared to 80 per cent in 1960.[8]

In the Transkei, the largest of the black areas, there was even the possibility of an absolute decline in the number of temporary migrants. More plausibly, it appears that temporary migration from the Transkei did grow, but not very significantly. Trevor Bell sums up the evidence by concluding that "if the total number of temporary migrants did indeed increase, this increase was relatively small compared with permanent migration. The latter, it must be noted, took place in the face of an increasingly stricter application of the influx control measures."[9]

"Settled" or "permanent", in the sense in which it has been used here was still a long way from corresponding to what Verwoerd meant by "economic integration". An African may have been "settled", but that did not make him "interwoven" with the economic life of the white man in the Verwoerdian sense. Yet no degree of semantic quibbling can ignore the fact that the imposing legal apparatus at Verwoerd's disposal could not, during his lifetime, prevent the proportion of permanently settled Africans in the urban areas from rising. Verwoerd may not have seen this as economic integration, but it was regarded in this light by many Nationalists less skilled in the use of words. For the Government, blacks in town may only have been temporary and separate labour units, a situation it saw as in no way altered by the growing evidence of permanent urbanisation amongst Africans. But this was clearly an attempt to evade a problem by defining it in such a way that it could hardly exist.

The increased severity of the application of the influx control measures may not have slowed down the rate of economic integration, but along with those other aspects of "negative apartheid" which so proliferated during these years, it could scarcely have failed to intensify discontent amongst the urban black population. One of the forms assumed by such discontent was the growth of black nationalism. The Nationalists of course denied that any such thing existed. The heterogeneity of South Africa's black population cut at the very roots of nationhood; there could be no single black nation in any acceptable sense, but only a number of separate black nations.

This reasoning, of which we have seen Verwoerd so dedicated an exponent, was not entirely unrealistic. A nation is not created simply by the rhetoric of an educated elite which has been exposed to Western influences. As the experiences of independent Asian and African countries have so remarkably shown, nationhood can only be the outcome of an inherently slow growth in societies which happen to be divided by differences of language, religion and race. It would have been surprising if many, perhaps most, of South Africa's blacks had not retained a strong sense of identity with their respective ethnic groups. These qualifications made, it remained true that by the 1950s a black nationalism had emerged in South Africa which to a large degree had managed to play down traditional tribal differences and was reaching out to a wider constituency than just a relatively small number of highly educated Africans.

African nationalists of the first half of the 20th century were men of the old school committed to moderation and reform within the system. Many had been trained in missions and, for a surprisingly long time, continued to believe in Christian understanding and human brotherhood in an environment where the scope for such values has always seemed unpromising. But mild manners and patience did not yield their expected fruits, while the body of discriminatory legislation grew steadily over the years, whichever government happened to be in power.

By 1950 South Africa and the world had changed. Rapid industrialisation was creating the urban mass basis for African nationalism which had hitherto been absent. A new generation of black nationalists was emerging, impatient with the ingratiating ways of their elders: The world was going through the first phases of decolonisation; the United Nations had been established and was already providing a forum for attacks on apartheid. Above all, the new South African government was displaying a doctrinaire commitment to universal racial separation, which was quite different from that of its predecessor, however committed both were to white supremacy. By 1948 black nationalists had come to expect little of Smuts; after 1948 they had no doubt that they could expect nothing at all of Malan and his equally unbending colleagues.

Industrialisation is no automatic solvent of divisions based on ethnic differences. In South Africa such divisions have persisted among urban blacks in spite of the rapid growth of the manufacturing sector during and after the war. Tribal clashes in the urban areas have been frequent. Nevertheless, it is still true that economic development in the post-war years encouraged the process of "detribalisation" and the emergence of an increasing number of urban blacks with no strong sense of ethnic identity. Such Africans also tended to be permanent inhabitants of the city. They had the most to lose by Verwoerd's ambition of tying them firmly to their respective "homelands" through stronger emphasis on their visitor status in the urban areas. They were the natural constituency of the African National Congress in its post-war attempts to establish itself as an organisation which derived its support from the urban black masses.

The new militant mood of the A.N.C. had its origins in the war years, but was much stimulated by the victory of the Nationalists in 1948. The Malan Government's politics of confrontation hastened the transformation taking place within black nationalism. The change of approach culminated in the Defiance Campaign of 1952, when the A.N.C. and the South African Indian Congress made common cause in a campaign of passive resistance which took the form of deliberate contravention of a number of apartheid laws. For reasons already discussed, the campaign was a failure, but it was not the end of the A.N.C.'s efforts to become a mass-based organisation. During the campaign the A.N.C.'s paid-up membership rose from 7,000 in June 1952 to 100,000 six months later. But by August 1953 membership had declined by 40,000.[10] It was essential to the A.N.C., if it wished to put effective pressure on the dominant whites, that it should have the support of many thousands of Africans who were willing to be mobilised against apartheid. Yet it was a goal inherently difficult to achieve. The A.N.C. was mainly interested in full political rights, while the black man in the street looked to the redress of immediate grievances, such as poor housing, and the harsh enforcement of the pass laws. If the A.N.C. wished for mass support, these issues could not be ignored, but additional strain would then be placed on its limited resources, with the further risk that the ultimate goal of full political equality would be lost sight of. Even so, the A.N.C. had little choice. Political effectiveness demanded the temporary shelving of its long-term aim of one man, one vote, and greater stress on those bread-and-butter issues which were the main concern of the ordinary African.

How did the Government respond to the changed tactics of the A.N.C.? Its reaction was to maintain that the correctness of its course all along was now in fact confirmed by the more militant black mood, that the choice lay between political equality and apartheid. Any compromise, as advocated by the United Party, was not feasible in the long run. No doubt the Nationalists were correct, but they ignored the extent to which their policies had led to a black reaction which left little room for manoeuvre. Also, apartheid at this stage closely resembled that compromise between political equality and "separate freedoms" which the Nationalists later came to condemn so vehemently as the *baasskap* policy of the United Party. As yet there was no prospect of separate development leading to anything but considerable local autonomy for the homelands within the framework of overall, and permanent, white rule. In response to a more militant black nationalism, the Government could not even offer the eventual prospect of full, but separate, political equality between black and white. Faced with permanent subjection as all they could ever hope for, black nationalists only became more uncompromising, which in turn strengthened the Nationalists in their conviction that apartheid was the only possible way for South Africa.

Verwoerd was ill-equipped to deal with African nationalism. We have seen that he had decided views about "black Englishmen", deracinated fellows who represented only themselves. He knew that the true representatives of the Africans were the tribal chiefs. One of his first actions as Minister was to abolish the Natives Representative Council, symbol of all those detribalising influences so dangerous to apartheid. His paternalism made it easier for him to get on with relatively primitive blacks. He liked to see them as children entrusted to his wise and benevolent, if strict, care. The relationship was one of inequality. That he could easily handle. The educated African was a different proposition altogether; Verwoerd was only prepared to deal with him if he were a "moderate", which in his book meant acceptance of apartheid.

The A.N.C. change in policy was not therefore sympathetically received by the Minister of Native Affairs. In 1953, after the Defiance Campaign, Verwoerd declared in Parliament that blacks once considered "reliable" by the Government could no longer be trusted. Referring to the new President of the A.N.C., Albert Luthuli, a former Zulu chief, deposed for his refusal to cooperate with the Government, Verwoerd said that he "always used to be considered by my Department as a moderate person", but that he now propagated "a policy of equal rights", which clearly put Luthuli beyond any acceptable pale for the Minister.[11]

The "new" African nationalism of the 1950s could evidently hope for no conciliatory response from the Government. Any advances for the African nationalist cause would have to be the result, not of white benevolence, but of effective bargaining power. But this was an aim only too likely to be frustrated. The A.N.C., as the main embodiment of black nationalism in South Africa, had both strengths and weaknesses, but it was the latter which proved decisive in the struggle against the Government. A good illustration is afforded by the A.N.C.'s opposition to a specific Government measure, the Native Resettlement Act of 1954.

This Act was part of Verwoerd's master plan to provide urban blacks with satisfactory living conditions, but without the right of freehold tenure. Under the terms of the Act, the Government would remove blacks living in Johannesburg's western areas to the new township of Meadowlands, where better housing would be provided. The difficulty was that in their existing residential areas, a fair number of blacks had freehold rights, which they would forfeit in Meadowlands. The A.N.C. decided on this as one of those bread-and-butter issues on which it would prove its value to the ordinary African. It announced its opposition to the impending removal, and set about organising a propaganda campaign that came to receive international publicity. However, it hardly got off the ground. The first removals took place in February 1955 with so little trouble that it seemed that Verwoerd had been right all along when he blamed the fuss on agitators, simply intent on their own selfish interests.

Agitators there certainly were, but the reasons for the A.N.C.'s failure perhaps lie deeper. Most obviously, there was the South African Government's ability, and manifest willingness, to use highly effective forms of violence whenever necessary. It had shown before that it had no marked scruples about the forcible suppression of demonstrations; there was little doubt that it would not have them now. Police "supervision" of the removals both prevented the A.N.C. from disrupting them and exposed its impotence when it could least be afforded by that organisation. The A.N.C. had invoked the Gandhian precept of non-violence in its resistance of the Government, but apart from misunderstanding how India achieved independence, it had made the mistake of thinking that non-violence could be of any possible relevance in a context where the "colonial power" lived on the premises, as it were, and had no intention of departing.

The A.N.C. also erred in assuming that ordinary Africans in the western areas would be universally opposed to the Government's scheme, which they were not. Better housing really was part of the new dispensation, a fact which became widely known after the first removals, and diminished support for the A.N.C. when the subsequent removals took place. Support for the campaign rapidly fell away. Faced with the very clear gains to be derived from the removal scheme, as well as the very considerable risks from opposing it, the black wage-earner sensibly decided that the time was not yet ripe for political martyrdom.

Much the same analysis applies to the A.N.C.'s opposition later in 1955 to the implementation of the Bantu Education Act. Unlike the new housing available at Meadowlands, Bantu Education was hardly an improvement on what had gone before. But, in common with the removals, the new system of education offered such advantages as to make widespread and overt resistance unprofitable. The boycott of Bantu Education which the A.N.C. tried to organise was also a failure. Support, at best, was patchy, and soon disappeared.

Not all Government measures offered such a blend of advantages and disadvantages as these. Many, probably most, laws passed during the 1950s which affected the urban African must have seemed onerous, with little to recommend them. But it was not easy to organise resistance without qualifying for the harsh penalties provided for by the Public Safety Act and the Criminal Law Amendment Act. When the A.N.C. did attempt to widen its appeal by opposing certain measures it found that they were not so patently loathsome to blacks as to inspire the barricade mentality. In addition, blacks in South Africa had registered steady, if uneven, improvements in their standard of living. The 1950s were not years of rapid growth and African real wages probably did not rise during the decade. But over the period 1935 to 1960 real wages for blacks in the industrial sector increased by more than 80 per cent. For the time being at least it seemed that blacks were content to enjoy their higher standards of living, however inadequate they may have appeared compared with those of whites. African nationalist leaders were themselves not exempt from such weaknesses of the flesh. After visiting black political leaders in South Africa in 1949, the famous Negro actor, Canada Lee, told Edwin Munger: "They never had it so good and they are afraid to die."[12]

The A.N.C. itself suffered from internal divisions and poor organisation. The leadership had decided during the 1940s to build a branch network, but the political campaigns led to the neglect of such efforts. The central leadership found it difficult to maintain control over the provincial branches in a country where the main cities lie at considerable distances from one another. Geographic divisions also tended to coincide with ethnic differences which, whatever the professions of the A.N.C., played a role in dividing the nationalist movement. There were other factors as well, but enough has been said to show why African nationalism in South Africa remained weak. Above all there was the State, which was prepared to go to virtually any length to suppress threats to white rule. To a large extent, therefore, the Nationalist argument that there was no one large black nation, but a number of smaller ones, was self-validating. Normally, a comprehensive black nationalism could have been expected to develop as the melting-pot of industrialisation gradually attenuated tribal loyalties.

Under apartheid it would not happen. Such a nationalist movement as did emerge failed to become a powerful mass movement and, faced with the continued futility of its protests, became increasingly divided as frustration turned inwards. After 1960 African nationalism was driven underground. As an organised movement within the country it was broken. In Britain and some African countries A.N.C. branches were maintained, but for the South African Government they had only minor nuisance value. The Nationalists had substantially succeeded in dividing South Africa's black population on ethnic lines. Overt black resistance to apartheid, till the 1970s, would be a resistance shaped by tribal mould. It would also take a different form from the traditional black nationalist demand for political equality in a common society. Yet the tribal dispensation was to yield benefits, limited but real, for the blacks which were foreseen neither by them nor by the Government.

6 A New Prime Minister

Verwoerd's plans for sweeping, all-encompassing racial separation had made him the most controversial figure in the Government. To his opponents he increasingly appeared a man hell-bent on personal power, intent on subjecting the great majority of the country's inhabitants to his own arbitrary rule. He had succeeded in building up what one opposition newspaper was to call his "Native empire", about which little was known except that it was the scene of rural unrest, as well as of "banishments, deportations, shootings, burnings, arson, closing of schools".[1] White political opponents, especially those with liberal inclinations, came to see him both as a bogeyman and as the strong man of the cabinet. A typical criticism of Verwoerd was made by the industrialist, Harry Oppenheimer, then still an M.P., and later head of the giant Anglo American Corporation: "When you have a man prepared to slow down his nation's welfare on account of political theories, then you are dealing with an impractical fanatic."[2]

Such a build-up could have done him no harm with the Afrikaners, to whom these attacks by the English-speaking were simply proof that he was doing the right things in the right way. Surprisingly, Verwoerd did not appear to be especially popular amongst the Afrikaners. He was not generally disliked, but he did not have the sort of personality which inspired warmth amongst the multitudes. He was aloof, and had neither the ability nor the inclination for that grass-roots fraternisation which both his predecessor and successor as Prime Minister possessed. The common touch was not his. He hardly ever took time off for socialising, dedicated as he was to the full-time job of saving the country for a white posterity. Despite such devotion, it seems that Verwoerd also had to face criticism on aspects of his policy by Nationalists whose special interests were affected. The proposal to remove the blacks from the Western Cape did not raise the Party's popularity amongst the farmers of the area. Although they did not say so in public, many Nationalists could not have liked Verwoerd's growing stress on "separate freedoms" for blacks, accustomed as they were to a no-nonsense master-servant relationship between the races. Verwoerd's insistence on strict limits to black access to the urban areas, little as came of it, was nonetheless a threat to the comfort of all whites, English- as well as Afrikaans-speaking.

His approach to black-white relations was, or at least seemed to be, so informed by a doctrinaire need for ideological rigour that it often failed to arouse the enthusiasm of those who were as convinced white supremacists as he. An especially remarkable example of "Verwoerdism" was the "church clause" of the Native Laws Amendment Bill. The original Bill aimed at simplifying and consolidating existing regulations governing the movement of urban blacks. The most controversial aspect of the Bill was the provision that made it compulsory for churches in white areas to apply for permission from the Minister of Native Affairs if they wished to hold services to be attended by both blacks and whites. In the wording of the original Bill: "No person may conduct in any area outside a location any church ... if a Native is to attend the church, unless he has first obtained the approval of the Minister."

The main English-speaking churches reacted by announcing that they would have no choice but to disobey the Bill if it became law. Public protest was vehement and unfavourable publicity overseas was widespread. Verwoerd had justified the original clause on the grounds that blacks should not be allowed to create disturbances for whites in the latter's own areas. The intention was not to interfere with freedom of worship, but the protests led him to amend the clause twice. The Minister would now proceed to exercise his power only after consultation with the local authority concerned, while it would no longer be the church in question which would be prosecuted, but the offending African. This was still not satisfactory to the offending church leaders, but it was all they were going to get. Verwoerd was prepared to concede no more, so that the Bill was finally enacted in May 1957.

Not only had Verwoerd been opposed from the usual quarters, he had also been criticised by both Nationalist and non-Nationalist Afrikaners. However sympathetic it may have been to apartheid, the Dutch Reformed Church could not be enthusiastic about Verwoerd's interference in church affairs and some of its leading spokesmen had expressed their concern. There was even criticism from the usually docile Nationalist press: *Die Burger*, as usual the most independent-minded, wanted to know whether greater flexibility was not desirable, and *Die Vaderland* in Johannesburg asserted that Verwoerd's justification of the "church clause" was not valid, for the real reason was ideological.[3]

This was a particularly good example of Verwoerd's ability to arouse controversy. Of course *Die Vaderland* was right: the reason for the church clause was ideological. This is where Verwoerd differed from so many of his fellow-Nationalists. Unlike them, he seemed to have a passion for consistency, irrespective of the human cost and no matter how absurd it made himself and his government appear. In broad outlines his policies were those that would have been pursued by any other Nationalist Minister of Native Affairs. Verwoerd's uniqueness was the dedication and vigour with which he applied policies that were not fundamentally new and his relentless pursuit of that "organically related system" which had been so deplorably absent before he became Minister. But his obsession with "system" often caused Verwoerd to pursue policies that were by no means essential for the maintenance of apartheid and the continuance of white rule. He seems to have found it difficult to distinguish between the more and the less important. In principle there was no difference between one man, one vote, and the attendance of blacks at churches in white areas: both involved a denial of the principle of racial separation, each had to be opposed equally relentlessly. Verwoerd, in short, was a born ideologue, and he had all the ideologue's impatience with whatever did not find room within his blueprint.

Superficially, the constant attacks and criticisms appeared to have little effect. To the public he seemed as forceful and imperturbable as ever. Increasingly, he emerged as the dominant figure of the Nationalist Government, too impersonal perhaps to inspire the same warm feelings amongst Afrikaners as Strijdom, but gifted with qualities of mind and personality that equipped him admirably as a future Prime Minister, a man who would not let political storms bend him from his course.

Verwoerd had one considerable advantage in any future struggle for power. His close ideological ally, Strijdom, had succeeded Malan as Prime Minister in November 1954. Malan, an old man of more than eighty, retired a bitterly disappointed man. His choice as successor was Havenga, whose Afrikaner Party had amalgamated with the Nationalists in 1951, and who had achieved some success as Minister of Finance. Havenga, moreover, was regarded as one of the less belligerent members of the cabinet. Malan and Strijdom were men who differed considerably in temperament and in their approach to politics. The bad feeling between them over Malan's decision in 1948 to form an alliance with the Afrikaner Party had never disappeared. Malan now openly supported Havenga and did everything in his power to secure him the succession. But it was Strijdom who won, primarily because he was the leader of the Party in the

Transvaal, now the main centre of Nationalist strength in the country. Strijdom was immensely popular in the province, where he had become known as "The Lion of the North". Malan had represented the Cape element in the Party, and had never really been comfortable with the more rigid northern thinking on Afrikaner issues. Havenga was a Free Stater, but had become identified with the Cape's more moderate attitudes, and its apparently more civilised way of practising discrimination. Strijdom was direct, averse to compromise, of limited intellectual capacity, and prone to frank statements about the white man's (i.e. the Afrikaner's) determination to remain on top. He differed strikingly from Malan in his brutal honesty and in his contempt for smooth talk. This was an important difference, for it reflected a cast of mind which saw politics in very simple terms, "as a succession of Gordian knots to be cleanly severed".[4]

Strijdom's triumph was one for Verwoerd as well. He had been frequently accused by the opposition press of aspiring to be Malan's successor, but in spite of his growing stature in the Party, such allegations were false. Verwoerd certainly had a driving ambition. While still a student he had told a fellow-student, Andrew Beyers, future Judge-President of the Cape, that he intended becoming Prime Minister one day, but this did not simply make him a ruthless careerist. He had his ambitions, but he had his principles and his loyalties too. Strijdom was his close political associate, with seniority in the National Party. Strijdom's principles were also Verwoerd's, however differently they chose to express them. Verwoerd regarded Strijdom as the logical and only acceptable successor to Malan. He actively canvassed for Strijdom and when the latter was unanimously elected, Verwoerd could justifiably feel that his own contribution to the new leader's success had been noteworthy.

Verwoerd's status in the Party was automatically enhanced. Malan had appreciated his ability, but could never quite bring himself to accept Verwoerd as one of his favourite colleagues. This was understandable, for their temperaments were quite different. They had disagreed over political strategy during the war years because Malan was soft on the republic and Verwoerd was not. Their disagreements reflected differences in political style and approach which could not be reconciled. Strijdom's victory meant that Verwoerd found himself with a far more congenial leader, who in turn treated him as one of his confidants.

Strijdom, compared with all South African Prime Ministers before him, as well as his successor, was an ordinary man. His short period of office, four years, was marked by no noticeable policy advances, but rather by a still more uncompromising assertion of apartheid in South African life.

The Coloureds were at last removed from the common voters' roll by the simple but dubiously moral device of enlarging the Senate and packing it with docile Party members to ensure that there would be the requisite two-thirds majority. Residential apartheid was further extended, invariably to the detriment of those without political rights. Under Strijdom the first steps were taken towards segregating South Africa's universities on an ethnic basis. Government policy during these years was one of rigour and still more rigour.

As the election of 1958 approached, evidence of divisions within the National Party became apparent. Malan's failure to ensure his favourite's election had exposed a north-south conflict within the Party, which to some extent coincided with differences in militancy and moderation. But subsequently another source of division seems to have emerged, namely, the role of Verwoerd in South African politics. As Minister he had easily become the most controversial member of the Government. He had tentatively been moving towards a concept of apartheid that emphasised "separate freedoms", however intangible they still were, instead of crudely asserting *baasskap*. Little had yet come of such advanced ideas, and a plausible case can be made that they were so much eyewash, designed to give apartheid a moral veneer it did not and could not possess. Even so, the mere expression of these notions challenged traditional Afrikaner concepts about the correct ordering of relations between white and black. Conservative discontent within the Party was to be expected. On a number of other issues he was also being attacked, both by political sympathisers and by enemies. Verwoerd had come across, rightly or wrongly, as a formidable personality who would stop at nothing to force through his plans for a racially separated South Africa.

Nationalists could not be expected to wash their dirty linen in public but there were clear indications that all was not well with the portfolio of Native Affairs. Verwoerd had told the Nationalist caucus at the end of the 1957 parliamentary session that he wished to resign his post as Minister of Native Affairs as he felt that it had become too identified with his own person, while he had merely been carrying out Party policy. He had said as much in a letter written at about the same time: "In my opinion it is injurious to any government for any specific government policy to become too identified with the name of the person implementing it."[5] Nevertheless, there were signs of other reasons for Verwoerd's professed desire to resign. His former private secretary cites the letter as proof that Verwoerd's wish to give up his portfolio "was not the result of fear of attacks, of which he had endured his full quota from both friends and

Verwoerd in his element, the central figure at gatherings of Afrikaner nationalism.

Editor of Die Transvaler, *the most vigorous and determined republican journalist in the country.*

The indomitable and immovable Afrikaner hero. The popular mythology which arose during Verwoerd's lifetime is splendidly captured by this statue in Bloemfontein.

Hendrik and Betsie Verwoerd in the early days of their married life. (Reproduced by kind permission of the SABC.)

Telling it as it is – and as it is getting to be. The Minister of Native Affairs taking his message, through an interpreter, to rural Africans.

A study in styles: Macmillan the urbane and Verwoerd the unyielding. The British Prime Minister and his host in South Africa in 1960.

Looking as benign as only he could: Verwoerd on his first day in office as Prime Minister.

Macmillan makes his "wind of change" speech to the hitherto unsuspecting joint Houses of Parliament. On his right is the President of the Senate, C.A. van Niekerk, and on his left are the Speaker of the House of Assembly, J.H. Conradie, Verwoerd, and the leader of the Opposition, Sir De Villiers Graaff. Above them is the famous painting of the National Convention which created the Union of South Africa.

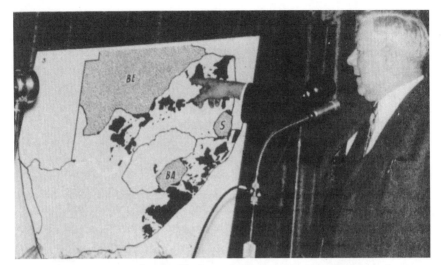

Verwoerd points to a map showing black population concentration which he had specifically drawn for use at political gatherings.

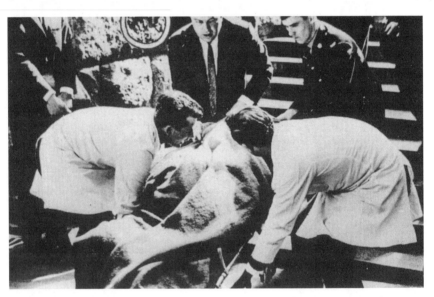

Dr. Verwoerd being carried on a stretcher down the steps of the House of Assembly. In the background is a policeman, holding the assassin's dagger (circled).

enemies". Yet Barnard suspected "that the increasing attacks and opposition to which he had been constantly exposed, added to the sheer burden of work ... were becoming too much for him".[6]

The United Party certainly thought political capital was to be gained by making it a "Verwoerd election", just as, ten years before, the Nationalists had managed to win (so went the conventional myth) by attacking Smuts's deputy, the liberal-minded J.H. Hofmeyr. Credibility was given to the rumour that Verwoerd was not the most popular man in his party by the statement at an election meeting of the Minister of Posts and Telegraphs, Albert Hertzog, that Verwoerd wished to resign because he could not "stand the suspicion of his own people".[7] It was apparently also his unpopularity with some Nationalists that made Strijdom decide to enter the election without indicating which post would be given to Verwoerd after the inevitable triumph at the polls.

Eight days before the election, however, Verwoerd announced that Strijdom, obviously in an attempt to scotch the rumours, had asked him to stay on in his post. Naturally, he said, he had no option but to accede. Verwoerd added that he realised that the United Party had made him its main election target. He accepted the challenge. He then issued one of his own: he would be happy to make his reinstatement a personal contest between himself and the leader of the Opposition, Sir De Villiers Graaff. If the Nationalists were defeated he would know what to do (although it is difficult to see what choice he would have had), while Graaff should know what to do if a strong Nationalist government were returned. One commentator remarks that Verwoerd's challenge was "typical of the self-assurance and self-confidence he displayed throughout his life".[8] No doubt this was so, but it was also revealing for another reason, for it required considerable resources of egotism to attempt to reduce the election to a personal contest between the leader of the United Party and himself, or even to suggest it as an election ploy.

In spite of, and probably to some extent because of, the tensions within the Party, the Nationalists chose to make Afrikaner unity the main theme of the election. There were sound electoral reasons for attempting to unite as many Afrikaners as possible behind the National Party, but clearly a resounding display of solidarity would also soften, at least temporarily, the divisions among Nationalists.

It was an appeal that succeeded even better than before. Afrikaner unity was still further consolidated, as Nationalist speakers had little difficulty in convincing their audiences that the Black Menace remained as threatening as ever. The future of the white race in South Africa was the issue, no less;

it could not be entrusted, the Nationalists argued with some plausibility, to an Opposition as colourless and as purposeless as the United Party had proved to be. On this question of race, Nationalists spoke with one voice, including Verwoerd. His version of white supremacy was more sophisticated than that of his colleagues, but he too made it plain that the whites would remain South Africa's top race. There is little doubt that this is how Nationalist voters saw it. For them separate freedoms and justice for all were at best interesting ideas, but white supremacy in their time, and most likely forever, was what they voted for.

The Nationalists were returned with an impressive majority, winning 103 seats as against the United Party's 53. Their overall majority was now 50, compared with the previous 33. Even so, it was still unlikely that this result represented an overall electoral majority, in spite of the Government's increased share of the votes. Many safe Opposition seats in the urban areas were uncontested, so that only estimates of the votes for and against the Government in these constituencies were possible. Nevertheless, it seems that a slight majority of voters continued to support the United Party. This was to be a consideration of some importance when Verwoerd, a mere two years later, decided as Prime Minister to hold a referendum on whether or not South Africa should become a republic.

He was now a member of the House of Assembly, having been returned for the seat of Heidelberg in the Transvaal. "Verwoerd knew that Strijdom's health was poor and wanted to take the necessary precautions in time. As Senator his chances for the Premiership would not have been good. The caucus would have hesitated to appoint a Senator as Prime Minister. He therefore wanted to get into the House of Assembly."[9] Soon there was to be a far bigger change in his political fortunes. Less than five months after the great electoral victory under his leadership, Strijdom died. He had been ailing for a long time, and there had been considerable speculation about a possible successor. Verwoerd, obviously, was going to be a prominent contender, but there were other strong men in the cabinet, which meant that his succession, no matter how close he had been to Strijdom, could not be considered a foregone conclusion.

The caucus of the National Party, consisting of 178 M.Ps and Senators, met on 2 September 1958 to choose a new leader, who would also become Prime Minister. It was the first such election in the Party's history; public interest was intense. Verwoerd had, predictably, allowed himself to be persuaded to be a candidate. As he put it: "When one receives a call from one's people, one does not have the right to say no."[10] Verwoerd was an ambitious man, but his sense of duty to the Afrikaners was profound.

Ambitious men generally have no problems in persuading themselves that the way of their ambition is also the way of their duty. Verwoerd's decision could not have been a difficult one. As a youthful professor he had become convinced that only political power could make South Africa a safe place for the Afrikaner. Partly for that reason he had himself entered politics. He had eventually been given political power, and had made such use of it that by 1958 he was easily the most controversial figure in South African politics. Now he was faced with the prospect of still more power, which, in his supremely confident way, he knew he could use, better than any of his colleagues, for the greater Afrikaner good.

He had two rivals, both senior to him in parliamentary experience and as members of the cabinet. There was C.R. Swart, Minister of Justice and leader of the National Party in the Free State. As the most senior Minister he had been acting Prime Minister since Strijdom's death. The other candidate was the Minister of the Interior, and Cape leader of the Party, T.E. Dönges. As Minister he had been responsible for introducing major racial legislation, such as the Group Areas Bill and the Separate Representation of Voters Bill. Dönges was seen, in spite of his record, and probably correctly, as the most moderate of the three candidates.

One of Verwoerd's main disadvantages was his inexperience as an M.P. He had been one only since April, with only two months' practical experience of the House of Assembly since the beginning of the session in July. There was also his reputation. His relentless drive to shape the country according to the design of racial separation had not made him popular with all his colleagues, especially those from the more genteel Cape. But, as might have been expected, it was this reputation that had endeared him to those many caucus members who believed in rigid separation between the races at all levels. It was unlikely that the more positive aspects of the Verwoerd approach had gripped the imaginations of many of them. To them he was the strong man, who would not tolerate any form of equality between white and black. The Opposition attacks over the years, in Parliament and in the press, had not really done him any harm in his own party, and amongst Afrikaners in general. Anyone so passionately disliked by the English-language press could not be devoid of many redeeming features. As usual in these matters, the Opposition tactics had been self-defeating. It had merely served to build up a man whom it had intended to destroy.

Verwoerd also had the inestimable advantage of being the favourite son of the Transvaal. He had been deputy leader to Strijdom in the province which had the largest number of votes in the caucus. As the elevation of Strijdom to Prime Minister had shown, the balance of power within the Party had decisively shifted to the north. If the Transvaal wanted him, there was little the other provinces could do about it. His other tremendous asset was, paradoxically, his lack of experience of the House of Assembly.

Verwoerd had been leader of the Senate for nearly a decade; his authority in that staid chamber was undisputed. The Coloureds had been removed from the common roll only because the Senate had been packed with an inordinate number of Party followers. It was quite natural that many, if not most, of these docile Party men should be awed by Verwoerd's personality and become his devoted followers.

Verwoerd's election was therefore no surprise. It was generally expected that he would win, yet it was no walkover. There were two ballots. In the first Verwoerd got 80 votes to the 52 of Dönges and the 41 of Swart. The last-mentioned being eliminated, 18 of his supporters voted for Verwoerd in the second ballot and 23 for Dönges, giving Verwoerd the victory by 98 votes to 75.

His triumph was sufficiently decisive to assure him of the loyalty of the caucus, but not necessarily of the cabinet. The evidence suggests that he had only minority support from his Ministers. Swart had been nominated by Ben Schoeman, a senior Minister, and seconded by Jan de Klerk, Strijdom's brother-in-law, both of whom had been determined to keep Verwoerd out. They supported Swart because they thought his chances of doing so were better than those of Dönges. The latter had been proposed by another senior Minister, F.C. Erasmus, but Verwoerd had to be content with nomination by one of the most junior members of the cabinet, De Wet Nel, later duly rewarded by being appointed Verwoerd's successor in the renamed portfolio of Bantu Administration and Development. It was only gradually, and with difficulty, that Verwoerd established that dominance in the cabinet which was so conspicuous a feature of his premiership after 1960. Such dominance, when it came, was in a sense inevitable, for power naturally gravitates to the office of Prime Minister. But all the evidence shows that Verwoerd dominated his cabinet to quite a remarkable degree, through sheer force of personality. The years between 1960 and 1966 can aptly be described as the era of Verwoerd.

The new Prime Minister addressed the people of South Africa in a broadcast the evening after his election. In what is practically obligatory for the leaders of Afrikaner nationalism on such occasions, he identified his choice with the will of God: "In accordance with His will it was determined who should assume the leadership of the Government in this new period of the life of the people of South Africa." He promised to defend democracy: "No one need doubt for a moment that it will always be my aim to uphold the democratic institutions of our country. It is one of the most treasured possessions of Western civilisation. The will of the people may not be impaired." He went on to promise: "The right of people with other convictions to express their views will be maintained."[11]

Verwoerd dwelt on a favourite Nationalist theme, especially with him. South Africa's colour policy had been misunderstood. Racial separation did not entail oppression, but envisaged "full opportunity for all", which could "only be planned and achieved for everyone within his own racial community". So far Verwoerd had been saying familiar, platitudinous things. Suddenly, he struck a new and controversial note when he made it clear that he would do all he could to bring about the establishment of a republic. The passionate Afrikaner ideal would now be vigorously pursued. But for Verwoerd the republic was no longer to be the embodiment of Afrikaner exclusivism, as it had been when he was editor of *Die Transvaler*. Then he had thought largely in cultural terms. The Afrikaner culture, and way of life, were threatened by those of the English. The republic as it was then envisaged would be both a means of self-defence, and of national self-assertion, against the English-speaking section. Now his thinking had acquired a more distinctly racial dimension, and the cultural aspect had receded. Once the Afrikaners had gained political power, it was natural that the perceived threat presented by the English should diminish. But South Africa was not immune to international developments. In a decolonising world increasingly sensitive about the rights of those subject peoples who were not white, the black man began to emerge as a far more imposing threat to the Afrikaner's continued existence than the English-speakers had ever been.

Verwoerd's years as Minister of Native Affairs had heightened his awareness of the problems created by black and white living together in one country. For him, it seems, the republic had now become an essential framework for the proper ordering of race relations in South Africa. It would be the realisation of an Afrikaner ideal, naturally, but it could no longer be the exclusive Afrikaner republic foreseen in that controversial constitution of 1942 he had helped to draw up. It would rather be an exclusive white republic in which the English-speakers would be seen as junior allies and not as traditional enemies. The pursuit of white unity was to be a keynote of Verwoerd's Premiership. For him it was an integral part of his ideal system of race relations in South Africa. But such unity could only be attained through the republic, for loyalty to the British

Crown had always divided English-speakers from the Afrikaners. Once this divisive influence was removed, whites could start dealing with the "real" issues, centring around black-white relations, on their merits. He was to state this more explicitly two months later, when addressing the Nationalist congress in the mainly English-speaking province of Natal: "In a republic South Africa will have a political set-up as in any other country. In such a system the clash between the two nationalisms – Afrikaner nationalism, founded on South Africa first, and English nationalism, founded on British imperialism – will disappear. The party system will lose one of the main divisive factors and the country will acquire a set-up as in any other country, for example, on the basis of conservatism versus liberalism."[12] Verwoerd was convinced that the opposition of so many English-speaking whites to the Government was largely artificial, that basically they agreed with the Nationalist racial policy, but were not prepared to vote for the Party as long as they retained their sentimental attachment to monarchical symbols. The republic, he presciently foresaw, would result in many English-speakers supporting the Government, while those genuinely believing in a common society for white and black would dwindle to a small, unimportant minority.

It did not mean that the Afrikaner identity would be submerged in a larger white identity. Verwoerd, particularly after 1961, when the republic finally arrived, gradually emerged as the spokesman for a white South African nationalism, but he never ceased being an Afrikaner nationalist above all. Afrikaner ambitions and interests were of supreme importance to him till the end of his life. It was rather a reflection of all that the Afrikaners had achieved for themselves since 1948, that their leading spokesman felt confident enough to speak in these terms. Verwoerd, in effect, had arrived at the position which was that of the much-maligned Hertzog in 1934. The basic difference between them, although they would both have denied it during the bitter internecine quarrels of those years, was one of timing. If the Afrikaner were to relinquish his hitherto rigid exclusiveness, it would be on his terms. The English-speaker would have to accept that in the South African republic of the future Afrikaner values would have primacy. It was in turn a reflection of their insecurity in a world where Britannia no longer ruled the waves, or much else, that to an ever larger extent they were prepared to do so.

But it was a policy fraught with ambiguity. It was not easy to be both an Afrikaner nationalist and an enthusiast for a broader white South Africanism at the same time. Nationalisms flourish on exclusiveness; many Afrikaners would only with difficulty, if at all, be able to mitigate that introversion and rejection of outsiders on which their political success as a people had been so largely founded. In spite of all the fine talk about "extending the hand of friendship" from Nationalist spokesmen, English-speaking sympathisers with the Government would find that acceptance within the National Party, particularly in the Transvaal, was no simple matter. At the grassroots level they would frequently encounter distrust, if not hostility. It could hardly have been otherwise; having been reared on suspicion of "the English" it was inconceivable that large numbers of Afrikaners would change their attitudes overnight. It does not detract from the significance of Verwoerd's new course, but it meant that the process of white nation-building would be gradual and protracted.

Verwoerd's election was greeted with unsurprising pessimism by his opponents. In a typical comment the *Cape Times* wrote: "As Minister of Native Affairs he has been an autocrat, contemptuous of criticism and public opinion. He is a declared racialist and champion of *baasskap*. He is an advocate of what he calls 'strong leadership' ..."[13] The Nationalist press was as euphoric as the *Cape Times* was bitter, ranging from *Dagbreek en Sondagnuus*'s perhaps not entirely happy description of him (in view of an earlier strong man of the same description) as a "man of steel",[14] to *Die Burger*'s view of him as someone recognised "as a power and phenomenon in public life, a man of destiny who has already made his mark on our fate and will continue to do so".[15] There was to be little in Verwoerd's record as Prime Minister that would persuade either side that it had been wrong.

To all appearances he assumed his new duties as if to the manner born. In the remainder of that parliamentary session he made three of those extremely lengthy speeches that had become his trademark. About the blacks he said nothing that was new, except to foreshadow the disappearance of the Native Representatives from Parliament. He had told the Senate before that he had received "representations from various leading Natives" advising that their supposed representatives were not doing their Job properly, only bothering to "come into regular contact with small cliques of agitators or their Native friends ..." He again affirmed his belief in "the principles of democracy", adding significantly, "as we know them", and declared himself against improving the white-black ratio in favour of the whites by unrestricted immigration, for many immigrants would be "unacquainted with conditions in this country", and would arrive "as the allies of those people who are prepared to allow intermingling".[16] This issue of immigration was one of the few on which Verwoerd was ever to change his mind.

Apart from the republic, Verwoerd was not overtly thinking of new policy initiatives. But if he was still finding his way, he was doing so with assurance. He never allowed his political opponents to rattle him, although they tried very hard to do so. When the United Party attacked him for an alleged breach of faith on a relatively minor issue, Verwoerd retaliated aggressively and effectively. He went into detail to explain why it was the opposition that had been wrong. He accused his attackers of conducting a "smear campaign" unworthy of decent people. This first full-scale attack on Verwoerd by the United Party was a premonition of things to come. It was a complete failure. None of their later onslaughts was to be any more successful.

A journalist who observed Verwoerd from the press gallery wrote about the effect he had on his opponents: "Dr. Verwoerd – although he did not have a good speaking voice (it often tended to tenseness and too high a pitch) seemed to mesmerize the Opposition with the sheer strength of conviction and the authority of his personality behind his words – physically and politically. Even professional pressmen in the gallery, who had heard him often over the years as Minister of Native Affairs in both the House of Assembly and the Senate, were filled with a new respect and awe for the man's debating abilities. Opposition English-language newspaper correspondents, in discussing his performance in the press rooms among themselves, used expressions such as 'talked circles around them' and 'slaughtered' and 'demolished' the Opposition."[17]

As Prime Minister Verwoerd maintained the same furious working pace as he had when Minister of Native Affairs. He often worked till two in the morning, and demanded nearly the same exacting standards from his staff. His memory had always been remarkable and coupled with his long hours it gave him an extraordinarily detailed knowledge of those topics on which he chose to speak, as well as of the day-to-day running of his department. He usually knew too much, and in the didactic manner of an academic could expound his policy for hours, when a briefer exposition would have been more effective. Only over weekends did he usually find time to relax.

Verwoerd was an excellent family man. He never allowed his huge workload to cause him to neglect his wife and children. His former private secretary wrote: "Dr. Verwoerd was a true family man who lived to be with them. The comradeship between the father and the mother could not be bettered."[18]

He had a strong practical flair and liked to work with his hands. In 1942, when editor of *Die Transvaler*, he bought a farm on the Transvaal highveld where he frequently spent weekends. He concentrated on dairy farming, and still possessed the property when he became Prime Minister. His duties then became so exacting that he could not continue farming, and eventually, in 1962, the farm was sold. Verwoerd still needed an outlet for his manual bent; he solved his problem by buying plots near Cape Town and Pretoria. Here he found relief from politics by working long hours as a carpenter, making such diverse objects as a workbench and mats for the bathrooms. His practical flair was not always fortunately expressed. When Verwoerd acquired his plot of land at Betty's Bay, about 80 kilometres from Cape Town, he himself designed his beach-house to the last details. His worshippers, of whom there were many at the time, found in this another proof of his genius. Undoubtedly it showed that he was versatile, but those qualified to judge were less happy about the final product.

It was an enlightening episode. Verwoerd never suffered from intellectual humility. He did not hesitate to pronounce on subjects or venture into fields where he could obviously not be an expert. A prominent Nationalist, who had to meet him frequently in the course of his work, has commented that Verwoerd seemed to think that he only needed three months in which to master any subject.[19]

His other love was fishing. At Betty's Bay he spent hours catching fish, sometimes informing his wife by the walkie-talkie he liked having with him of his successes. Once, early in 1964, Verwoerd the angler even made the front pages of the newspapers, standing with a delighted smile next to an enormous tunny of nearly 500 pounds that he had boated.

The public knew little about these aspects of Verwoerd's life. To the outside world he appeared hard, inflexible and doctrinaire. He was indeed all these things, but there was a more attractive side to his personality which he scarcely bothered to reveal to the public. Perhaps he thought it would be difficult to reconcile this with the tough talk and protestations of relentless determination for which he was noted. Whatever the reason, Verwoerd's personality had puzzling features. Overseas visitors invariably testified to his courtesy and charm. Lord Montgomery found his meeting with Verwoerd a "pleasant surprise" and described him as "this obviously sincere, quiet-spoken and kindly man". A British Labour M.P., John Dugdale, had similar impressions, and even spoke in the House of Commons about Verwoerd's great charm, adding that he found it difficult to believe that this man was responsible for the shooting of Africans at Sharpeville.[20] Closer home, his former private secretary, Fred Barnard, wrote a hero-worshipping account of his years with Verwoerd, in which he admits that the boss was a demanding taskmaster who could on occasion be impatient and domineering. Nevertheless, the portrait that emerges is of a man who was usually friendly and considerate, and quite lacking in self-importance. At the totally uncritical level there is the account by Mrs. Verwoerd's private secretary, Annetjie Boshoff, who found Verwoerd a paragon without taint or blemish, apparently as nearly perfect as it was possible for a human being to be. (It hardly needs saying that Verwoerd, the stock Afrikaner hero, also stalks through the pages of both Barnard and Miss Boshoff. He is unyielding in his adherence to principle, far-sighted and, of course, God-fearing.)

Still, there is plenty of evidence that Verwoerd could be difficult, if not impossible. He certainly did not like disagreement by fellow-Nationalists. He was hostile for years to a leading Afrikaans journalist who had mildly questioned some of his policies. Piet Meiring found that Verwoerd had a weakness for sycophants, very willing to be impressed by those who genuflected before him. He found it decidedly difficult to forgive dissent from the truth once it had been revealed by him. There is the testimony of the hedonistic Paul Sauer, a member of the cabinet from 1948 to 1964, who complained that "Dr. Verwoerd did not trust others to carry out his wishes to the letter. He trusted only those who accepted what he said without question. If you differed slightly from him, he held it against you." Malan, said Sauer, never bore a grudge against anyone for disagreeing with him; Verwoerd did.[21] There were others who, even when not exposed to his animosity, found him a cold fish, impersonal and aloof.

But then there is the quite different testimony of Ben Schoeman, whose outstanding abilities made him a member of the cabinet for twenty-six years. Schoeman had detested Verwoerd since the early years of the Second World War. As an ex-Hertzogite he had been repelled by Verwoerd's vindictiveness and animosity to the former Prime Minister. Although on the same side after 1939, they had a strong aversion to one another. It did not abate with the years. After Verwoerd became a Minister in 1950 he and Schoeman were involved in frequent bitter exchanges at cabinet meetings. After Strijdom's death Schoeman had supported Swart as his successor, not because he was the best of the three candidates but because he wanted to keep Verwoerd out at all costs. When the latter won Schoeman was convinced that his days as Minister were over. He was astounded when Verwoerd assured him that he was virtually indispensable and suggested that they should forget the past and make a new start.

For some time still Schoeman remained suspicious. He could not believe that the Verwoerdian leopard could so readily change his spots. He constantly expected the new leader to commit "some or other reckless action". Schoeman admits he had been wrong: "I gradually discovered, rather to my surprise, that Verwoerd had much charm and an attractive personality, which all the years I never wanted to notice. I had of course long been aware of his intellectual prowess, his exceptional ability, his energy and purposefulness, his pertinacity and his determination which was frequently akin to obstinacy, but Verwoerd was now a completely different person from the man whom I knew since 1940 and could not bear in my sight. Gradually my antagonism disappeared and it was only now, after all the years of quarrelling, that we would learn to know and appreciate one another."[22]

Superficially, all this conflicting evidence presents us with an enigma. Dugdale of the Labour Party came to such a conclusion when he said that Verwoerd lived "a sort of Jekyll and Hyde life". But perhaps it is unnecessary to be so frankly defeatist, without at the same time falling into the pitfalls of psycho-history (that latest fad of academic historians who should know better). Basically, Verwoerd was a natural autocrat, convinced of his own rightness. A man not prone to random displays of warmth, he relaxed most completely with his family, but he could turn on the charm for foreign visitors, potential converts as they were and confident as he was that his case was so foolproof that it had only to be stated to win their acceptance. Quite often he succeeded, as witness the celebrated example of Lord Montgomery. For the rest he seems to have reserved the warmer side of his personality for fellow-Nationalists and colleagues like G.D. Scholtz who agreed with him on virtually everything. He could also be genuinely friendly to those whose station in life did not equal his, especially if their attitude was one of uncritical hero-worship, as it was with Barnard and Miss Boshoff. But apparently he did not establish warm, friendly relationships with his political peers, unless they were his special intimates, and these seem to have been few. The case of Ben Schoeman was probably exceptional. Schoeman was very much his own man, of independent financial means and known for his outspokenness and bluntness. He was also an extremely competent Minister. Verwoerd was probably perfectly sincere when he told Schoeman that he was nearly indispensable. He must have known that the only way to retain Schoeman's services was to conciliate him and to tolerate his occasional differences with his own point of view. But most of his colleagues were cast in a different mould. Verwoerd was impersonal and detached with them, except when they ventured to disagree. For the latter he reserved the hostility one feels for an apostate from the same faith. The Opposition, naturally, did not matter, but fellow-Nationalists should know better: In the final analysis, Verwoerd knew he was right. To question his judgement was heresy. This is as far as the available evidence takes us. It is quite possible that these surface phenomena were manifestations of a personality far stranger, and more complex, than Verwoerd watchers could ever have imagined, but psychoanalysis of a dead man is usually an unrewarding task.

Whatever the intricacies of his personality, Verwoerd dominated his cabinet. It was mentioned above that initially his position was an unenviable one, surrounded by colleagues most of whom had not voted for him. Gradually, the situation changed, and Verwoerd ended by establishing his complete authority over the other Ministers. Edwin Munger recalls that he "will never forget waiting to see him outside his Cape Town office one time when an informal Cabinet meeting was going on inside. As the meeting broke (after – one learned later – considerable strong criticism from the Prime Minister) the Cabinet shuffled out the door as though they were chastised bad boys."[23] Verwoerd largely dominated his cabinet through the force of his personality, the strength of his convictions, his sureness of just where he wanted to go. In these respects he could not be equalled by any of his Ministers. The only other South African Prime Minister who had so overawed his colleagues had been Smuts. The corollary was that Verwoerd, like Smuts, tended to be sole policy-maker. Once he had decided, so had the cabinet. It was not always seen as his most endearing feature. Another foreign observer, giving his source as a "personal communication", wrote that "even among his Cabinet colleagues there were some who resented his domineering style, his inclination to interfere and make *ex cathedra* statements, but Verwoerd's convictions about the road to be followed and his role as leader of white South Africa never faltered".[24]

Such undisputed dominance made for strong leadership. It does not seem to have been accompanied by any profound insight into character. In addition to his weakness for sycophants, Verwoerd had no marked ability for choosing the right man for the job. He appointed some outstanding mediocrities to some of the most important posts in his cabinet. As with Smuts, he surrounded himself, though to a lesser degree, with men very much inferior to himself in ability. Like so many forceful personalities, Verwoerd did not encourage independent thinking. He thus gave coveted posts to a number of men who were noted not for their competence, but for their subservience to him. But they undoubtedly helped to establish his unquestioned authority in a cabinet which was not at first particularly well disposed to the new Prime Minister.

194

7 A Change of Course

Important as the republic was to Verwoerd, and determined as he was to achieve it, he regarded relations between the races as still more fundamental. This was a clear shift in emphasis from his editorial days, when the republic was the one true end of Afrikaner aspirations. He had come to realise that while a republic would be fine and proper the continued existence of the Afrikaners as a national entity required, above all, a satisfactory solution to the race problem. He now saw the republic as an essential means of solving the problem, through the white unity he fondly anticipated, but it was only one means and not the most important.

As Minister of Native Affairs he had stressed, in emphatic terms, that it was not the Government's policy to grant independence to the various black ethnic groups. Their ultimate constitutional destiny, he apparently thought, would be a problem for future generations. It would be enough for the present if he consolidated traditional authority in the reserves, while attempting to control the flow of blacks to the white areas. As late as March 1959 his Secretary for Native Affairs, Eiselen, denied that the "Bantu areas" would ever become independent. It seemed to him "and to most members of the European electorate ... that the maintenance of White political supremacy over the country as a whole" was "a *sine qua non* for racial peace and economic prosperity in South Africa". Eiselen thought it unlikely that Parliament would ever grant the reserves a degree of administrative autonomy which would exceed the "actual surrender of sovereignty by the European trustee". But, in any event, these were "problems for the future".[1]

The views of Eiselen, who had worked so closely, and so harmoniously, with Verwoerd for so long, expressed in an article in *Optima* in the same year as the policy of Bantu Homelands was announced, suggests that Verwoerd's "new vision" was very new indeed. In January of that year he was still determined to keep it as vague as possible, a problem for their children's children: "We are giving the Bantu as our wards every opportunity in their areas to move along a road of development by which they can progress in accordance with their ability. And if it should happen that in the future they progress to a very advanced level, the people of those future times will have to consider in what further way their relationship must be reorganised."[2]

Verwoerd, it is true, went on to describe those territorial authorities which had been created as "independent bodies in the first stage of development ... We must ensure that the outside world realises, and that the Bantu realises, that a new period is dawning, a period in which the White man will move away from discrimination against the Bantu as far as his own areas are concerned, that the White man is leading him through the first stage towards full development."[3]

It was hardly clear yet what "full development" meant. Verwoerd was still doing his best to keep his options open, but his announcement, vague as it was, further helped to polarise the United Party, traditionally divided between conservatives who differed little from any Nationalist on the race issue, and mild liberals who accepted that South Africa was a multiracial country which had to be governed, so they seemed to think, on the lines of 19th century Britain. The U.P. conservatives decidedly regarded Verwoerd's statement as a godsend, enabling them, they confidently assumed, to make hair-raising electoral propaganda against the Government for betraying white supremacy. Douglas Mitchell, Natal leader of the U.P., and one of the most conservative of the lot, typically attacked Verwoerd for being, of all things, a liberal who was being too decent to the blacks.

Verwoerd's response was to become even more "liberal", for some months later, in May 1959, he made it more explicit than ever before. The Government had introduced a Promotion of Bantu Self-Government Bill, which proposed to abolish the existing system of representation of blacks by whites in the central Parliament. Verwoerd had for long been highly dissatisfied with the role of the Native Representatives in Parliament, partly because, so he claimed, they represented only "small cliques of agitators and their Native friends", and partly, perhaps mainly, because of their unrelenting hostility to him and his policies. For him it was a logical step on the road to black self-rule. Africans could have political power in their own areas, but not in the white man's Parliament, even if it took such an insignificant form as representation by seven white M.Ps and Senators. Verwoerd was a great lover of logic when it suited him; he thus chose to believe that the system of territorial authorities had developed so far that abolition of Native Representation was justified. There could be no peaceful co-existence between two systems founded on fundamentally incompatible premises. The presence of Native Representatives in the central Parliament would only strengthen the hopes of all those, black and white, who believed in "integration".

This issue had been discussed in the Nationalist caucus, and not all M.Ps had been happy about the removal of the Native Representatives at this time. No final conclusion had been reached; the issue was to be discussed again, but before this could happen Verwoerd made up his mind, and announced in Parliament that the Native Representatives would have to go. It was a typical high-handed action by Verwoerd and accepted with typical docility by his party. There was one exception. One of the younger Nationalist M.Ps, Japie Basson, refused to support the Promotion of Bantu Self-Government Bill because it provided for the removal of the Native Representatives, which, he argued, would only be justified once the black homelands had become politically independent. Verwoerd did not see it that way, and Basson was expelled from the Nationalist caucus. Later he claimed that other Nationalist members had initially opposed the measure as well. Basson's criticism of the Bill was persuasive; it would have been surprising if he had been the only Nationalist with doubts. But Party discipline had always been firm. Nationalists, with rare exceptions, do not wish to incur the odium of having split the *volk*, and Verwoerd was not the person to tolerate opposition from within, so Basson had to go into the wilderness on his own. It was the only open revolt Verwoerd had to face from a member of the Nationalist caucus while he was Prime Minister.

Verwoerd had to provide at least superficially meaningful compensation for the abolition of the old system of separate representation. He now explicitly spoke of the prospect of complete independence for the black areas: "If it is within the power of the Bantu, and if the territories in which he now lives can develop to full independence, it will develop in that way." Eiselen's article, in which such a possibility had been rejected, Verwoerd dismissed as having been "written months before the statement I made in the beginning of the year".[4]

Verwoerd concluded what was probably the most important speech of his career, by asserting that the National Party was "prepared to develop the areas where the Bantu's control may be extended under the leadership of the White man as the guardian, and on the understanding that even if it should lead to Bantu independence, it would be ensured by wise statesmanship, that that development takes place in such a spirit and in such a way that friendship will remain possible although the White man will never be under any form of Bantu control, whether in Federal form or in the form of Union."[5]

The Promotion of Bantu Self-Government Act provided "for the gradual development of self-governing Bantu national units", as well as "for direct consultation between the Government of the Union and the said national units in regard to matters affecting the interests of such national units". Eight black national units were recognised, of which the Xhosa unit was the largest, with the best prospects for independence, occupying as it did the Transkei in the Eastern Cape, a large and compact territory, but, like all the others, extremely backward economically. Five white Commissioners-General were to be appointed to act as links between the Government and the ethnic units, which were reduced to five for administrative and political purposes. Urban Africans were to be linked to their respective territorial authorities through tribal representatives appointed by the new political units.

1959 stands as the decisive year in the evolution of Nationalist policy toward the African. This "new vision" of Verwoerd was not the inevitable outcome of his, and the Government's, previous policies. As Minister of Native Affairs, Verwoerd had explicitly denied that independent black states were the logical result of apartheid as conceived by him. It was just Opposition propaganda. Now he announced that such independent states actually were part of the apartheid scenario. What made him change his mind? The indications are that his thinking evolved rapidly after he became Prime Minister. There is no reason to doubt his statement that Eiselen's article of March 1959 had been written months before his own speech in January. But this means that late in 1958 Eiselen was still thinking in terms of permanent white rule over the whole of South Africa. It is hardly likely that he would have written as he did, had it not reflected the views of the man who was the political head of his department till September that year. But only four months later Verwoerd was thinking along distinctly different lines. Another four months later he made this quite clear. The principle of independence was accepted.

As Minister Verwoerd was subject to some constraints which automatically disappeared when he became head of the Government, but there is no evidence that he now felt free to announce a policy which he had long believed in but thought would be effectively opposed by his colleagues. He simply changed his mind after he became Prime Minister. Internal Party pressures were probably not responsible. The majority of Nationalist M.Ps would doubtless have been quite happy to continue on the same course of what, in terms of the new policy, had actually been *baasskap*. It had served them well. From their constituents there had never been any clamour for "separate freedoms." It is true that there

198

were some Afrikaner intellectuals whose sensitive consciences demanded a more ethically justifiable policy toward the blacks, but their voting battalions were few. From the electoral point of view the potential risk was indeed considerable, or so it must have seemed. Traditionally conservative Nationalist voters would now have to live with ideas about black freedom and equality which to many were revolutionary. Verwoerd's own subsequent caution in proceeding along this new road he had mapped was at least partly due to such considerations. It seems that external factors were largely responsible for the Bantustan policy, as it was popularly known. Verwoerd had come to realise that the growing criticism of apartheid abroad demanded changes which would give the policy some moral basis, however specious and expedient it may have seemed to critics. The attacks reflected a changing international environment, increasingly hostile to discrimination by white against black, if not to other forms of oppression. Verwoerd was to state this realisation clearly in his January speech: "… we cannot govern without taking into account the tendencies in the world and in Africa. We must have regard to them. Our policy must take them into account. And we can only take them into account and safeguard the White man's control over our country if we move in the direction of separation – separation in the political sphere at any rate."[6]

In April 1962 he was to put it more explicitly still when he told the House of Assembly that he "did not envisage that the position in Africa and in the world and locally would be such that it would be necessary for these steps to be taken already … The position which arose during the last few years forced us however for the sake of our country's safety and progress to allow measures to be taken sooner than we expected."[7]

In announcing his Bantu Homelands policy, then, Verwoerd was responding very much to changing circumstances. He was no wise, far-sighted planner who produced the intellectual ace he had up his sleeve all along when he judged that the time was ripe.

Confident as he invariably was of his own rightness, Verwoerd did not claim originality for his policies. He liked to think of them as rooted in those Afrikaner traditions he so revered. And the last accusation he wanted to hear was that this Dutchman was imposing his foreign ideas on true Afrikaners and Nationalists. When he was Minister of Native Affairs he was at pains to emphasise that he was only carrying out Party policy as formulated in its pre-1948 programme of principles. But the policy of independent black states was nothing if not original. A few Afrikaner intellectuals, ensconced in their ivory towers, had toyed with the idea before, but no Nationalist politician had ever dared to suggest, or perhaps even to think, that this could be the ultimate outcome of apartheid. But even here Verwoerd felt compelled to find a respectable ancestry for his new policy. In January 1963, perhaps in an attempt to counter criticisms that Bantustans were un-Nationalist, he told Parliament that he had discussed these questions with Malan and Strijdom when he was still a Minister. The former had wanted to know why the Transkei should not be given a Parliament, while Strijdom had considered legislation to give the Transkei self-government, "but his death prevented him from doing so".[8]

Verwoerd's remarkable memory was presumably serving him well, but even so there is nothing here to suggest that more than a limited form of local government had been contemplated by his predecessors. Anything else would have been startling. Malan had never been much interested in Native policy. He was not the man to innovate in this field. Strijdom's interest had been far greater, and he had steadily been becoming more aware of developments in Africa, with all their implications for the Afrikaner. But he was a limited man, with a mind more attuned to continued white domination or *baasskap*, than to evolving black freedoms. Even less than Malan would he have had Verwoerd's sweeping ideas about the future. The truth was that, in the political context of his time, Verwoerd was being highly original, however reluctantly he may have decided to give history a push. All the evidence suggests that after he became Prime Minister he rapidly became aware that changing circumstances required changed policies. He now acted with a renewed sense of urgency and, in doing so, imposed a new framework on South African politics.

It was a framework which the United Party welcomed – mistakenly as it transpired. Verwoerd's proposals of partition made the Opposition's policies look quaintly archaic. The United Party rejected apartheid, but believed in permanent white supremacy with a limited number of white representatives for blacks in the central Parliament. Its right wing was convinced that plenty of political capital was to be made out of exploiting Afrikaner fears that the Government was being too kind to Africans. It was certainly worth trying. In reply, the "progressives" in the U.P. believed that Verwoerd's "new vision" required more liberal policies. As one of them put it years later, the lengthy discussions in caucus revealed "an absolute cleavage on basic principle on the colour question".[9]

The United Party's fragile unity was shattered at its congress in August 1959. The break came over the proposal by the leader of the Opposition's right wing, Douglas Mitchell, that the Party oppose further purchases of land by the Government for black occupation. Such land, he argued with a sophistry worthy of Verwoerd, would be used for Bantustans, which would eventually become independent and result in the "Balkanisation" of South Africa. But once the Party returned to power such purchases would be entirely legitimate for they would no longer lead to the fragmentation of the country. Partly an attempt to drive the "left" out of the Party, and partly an opportunistic ploy to catch Nationalist votes, the resolution, based on Mitchell's proposal, which was finally adopted to some extent, achieved its first objective. Eleven M.Ps who believed that Verwoerd's new policies did not diminish the U.P.'s obligation to support the purchase of additional land for blacks, now resigned from the Party. They proceeded to form the Progressive Party, which advocated a non-racial franchise based on educational and property qualifications, with constitutional safeguards for minority groups. This policy was certainly more humane and enlightened than that of the Government, or of the United Party, but suffered from the considerable liability of being largely irrelevant in the South African environment of racial polarisation. Neither the whites were much interested in the Progressives, as their electoral fortunes were to show, nor were the blacks, whose leaders, even when "moderate", insisted that their demand for one man, one vote was not negotiable.

The United Party's other objective in adopting the land resolution, namely to make effective racist propaganda at Nationalist expense, was a complete failure. Justifiably, conservative Afrikaner voters needed a lot of convincing that the U.P. would be better than the Government at upholding white supremacy. Claims that Verwoerd had suddenly become a prominent liberal were too laughable to be taken seriously. The United Party continued to proceed from electoral disaster to electoral disaster, a travesty of what a respectable opposition should be. But in one respect the U.P.'s *Swart Gevaar* (Black Menace) propaganda may have been effective. It became a favourite criticism of the Opposition by the Nationalist press that the U.P.'s unashamed appeal to right-wing prejudices inhibited the more rapid implementation of separate development. Verwoerd, it is true, had always been particularly sensitive to a possible threat from the right. He himself had been the "right-wing" candidate in the contest for the Premiership. He had been seen in this light not only by the Opposition and its press, but also by those members of the Nationalist caucus who believed in tough uncompromising racial policies. Without their support he would have lost. Previously, when Malan retired, it was the "extremist" Strijdom who triumphed over the "moderate" Havenga. So it was understandable that Verwoerd should not have wanted to antagonise the strong right wing of his party, personified by such men as Albert Hertzog. Here, it seems certain, the United Party propaganda left its mark. One commentator, himself an extreme rightist, in an "inside", to-be-used-with-caution account of Afrikaner political events at the top during these years, has recorded that what really bothered Verwoerd "was the increasing evidence he was receiving that loyal supporters of the Party were becoming refractory because he was cutting up the country into small Bantu states".[10]

Verwoerd's natural inclination was to hasten slowly with the constitutional development of the black areas. As Minister he had said plenty about the wonders of slow, organic growth. As Prime Minister he had announced the homelands policy mainly because he had become impressed by the converging international pressures on South Africa. Once the principle of independence had been accepted, it seems, Verwoerd was content to believe that provisionally he had done enough. Autonomous black states were still far in the future.

There is no doubt that Verwoerd genuinely believed in his policy, that it was not mere eyewash intended for difficult foreigners. "He often spoke – not for quotation – of both the moral and pragmatic need for an outlet for Bantu political aspirations." Yet it was "doubtful whether he ever convinced the rank and file within the National Party of the validity of the Bantustan concept. More than one Nationalist M.P. spoke privately of the Transkei as a smokescreen to deceive world opinion."[11] Verwoerd was vulnerable to attack from the right, and knew it. Many thought that he was unduly sensitive to the threat of conservative opposition from within the Party, but Verwoerd could never ignore the uncomfortable prospect of being outflanked on the right. It had happened to other Afrikaner leaders; it could happen to him. In the final analysis, then, it appears that Verwoerd was intellectually convinced that the pace of the ox was proper for the political evolution of the Bantustans, but that he felt inhibited in following even this tardy course by the possibility of internal repercussions in the National Party. The Opposition's more ardent racism must have strengthened such inhibitions. It was a paradoxical development. Verwoerd's Bantustan policy had precipitated a split within the United Party and weakened it still further, but what was left of the official Opposition now felt free to attack the Government from an outspoken reactionary standpoint. As an attempt at vote-catching it had little success, but to the extent that it reinforced conservative Nationalist convictions that the homelands policy was a danger to the white man, it weakened Verwoerd's ability and inclinations to pursue a genuinely new course.

1959 was a watershed in the development of apartheid. For the first time a South African government had accepted the principle of independence for the country's black areas. But it was a year memorable for another major item of apartheid legislation, although it was inevitably overshadowed by the Bantu Self-Government Act. It was not a new departure, but the final realisation of an intention first announced in 1955. This was the Government's aim to segregate South Africa's few "open" universities on a racial basis.

Previously, universities had been free to accept as students whom they pleased. Three predominantly white universities, all English-speaking, had also enrolled students of other races, although one of these, the University of Natal, had itself enforced segregation by providing a separate non-white campus. The other two, the University of Cape Town and the University of the Witwatersrand, prided themselves on being "open", but it was only true in a very partial sense. Each university had a small number of non-white students, no more than three to four hundred, compared with a total student body of five to six thousand. It was not simply because so few non-white students were qualified for admission to these liberal institutions or because they could not afford the admission fees, but because the universities operated their own quota system. They accepted non-white students, but strictly in limited numbers, not enough to cause discomfort to their white fellow-students and to the staff, but enough to give these whites a glow of pride in their enlightenment in the morass of backwardness and obscurantism that was South Africa's racist society. Those students who were admitted, whether African or Coloured or Asian, were free to attend lectures, but were not allowed to participate in sport or social activities, should they ever have been so daring as to try to do so. It was a not unfamiliar brew of egalitarianism tempered by expediency. As it turned out, when the time came to protest against the Government's determination to impose academic apartheid, these institutions did so because it constituted interference with university autonomy, not because they rejected the principle of segregation. On the contrary, they accepted it, but wished to enforce it in their way, instead of being told by the Government how to practise discrimination.

There is of course no doubt that the Nationalists' attempt to segregate the universities completely was destructive of university autonomy and academic freedom. But equally there is no doubt that much of the protest against such interference was only speciously liberal and hardly concerned with the interests of non-white students. This did not prevent the struggle over academic apartheid from being one of the most hard-fought and bitter under Nationalist rule.

The Government announced its intention to segregate the universities in May 1955, but it was only in April 1957 that it introduced the Separate Universities Education Bill. Opposition to it was vehement, both within and outside Parliament, and on a wide front. Protests from overseas came flooding in. For a time it looked as if the Government might change its mind; when the 1958 general election was held the issue was still unresolved, but the much enlarged majority of the Nationalists now only made them more determined to proceed with university segregation. The Extension of University Education Bill was introduced in August 1958 and, after a further bitter struggle in Parliament, with the Opposition continuously forcing divisions and the Government resorting to the guillotine, it was finally enacted in June 1959.

The new law provided for the establishment of four ethnic university colleges, in addition to Fort Hare in the Eastern Cape, hitherto the main source of black university graduates. They were for Coloured, Indian, Zulu and Sotho-Tswana students respectively. No non-white student could in future register at an "open" university without special permission from the Minister of Education. Although the act applied to all non-white students, it was a logical culmination of the policy of Bantu Education since its inception in 1955. Verwoerd had not introduced this measure, but it was in complete accord with his approach and objectives as set out six years before. On the last day of the debate, he had produced one of his typically long and didactic speeches. To those familiar with his ideas as he had expounded them over the years, it was unoriginal, replete with the standard Verwoerdisms. There were specious arguments about academic freedom, and the dangers of the "open" universities as the thin end of the wedge, which would eventually lead to "social integration" and a mixed society dominated by non-whites. Separate universities were to be a healthy counteracting force which would further the ideal of separation and thus reduce possible areas of friction. They would save the youth of the different racial and/or ethnic groups for the values of their own respective communities, etc., etc.[12]

It had been a hard, acrimonious struggle, which did not reflect too well on many of the participants. It testified to the Government's utter determination to impose apartheid even in that sphere where racial barriers can have least justification, namely, higher education. The word "fanatical" has frequently been used by opponents of the Nationalists to describe their approach to race. Trite as it is, it is difficult to think of a better term for this insistence that a proper university education could only be provided on an ethnic basis. But the controversy was also revealing about much of the opposition to the Government. The main thrust of the protests was that the proposed legislation was an unwarranted interference with the rights of the "open" universities. Apartheid itself was not the important issue. Neither had it been a major grievance of the Torch Commando at the beginning of the decade. Then the protest had been over the Government's plans to circumvent the entrenched clauses of the constitution in order to remove the Coloured voters from the common electoral roll. Had the Coloureds been disenfranchised through proper constitutional procedure, the Torch Commando would never have existed, and resistance from the white community would probably have been minimal, as when blacks were "properly" taken off the roll in 1936. In short, English-speaking whites in South Africa never found it easy to become passionately involved over the deprivation of the rights of the non-whites. What mattered to them was that their institutions, such as some English-speaking universities, were being attacked by an exclusively Afrikaner government, or that the circumvention of the entrenched clauses with respect to the Coloured voters might endanger the status of English, which had been similarly entrenched as an official language. The whole unpleasant episode cast a sharp light on the South Africa of the day, its prejudices, its antagonisms, and, not least, its hypocrisies.

The 1950s had been a turbulent decade. Non-Nationalists of different views and colours had had considerable difficulty in adapting to a government which rode roughshod over the civil liberties of so many South Africans. Verwoerd's election brought no change in the prevailing unrest.

The second half of the decade saw an intensification of rural violence, in the Eastern and Western Transvaal, and, especially, in Pondoland in the Eastern Cape. The causes of the unrest were diverse. In Sekhukuneland in the Eastern Transvaal, resistance to the introduction of the Bantu Authorities system was widespread and militant, resulting in three hundred arrests and twenty-one convictions for murder. In the Western Transvaal there were particularly bitter protests against the compulsion of African women to carry passes or, as they were euphemistically known, reference books. Large numbers of these were burnt in protest. But it was in Pondoland that rural violence became endemic, as Africans seemed determined to reject anything associated with the Government, from Bantu Authorities and Bantu Education to agricultural betterment schemes. Whatever the form of rural violence, in all areas the common denominator was opposition to the enforcement of controls by a government seen as hostile to blacks.

In the urban areas too discontent erupted easily. In January 1960 nine policemen, white and black, were killed in a raid for illicit liquor in the black township of Cato Manor near Durban. Less than a year before demonstrations by African women in Pretoria against the carrying of passes were forcibly broken up by the police. Against this background of continuous unrest, the black nationalist movement was increasingly subject to internal strain. The advocates of a new strategy were becoming more and more disenchanted with the ineffectual old ways which had so patently achieved nothing.

For them the definitive proof that they were right came with the 1958 general election. It had been the A.N.C.'s policy to collaborate with other racial groups in what was known as the Congress Alliance. The Defiance Campaign of 1952 had been conducted in alliance with the South African Indian Congress. After the campaign the Alliance acquired another member in the Congress of Democrats, supposedly a body of whites who endorsed the A.N.C.'s ideal of a black-ruled multiracial South Africa, but in fact a front organisation for the illegal Communist Party. Within the A.N.C. a group emerged, increasingly vocal as the failures accumulated, which was bitterly hostile to alliance with members of other racial groups, especially the Congress of Democrats which, they were certain, diverted black nationalism from its true objectives in the interests of irrelevant ideals such as the nationalisation of the "commanding heights" of the economy. In an attempt to recover lost prestige for the A.N.C., its left wing had persuaded Albert Luthuli to support a stay-at-home strike of workers which would coincide with the general election of 1958. The strike was not a success: few Africans were prepared to risk their jobs and their livelihoods in a venture which was so unlikely to yield any tangible rewards. The A.N.C. emerged with its reputation diminished and with poor prospects of regaining its former mass support.

For the Africanists in the A.N.C., drawn largely from its militant youth wing, continued membership of so futile an organisation was pointless. At the A.N.C.'s Transvaal conference in November that year, Robert Sobukwe led a walkout, followed in March 1959 by the formation of the Pan Africanist Congress, with Sobukwe as President. The P.A.C. claimed to believe in "political democracy as understood in the West", but its mood was decidedly more aggressive than that of the A.N.C., and its commitment to non-violence more dubious. It was frankly exclusivist. There was to be no cooperation with whites, or with Communists. Blacks had to liberate themselves; true liberation would not come by working with groups whose interests were so fundamentally different from theirs.

The split within African nationalism hastened the process of racial polarisation. The A.N.C. was initially relieved at the departure of the dissidents, but soon found that it was in danger of being pre-empted by the more activist approach and the rabble-rousing speeches of the Pan Africanists. In the competition for mass support, the A.N.C. found itself responding in the same way, thus helping to confirm the worst white fears about the nature of black nationalism in South Africa.

1960 was to be a jubilee year for white South Africans. The Union of South Africa had been established in 1910, the outcome of the deliberations of an exclusively white National Convention. Black nationalists had always seen it as a year of betrayal, when Britain had allowed the dominant whites to entrench the colour bar in the constitution and thus to subject the Africans to permanent inferiority. The A.N.C. decided in December 1959 to mark the 50th anniversary of Union with huge demonstrations against the pass laws, to be held on 31 March 1960. But the P.A.C. had similar plans, and intended to get in first. It would also protest against the pass laws, in a manner which would be far more uncompromising and defiant than that of its parent body. If nothing else happened, 1960 would at least be remembered for the massive rejection of the pass laws by the Africans. But 1960 was to be memorable for many other reasons.

8 The Start of a Remarkable Year

The year began on a controversial note when Verwoerd chose to announce at the beginning of the parliamentary session, on 20 January, that a referendum would be held later in 1960 on whether or not South Africa should become a republic. It had been a difficult decision. The result of the 1958 general election suggested that the United Party still had the support of a small majority of the electorate. This was confirmed by an inquiry conducted by secretaries of Party branches in the latter half of 1959 throughout the country, on Verwoerd's instructions. They had been instructed to calculate, on the basis of the available evidence, including the 1958 election results, what likely result a referendum on a republic would produce. Their findings were discouraging. It appeared that if 90 per cent of the electorate were to participate in such a referendum the anti-republican majority would be between 60,000 and 70,000 votes. This was a dismal prospect but, if the memories of Verwoerd admirers are reliable, not one to deter him in the least. "Fellows," he said, "we are going ahead and we are going to win with a big majority."[1]

Why did Verwoerd decide to hold a referendum at such an inauspicious time? There were many Nationalists, perhaps a majority, who would have preferred to wait until there was evidence of greater electoral support. Here it seems the urgency of the race question was vital. As Verwoerd was to recall later: "During the last few years before Advocate J.G. Strijdom's lamented passing, we all had begun realising that if the republic was not brought into being within the following five-year period, the time would be lost forever. There were those who considered that greater unity of the people and more progress with the non-white question should be effected first. Advocate Strijdom and I, however, were among those who believed exactly the opposite. We were satisfied that the republic should come first, and then the language groups would grow closer and then tackle the problem together."[2] In brief, a republic was essential for white unity, in the face of an overwhelming black majority, and if it did not come soon, it never would.

Having decided on a referendum, there was the question of what kind of republic it would be. Verwoerd's own earlier preference, as expressed in the constitution he had helped draw up during the war, was for an authoritarian Afrikaner republic as far outside the Commonwealth as possible. These preferences had changed remarkably little over the years, if Beaumont Schoeman's account of a conversation between Verwoerd and Albert Hertzog is correct.[3] Hertzog, on whose diaries Schoeman relies very heavily in his behind-the-scenes picture of Afrikaner politics, was the National Party's leading reactionary, and his remarks may have been coloured by an unconscious desire to portray the Prime Minister as sharing views as right-wing as his. Yet the account rings true, for it sounds very much like the Verwoerd of old. As we know, he was prepared to modify his views if he deemed it in the Afrikaner or, increasingly, the white interest. But it is likely that his remarks to Hertzog expressed his true emotional preferences as a very committed Afrikaner nationalist.

Verwoerd told Hertzog that he was not yet sure whether the republic should be based on the American model, with the president as chief executive, or on the pre-de Gaulle French model, in which the president was a figurehead and symbol. He had no doubt about the Afrikaners' desire. They wanted a president chosen by the people (*volk*) but he doubted the wisdom of this as such an elected president might possibly not be "one of our people". Verwoerd did not elaborate on this remark, at least not in Schoeman's account, so it is not clear why he should have been uncertain of the people's choice of the president. It is, on the face of it, a surprising statement, for if there were enough votes for a republic, there would presumably also be enough to elect a president who was indeed "one of our people". A likely explanation is that Verwoerd, in view of the fine balance between Nationalist and non-Nationalist as revealed in the last election, was depending upon many political opponents to vote for the republic, for in principle it was not a party political issue, but knew that they could obviously not be relied upon to help elect a president with the right views, "one of our people". If Hertzog's memory was not at fault, it showed that for Verwoerd his ultimate loyalties were still with the Afrikaners. He undoubtedly believed in white unity, for extremely hardheaded political reasons, but for him it was only acceptable on the basis of Afrikaner domination. On any other terms it was not worth having.

Verwoerd was also worried about the republic's relationship with the Commonwealth. Should it remain a member or be outside? His own ardent wish was for a republic which from the start would be outside the

Commonwealth. It would then sign a treaty of friendship and cooperation with Britain. But he knew full well that many Nationalists were opposed to such a course. In these circumstances, he thought it may initially be desirable for the republic to remain inside the Commonwealth.

This first conversation with Hertzog was on the last day of the 1959 parliamentary session. When Verwoerd again spoke to Hertzog, on 10 January, he had finally decided. The republican issue could no longer be delayed, for propaganda against the republic would become continuously more intemperate; voters, especially the farming community, might be persuaded that it was not in the country's best financial interests. He had also decided that at first there would be no drastic changes in the form of the republic. Verwoerd feared that if the known set-up of government were to be changed radically, it would deter many potential republican supporters. This he believed to be a certainty if he were to declare himself in favour of a Paul Kruger type of republic. While many Transvalers would be delighted, it was sure to alienate many voters in the Cape Province. So too would many potential supporters be alienated were he to opt for a republic outside the Commonwealth. It was vitally important to consider the feelings of English-speaking voters, for Verwoerd calculated that the Nationalists, in spite of their comfortable parliamentary majority, were still polling approximately 70,000 votes less than the United Party.

Speculation about the republic had long been in the air, but few South Africans expected 1960 to be the year of decision. On 14 January the usually well-informed Cape Nationalist daily, *Die Burger*, reported that a "tame" parliamentary session was expected in view of the impending Union festival. The republic, it added, would perhaps be a feasible prospect by 1963.

Verwoerd's cabinet fully supported his decision that the time for a republic had come. It was agreed that the public would be asked to decide in a referendum in which no other issue would be considered. Verwoerd told his colleagues, in one of those remarks that speak volumes, that he had himself been opposed to a referendum when Malan and Strijdom had supported the idea, but that he was now inevitably committed to one.[4]

The next step was to inform the Nationalist caucus. The news was received amidst scenes of rejoicing and emotionalism which are best left to Scholtz to describe: "This news was a great and dramatic moment in the lives of most of those present. They who had so long yearned for the fulfilment of the greatest ideal of their people, but who had repeatedly been told in the past that the time was not yet 'ripe', were now suddenly given news which filled their hearts with the greatest joy and enthusiasm. Verwoerd's words were truly sweet music to their ears."[5]

The caucus was sworn to secrecy until Verwoerd made the announcement in the House of Assembly. Certainly it came as a complete and thoroughly unpleasant surprise to the Opposition. The Governor-General, in his speech from the throne which had opened the session, had not referred to the republic, and the Opposition had no reason to expect that in this festival year the electorate would be asked to decide on so controversial and so emotional an issue. On the day that Verwoerd informed his caucus about the referendum, the leader of the United Party, Sir De Villiers Graaff, introduced the customary motion of "no confidence" in the Government. So sure was he that the republic was a non-issue for 1960 that, unlike in his speech the previous year, he ignored the subject and concentrated on the evergreen issue of race relations.

When Verwoerd rose to reply the next day, 20 January, he first dealt with some of the points raised by Graaff. Then he continued: "The problem which now comes within the realm of practical politics is the attainment of a republic in South Africa."[6] Then followed one of the memorable scenes in South African parliamentary history. Verwoerd's statement was greeted with stormy applause by his own followers. The members of the Opposition sat as if stunned. They had prepared themselves for a run-of-the-mill no-confidence debate, in which all the pros and cons could be readily anticipated. Now they had to adapt to an entirely new, unexpected and dramatic situation, which none of them welcomed.

Apart from the predominantly English-speaking Natal, with its touching and increasingly archaic allegiance to the British Crown and its symbols, the United and Progressive Parties had few supporters who were enthusiastic monarchists. At most they favoured the royal connection for sound material reasons; they believed that South Africa benefited economically from membership of the Commonwealth. These economic advantages would be endangered if South Africa became a republic. In any event, there was no pro- or anti-republican consensus within either Opposition party. Nor did the recent split which had produced the Progressive Party suggest that a fight against the republic would be well concerted. The Opposition was quite sure that sleeping dogs were best left to lie.

Verwoerd explained to the Nationalists and the badly shocked

Opposition what kind of republic he envisaged and how he would ask the electorate to decide. In accordance with the decision of the cabinet taken two days before, changes in government procedure would be minimal. A referendum would be held in which only whites would take part, with each voter being given the simple choice of deciding for or against a republic. Most controversially, he made it clear that a majority of one either way would be sufficient to decide the issue. This clearly contradicted Strijdom, who had publicly committed himself to a previously specified majority, without which a republic could not be established. Verwoerd and Strijdom had always disagreed on this issue. As he later explained, Verwoerd's view was that "if one stated a figure, say 20,000 or 40,000, the sceptics and opponents would immediately name something like 100,000. In this way one merely lands in an argument over numbers. Should you propose a two-thirds majority, opponents would begin binding themselves to a three-quarters majority – all to make the achievement impossible. Therefore I always pleaded for the principle of a bare majority, which one would have to admit meant a majority of one."[7]

Verwoerd promised that there would be no radical changes in the form of the republic. It would be Christian and democratic, and the language rights of both the white communities would be fully protected. The monarch as head of the State would be replaced by a president, who, unlike the presidents of the Boer republics, would have no executive power. Verwoerd was not prepared to say whether it was the Government's policy that the South African republic should remain within the Commonwealth, but gave "a clear and unequivocal promise" that the Government would make its policy known before the referendum. It was a decision that would be taken in the light of the situation in other Commonwealth countries, especially Britain, for if there were prospects of a Labour Government, membership might not be worth having. The basic consideration would always be the interests of South Africa.

As Verwoerd sat down to Nationalist applause, he was succeeded, appropriately enough, by the United Party's leader in Natal, Douglas Mitchell, irascible, conservative and now plainly furious. His first words reflected the unpleasant surprise of a man who, with his colleagues, had been expecting a "tame" session. He bitterly attacked Verwoerd for coming forward, in a year where it had been understood that there would be none, with "contentious legislation with a vengeance". With some justification, as the speech from the throne had not referred to the republic at all, Mitchell accused Verwoerd of being "guilty of *suppressio veri* ... and possibly of worse". But his next remark was a wild swing which was hilariously received by the Nationalists: "I am more than ever convinced that the speech of the Prime Minister this afternoon is the last throes of a man who sees his party leaving him and breaking up (laughter). It is the last carrot he is holding in front of the Nationalist Party donkey." His last words were an only too accurate indication of what the feelings of the United Party's followers in Natal would be: "It is something which will render us asunder and make it a day of mourning instead of a day of celebration."[8]

Mitchell's sentiments were highly coloured and genuine, but, at best, most members of the Opposition could only be lukewarm anti-republicans. For them the British monarchy was not a focus of intense emotions; still less did it command their ultimate loyalties. They would of course oppose the republic, for the best of party political reasons. They had no wish to jeopardise their political futures. And there was always the irresistibly tempting prospect of the referendum going against the republicans. However frequent the disclaimers of the Government that it was a struggle outside party politics, everyone knew that an adverse result in the referendum would be a bad blow for the Nationalists and, especially, for Verwoerd. Indeed, if the United Party believed its claims, frequently repeated over the years, even after 1958, that it was supported by the majority of the voters, then the republic was likely to be rejected, unless enough voters should be persuaded that it had really nothing to do with party politics. The indications were that, in spite of the continuous erosion of United Party support since 1948, the Nationalists still did not command an overall majority of votes. Verwoerd's own strong emphasis on the non-party political nature of the conflict was largely due to his own awareness of this all too likely outcome. But it remained true that the opponents of a republic could never be as vigorous in their cause, and as emotionally committed to it, as the republicans would be. Verwoerd had caught the Opposition badly off balance, and had immediately seized the initiative. He would maintain it for the duration of the referendum campaign. As the political correspondent of *Die Burger* was to write the next day: "His declaration was the biggest sensation experienced by the House of Assembly in many years."

Verwoerd's status amongst Afrikaners was immeasurably enhanced. He was not the stuff of which popular heroes are made. His rise to power in the National Party was due to a force of personality and mind which could not be ignored, however unlovable the impression. But as the man who had suddenly made the republic, the focus of so many Afrikaner aspirations and emotions, a realisable ideal, Verwoerd for the first time became an object of popular hero-worship and enthusiasm. Nonetheless, it was a calculated risk. Whatever his outer display of confidence, and this never faltered, Verwoerd knew that defeat in the referendum could be the end of his political career. He could go down in history as the Man who Brought the Republic, but the figures at his disposal suggested that his chances of doing so were rather less than even. If he lost the referendum he could try to brazen it out by calling a general election and proclaiming a republic after the inevitable victory. Or he could do so simply by using his existing parliamentary majority. Verwoerd was no democrat in any acceptable sense of the word, and some of his remarks in the campaign were to suggest that he was thinking along these lines. It was certain, however, that even if the republic was established in this way, a referendum defeat would have been a very serious blow indeed for Verwoerd's prestige. His decision to proceed with the referendum, when it would have been so much more convenient not to do so as far as his personal position was concerned, was without doubt an act of considerable political courage.

Verwoerd had said that the referendum would be for whites only. While blacks were destined for their separate freedoms and Indians had never enjoyed the franchise, those of the Coloured community who were suitably qualified had until recently been on the common voters' roll with the whites. Both the United and Progressive Parties criticised the Government especially harshly for the exclusion of the Coloureds from the referendum. But for Verwoerd their participation was never a possibility. Historically, he argued, the republic had been an issue between the whites; it had nothing to do with the Coloureds. Factually, Verwoerd was correct. The Coloureds had never participated in the pro- and anti-republican struggles of the past. As a reason for excluding them from the referendum, the argument could not stand up to close analysis. However, this was no concern of Verwoerd's. Democracy in South Africa was the special preserve of the whites. Moreover, he knew that if the Coloureds did participate, the referendum was all but lost, as they would certainly seize this splendid opportunity of expressing their grievances against the Nationalists by rejecting the republic.

On a related issue, Verwoerd showed rare but understandable flexibility. In his speech on 20 January he had made it clear that the voters of South West Africa would not be allowed to participate as the territory was not constitutionally part of South Africa. Sir De Villiers Graaff saw

214

this as an opportunity to make political capital. He believed that South West should take part in the referendum, and vigorously criticised Verwoerd's decision. The Prime Minister now announced that he had reconsidered: the inhabitants of the territory would be allowed to vote after all. *The Cape Argus* in Cape Town, the only Opposition newspaper which did not reject the republic out of hand, commented: "It is clever politics but dangerously lacking in scruple."[9] In fairness to Verwoerd it must be added that he had been repeatedly urged by both the M.Ps from South West Africa and many of its inhabitants to permit their participation. Since South West Africa was represented by six M.Ps who were all Nationalists, it was reasonably certain that the territory would be strongly pro-republican. It could not have been very difficult, just this once, for Verwoerd to admit that he had been wrong.

The republic was itself a dramatic issue. Inextricably it became bound up with other events and issues which made 1960 the most dramatic year in South African history. The country was still recovering from the surprise and, for many, the shock, of Verwoerd's announcement, when the British Prime Minister, Harold Macmillan, arrived in South Africa at the end of an extensive tour of Africa. He had come to announce, unbeknown to the Government, the parting of the ways between Britain and South Africa, that his countrymen could no longer afford to be seen as fellow-travellers of apartheid, much as they could still afford to trade with South Africa. On 2 February 1960 Macmillan gave what was destined to be his most famous speech to the combined Houses of Parliament in Cape Town. Verwoerd had no idea of what he was going to say, although Macmillan had been his personal guest at the official Prime Minister's residence of *Groote Schuur*. The speech had been drafted two months before by the British High Commissioner in South Africa, Sir John Maud, who had visited London for the purpose. Since then it had been rewritten and touched up throughout Macmillan's African tour. His behaviour suggests that he was determined to cause a sensation; the normal rules of courtesy were deliberately flouted when he failed to give Verwoerd an advance copy of his speech, or even to give him any notion of what he was going to say. A frantic last-minute attempt by Verwoerd's private secretary to obtain a copy from one of Macmillan's aides was politely ignored. It soon became evident why secrecy had been so important. Macmillan's message was clear and unequivocal: Britain was dissociating itself from South Africa's policies, and was publicly siding with the emerging nationalisms of the African continent. African nationalism he cleverly compared with Afrikaner nationalism: "The most striking of all the impressions I have formed since I left London a month ago is of the strength of this African national consciousness. In different places it may take different forms, but it is happening everywhere. The wind of change is blowing through the continent. Whether we like it or not, this growth of national consciousness is a political fact. We must all accept it as a fact. Our national policies must take account of it. Of course, you understand this as well as anyone. You are sprung from Europe, the home of nationalism. And here in Africa you have yourselves created a full nation – a new nation. Indeed, in the history of our times yours will be recorded as the first of the African nationalisms."

Macmillan affirmed that it had been British colonial policy "not only to raise the material standards of living but to create a society which respects the rights of individuals – a society in which men are given the opportunity to grow to their full stature, and that must in our view include the opportunity to have an increasing share in political power and responsibility; a society in which individual merit, and individual merit alone, is the criterion for man's advancement whether political or economic."

British aims were not South African aims; for this reason apartheid could expect no aid and comfort from the United Kingdom: "As a fellow member of the Commonwealth, it is our earnest desire to give South Africa our support and encouragement, but I hope you won't mind my saying frankly that there are some aspects of your policies which make it impossible for us to do this without being false to our own deep convictions about the political destinies of free men, to which in our territories we are trying to give effect."[10]

Verwoerd had been completely unprepared for this. As Macmillan's message came across he must have been under some strain; such was certainly the impression of his private secretary, Fred Barnard, who was watching him closely. But if he was, he gave no sign of it as he rose to make the off-the-cuff reply which had been forced on him by his guest's bad manners. Verwoerd thanked Macmillan for his frank statement of his position; however, he denied that South Africa "was in any way out of step: "If our policies were rightly understood we believe … that it would be seen that what we are attempting to do is not at variance with a new direction in Africa, but is in the fullest accord with it." On the contrary, it was all too possible "that there may be great dangers inherent in (British) policies. The very objective at which you are aiming may be defeated by them."

Verwoerd forcefully stated a position which not only Nationalists but nearly all South African whites would endorse in the strongest terms:

"The tendency in Africa for nations to become independent and, at the same time, the need to do justice to all, does not only mean being just to the black man of Africa but also being just to the white man of Africa. We call ourselves Europeans but actually we represent the white man of Africa … We also see ourselves as a part of the white world, a true white state in Africa, notwithstanding the possibility of granting a full future to the black man in our midst."[11]

Verwoerd's reply, concise, direct and lucid, to Macmillan's long and carefully prepared speech, bears no trace of its impromptu nature. To have made the response he did to a statement which came as such a total surprise, testifies to formidable qualities of mind and personality. It was probably his finest hour.

There were also distinct political benefits. Verwoerd's frank assertion that South Africa's whites were entitled to justice, and that they had no intention of leaving their motherland, raised his prestige among the English-speaking in proportion to their sense of betrayal by Britain, which they had naively, if understandably, expected to support permanent white minority rule everywhere in Africa. Once more it was Douglas Mitchell who best expressed the agonies of those whites who had never concealed their pro-British sentiments. Speaking in Cape Town, he referred to "the reaction by a large section of the public who believed that Mr. Macmillan had said something strange and incredible that he had announced something they did not think could happen". He added: "Why do we find it strange? This one thing is certain. Britain is getting out of Africa … Britain is out for eternity, you cannot bring her back …" And Mitchell went on to ask the question which had suddenly been given new relevance by Macmillan's speech: "What matters is: does the White population survive in this southern part of Africa or not?"[12]

Macmillan's speech created a sensation, both in South Africa and in Britain. In South Africa it meant sheer political gain for Verwoerd. From this time on he came to be seen to an ever-larger extent by his fellow whites as the pillar of strength which stood between them and the kind of chaos that had erupted in the Congo in 1960. For the republican cause Macmillan could only have brought additional votes from Opposition supporters. He had made it clear that neither South Africa's constitutional status nor its membership of the Commonwealth would in the least influence Britain's pursuit of its perceived national interest. Verwoerd made the point in Parliament the following month: "It was not the Republic of South Africa that was told, 'We are not going to support you in this respect.' Those words were addressed to the monarchy of South

Africa, and yet we have the same monarch as this person from Britain who addressed these words to us. It was a warning therefore that was given to all of us, English-speaking and Afrikaans-speaking, republican and anti-republican. It was made clear to all of us that as far as these matters are concerned, we shall have to stand on our own feet."[13] It was a valid observation, well made.

Verwoerd knew this long before Macmillan had said it. To him it was not news, but in so far as he was speaking for a growing number of white South Africans, he reflected a new awareness of some rather old realities. It was an awareness that could only further the republican ideal, as well as hasten the development of Afrikaner nationalism into a broader white nationalism.

The new white South African attitudes were only reinforced by the acclaim which greeted Macmillan's speech in Britain, where it was seen as an unprecedented rebuke to South Africa. So it was, and all the more resented in the Union, because of Macmillan's typically British justification of his country's pursuit of its national interest in terms of the most elevated morality. British policies being what they were in Africa, it was inevitable that South Africa's English-speaking whites would find their traditional loyalties placed under immense strain. Macmillan and his speech were not essential for this transformation. But his declaration that the wind of change was blowing through Africa was nonetheless a landmark in the development of English-speaking, as well as of Afrikaner, attitudes in South Africa. After Supermac things could never be quite the same again.

9 Sharpeville

As if in immediate confirmation of Macmillan's words, South Africa now entered one of the greatest crises of its history. Hitherto it had seemed that 1960 would be remembered as another year of intense conflict between whites, on issues which were of considerable importance to them, but hardly at all to the other races. Yet the whites had long been disputing with one another against a background of rising racial tension. When it finally reached a climax at Sharpeville on 21 March 1960, it became clear to all that this was to be a year which was truly different.

The African National Congress had intended to demonstrate against the pass laws on 31 March. Largely a response to the challenge of the newly formed Pan Africanist Congress's disturbing popular appeal, the decision elicited a counter-response. Robert Sobukwe of the P.A.C. announced on 18 March that his organisation would now initiate a campaign against the pass laws, beginning on Monday, 21 March. Members and supporters of the P.A.C. throughout the country would on this day leave their reference books at home, and present themselves at the nearest police station for arrest. Sobukwe himself informed the Commissioner of Police of the P.A.C.'s intentions. He had also stressed that the campaign was to be non-violent. Simply by filling South Africa's prisons to overflowing with offenders against the pass laws, the system would collapse of its own accord. The P.A.C.'s slogan was "no bail, no defence, no fine". It was a campaign intended to bring "freedom and independence" to South Africa by 1963.

As with non-violent campaigns in other parts of the world, the intentions bore little relation to the outcome. Certainly very few whites saw any reason for concern. On 21 March *Die Burger* reported on its front page that the P.A.C.'s campaign was expected to gain little support. A "senior police officer" was quoted as saying that the presence of Saracen armoured cars would be enough to encourage the appropriate attitudes of calm. At Philippi, near Cape Town, events did go very much according to plan. Fifteen hundred Africans went to the local police station and demanded to be arrested. After the police had lined them up in queues and taken their names, they warned them to appear in court the next week. The blacks then dispersed quietly. But at Sharpeville events were to leave their indelible mark on South African history.

At this township outside Vereeniging in the Transvaal, a crowd of about 15,000 to 20,000 blacks had eventually gathered outside the police station after the police had refused to arrest those who had first presented themselves without their passes. Reinforcements eventually brought the number of police up to about 150 men. As the number of Africans increased and the day wore on, their mood became more and more aggressive. Arrests were made and stones were thrown at the police. In January that year the Cato Manor massacre near Durban had claimed the lives of four white and five black policemen, all killed by a mob of Africans. This event was probably uppermost in the minds of the police at Sharpeville. Finally, the nerves of one policeman gave way; he opened fire, and this was interpreted by his colleagues as a command to do so as well. The blacks immediately ran away, but by then it was too late. When the firing ceased 67 Africans lay dead, most of them shot in the back. 186 had been wounded.

At Langa, near Cape Town, some more blacks were killed later that day after a demonstrating crowd of blacks had refused to disperse. The casualties here were relatively light, with two Africans killed and a number wounded. After the demonstrators had been driven away, they went on the rampage, burning cars and buildings. Order was only restored by midnight.

The House of Assembly had met on the afternoon of the 21st to discuss the vote for the Prime Minister's Department. As the members were debating the republic and the referendum, news began to filter through of the violence in the Transvaal. The full extent of the tragedy only became known the next day, but Verwoerd was satisfied that he knew enough of its causes to be able to say later that afternoon that anti-Government propaganda "necessarily had an inciting effect on the Bantu."[1] On 22 March he felt able to say a good deal more. He was dubious about Sir De Villiers Graaff's request that a commission of inquiry be appointed, as this could provide a platform for agitators, which could only lead to further trouble. He knew, in any event, that the disturbances had nothing to do with apartheid. It was a symptom of the times, in Africa and elsewhere, as "a result of all sorts of ideas expressed in the world and inspired in other parts of the world". Like the author of Ecclesiastes, Verwoerd was apparently convinced that there was no new thing under the sun. Such disturbances were periodic events "which came in cycles as a result of incitement in regard to some or other matter of law". In South Africa the troubles had in fact not been so severe as those which had recently occurred in other parts of Africa, such as Nyasaland, Brazzaville and Katanga. If an unusually large number had been killed on this occasion it was because they were "now more bold than before". There had been considerable unrest under the Smuts Government, and in 1946–7 51 had been killed and 1,590 wounded in disturbances. As far as he was concerned, Sharpeville was largely due to agitation arising from sustained attacks on the Government over the previous ten or twelve years by liberals and the sensationalist press.[2]

If nothing else, Verwoerd was always good at explaining away unpleasant facts and events. When he had finished, the shootings were close to resembling only a ripple on the usually placid surface of South African life. The unreality of Verwoerd's approach is well captured by Anthony Delius of the *Cape Times*, who watched the performance from the press gallery: "The Prime Minister looked out over the bodystrewn locations of yesterday in his mind's eye, and took a detached, almost academic, view of the tragedy. It had all happened before, he implied – these things come in waves. The main thing was to have a firm police force."[3]

Verwoerd understood little about the causes of Sharpeville, but he knew how to deal with disturbances. A firm police force was indeed the answer. He had blamed both the A.N.C. and the P.A.C. for the violence, in spite of the former's refusal to have anything to do with Sobukwe's campaign. Both had contributed, he knew, to the atmosphere of lawlessness and the false propaganda which had led to the tragedy. The Government now acted against both organisations, and against everyone else who might be regarded as a threat to law and order. Public meetings were banned in specified magisterial districts. A week after Sharpeville, the Government introduced the Unlawful Organisations Bill, designed to ban the A.N.C. and the P.A.C. The penalties for intimidation were increased tenfold. On 30 March a state of emergency was declared, while 12,000 people of all races were detained in pre-dawn arrests. Eventually more than 18,000 were detained under the emergency regulations.

The Government's strong-arm methods were unprecedented; so was the reaction overseas. The American Government publicly regretted "the tragic loss of life" and expressed the hope that "the African people will be able to obtain redress for legitimate grievances by peaceful means. Press condemnation was universal; papers devoted half their front pages to enlarged pictures of the "battleground" of Sharpeville, showing the twisted bodies of the dead and the dying. Comparisons between apartheid and the Nazi persecution of the Jews were common. The South African consulate in New York was picketed, and a protest meeting in Trafalgar Square in London outside South Africa House drew 13,000 people. The Security Council of the United Nations condemned South Africa and demanded that apartheid be abolished. Gold shares on the stock exchanges slumped.

Although the A.N.C. had not been involved in the anti-pass laws demonstrations which led to Sharpeville, it now proclaimed 28 March as a day of mourning for those who had been shot. Everyone was asked to stay away from work and mourn in their homes. The intervening week was one of sustained violence, which took the form of riots, the burning of passes, stone-throwing, murder and arson, especially on the Rand. On 26 March the carrying of passes was temporarily suspended; it was followed the next day by the public burning of his pass by Albert Luthuli of the A.N.C. The day of mourning, when it came, was disturbing evidence of the economy's dependence on black labour. In Cape Town 50,000 to 60,000, more than 90 per cent of the total number of black workers, stayed at home, causing widespread disruption of economic activities in the Cape Peninsula. In Johannesburg an estimated 85 to 90 per cent stayed away, and in Port Elizabeth it was 85 per cent. In Durban, where no more than 25 per cent stayed at home, and in the smaller towns, the day of mourning was a relative failure. On the Rand there was widespread rioting in the black townships.

The Government was to claim that many blacks did not go to work because they were intimidated. It was undoubtedly true that intimidation did occur, but it is equally true that the very high rate of support for the day of mourning in Cape Town, Johannesburg and Port Elizabeth could have had little to do with intimidation. Two days later Cape Town was to provide spectacular disproof of the "agitator" theory of the disturbances.

The A.N.C. had called for only one day of mourning, to end at midnight on 28 March. But the P.A.C. wanted a continuing campaign, and did not support a return to work. In Cape Town, on 29 March, many Africans stayed at home. This was followed the next day by a march on Cape Town of 30,000 blacks under the leadership of 23-year-old Philip Kgosana of the P.A.C. The intention was to present themselves at the police headquarters in Caledon Square for arrest as being without their passes, as well as to demand the release of Sobukwe and their other leaders who had been arrested. Parliament, in close proximity, met under the protection of Saracen armoured cars and steel-helmeted troops. The march from the African townships to the city had throughout been orderly and well disciplined, but the anxiety of the whites who observed was intense. A single panic reaction, as at Sharpeville, could abruptly transform order into anarchy in South Africa's legislative capital. This, fortunately, and to the relief of Cape Town's whites, did not happen. Kgosana was received by the Commissioner of Police, who left him with the impression that his request for an interview with the Minister of Justice would be granted. On receiving the news the Africans quietly returned to their homes. There had not been another Sharpeville, but for the many whites who saw the procession it had been an impressive and frightening spectacle. It was the most threatening moment of the entire crisis. It also proved conclusively that blacks had strongly felt grievances and that, as long as nothing was done to satisfy them, the potential for disorder was fearsome.

That afternoon, in a heavily guarded Parliament, Verwoerd stood up to make a statement on the general situation in the country. He referred to the march on Cape Town and gave another reassurance to the House and the country that the Government would not hesitate to use whatever force would be necessary to maintain peace and order. He also warned those who used their influence with blacks to incite them of the likely consequences to themselves. It was a typical Verwoerd performance, abounding in tough talk and affirmations of unyielding resolve.[4]

It was immediately after Verwoerd's speech that the Minister of Justice declared a state of emergency in 122 of South Africa's 265 magisterial districts. Among the thousands arrested Philip Kgosana was one of the first. The black townships of Langa and Nyanga on the outskirts of Cape Town were cordoned off when the arrests led to further demonstrations. For a week the inhabitants of these townships were cut off from the outside world. Then, as their resources became exhausted, they gradually went back to work. Throughout the country, after the state of emergency had been declared, the police rounded up thousands of blacks suspected of incitement and intimidation, as well as many who had no permits to be in an urban area.

By the beginning of April the Government had the situation well under control. In retrospect it is clear that there never had been any serious danger of the Nationalists being overthrown, still less of white control being weakened, whatever Sobukwe's aspirations may have been for black rule by 1963. But the atmosphere of crisis and tension remained. Talk of reform and far-reaching change was in the air, not only among opponents of the Government, but also among many Nationalists. Even before Sharpeville there had been signs of tension in the National Party, partly because some Nationalists, mainly from the Cape, wanted to soften the rigidity of Verwoerd's policy towards the Coloured people, partly because some (frequently the same people) felt that a more conciliatory policy towards the outside world was necessary. This cleavage was now accentuated by Sharpeville. It was at this time that rumours of a coalition government consisting of elements of the two main parties began doing the rounds. From Afrikaners who stood outside politics there were demands for change as well. Perhaps most significant, nine prominent ministers of the Dutch Reformed Church, including three moderators of regional synods, urgently appealed to the Government "to apply its policy in such a way that it did not do harm to human relations".

How did these appeals for change and reform affect Verwoerd? He undoubtedly took them very seriously – but as signs of weakness that made the Government's task so much more difficult. They had to be resisted at all costs. Mrs. Verwoerd noted his frame of mind in the entry in her diary for 3 April: "He wants to end the situation by drastically limiting the number of Bantu. Manufacturers will complain, but it must force them to border industries. 'If I cannot save the country, then I would rather resign. I will *never* be an accomplice to the destruction of our people by abandoning our policy!'"5

Beaumont Schoeman gives us a particularly good example of the Verwoerd stand in operation. At a cabinet meeting at the beginning of April which was dominated by discussion of the crisis and the many demands for reform, three senior Ministers, Dönges, Sauer and Schoeman, made a strong plea for considering the abolition of the reference book system. But Verwoerd was "very decidedly and visibly irritated by this attitude". He immediately said that this was out of the question, as the system had to perform certain functions, namely, to control the black influx to the white areas, to identify an African to his employer, and to protect current urban black wages by preventing an unlimited inflow to the towns. "The supporters of the abolition of the reference book system put up little resistance after Dr. Verwoerd had expressed himself so strongly on the subject. It was as if they suddenly recoiled from their own proposal. The matter was simply left there and considered as settled."6

Continuing on the old course presented no difficulties to Verwoerd. He knew that blacks had nothing to complain about. Agitators were responsible for all the trouble. He gave a full exposition of his theory of black unrest five days after Sharpeville, at Meyerton in the Transvaal, to a gathering of 70,000 to 80,000 people, the largest crowd ever to be addressed by a South African Prime Minister. In his first public appearance since the tragedy Verwoerd urged everyone to keep calm: "Nobody should

224

be at all upset. Nobody should think that law and order cannot be maintained in the country … I would like especially to call upon the whites not to get the wrong impression of the blacks in the Union of South Africa. These troubles are not troubles caused by the black masses. The black masses of South Africa – and I know the Bantu in all parts of the country – are orderly. They are loyal to the government of the country. The masses are beginning to realise that we are also thinking of their interests, that we too can see what they need, that we know and recognise their rights. The groups of people seeking their own gain are small and they make use of mass psychology at mass gatherings, and by threats and other means are sometimes the cause of trouble."[7] As a former professor of psychology, Verwoerd presumably knew what he was talking about.

There is no reason to believe that if Verwoerd had been strongly impressed by the reality of black hardship he would have spoken differently. It was after all his job to save the *volk* from destruction, and a full-time job it was too, for Verwoerd was prone to see threats to Afrikaner existence everywhere, whether they came from yielding to the demands of black agitators or allowing racially integrated sporting teams to tour South Africa. But it must have been a comfort to know that, whatever the overt evidence, the "black masses" believed as strongly in the Government's hard line as he did.

It was less than three weeks after Sharpeville that Verwoerd had his narrow escape from death. He had gone to Johannesburg to open the Rand Easter Show on 9 April. Verwoerd had just sat down after completing his speech when a slightly-built white man approached him, in full view of the crowd. Upon reaching the Prime Minister, he called out "Verwoerd!" As Verwoerd looked up at him he fired two shots into his victim's head at point-blank range with a small-calibre revolver he had quietly and unsuspectedly taken from his pocket. Verwoerd fell back with blood streaming from his face, while security men and bystanders overpowered his attacker in the midst of total pandemonium. Gravely hurt, Verwoerd was hurried to hospital, where at first it was feared that he would not survive.

Verwoerd recovered. The two bullets had almost been fatal. Even Verwoerd had thought he was going to die when he knew that he had been hit. In hospital, when he realised that he was still capable of coherent thought, he decided that he would resist death with all his remaining strength. This iron determination, together with the expert medical attention he received, were responsible for a remarkable recovery. The bullets were removed nearly a month later. On 15 May

Verwoerd returned home and five days later addressed the nation in a radio broadcast. It was the first but not the last attempt to assassinate a South African Prime Minister.

His would-be murderer was judged mentally disordered and unfit to stand trial on a charge of attempted murder. He was David Pratt, a wealthy Transvaal farmer with a record of mental instability. In court he was to claim that he had not intended to kill Verwoerd, but only to maim him. The Prime Minister's period of recovery "would at least give him an opportunity to reconsider some of the things that were going on". Pratt was sent to a mental hospital, where he committed suicide the following year.

The absence of Verwoerd's strong hand while he was in hospital allowed reform-minded Nationalists to express themselves more freely. Coalition became a topic of frequent discussion within the Nationalist caucus, and demands for a more conciliatory race policy were now often heard from prominent Nationalists, mainly from the Cape. The Minister of Lands and acting chairman of the cabinet in Verwoerd's absence, Paul Sauer, easy-going and not noted for his addiction to ideology, gave best expression to these currents of Nationalist thinking in his famous Humansdorp speech on 19 April. Sauer announced that "the old book of South African history was closed at Sharpeville". A new approach was needed, especially with respect to the system of reference books, the prohibition of liquor sales to blacks, the right of Africans to some degree of local government in the urban areas, and the problem of black poverty.[8]

Sauer was flying a kite, but it was not airborne for long. He received too many wrong responses. It was too enthusiastically welcomed by the Opposition, which now saw him as a key figure in any political realignment. But within the Nationalist caucus there was strident opposition to Sauer's proposals. The majority clearly rejected them, and it was decided that they would not be further discussed until Verwoerd's return.

It was in fact the latter's decisive intervention, when still recuperating, which prevented any major change from the plotted course. Although still unfit to attend Parliament after he returned home, he prepared a lengthy statement which the Cape Nationalist leader, T.E. Dönges, read to the House of Assembly on 20 May. It was intended more for reformists within his own ranks than for those outside, whom he had long ignored and would continue to ignore. The message was simple: the Government (i.e. Verwoerd himself) knew better what the country needed than all the well-meaning people who had been so free with their advice after Sharpeville. They were inadequately informed, not having the Government's access to facts, and the opportunity to consult with experts. "In addition," and this seemed to be aimed directly at Sauer, "we must guard against the tendency which has arisen in certain quarters as a result of internal and external propaganda to see the disturbances in the wrong perspective; and in the second place against the attempts of opponents to try to encourage a change to a supposedly altogether new policy or a revision of policy. This in the end appeared to be nothing but an attempt to revitalise the policy of integration which has already failed here and elsewhere in Africa." Verwoerd proceeded to re-open that old book of South African history which Sauer had declared closed at Humansdorp: "The Government sees no reason to depart from its policy of separate development as a result of the disturbances. On the contrary, the events have now more than ever emphasised that peace and good order, and friendly relations between the races, can best be achieved through this policy." Considered out of context, this was unexceptional stuff, with which any good Nationalist could be expected to agree. But as all deviationist tendencies had just been branded as the high road to integration, Verwoerd was saying in effect that there was only one true way, and that was through him and him alone.[9]

Not that Verwoerd's own suggested improvements were so different from Sauer's. It was the tone of unbending resolve which distinguished Verwoerd from his more conciliatory colleague. Verwoerd too was prepared to give urban blacks a larger measure of autonomy in their residential area in the towns and cities. The amendment of the liquor laws prohibiting the sale of spirits to blacks had long been under consideration, for the system of police raids in search of illicit liquor dealers and shebeens had been considered unsatisfactory by the police themselves. Verwoerd was not prepared to make significant changes in the pass laws, although it was clearly one of the major sources of urban black discontent. Reference books and influx control would remain. Even here Verwoerd was making a valid point when he stressed that abolition of the system, by allowing a much greater inflow of blacks to the towns, would lower the existing wage level of urban black workers. As for low wages, apparently the most considerable of all the grievances, Verwoerd offered no hope of improvement through action by the Government. This was held against him, but it is difficult to see what was so specially iniquitous about his attitude, or indeed what he could have done. As Verwoerd truthfully pointed out, this was a concern of the employers. No laws prohibited them from paying more than the minimum statutory rates. He thought it wrong that the Government should force employers to pay more. Although he did not say so, Verwoerd could have added that the probable effect of such compulsion would have been a higher level of black unemployment, as employers tried to reduce their labour costs by employing fewer black workers.

Verwoerd's vigorous response, while still convalescing, effectively scotched the rumours that big changes were under way. Nationalist reformers were now more careful about what they said in public. But in private it was another matter. There would still be demands for policy changes, especially with respect to the Coloured people. They would remain a continual challenge to Verwoerd's domination of the National Party, to his unyielding determination to keep it on the only true way to separate development. But, as it transpired, it was a challenge Verwoerd beat off with relative ease.

So much has been written about the events leading to Sharpeville and those which came after, that it comes as a surprise that there is still no plausible explanation why it happened. Why was there a Sharpeville? There are two broad explanations, one only slightly less implausible than the other. The one which has been contemptuously rejected by liberals and academic critics of apartheid (often but not always the same people) has been the Verwoerd and general Nationalist contention that it was simply due to agitators, usually Communist-inspired. These critics have fallen over one another to make the obvious point that effective agitation requires a susceptible audience, that people must feel that they are being pretty hard done by before they start mounting the barricades. This is true enough, and the agitator theory of the disturbances deserves all the contempt which has been so copiously poured over it. But the critics' alternative explanation is hardly much better. It is implicit in their rejection of the Nationalist interpretation. Blacks had plenty of grievances, their suffering was so intense, that something like Sharpeville was inevitable, sooner or later. It had to happen. It was all due to oppression.

The policy implication was clear. Future Sharpevilles could only be prevented by redress of grievances. In particular, the pass laws had to be substantially modified, when not abolished altogether, and black wages had to be raised. However sound a prescription for avoiding other Sharpevilles (and it was really not all that persuasive), the liberal conventional wisdom as an explanation of what happened on 21 March and after has an element of truth. Africans must have been dissatisfied with something, even if only imaginary, to have behaved the way they did. To any impartial observer it was indeed obvious that apartheid had given them much to complain about. But it has become one of the oldest, and one of the few sound clichés of the social sciences that there is no self-evident correlation between great hardship and political violence.

The famous revolutions of the Western world took place in societies where economic development was rapid and material conditions were improving, however considerable the injustices which may still have existed in England, France and Russia when they were hit by social upheaval. Eric Hoffer is worth repeating in this context: "It is not actual suffering but the taste of better things which excites people to revolt."[10]

What is needed therefore is an explanation of Sharpeville that goes beyond the stock platitudes about oppression and suffering. These certainly existed, and there had indeed been six major protests against the pass laws between 1910 and 1960. But none had led to violence on the same scale as Sharpeville. Could it simply have been an accident, the unforeseen outcome of the panic reaction of an inexperienced young policeman? But then why did it lead to such large-scale disturbances in other parts of South Africa? What can explain the events of 21 March and their ramifications?

Taking an analogy from the French and the Russian revolutions, could one argue that the crisis had been at least partly due to rising expectations, what Hoffer calls "the taste of better things"? Probably not, if it is taken in strictly material terms. The 1950s was not a period of exceptionally fast growth, and what growth there was did not lead to a rise in the average per capita incomes of a rapidly growing black population. In this sense, therefore, it is unlikely that the Sharpeville upheaval was the outcome of the rising but frustrated material expectations of South Africa's blacks. Undoubtedly they desired higher incomes, but their experiences over the previous decade could hardly have led them to expect that their aspirations would be realised.

It is true that low wages were a major grievance, as well as the reference book system and the difficulty of voicing their discontent. This had been the finding of the one-man commission appointed to investigate the shootings at Langa, and there is no reason to assume that these conditions were peculiar only to this area. (The Government had eventually appointed two judges to investigate respectively the violence at Sharpeville and Langa, in spite of Verwoerd's initial misgivings. The commissioner investigating Sharpeville, Justice P.J. Wessels, did not attempt to go beyond a factual account of what happened. Justice M.A. Diemont, who investigated Langa, went deeper and tried to discover why the violence took place. Neither account was published, but their findings were made known to the press.) But these were long-standing complaints. They do not explain the actual timing of Sharpeville. Why 1960? Why not sooner, or later? What, in other words, were the *new* factors which precipitated the crisis?

It can best be understood if it is seen in the context of Nationalist rule till then. The decade of the 1950s was a time of mounting physical violence by groups which resisted Government policies, of violence by the Government in suppressing them. Most of the previous decade had been markedly different, even if such events as the 1946 miners' strike are taken into account. The A.N.C. had shared the general optimism about the South Africa that would emerge after the war. In 1945 it published a Bill of Rights, strongly influenced by the Atlantic Charter, which called for one man, one vote, the abolition of the industrial colour bar, and recognition of Africans' right to collective bargaining. Although the demands were very different from before, the tone was still moderate. There were as yet no threats or ultimatums. It was a document which embodied the hope and expectation that the great ideals for which the war had ostensibly been fought would also find their application in South Africa. It was a hope which was already beginning to turn sour by 1948, faced as blacks were by the indifference and conservatism of the United Party. The victory of the Nationalists and the policies they so relentlessly pursued only heightened the disillusionment and sense of frustration. It is against this background that Sharpeville must be seen, of rising black expectations during the 1940s, particularly after 1945, but which were sharply disappointed towards the end of the decade, and even more so during the 50s. Such disappointment would have existed under any government committed to white supremacy, but it was the Nationalists' peculiar talent and ability to intensify it in many unexpected ways. Hence the Defiance Campaign of 1952, a challenge to the Government which evoked the response of unprecedentedly harsh legislation as a future deterrent. Temporarily such laws had the desired effect; normally it could have been expected that black ambitions would adjust realistically to prolonged frustration and defeat. But the international climate had changed irrevocably since the war. The end of empire and what one political scientist has called "the rise to self-assertion of Asian and African peoples" meant that white minority rule was now totally disreputable as a principle of government. Therefore, in spite of both the Nationalists' manifest willingness to use force in suppressing black dissent and the failure of their living standards to rise, the hopes of Africans were kept alive. History was on their side; all they needed was patience.

Sharpeville was thus not an isolated event. It was rather the culmination of a crisis which had begun in the late 1940s, even before the Nationalists came to power. The crisis arose out of the discrepancy between new black expectations and time-honoured South African reality. Oppression and discrimination do not in themselves explain the course of events. They were necessary, but not sufficient, conditions for what did eventually happen.

As for the timing of Sharpeville, this can be explained by the emergence of a new factor, namely, the P.A.C. Its militancy, its insistence on making extreme demands and its blatant over-optimism (*vide* Sobukwe's "black rule by 1963") struck a responsive chord in the African masses. A final quotation from Hoffer is apposite: "A rising mass movement preaches the immediate hope. It is intent on stirring its followers to action, and it is the around-the-corner brand of hope that prompts people to act."[11]

In a situation which was already tense, the British Prime Minister arrived and spoke about the wind of change. Nationalists were only too prone to see Macmillan's speech as the direct precursor of Sharpeville. For them it was part of "a cumulative process whereby external critics, by continuously telling the non-whites that they were unfairly treated, that they were oppressed, that they should demand their just rights, and that radical changes were on the way, had created a situation of frustration and discontent which had resulted in conflict and tragedy." The Minister of Foreign Affairs, Eric Louw, cast Macmillan as a meddling outsider in a speech he made in the House of Assembly at the end of April, citing in support an article in the London *Economist* which had suggested that Sharpeville was the climax of a crisis which began eight weeks before, with Macmillan's address in Cape Town. "But this seems very questionable. The most that could be said is that Macmillan had exacerbated an already tense situation. He had certainly not created it."[12] Sharpeville was indeed the climax of a crisis – but it was a crisis which had begun even before the Nationalists came to power.

In spite of the state of emergency, it was not a crisis which came even close to threatening white rule. One essential ingredient was lacking: access to armed force. The State retained its monopoly over police and military power. After the initial shock the Government reacted quickly, decisively and harshly. There were no old-fashioned inhibitions about the rule of law and habeas corpus. Many were detained, of whom less than a third were convicted and sentenced for various offences. Sobukwe himself was sent to prison for three years, but after his release was detained for another six years under a special law renewed each year. Luthuli and his A.N.C. colleagues who had destroyed their reference books were each sentenced to a year's imprisonment or a R200 fine. The atmosphere of crisis persisted, but after a few weeks the Government was as firmly in control as ever.

10 The Republic

Verwoerd's recovery from Pratt's murder attempt had been remarkably swift. His renewed participation in public affairs came nearly as soon. A few days after his return home on 15 May, he prepared the statement read in Parliament by Dönges which put an end to the hopes of far-reaching reform aroused by Sauer's Humansdorp speech. On 31 May he was the main speaker at the celebrations in Bloemfontein which marked the fiftieth anniversary of Union.

The attempted assassination had left no overt psychological scars. When he referred to it he did so with the utmost calm. Two weeks after the attempt he told his bodyguard, Major Richter, that he had no reproaches against anyone: "I am only one of the martyrs of the Afrikaner people." When urged to bring a claim against his assailant, he refused to do so, saying, "I cannot even feel embittered toward Pratt."[1] Perhaps subconsciously, he even felt grateful, for the emotional and political rewards were substantial. Verwoerd's readiness to cast himself as a martyr for the Afrikaner cause shows once more his intense identification with his adopted people, as well as his desire to be accepted by them. Verwoerd had to work at being an Afrikaner. As an Afrikaner by choice and not by birth, he must inevitably have had his moments of isolation, when he felt that he could never be quite like other Afrikaners. He could never be quite sure that Nationalists whom he had offended would not mutter to each other: "What can one expect of a Dutchman?" Verwoerd had to prove himself continuously. As one prominent Nationalist put it: "He believed in being an Afrikaner seven days a week."[2] Or, in the words of his colleague, Ben Schoeman: "Before he became Prime Minister, he was a fanatical Afrikaner. He always spoke about *our* ancestors, our glorious past and *our* Afrikaner heroes, although he was no born Afrikaner. It was as if he wanted to convince himself and his supporters of his Afrikanership."[3] Now, after Pratt, everything was different. A close observer of Verwoerd's political career has found the unsuccessful assassination attempt "the turning point for Verwoerd as leader of his party. Up until then many in the party had been uncertain about him, about his aims and his motives. They had not been able to find in him the personification of their people's struggle … But now he had suffered grievously in the cause of Afrikanerdom; the onslaught on his life was an onslaught on their cause, and the human sympathy that went out to him became in the case of many an enduring love for a hero who so miraculously survived the ordeal to lead them on."[4] This is confirmed by a journalist who had worked under Verwoerd on *Die Transvaler*, when he says that his wounds and his escape created "a mystical bond" between him and the Afrikaner people. Many saw his almost inexplicable survival "as a sign from Above". Verwoerd's position was increasingly strengthened "until eventually he stood more strongly than any Prime Minister before him".[5]

Even the normally sophisticated *Die Burger* commented: "In this miraculous escape, all believers will see the hand of God himself."[6] Verwoerd was one of those who knew that his escape was no accident, and said as much in his broadcast to the South African people on 20 May: "I trust that I will be permitted to testify to my conviction that the protection of Divine Providence was accorded one with a purpose, a purpose which concerns South Africa too. May it be given to me to fulfil that task faithfully."[7]

When convalescing Verwoerd had been flooded with messages of goodwill and sympathy from members of all language and race groups. This spontaneous response was an opportunity to include in his broadcast a theme which was to be a keynote of his remaining six years as Prime Minister: "This proves that South Africa is not nearly as divided or filled with hatred as is so often stated. The realisation that many English- and Afrikaans-speaking people are becoming one nation; that we have to face our problems together … has perhaps never been felt so clearly by so many. The fundamental consciousness of a real South Africanism which overrules everything else is beginning to predominate over differences of origin, language and outlook."[8] Noticeably, he had not included differences of race. He had received many messages of goodwill from members of other race groups and their organisations. Verwoerd made a point of referring to these, but it was clearer than ever that his "real South Africanism" was a special white preserve, that the South African nation was a white nation.

At Bloemfontein white unity was again his special concern. On this ostensibly non-political occasion Verwoerd underlined his conception of the republic as rooted in a white national unity which transcended partisan differences. His appeal was to the English-speaking. He urged them to forget the conflicts of the past and to cooperate with the Afrikaners in solving their common problems. He foresaw a republic "of the English and Afrikaans-speaking sections alike, one united white nation governing what is the heritage of white South Africa, joined together as one by the very task set before them at this time, and through this unity cooperating in solving its special problem of race relations so totally different from problems anywhere else in the world ..."[9]

There was more than a touch of ingenuousness in this appeal. Verwoerd was no doubt sincere in believing that the republican ideal was not a party political issue, but in view of his equally strong conviction that the differences between the National and United Party race policies were basic and irreconcilable, it is difficult to see how he could not have envisaged marked partisan benefits with the coming of the republic. What else could he have meant when he spoke about the cooperation of the white groups in solving their "special problem of race relations"? It would only be possible if there were agreement on fundamentals, and this meant acceptance of Nationalist policy. For Verwoerd the attainment of the republic would be the outcome of a non-party struggle, but it was expected to do the National Party a power of good.

Verwoerd had not always been so conciliatory. The week before Sharpeville he told a meeting of Nationalist M.Ps' wives: "Our chances of winning are great, provided that we can harness all the forces of the people. If we do not win now, the fight becomes harder, and I am afraid, also more bitter. We are now fighting with gentle means. If we lose, we will fight harder and with more forceful means."[10]

This came ominously from someone who had been claiming that a republic would heal the wounds inflicted by years of white disunity and conflict. Verwoerd said later that he had not been aware that the press had been present, which only confirmed the impression that he came in two versions: the public, conciliatory Verwoerd, and the private unreconstructed Verwoerd, utterly determined to achieve his ends and not overly nice about his means. When pressed in the House of Assembly, he tried to explain. The Opposition had alleged that the exclusion of the Coloureds made the election a fraud. Therefore, "If we do not succeed then in the light of this attitude they adopt, and if it should be maintained, I would not be in favour of holding one referendum after another. I would prefer to say frankly that next time we will adopt the normal method adopted by all countries of allowing all decisions to be taken by the majority in Parliament elected for that purpose."[11]

It seems quite clear that Verwoerd had decided to establish the republic whether a majority of voters were in favour of it or not. If he lost the referendum he would either call a general election and, after the inevitable victory, use his majority in Parliament to frustrate the will of the (white) people, or he could do so without calling an election at all. He must have known what the cost would be in terms of the white unity which he so claimed to cherish. If he genuinely did believe in this ideal, as was probable for the very best reasons of Afrikaner self-preservation in a hostile environment, he must have calculated that eventually, in a longer run than he had hoped for, it would still be realised under a republic, once the bitterness aroused by the way it had been established had faded. Fortunately for Verwoerd, the course of events in 1960 played into his hands. After the referendum he would indeed be able to say that by establishing a republic, he would only be acting on the broad basis of the people's will.

The republican campaign coincided with a period of economic crisis. Large amounts of capital flowed out of the country as foreign investors lost confidence in its political stability. For an economy which relied so much on considerable injections of foreign capital, this was extremely serious. South Africa's high propensity to import usually resulted in a deficit on the current account of the balance of payments, which was normally covered by foreign investment. As capital fled the country, and gold and foreign reserves fell, South Africa faced its most serious balance of payments crisis since 1932. The Government's reaction was as tough as it had been in suppressing black dissent. It imposed stringent import and foreign exchange controls, which helped to reduce economic growth almost to zero. While capital was fleeing the country, so were many of its inhabitants. Thousands of English-speaking whites had found their morale grievously shocked by the prospect of a "Verwoerd republic" (as Opposition propaganda had it), by Macmillan's "betrayal", by Sharpeville, and, not least, by the chaos in the Congo, which had recently gained independence, only to prove immediately that it had no idea what to do with it. Many English-speakers now desperately sought refuge and greater security in more genuinely Anglo-Saxon parts of the world, notably Australia. Foreign immigration, which had in any event declined since 1948, reached its lowest point since the war.

None of this interfered with Verwoerd's intense pursuit of the republic. He had not yet announced when the referendum would be held. He now did so, informing the electorate at the beginning of August that they would be asked to make their choice on 5 October. In his broadcast speech Verwoerd specifically dealt with the most common objection to a republic, namely, that its establishment would endanger South Africa's membership of the Commonwealth. He gave the unequivocal assurance that the Government would apply for continued membership if a majority voted for a republic. He was confident that such an application would be granted in view of past precedents. "An adverse decision," Verwoerd rightly noted "would indicate an important change in the character of the Commonwealth. It would mean interference in the domestic policies of member countries, which in this instance would actually be aimed at the right of the white man in this country to retain control over what he had built up for himself. It would also mean that younger non-white member countries would be exercising a predominating influence in this matter. Such a change of character would prove a threat to South Africa and her white citizens even if she remained a monarchy."[12]

A non-Nationalist would have used different phraseology, but there was nothing essentially wrong with Verwoerd's analysis. Even if South Africa did not become a republic, continued membership of a Commonwealth ever more outraged about white supremacy would have been impossible. But there were few anti-republicans who thought so at the time. For them the Commonwealth represented security in a threatening world, apart from the real sentimental attachment of many to the Crown and "home". Even those who were prepared to entertain the thought of a republic within the Commonwealth, recoiled at the prospect of a republic outside the "club", deprived of Commonwealth trade preferences, friendless, isolated and insecure. It was an awful prospect, which did not even need the stimulus of a strong imagination. The Opposition parties were to make the most of it in the two months that lay ahead.

The other main theme of Opposition propaganda was summed up in the odd expression, "Verwoerd Republic". It was meant to convey the threat to civil liberties and democratic procedures that such a state would embody. It was true that Verwoerd and his colleagues had since 1948 shown scant respect for the rights of many South Africans, especially those who were not white. But none of the propagandists bothered to explain why a Verwoerd Republic should in this respect be any different from a Verwoerd Monarchy. And, in any event, most anti-republicans believed as firmly in white supremacy as did Verwoerd. Nevertheless, the cry persisted, and must have persuaded many that a republic would mean the advent of a dictatorship under which even the formal trappings of democracy would be rejected with contempt.

Verwoerd flung himself into the campaign with an ardour and a determination which showed how close the republic lay to his heart. He

236

addressed large and enthusiastic meetings all over the country, emphasising the need for unity, continuously appealing to the English-speaking to join the Afrikaners in building a South Africa which would be safe for "white civilisation". At one meeting at the Goodwood Showgrounds near Cape Town, which must have been typical of his performances elsewhere, the author can recall that he spoke for two hours without notes, never searching for a word, always in command of his arguments. Delivered in his characteristic high-pitched voice, it was a speech which impressed, indeed mesmerised, for precisely these reasons, for Verwoerd was no natural orator and was rarely able to play on a crowd's emotions.

Towards the end of the campaign republican propaganda struck a new, unsavoury note. The Government found it irresistibly tempting to exploit the mess in the Congo by resorting to the same black peril propaganda which it had always found so reprehensible in the United Party. In Johannesburg posters appeared which read: "To re-unite and keep South Africa white, a republic now" (the Afrikaans version carried much more punch: *Ons republiek nou, om Suid-Afrika blank te hou*). It was reported by the ultra-liberal *Rand Daily Mail* (which later impressively revealed the contents of Verwoerd's "pro-republic" letter to all voters, well in advance of its being sent) that the decision to concentrate on white racial fears was made at a meeting of Nationalist officials in Johannesburg addressed by Verwoerd himself. "White fortresses in Africa are being overrun further and further south," he said.[13] From now on the black menace featured prominently in Nationalist propaganda, giving a field day to less subtle members of the cabinet like Albert Hertzog. The *Rand Daily Mail* caustically observed that Nationalists "have been given the green light to go ahead on the straight issue of White versus Black. The whole republican referendum is reduced to the simple question of whether you want your daughter to marry an African or, more to the point, be ravished by a Congolese soldier."[14]

The same note was sustained by Verwoerd in the letter in his handwriting of which a million printed facsimiles were posted to voters throughout the country. Dated 21 September 1960, it stressed the "chaos in the Congo. Internal conflict and the elimination of the White man seem imminent in most other parts of Africa." Putting his foot down hard on the accelerator, Verwoerd predicted that, unless South Africa became a republic now, "we ourselves may possibly, but our children certainly, will experience all the suffering of the Whites who are being attacked in and driven out of one African territory after the other".[15]

Verwoerd was undoubtedly aware of events in the Congo. The

circumstances of South Africa were quite different, but, like other white South Africans, his eye for nuances in these matters was poor. He took the tempting way out, drawing superficial analogies and hoping for the political gain which was only too likely to follow. It probably did win him a substantial number of votes, but his willingness to resort to this kind of propaganda was one of the less elevating episodes of his career.

In spite of his outer confidence, Verwoerd must have had his full share of anxiety about the outcome. It has already been suggested that the decision to push the republic was a calculated risk, which required plenty of courage. Beaumont Schoeman comments on a conversation Verwoerd had with Hertzog towards the end of the campaign, which reflected his inner turmoil: "Doubt about the outcome of the referendum and the personal consequences for him of an adverse result, must undoubtedly have consumed him with worry. He admitted very honestly that only a small percentage of the English-speakers would vote for the republic. Therefore he hoped that large numbers of them would fail to vote."[16]

Verwoerd was right about the response of the English-speaking. Few of them did vote for the republic. But not many stayed away from the ballot box. In Natal, the centre of anti-republican sentiment, the voters' response was the heaviest of all four of the provinces. In the Transvaal and the Orange Free State, where republican sentiment was concentrated, the percentage poll was lower than in both Natal and the Cape Province, where the republicans had a majority of less than 2,000 out of more than 540,000 votes cast. Even so, Verwoerd and his republican cause were victorious. In a total poll of more than 90 per cent, the republican vote came to 850,458 compared with 775,875 votes against. The majority was 74,580; just over 52 per cent had voted yes. Verwoerd's prediction when he decided to go ahead with the republican issue, after he had been shown the pessimistic forecasts of his Party officials, was only partially correct. They had won, but not with a big majority.

Why did the republicans win? Partly it was simply a continuation of the electorate's pro-Nationalist trend since 1948. The results of the 1958 general election showed that the Government was close to having the support of an absolute majority of the voters; it was only a matter of time. Although it was ostensibly a non-party issue, and some opponents of the Government certainly did vote for the republic, there were probably not too many of them. The outcome was therefore a fairly accurate indication of the support for the Government in the country at the time. It showed that since 1958 there had been a swing of three per cent in favour of the Nationalists.

How was this swing affected by the events of 1960? Probably they helped to make it more pronounced than it would otherwise have been. Sharpeville and its aftermath, the Congo and its disasters, brought home to the white population as never before the perils of living in an overwhelmingly black continent. A republic outside the Commonwealth, so consistently (and accurately) predicted by the Opposition parties, would be friendless and alone, or so it seemed. Apart from the sentimental attachment of many whites to things British, this had probably been the most important reason for opposition to the republic. But, after Macmillan's speech, was membership of the Commonwealth really such an asset? He had made it abundantly clear to the whites of South Africa that they would get no British support in the difficult times ahead. Inside or outside the Commonwealth, they would have to remain on top by their own efforts. It was a disturbing thought, and must have persuaded many voters that if they were to go it alone, it had best be done by a white population no longer divided by obsolete constitutional issues. There was also the personal sympathy arising from Verwoerd's close escape from death in April. It could not have lost him any support, and must have induced some to vote for the republic. But, above all, Sharpeville and the Congo stressed the necessity for a strong government. A defeat in the referendum would not have led to the fall of the Nationalists, but it would have been an undeniable blow to their prestige. Yet the United Party looked less and less capable of governing every day. As they had so conclusively shown since 1948, and especially in that fateful year of 1960, the Nationalists were ruthless, but at least they did not crack easily. A strong government they certainly were, too strong indeed for any refined liberal taste. It was this kind of consideration, now-is-the-time-for-all-good-whites-to-unite-behind-the-Government, which must have been a powerful inducement for voters to support the republic. On balance, therefore, the events of 1960 favoured the Nationalists, but probably they merely contributed to that swing to the National Party which, since 1948, has been the most striking feature of white South African politics.

Having won, Verwoerd was conciliatory. Two days after the referendum, he addressed the nation over the radio. A momentous decision had been taken, he said. The high percentage poll left the issue in no further doubt. "But I also wish to thank all voters for the spirit in which they did their duty. This is one of the most encouraging aspects of the referendum contest, since it shows that that fundamental goodwill is present which will make it possible to go forward together in spite of differences … The good-natured conduct of nearly the whole electorate on both sides demonstrated that even the bitterest and most personal attacks, and the call on group emotions and prejudices, particularly by a mighty press, can no longer rouse universal antagonism as before. The voters generally approached this great problem with a maturity wonderful to behold." Verwoerd saw the republic as the beginning of a new era; he promised "to lead our nation in such a way that without sacrificing or compromising on principles, either by the one party or the other, we need never again feel like two nations in one state". And he urged the winners not to rejoice too openly: "It would really be wonderful if those who have opposed the birth of a republic so far, could nevertheless now be made to feel at home even on occasions of thankfulness and rejoicing."[17]

In the transition to the republic Verwoerd obviously saw it as his main duty to play the unfamiliar role of conciliator. It was for him to help heal the wounds inflicted by partisan strife, to make it as painless as possible for opponents of the republic to accept the new era he had so confidently announced. On 10 October at the Kruger's Day celebrations at Kroonstad in the Free State, he continued in this vein, even managing to include *Die Transvaler*'s favourite villain of the 1940s, General Smuts, among those "fellow builders of our state" who would increasingly be remembered for "their greatness and what they meant for their generation and for us thereafter".[18] But the acid test of Verwoerd's ability as conciliator would only come the following year, when he was scheduled to attend the Commonwealth Prime Ministers' meeting in March. His mission would be to ensure the South African republic's acceptance as a member of the Commonwealth. For the anti-republicans were unanimous: if they had to live in a republic, it should at least be a member of the Commonwealth.

Verwoerd's opponents took their defeat badly. Sir De Villiers Graaff issued a statement in which he emphasised the small majority of the republicans and then went on to argue, rather strangely, that a republic created with such a precarious mandate would "be a sectional republic and not a South African republic", as if retention of the monarchy would in the circumstances not have been even more sectional. Graaff tried to erect a final obstacle to the republic by asserting that the Government was not entitled to introduce legislation to establish a republic until it was certain that South Africa would be allowed to remain in the Commonwealth.[19] The United Party leader in Natal, Douglas Mitchell, led a delegation from his province which asked Verwoerd for greater autonomy, as well as for the entrenchment of a variety of rights in the new constitution, so intensely did they fear what awaited them in the Verwoerd Republic. Naturally, neither Graaff nor Mitchell had any success. Verwoerd had said quite unequivocally before the referendum that a favourable vote would result in the establishment of a republic, whether inside or outside the Commonwealth. Equally plainly, he had emphasised that the existing constitution would be changed in one respect only, the substitution of a president for the monarch.

Six weeks after the referendum, Verwoerd announced that South Africa would become a republic on 31 May 1961, hitherto celebrated as Union Day. On 23 January he introduced the Republic of South Africa Constitution Bill in the House of Assembly. It was as Verwoerd had promised: the only major change was that South Africa would now have a president as head of state, and no longer a monarch represented by the Governor-General. But before the Bill had passed through all its stages, South Africans heard that their country would cease to be a member of the Commonwealth.

Verwoerd had promised to do everything in his power to retain South Africa's membership. He had said as much in his New Year message for 1961, but had added a proviso: "While I shall sincerely endeavour to ensure South Africa's continued membership of the Commonwealth, it must remain understood that South Africa will not be prepared to pay the price for this by allowing interference in her domestic policies, of sacrificing principles on which her government has been repeatedly elected since 1948, or of submitting to any reflection on her sovereignty or her national honour."[20]

Verwoerd was ready for the unpleasantness which he knew awaited him in London when he left to attend the Commonwealth Conference, both from demonstrators and, not least, from some of his fellow Commonwealth Prime Ministers. He was right. There was perhaps even more unpleasantness than he had bargained for, but his ability to remain smiling, friendly, and yet formidable, much impressed his British audience. For two weeks he held the headlines in the British press, which colloquially referred to him as "Dr. V". From the outset he made it perfectly clear to the newspapermen who interviewed him that apartheid would remain; there was nothing the Commonwealth could, or would be allowed to, do about it. His ever-ready willingness to answer questions produced a phrase he was never allowed to forget, for on being asked whether "white supremacy" would continue to be South Africa's policy, Verwoerd replied that his Government believed "in the survival of both groups", which he preferred to describe not as supremacy, but as "a good neighbour policy". That memorable statement set the tone for Verwoerd's stay in London. It marked the gulf of incomprehension between him and his critics. To him apartheid was just that, good neighbourliness; to them, once they had recovered from their amazement at this unusual choice of words for what they had no doubt was the oppression of a black majority by a white minority, it simply did not begin to make sense. There was never any meeting of minds, only a reiteration on both sides of views and prejudices which were by then only too boringly familiar.

The prospect of any common ground at the Prime Ministers' Conference was therefore negligible. Verwoerd had gone to London determined, despite his own private predilection for being outside the Commonwealth, to do all he possibly could to ensure South Africa's continued membership as a republic. White national unity depended upon it. He was apparently confident of success. Had not the republics of India, Pakistan, Ceylon and Ghana been accepted as members of the Commonwealth? He had also been left with this impression by Macmillan, who had in 1960 canvassed Commonwealth Prime Ministers about South Africa's membership, finding little enthusiasm but also a reluctance to push for a final break.

When the Prime Ministers eventually met in March 1961, some attitudes had hardened. Macmillan found the Afro-Asian members now much less amenable to apartheid. Verwoerd, by contrast, was remarkably conciliatory. He agreed, though with reluctance, that apartheid be discussed at the Conference. It must have been an extremely unpleasant decision, but it was part of the price he was prepared to pay for continued membership. It was not high enough. The discussion, frequently acrimonious, revealed an intensity of feeling about apartheid that made it quite clear that, even if South Africa were allowed to remain in the Commonwealth, it could only do so in increasingly uncomfortable circumstances. The lack of intellectual contact was total. Nehru of India and Nkrumah of Ghana emerged as uncompromising opponents of South African membership, while it was saved from appearing an outright East-West confrontation by Diefenbaker of Canada's intensely emotional, verging on the sanctimonious, rejection of apartheid. Verwoerd himself did little to further understanding. He revealed his utter inability to grasp why apartheid was so universally condemned when he trotted out the hoary argument that blacks were materially far better off in South Africa than anywhere else on the continent. True perhaps, but irrelevant. Apartheid was offensive because it was racial discrimination of a particular kind – by whites against blacks. Black living standards or white benevolence were beside the point, as was the issue of discrimination as such. It was a waste of time to talk, as Verwoerd did, about the problems of minorities in Malaya and Ceylon.

Macmillan, in his British way, tried hard for an acceptable compromise. It would be in the form of a communiqué confirming South Africa's membership of the Commonwealth, but recording the strong feelings of the other ten leaders about apartheid. Even this Verwoerd was willing to accept, once more with the utmost reluctance, but the proposed compromise was a further waste of time. By now some of the Prime Ministers had decided that they wanted South Africa out, and told Macmillan so. When Verwoerd was informed he realised that the struggle was over: South Africa could only remain a member on those demeaning terms he had rejected from the outset.

On 15 March Verwoerd informed the Conference that he was withdrawing South Africa's application to remain a member of the Commonwealth after it became a republic. He read a carefully prepared statement which gave the reasons for his withdrawal, concluding, "I am, however, sure that the great majority of the people of my country will in the circumstances appreciate that no other course was open to us ... I must admit that I was amazed and shocked by the spirit of hostility, and at the last meeting even of vindictiveness towards South Africa shown in the discussions, in spite of the lengths to which we were prepared to go in the various draft communiqués ... The character of the Commonwealth has apparently completely changed during the last year."[21]

Verwoerd's decision, though not wholly unexpected, still caused a sensation, both in Britain and South Africa. It was the first time that a country had virtually been forced out of the Commonwealth, and it received appropriate banner headlines. But in South Africa it was more than a wonderful news story. Verwoerd's visit to London had been his first major attempt at post-referendum nation-building. Now there was every prospect of a spectacular failure. He had really done his best, but were the English-speaking going to believe him?

They would not if it depended upon some of their newspapers. The *Cape Times* reacted stridently and predictably. In a typical editorial it wrote: "The plain meaning of the events in London last night is that we have been thrown out of the Commonwealth, out of the group of the most tolerant, the most civilised, the most fairminded peoples in the world. And we have been thrown, out because of the narrow-minded, inflexible doctrines of racism which began the sabotage of South Africa in 1948 and came to their climax under the direction of Dr. Verwoerd."[22] In Johannesburg *The Star* also singled out Verwoerd as the villain: "He has been a disastrous failure and it would be in the interests of the country if he could be persuaded to resign."[23] These were some of the most acerbic press comments. In Natal there was the usual secessionist posturing from white supremacists who would have been as unwelcome in the Commonwealth as Verwoerd and his colleagues. In Parliament and outside Opposition spokesmen made it a personal issue: Verwoerd alone was responsible. One of the most vehement critics was the dedicated white supremacist, Douglas Mitchell, who used the familiar Hitler analogy: the policies of the Nationalists, like those of the Führer, would "bring them crashing to the ground".[24]

There was plenty of understandable resentment amongst the English-speaking as a group. It was years before they would start supporting the Nationalists en masse, and then only after Verwoerd's death. But it could have been worse. Natal once more did not secede, the massive protest marches and demonstrations of the early 1950s did not recur. When emotions had subsided it became clear that Verwoerd had genuinely tried very hard to keep South Africa in, that any white supremacist government would have failed in its attempt to remain a member of the Commonwealth. There was the testimony of Sir Robert Menzies, Prime Minister of Australia, who said, "I would have withdrawn the application if I had been in his place." Soon it was apparent that the referendum scare propaganda about the consequences to South Africa of the loss of Commonwealth trade preferences had been hopelessly exaggerated. Trade concessions were retained by the Republic; economic links between Britain and South Africa remained firm. During the great economic boom that followed, the predictions of disaster could only be seen as amusing memories of a bygone era, reflections of an emotional insecurity that did not accord with the country's new mood of self-confidence.

Amongst Afrikaners there could of course be no doubt. What seemed a failure to everyone else was for them a singular triumph. A republic within the Commonwealth would have been a regrettable compromise, accepted only in the interests of white unity, and because it would be preferable to no republic at all. It would never have had the same emotional appeal as a republic which had broken all constitutional ties with the historic enemy. Verwoerd had now achieved the historic ideal and returned home a hero of the first magnitude. In spite of his own apprehensions about how he would be received, he was greeted on 20 March at Jan Smuts airport near Johannesburg by a wildly enthusiastic crowd (variously estimated, depending on the source, as ranging from 15,000 to 60,000), whom he informed that "what had happened in London was not a defeat but a victory ... We have freed ourselves from the Afro-Asian states." Mrs. Verwoerd was to describe this welcome at Jan Smuts as "probably the highest high point of his life". That same evening in Cape Town he told another cheering crowd: "What happened is nothing less than a miracle. So many nations have had to get their complete freedom by armed struggle ... but here we have reached something which we never expected."[25]

The final transition to the republic still remained. The signs were that it would not be smooth. Verwoerd's return coincided with the first anniversary of Sharpeville, and all commemoration meetings were banned. But, in spite of the Government's drastic resort to force the previous year, black dissent was again becoming overt. An "all-in" conference had been held in Pietermaritzburg towards the end of March, attended by more than a thousand blacks, mainly ex-members of the now banned A.N.C. It demanded a non-racial national convention, to be held not later than 31 May. If the Government refused blacks would come out in their thousands to protest against the republic. They would be called upon to refuse cooperation with any government which rested "on force to perpetuate the tyranny of a minority". A National Action Council was appointed to direct the campaign, while the Indian and Coloured communities, as well as "all democratic whites", were invited to join in opposition "to a regime which is bringing South Africa to disaster".

It was not the Government's style to risk liberty turning into licence. The month of May was a time for *kragdadigheid*. A bill was rushed through Parliament which extended the security legislation, and 8,000 to 10,000 blacks were detained in large-scale raids for alleged breaches of various laws. The National Action Council responded by calling for a stay-at-home for all Africans, starting on 29 May and lasting for three days. All police leave was cancelled, and the Active Citizen Force was mobilised.

The end of May was an anti-climax for all the protagonists. The stay-at-home was a near complete failure. On the first day only between 50 and 60 per cent of Johannesburg's black workers stayed away. In the other urban centres the boycott was even less impressive. Employers had been unsympathetic and refused to pay wages to absentees from work, even threatening them with dismissal. The underground P.A.C. had discouraged the stay-at-home, distributing leaflets which urged workers not to take part in "sterile demonstrations".

For the republicans too the long-awaited new era could have arrived more auspiciously. 31 May 1961 was a wretched day. It rained heavily and continuously as C.R. Swart, the former Minister of Justice and later Governor-General, was sworn in as the first President of the Republic of South Africa in Church Square, Pretoria.

But nothing was going to spoil the occasion for the man chiefly responsible for the stirring event. Proposing the toast to the new President at the subsequent banquet, Verwoerd assured him that he would "play an essential role in our country because we who must build and fight will inevitably have different ideas about how South Africa's future is to be developed. We shall inevitably from the depths of our convictions quarrel with one another. But notwithstanding all this, there will be the basic unity of one people of the Republic of South Africa and you will have to be the tie to bind us all together."[26] It was the expression more of a hope than of a reality. Nor had the choice of president made it any easier. Swart, in his political days, had been an extreme partisan. He could not now, overnight, become a symbol of national unity, which really meant white unity.

The sole eligibility of whites for membership of the nation had been implicit in Verwoerd's whole speech; later he was to make it completely explicit when he reverted to his more congenial role of Nationalist politician. But even in this exclusive sense, there was still no South African nation. White unity would only develop gradually and precariously after 1961. It would not come in Verwoerd's time, and more than ten years after his death was still more honoured in the rhetoric of politicians than in the practice of English- and Afrikaans-speaking white South Africans. Memories of the wrongs and conflicts of the past were still too recent. As for Joyce's Stephen Dedalus, for South Africa's whites, and indeed for all the people of the country, history was a nightmare from which they were trying to awake. Ironically, no one had done more in his day than Verwoerd to prevent them from awakening.

The republic had arrived, but the pressures on Verwoerd were still enormous. Black nationalism as a political movement had been driven underground, yet the natives were clearly still restless. He had been attempting to conciliate the English-speaking, but it was only the beginning; they were still in no mood for the white unity he was preaching. Amongst Nationalists themselves there were those who wanted to gain what he could only see as a temporary respite by making "concessions" to the non-whites. To Verwoerd it was clear that he needed five assured years in which his policies could unfold. He decided to hold a general election, both to strengthen the authority of the Government and his own authority in the National Party. It was scheduled for October 1961, although the next election had been due only in April 1963.

Verwoerd was anticipating stormy times. He gave an early indication of his expectations when, in August, he appointed a new Minister of Justice. B.J. Vorster had been made a Deputy Minister by Verwoerd in 1958, and in his eight years in Parliament since 1953 had shown himself an aggressive and formidable debater. He had been, if he was not still, a man of militant convictions. During the war he had spurned the tame ways of party politicians; he was instead an enthusiastic admirer of Hans van Rensburg. He became a "General" in the Ossewabrandwag, and was later interned by Smuts. Vorster's appointment to such a key post was a sign of the authoritarian times. If the dissenters from white supremacy were to be dealt with harshly, then he was indeed the man for the job.

That same month Verwoerd came out with his election cry. Speaking at Balfour in the Transvaal, he appealed to the electorate to "defend the White Republic".[27] Obviously, for him the only intelligent way of doing so was by voting Nationalist. Less than a month later, when opening the Transvaal Nationalist Congress, Verwoerd unequivocally stated his views about nationhood: "Let me be very clear about this; when I talk of the nation of South Africa I talk of the White people of South Africa. I do not say that in disparagement of any other racial group of South Africa. I do not see us all as one multiracial state descending from various groups."[28] It was one of his most controversial speeches, but no one had any right to be surprised. It had been apparent all along that whenever Verwoerd spoke of "the nation" he actually meant the whites, if not the Afrikaners (for whom, however, the more mystical expression "*die volk*" was usually reserved).

Here were two of the dominant themes of Verwoerd's remaining years as Prime Minister: his determination to go to any lengths to retain white control over the country and, as ultimately essential for the maintenance of that control, the need for white unity. Both, he had no doubt at all, required the unchallengeable ascendancy of the National Party.

The result of the election was predictable and gratifying to Verwoerd. The Nationalists gained their most considerable victory yet, and were returned with 105 seats, compared with 102 in 1958. The United Party regained the seats of ten of the eleven M.Ps who had defected to form the Progressive Party, although this party polled more votes than had been anticipated. The conservative-liberal polarisation which Verwoerd had hoped for and anticipated under the republic, seemed to be emerging – at the expense of the United Party, which had gone into the election with nothing more substantial than the meaningless slogan of "race federation" and a pact with Japie Basson's virtually (as it transpired) non-existent National Union. But while the United Party had no capacity for growth, it would take an unconscionable time dying. The Progressive success had been misleading. In part it reflected protest against the official Opposition's failure to oppose effectively; in part it revealed a post-Sharpeville awareness, which soon faded, that new times required new policies. In fact, the U.P. was to continue to lose conservative support to the Nationalists, but was to concede very few liberal supporters to the Progressives, whose electoral performances for more than a decade were almost unrelievedly wretched. In short, it was still too early for Verwoerd's vision of the ideal party system, namely, a huge conservative party confronted (if that is the word) by a very small liberal party. The U.P. pre-empted a large middle ground, more conservative than liberal in so far as it had any policies at all, but by its very existence helping to frustrate Verwoerd's ideal of massive English-speaking support for the Government. This also meant that white unity, as seen by Verwoerd, could not be easily realised either, for, often as he may have professed the belief that this was perfectly compatible with party political differences, there can be little doubt that he saw support of Nationalist policy as the only true basis for the unity that would guarantee the future of the white republic.

11 Prosperity and Dissent

The remaining years of the Verwoerd era coincided with the greatest economic boom in South African history. This can hardly be over-emphasised, for the prosperity of the 60s left its stamp on all aspects of South African life, on white attitudes and on black discontent, on the practice of foreign policy, and, not least, on political change. Over the whole period 1960–70 the economy grew at the average annual rate of 6 per cent, while per capita incomes increased by nearly 3 per cent yearly. During the years 1963 to 1965 the growth rate actually exceeded 7 per cent. Expansion was especially impressive in the manufacturing sector, which increased its gross output by more than 70 per cent during the first half of the decade, compared with 48 per cent for gross national product as a whole. The Government's own mood of confidence after the coming of the republic was reflected in the active encouragement of that immigration to which it had previously been so hostile. Its efforts were rewarded: 180,000 immigrants came to South Africa during the 1960s with 1966 registering a record number of more than 50,000. Foreign capital, which had fled the country so frantically after Sharpeville, gradually flowed back to one of the most hospitable investment climates in the world. Local businessmen regained confidence and invested more heavily than ever before.

Why this amazing recovery? The political climate was at first hardly favourable, with Sharpeville a recent memory, South Africa no longer a member of the Commonwealth, attacked with unprecedented virulence at the United Nations, and the newly independent states of Africa doing their best to discredit the early optimism of Western liberals about their prospects as infant democracies. But the Government did much to restore confidence. Its harsh determination to maintain law and order, no matter what the human cost, was clear proof that the end had not yet come for white South Africa. More basically, the boom of the 1960s can be seen as the resumption and acceleration of the post-war trend of high economic growth, temporarily interrupted between 1958 and 1961: "The main cause of the revival ... probably lay in the inherent strength of the economy, which between 1945 and 1957 had shown its capacity for rapid and sustained growth."[1]

Whatever the reasons, the high growth rate had profound political and social implications for South Africa. Most obviously, per capita incomes rose, for both whites and blacks. Yet the so-called wage gap did not narrow, for while black incomes rose significantly, white incomes kept pace with the increase. This was not at all inevitable, or inherent in the very nature of a racially repressive form of capitalist development, as left-wing writers on South Africa would have it. The narrowing gap since 1971 is enough to suggest that there are more serious explanations of income distribution than those of radical mythology. But what were the consequences of this trend? Higher incomes, we know, do not necessarily lead to less discontent. It is quite likely rather to heighten existing feelings of frustration. In South Africa, especially, with its large majority of second-class citizens, such an outcome was not at all improbable. Black incomes were rising significantly, but so were white incomes. The Africans' sense of what sociologists call relative deprivation must have been acute. At least, it seems a plausible hypothesis, but is it valid? In the final analysis, it comes down to expectations. Were the hopes of blacks rising? If they were, then the argument is probably correct. Inevitably such hopes would be frustrated by the brutal realities of apartheid. On general grounds there is strong reason to believe that black expectations were being heightened, because of greater prosperity and the achievement of independence by more and more African colonies. On the other hand, the calamities of 1960 bitterly disappointed many hopes and must have induced a more sober appreciation of political possibilities in the apartheid state. The forcible suppression of the A.N.C. and the P.A.C. could only have contributed to a greater sense of realism. No longer could rival black nationalists publicly compete with one another by promising utopia round the corner. This also pointed the way to an effective strategy by the Government. In the circumstances of the time, it was no doubt impossible to prevent South Africa's blacks from having great hopes about a future destined to be theirs. But at least Government policy could both help determine the form of such expectations and frustrate those which were most hopelessly unrealistic.

It required a judicious blend of the carrot and the stick. The carrot was the prospect of a better deal for blacks in "their own areas", the ethnic homelands. Here they could have as many hopes as they liked; in theory the sky was the limit. Left-wing opponents of the Government condemned the Bantustan policy as a fraud, and it could certainly never deliver on all its promises. For permanently urbanised Africans in particular the policy could only be a second best. But, and this is the crucial point, faced with the frustration of their hopes for majority rule in the whole of South Africa, it was likely that many blacks would settle for this second best rather than nothing at all. Such a best possible outcome for the Nationalists demanded that it be made quite plain to the black population that there was really no other prospect of political change in South Africa. If they rejected Bantustans they would end up with nothing. Here the stick had to be flourished. It would be Government policy to show that it was prepared to go to any lengths to maintain white rule over the larger part of South Africa. It meant a willingness to resort to strong-arm methods whenever "the safety of the State was threatened". The years 1961 to 1966 were in fact marked by levels of coercion hardly known before in South African history. It is only a superficial paradox that "separate freedoms" and a common unfreedom went hand in hand; they were indeed two sides of the same coin.

It is one of the ironies of recent South African history that the same economic boom which helped to heighten black expectations, also considerably enlarged the Government's ability to frustrate such hopes. Greater prosperity in the most advanced economy in Africa meant that the Government now, more than ever before, had the material resources to make a success of white supremacy. The Nationalists were well aware of their own stake in economic development. The day after Sharpeville Verwoerd announced the establishment of the Economic Advisory Council. Consisting of representatives of the private and public sectors, the Council was designed to co-ordinate relations between the two sectors and to advise the Government on current economic problems. There were other indications of Verwoerd's awareness that economic progress was essential to white survival. In a speech to the *Afrikaanse Handelsinstituut* (Afrikaans Institute of Commerce) towards the end of 1961, he emphasised that it was Government policy to advance industrial development in every possible way, to promote the sales of South African products at home and abroad, and to keep taxation as low as possible.[2] All this was a far cry from the anti-capitalist and anti-Semitic Verwoerd of the days of *Die Transvaler*, but had circumstances not changed? In particular, had the "British-Jewish democracy" not been overthrown, and had a vigorous Afrikaner capitalism not been an impressive by-product of South Africa's post-war growth? Verwoerd was now prepared to see merits in private enterprise to which he had previously been blind. Economic strength made

251

possible military strength; under Verwoerd defence expenditure, relatively low hitherto, went rocketing upward.

There was a further irony. The same economic prosperity that made it possible for the Government to treat internal dissent with impressive *kragdadigheid* and to remain invulnerable to external attack, was dependent on an unremitting flow of black labour to the white areas. Between 1960 and 1970 the number of blacks employed in manufacturing virtually doubled, from more than 308,000 to nearly 616,000. Few of these were employed in the border industries. The Tomlinson Commission had spoken of the annual creation of 50,000 jobs in the black areas. Ten years later, by the end of 1966, less than 45,000 jobs had been created for Africans in the border areas and the reserves. These are merely a few of the statistics which point to the overwhelming dependence of white prosperity on continued and growing supplies of black labour. In one of his first speeches as Minister of Native Affairs, Verwoerd had warned against the concentration of black workers in South Africa's industrial complexes. It "could bring about the death of White civilisation in South Africa." But, he continued impressively, in one of those melodramatic now-the-time-has-come-to-choose pronouncements at which he was so adept, "the survival of white civilisation in South Africa is of more importance to me, even more important than expanded industrial development".[3]

Damning words in retrospect, but few of the Afrikaners so intent on jumping on the prosperity bandwagon of the 60s had many thoughts to spare for the survival of White Civilisation. They would not hold Verwoerd's failure to live up to his splendid words against him. On the contrary, they were only liable to revolt if he did live up to them – and proceeded to make a mess of the economy. Verwoerd was of course being perfectly sincere, but there was really very little he could do. Warnings about the awful consequences for white survival of economic dependence on a numerically superior and politically inferior black proletariat were the fashionable stock-in-trade of Nationalist politicians. Little was done about it, and that little after Verwoerd's death. This was the great internal contradiction of apartheid. Only a strong economy could allow the Government to be tough with local dissidents and to defy the outside world; in short, to remain on top. But all too obviously, economic strength was only possible through the frustration of the Nationalists' great aim of separating black and white on a territorial basis. Even if economically feasible, it was politically impossible. Certainly during Verwoerd's public career there were no serious attempts at territorial segregation. He and his colleagues took their refuge in the not so immediate future. 1978 would be the turning point, when the rate of economic integration would begin to decline.[4] Thus, as long as Verwoerd was Prime Minister, the Nationalist Government could, without too many qualms, continue to have the best of both possible worlds.

Such was the background to political events between 1961 and 1966. Not all Nationalists were enthusiasts for all of Verwoerd's policies. Some came from the right, others were, in later terminology, Nationalists of the *verligte* (enlightened) variety. Verwoerd's handling of internal dissent tells us much about the man and his technique as a politician.

A sympathetic foreign critic of the Government, Edwin Munger, has written: "It is fair to say, although there are those who disagree, that Dr. Verwoerd began on the right wing of his Cabinet and over time 'moved almost to the left – especially in his emphasis on at least theoretically radical solutions."[5] If this is true, it is only so in a very qualified sense. His Bantustan policy was certainly radical, in theory. Here Munger is right. The only very partial translation of theory into practice during Verwoerd's lifetime is usually blamed on the strength of right-wing sentiment in the National Party. Many, if not most, Nationalists thought independent black states were fine, as long as they remained only a wonderful ideal. Verwoerd always felt this constraint and could not go as fast as he wanted to. This is the usual argument of Verwoerd's apologists. Probably it contains a kernel of truth. Verwoerd had to endure plenty of criticism from Nationalists, particularly from the rural Free State and the Transvaal, that the Government was "doing too much for the Natives". He had to spend much of his time pacifying such critics, persuading them that his policies were really in the best interests of the white nation. But his behaviour with respect to the other racial groups in the country suggests that much of his radicalism was only theoretical, that given the opportunity to be more "left" he would not have seized it with both hands.

Verwoerd had always prided himself on the "logic" of his policies. To him there were only two ways: "integration" or "separate development". It was a favourite and unanswerable criticism of his that the United Party rejected both, that it stood for permanent white supremacy and that its policies were thus devoid of moral foundation. If the African were not given his freedom on a territorially separate basis from the white man then he had to be given the same rights in an integrated society, which would inevitably result in black majority rule. There was no middle way. The logic was indeed impeccable, but how did it apply to the other non-white races, the Coloureds and the Indians? Clearly, in the absence of a homeland for each group, both morality and Verwoerdian logic pointed to their integration with the whites.

The position of the Coloureds and that of the Indians was in principle the same, but it was the former who became the focus of Nationalist controversy. Unlike the Indians, the Coloureds were not only indigenous to South Africa, but had enjoyed real if limited voting rights on a common roll with the whites until they were finally removed from that roll in 1956, after a prolonged constitutional crisis. Since then they had elected four white M.Ps on a separate roll to represent them in the House of Assembly. The relatively small poll in these elections was only one of the many ways in which the Coloureds showed their disgust at the version of separate development foisted on them. Some influential Cape Nationalists, probably more noted for their education and intelligence than their numbers, had long felt that the Coloureds, both historically and culturally, "belonged with the white man". Not only was it right that they should be given a new deal, but political realism demanded it, as they might otherwise make common cause with the blacks.

The Nationalist daily in Cape Town, *Die Burger*, was the most prominent exponent of this line of thought. After the successful referendum, heralding as it did a new age, the paper decided that the time had come for a better dispensation for the Coloured people. Even before, in July, the editor, Piet Cillié, had written with obvious approval in his weekly column that many Nationalists strongly supported a new policy with respect to the Coloureds. In particular, they felt that the Coloureds in the Cape should be allowed to elect four members of their own race to Parliament. "This of course is only one part of the complex of plans which are being discussed by thinking people."[6]

Shortly after Sharpeville, the pro-Government South African Bureau of Racial Affairs (Sabra) appointed a commission to investigate the situation of the Coloureds. Its report, which was submitted in January 1961, was never published, nor were its recommendations accepted by Sabra, because, as one of the organisation's officials later explained, some of the commission's members wished to use the report to embarrass the Government. There can be little doubt that the recommendations would have done so. They were, it became known unofficially, that the Coloureds should be given the opportunity of becoming full citizens, and that they should be represented in Parliament by their own people.

Verwoerd did not have to wait till January to know that the commission's findings would be unpalatable. Talk of reform was in the air; the mere appointment of such a commission was ominous, suggesting as it did that existing policy towards the Coloureds was not wholly perfect. He now acted swiftly, to scotch all revisionist rumours of a change in the Party line. In a press interview after the referendum he once more trotted out his favourite argument that "small concessions" would inevitably lead to big ones; that it would all end in biological integration and a nation of coffee-coloured South Africans. If a Coloured had the right to enter Parliament he was liable to marry your daughter too. Verwoerd confirmed the eternal nature of Nationalist policy: it was "one of parallel streams and in the sense of separation, but within every stream it is the goal to achieve the fullest rights and opportunities for a particular population group, to protect them and to extend them". For the Coloureds, it came as no surprise to learn, the most immediate priorities were not political at all, but economic and educational. Training and experience in local government were also desirable. But every move to multiracialism, especially in the governing of the country, would lead to continuous "civil war" as each group tried to ensure its own existence. Ultimate justice for all was only possible through "separate, parallel development".[7]

Verwoerd's statement came as an unpleasant surprise to the Cape revisionists who had been hoping for better things under the republic. It was followed by weeks of vigorous polemics in the correspondence columns of *Die Burger*. Many Nationalists were clearly unwilling to accept that Verwoerd had spoken the final word about the future of the Coloureds. It was a new situation for him, accustomed as he was to laying down the law without fear of contradiction. He put it beyond doubt when he addressed a Nationalist conference on the Rand a week later. In what was to become one of his most notorious statements, Verwoerd told his audience that Nationalist leaders would have to stand "like walls of granite" on their colour policy: the existence of a nation was at stake.[8] Hitherto Verwoerd had been making those *ex cathedra* pronouncements at which he was so adept. It was a measure of his concern about the dissent in the Cape that he now convened a rare meeting of the Federal Council, the supreme authority of the National Party, which, with unsurprising docility, gave him the full support he demanded.

A few weeks later, on 6 February 1961, Sabra announced that its conference on "The Position of the Coloured People" had been post-poned indefinitely. Verwoerd's triumph became complete later that year when Sabra was purged: its new executive committee would henceforth consist of those whose conformity to Government policy was total and unquestioning.

The position of the Coloureds was the great "liberal" issue within the National Party under Verwoerd. Yet his victory over the revisionists was gained before the republic had really begun to function. From now on there would be no more serious proposals in public by Nationalists that Coloureds should sit in Parliament. The most they could expect, as Verwoerd made clear, was the right to self-government in their own residential areas. They would be able to control their schools and hospitals and so on, but their political rights would always be limited.

Verwoerd had not up till now given much thought to the Coloureds, taken up as he had been by native policy, the republic, unrest and foreign affairs. Now he applied his mind to the issue, to produce one of those specious rationalisations which sound as if they were made by someone who had been living on the lunatic fringe all his life. In an interview with *Die Transvaler* he said: "According to the theorists, there cannot be a state within a state. But when it concerns the future of a nation, a state structure can and must be created which, in practice, amounts to a state within a state. South Africa has reached a stage where it has become essential to give certain rights to the non-White groups ... If the price for their continued existence is that the theoretically impossible state within a state must be created, the Whites must be fully prepared to pay for it."[9]

No one ever took this mumbo-jumbo seriously, not even Verwoerd himself, for he was to make no attempt to refute the "theorists" by proving that there could indeed be such a thing as a Coloured state within a white state. It was patently an attempt to give respectability to his all too apparent determination to keep the Coloureds in a state of permanent political inferiority, in spite of all the self-righteous Nationalist accusations against the United Party that it wanted to keep the blacks in subjection forever.

So much is obvious. What is perhaps not so obvious is why Verwoerd had so little difficulty in putting the reformists in their place. The best answer is probably that they represented no one except themselves. A new deal for the Coloureds was an intellectual's issue, the cause of those Nationalists whose consciences had been bothering them about the way this minority was being treated. But political parties represent particular interests, and few of the interests represented by the National Party had much to gain by more justice for the Coloureds. There was, in short, little incentive for most Nationalists to get excited over Coloured rights. Their self-interest was not obviously involved, except in some uncertain long run when the Coloureds might decide, out of sheer gratitude, to make common cause with the whites if it ever came to a showdown with the blacks. It was not a good reason for being nice to the Coloureds; ordinary Party members and supporters cannot be blamed for not finding it persuasive. As for the continued injustice imposed on the Coloureds, this was unlikely to cause many Nationalists sleepless nights. People are expert at believing what they want to believe and had not Verwoerd himself, displaying again that fine talent for ingenious sophistry which had stood him in such good stead at the Poor White Conference in 1934, assured the whites that the Coloureds had never had it so good?

Rights for the Coloureds was therefore an issue for the educated and articulate few. Verwoerd's tough line was unlikely to have a high cost in electoral terms, as the result of the 1961 election was to show so decisively. But why was he so adamant in his insistence on no concessions at all to the Coloureds? Was this just another Verwoerd obsession? Would a more flexible man have responded in a more conciliatory way?

The manner of this response was indeed all Verwoerd. No one else could have combined such an unyielding stance with such preposterous arguments. It was simply absurd to maintain, as he did, that a concession in one sphere would inevitably lead to large-scale miscegenation, and to the disappearance of the Afrikaner with his precious white skin. The emergence of multiracial sport in South Africa after his death, another issue to which he applied his "thin-end-of-the-wedge" argument, has not led to far-reaching changes elsewhere, but simply to more multiracial sport. Here in fact was Verwoerd the super-Afrikaner again, intent on saving his adopted people from all kinds of strange perils, conjured up by his fantasy-prone mind. His mental state is strikingly conveyed in the remark he repeatedly made to his wife: "I am not going down in history as the man who led the Afrikaner people to bastardisation. If the majority is in favour of it, then I will resign."[10]

But, in a more basic sense, the nature, in contrast to the manner, of his response could have been little else. We have only to look at the heavy weather Verwoerd's entirely more pragmatic successors made of trying to be just to the Coloureds, to realise that Nationalist policy operates within pretty fundamental constraints. The crux of the matter is simply that any genuine policy of non-discrimination towards the Coloureds (and the Indians) must result in a loss of Afrikaner political control. The whites as a whole outnumber the Coloureds, but the latter and the English-speaking together outnumber the Afrikaners. Four Coloured M.Ps would only have been a drop in the ocean of the huge Nationalist majority in Parliament, but it could not have remained at that. As the Coloureds developed, pressures would have built up for more substantial parliamentary representation. Eventually, if the logic of democracy were accepted, not to mention the ostensible principles of the National Party, there would have been full political equality between white and Coloured. From being in a political majority, the Afrikaners would now have been in a political minority. It was only a distant prospect, but, given the premises, inevitable. It is doubtful whether the early *verligtes* who were so enthusiastic for a new deal for the Coloureds were fully aware of this dilemma. Probably they gave it little thought, which contrasts remarkably with their insistence on thinking through with remorseless logic the consequences of any policy of "integration" between black and white. Perhaps the difference lay in their realisation that whatever policy was pursued toward the Coloureds, they would always be outnumbered by the whites as a whole. They could never be as great a threat to white survival as the blacks.

Whatever the explanation, Verwoerd was only being brutally realistic when he so adamantly resisted all talk of reform. Fine words about moving away from discrimination had no effect when Afrikaner domination was threatened, even if only as a prospect for the remote future. Naturally he could not advance this as a justification, but with his famed sense of logic he must have been aware of it. He certainly believed in his publicised rationalisations and may even have attached more importance to them. But the basic similarity between his reaction to the demand for genuine political rights for the Coloureds and that of Vorster and P.W. Botha, despite their quite different expressions, suggests that *de facto* and permanent injustice to the Coloureds is a basic feature of Nationalist policy, not to be altered by the protestations of a few intellectuals.

If Verwoerd had to be so careful of such fundamental constraints, does it follow that he had little choice in his policies toward the Coloureds? Does it make any sense to criticise him for not being "liberal" enough to them, if there was not much else he could do? The answer is that while continued Afrikaner rule precluded any genuine policy of non-discrimination with respect to the Coloureds, there were many forms of discrimination which could have been softened or eliminated altogether. Vorster removed some of them to no electoral cost to himself. Verwoerd could have done likewise, had he felt so inclined.

Four Coloured M.Ps, or ten, or twenty, would certainly not have satisfied Coloured demands for full equality. Verwoerd was correct when he claimed that such limited representation could, by its very nature, be no solution to the problem of Coloured political rights. Here his "logic" was sound. But it was scarcely more logical to pose the only alternatives for South Africa as "integration" and "territorial separation" and then to reject both of them for the Coloureds. Neither the "liberal" policy of limited parliamentary representation for the Coloureds by their own people, nor the existing policy of representation by four white M.Ps, could be satisfactory if non-discrimination were the criterion. Equally, however, there could be no doubt which was the less unsatisfactory. Faced with these alternatives, Verwoerd unhesitatingly chose the course of more discrimination, incompatible though it was with the basic assumptions of his race policy. There is no reason to think that the political dangers, in terms of reduced electoral support from Nationalist voters, of a strictly limited number of Coloured M.Ps were considerable. It was only the implication of eventual political equality that was unacceptable – but such equality was hardly inevitable. In other words, even within the existing constraints on Government policy, Verwoerd could have done far more, at least with respect to the Coloureds, to show that "moving away from discrimination" was not just an empty phrase. That he did not do so suggests that Munger's view of him as gradually moving to the left during his political career is largely devoid of substance. Never, in truth, did he appear in a more totally unattractive light than in his refusal to tolerate the slightest overt dissent on this score within his own party, and in his unrelenting insistence on permanent subordination for the Coloureds. He thought he was standing between the Afrikaners and their "bastardisation"; in fact he was displaying to the whole world that invincible core of race prejudice that guided all his policies.

There is an instructive lesson to be learnt from this whole episode. "Liberal" reformers in the National Party could not command the support of effective interest groups; hence they failed. Successful pressure would have to come from outside the Party, whether within or outside South Africa. It was the worldwide condemnation of apartheid that made Verwoerd embark on his Bantustan enterprise, but he managed to resist all other pressures for "liberalisation". His successor, Vorster, had a less rigid view of what constituted capitulation; apartheid was considerably modified in carefully chosen fields such as sport and attendance at theatres, but there was no sharing of political power with the Coloureds and the Indians, let alone with those blacks who, to all intents and purposes, are permanent inhabitants of the urban areas.

Traditionally, Nationalist governments have been sensitive to pressures from the right. While the Nationalist "left" could always be disregarded at no serious electoral cost, the traditional conservatism of the Party rank and file made a similar disregard of its views an entirely more hazardous enterprise. It was on the right that power lay in the

National Party. Malan's first three successors, Strijdom, Verwoerd and Vorster, were the candidates of the right when they in turn became Prime Minister. (P.W. Botha narrowly defeated the right-wing candidate, and only because of the latter's involvement in the Information scandal.) Verwoerd was thus always exceptionally sensitive to pressures from the right. Even when, in spite of such pressures, he did not deviate from his Bantustan policies, he took immense care to explain why it was essential not to do so. That he was subject to constant criticism from within the Party for going too far in giving "separate freedoms" to blacks is certain. Thus, when opening the Free State Nationalist Congress in 1962, Verwoerd paid special attention to criticisms which had supposedly been made by Graaff, but which were really implicit in the issues for discussion which had been submitted by various branches of the Party. His response to the common complaint that the Government was doing too much for the blacks was astute. To his credit, he made no attempt to deny the charge, but justified his policies in terms of white self-interest. What was being done for the blacks was for the benefit of the whites themselves. It was really an enterprise in white survival.[11]

Critics from the far right would never be silenced as long as Verwoerd was Prime Minister, but he managed to contain them quite comfortably. Prophecies of doom could virtually be disregarded at a time when South Africa was entering the most prosperous period of its history. Nor, during his lifetime, did the whites have to make substantial economic sacrifices for the development of the homelands. Some of the extremists did eventually come into the open. They formed the Republican Party to contest the 1966 general election under the slogan of "white *baasskap* over the whole of South Africa", but for them the outcome was disastrous. The strong electoral support they claimed proved to be a figment of their imagination: all 22 of their candidates lost their deposits. They probably were right in claiming support, but this was for their views; their defeat was partly a reflection of the fact that the Government had actually not done all that much for the blacks.

This was the ultimate constraint on the Government's freedom to act: the imperative of not being seen as too liberal to Africans. Within these limits, and provided that separate freedoms did not seriously jeopardise a high rate of economic growth, the Government was free to do pretty much what it liked. A political scientist has commented: "While it is true that developments in parliamentary systems in the past half-century have tended to exalt the executive at the cost of the legislative, this tendency has been carried to its furthest point in the South African governmental system. In constitutional terms there has developed a remarkable degree of cabinet cohesion free of the stresses and temperament which often characterise British cabinet ministerial relationships … The clue to understanding what passes for much of the political activity in South Africa lies in knowing that neither 'pressure groups' nor 'people' – to use Truman's words – are in control. South African ministers are themselves able to turn a deaf ear to the pleas which come from many quarters."[12] In the final analysis, it seems, the overriding imperative of maintaining white supremacy has concentrated power to an extraordinary degree in the hands of the South African Government.

In practice, in the first half of the 1960s, this really meant Verwoerd. By all accounts, he dominated his Ministers. One of them, Frank Waring, has said it in so many words: "Verwoerd was a man who would listen, ask you questions and show that he knew a great deal about your portfolio. But then he said, 'This is what we will do.' And that was that. Verwoerd wanted to make all the decisions. Verwoerd was a very strong character and he dominated the cabinet completely … Verwoerd was so overwhelming and dominating as Prime Minister that it was simply inconceivable that the time would arrive when he was not there …"[13]

There was thus no strong, effective dissent to him within the National Party. The Opposition, as represented by the United Party, was weak and divided, and was in any event to support the Government in some of its most coercive measures. It is true that the English-speaking were not as yet voting for the Nationalists in large numbers, though Verwoerd went to considerable lengths to conciliate them. Towards the end of 1961 he took the unprecedented if unsubtle step of appointing two English-speakers to his cabinet, the former United Party M.Ps, Alfred Trollip and Frank Waring. Yet white unity did not come quite so easily. The very existence of the National Party was based on that kind of Afrikaner exclusiveness that Verwoerd himself once did his best to propagate. Its continued cohesion would still largely depend on Afrikaner values and traditions. Many years would have to pass before English-speakers would even begin to feel at home in the Party. But Verwoerd's policy was to show marked dividends. Increasingly, he came to be seen as the embodiment of a white South African nationalism, of the whites' determination to remain on top and survive. If not many English-speakers joined the National Party a considerable number began to support it at the polls, as the result of the 1966 general election was to show for the first but not for the last time.

While Verwoerd had little to fear from white political opponents, inside or outside the National Party, black opposition was another matter. The A.N.C. and the P.A.C. had been banned, but African nationalism did not cease to exist or, in Verwoerdian terms, "agitators" would still be prepared to play upon the emotions of the ignorant black masses. The unrest and disturbances, which had reached a climax with Sharpeville, did not subside after 1960. They continued, but inevitably in different forms. They also provoked a Government reaction which contributed to making the years between 1961 and 1965 among the most violent in South African history. It was a time of growing prosperity, but also of coercion and repression.

After the failure of the general strike during the inauguration of the republic, its organiser, Nelson Mandela, and other former A.N.C. leaders decided to form an underground revolutionary movement openly committed to violence as the only means of overthrowing white supremacy. It was called *Umkhonto we Sizwe* (Spear of the Nation). They had at last realised that in the South African environment, there was no future for Gandhian precepts of non-violence. They belonged to a different time and a different place, but not to a South Africa where peaceful resistance had only led to fewer rights and more repressive legislation.

Umkhonto's way of continuing the struggle was through sabotage. It would blow up Government offices and disrupt communications and power lines. Endearingly old-fashioned as they may seem in the present age of terror, the saboteurs would take care not to endanger human lives. The expectation, or rather the hope, was that public order would collapse and with it, eventually, white supremacy too.

Umkhonto's first acts of sabotage were on the Day of the Covenant, 16 December 1961, when post offices and other government buildings in Johannesburg, Port Elizabeth and Durban were attacked. Over the next three years there was to be widespread sabotage throughout South Africa. *Umkhonto* was probably the main force behind the violence, but it was not alone. There were two other underground movements dedicated to the overthrow of white supremacy. One, much the most brutal of the three, was an offshoot of the P.A.C. and called itself *Poqo* (Pure). It was bitterly anti-white and probably had a substantial mass following, mainly in Cape Town and the Transkei. The third, much the most ineffectual of the three, was the African Resistance Movement, a multiracial organisation consisting mainly of white professional men and students.

1962 was a year of exceptional violence. *Poqo* had no scruples about taking lives. It was responsible for attacks upon African chiefs and policemen, three of whom were killed in the Langa township near Cape Town. In November, at Paarl, also near Cape Town, some *Poqo* members were arrested for the suspected murder of black officials, whereupon a mob attacked the police station, burnt homes and shops, and killed a white man and woman. The following February *Poqo* members hacked five whites to death in the Transkei. All this was taking place against a background of continuous sabotage attempts by *Umkhonto* and the A.R.M., while chiefs and headmen in the reserves who collaborated with the Government were assaulted and sometimes murdered.

These stories are unexciting today, but at the time they were incredibly alarming. The Government took to itself unprecedented powers to suppress revolt. There were already many repressive laws on the statute book, but the General Laws Amendment Acts of 1962, 1963 and 1964 immeasurably widened the range of arbitrary power which could be exercised by the authorities, as well as the capacity of the security police to deal with anyone even suspected of dissidence, let alone of subversion. The first of these laws, generally known as the Sabotage Act, broadened the definition of sabotage and made it a capital offence. The Minister of Justice was given the power to place anyone under house arrest. A year later the police were given the right to detain suspects for any number of periods of ninety days, without bail, and in solitary confinement. In 1964 the Minister was given the power to extend banning orders before they lapsed. In 1965 the Criminal Procedure Amendment Act empowered the Attorney-General to hold witnesses in prison for a period of up to 180 days. There were other laws, but these suffice to give the flavour of the new legislation.

As Minister of Justice, B.J. Vorster was the ideal choice for under-taking a campaign of mass repression. Like Verwoerd when he became a member of the cabinet, Vorster was a man with a past, of which he was frequently reminded during his dramatic career as Minister. Even the National Party at first held his O.B. record against him, and rejected him as one of its candidates in 1948 for this reason. Vorster nonetheless stood as an independent, to become famous overnight as the man who lost Brakpan by only two votes. He eventually entered Parliament after the 1953 general election, soon making a favourable impression on his fellow-Nationalists by his formidable abilities as a debater. Verwoerd made him Deputy Minister of Education, Art and Science in October 1958; three years later he was appointed Minister of Justice.

His predecessor, F.C. Erasmus, had not impressed his colleagues with his handling of the internal situation after Sharpeville. To outsiders it comes as a surprise to learn that he was regarded as insufficiently ruthless. No one was ever to accuse Vorster of this serious shortcoming in a South African Minister of Justice. From the very first he used the powers given him with great gusto, even with apparent relish. The figures speak for themselves: when the 90-day measure was suspended in January 1965, 1,095 persons had been detained during the 18 months of its operation, 575 had been charged with specific offences, 272 were convicted, 210 were discharged, and 93 were at the time still awaiting trial.[14] In his five years as Minister of Justice, Vorster banned 453 persons. During 1964 671 had been charged with contravention of the security laws. Five were sentenced to death, nine to imprisonment for life, and eight to twenty years' imprisonment. Most of those convicted were sentenced for belonging to banned organisations or for furthering the aims of these organisations; 285 went to prison for five years and 19 for five to seven years.[15]

Defending his exceptional harshness as Minister of Justice, Vorster was to invoke the ultimate justification of all authoritarians: it was essential for the safety of the State, of which he was the best judge. In spite of the Suppression of Communism Act of 1950, the menace from the extreme left remained. The State was threatened by a Communist conspiracy, liberals were knowingly or unknowingly being used as Communist tools in furthering the proletarian revolution. Vorster was not going to send out his police to fight the Communists with "bare hands": "With our experience of Communism we have found it necessary to acquire greater powers than are absolutely essential in order to block all loopholes."[16]

It was a familiar formula, but exceedingly effective. The consequences for the radical opponents of white supremacy were devastating, whether they were Communists or not. *Poqo* was crushed by the middle of 1963. *Umkhonto*'s leader, Nelson Mandela, was captured in August 1962. The following July its other leaders were seized on a farm at Rivonia, near Johannesburg. The African Resistance Movement had been committing ineffective acts of sabotage and in July 1964 most of the leaders were captured, although one of them, John Harris, was still to commit the most shocking act of violence of these years by exploding a bomb at the Johannesburg railway station. One person was killed and fourteen others seriously injured. Harris and a number of *Poqo* members were hanged while other leaders of the revolutionary movements were sentenced to long terms of imprisonment. By the end of 1964 the campaign of violence to break the South African Government had itself been broken by violence.

The cost to civil liberties had been immense. South Africa had by now acquired a body of repressive legislation which was to be steadily enlarged by successive governments over the years. Vorster was to claim that these powers had not been abused. No one had been detained without good reason; the police had been given strict instructions not to misuse their powers over detainees. Unfortunately, so he admitted, there were a few isolated cases of police ill-treating their prisoners, but of course it was well known that neither in Russia nor in South Africa was it possible to make an omelette without breaking eggs. When it did happen, Vorster asserted, he acted "quickly and decisively" against the culprits,[17] a claim which must be seen in the light of the total failure of Vorster's Government to establish which police official or officials had been responsible for the death of Steve Biko, who died in 1977 as a result of injuries while in custody.

Two conclusions are appropriate. There was never much of a Communist threat, nor was the safety of the State in any considerable danger. Of the three main underground movements, Communists played a leading role only in *Umkhonto we Sizwe*, which was nonetheless controlled by former members of the A.N.C. Its leaders were to justify such co-operation on the grounds that theoretical differences were a luxury which could not be afforded in the fight against repression. Later in 1964 leaders of the Communist Party were convicted for belonging to an unlawful organisation, but there was never any proof that they had participated in the sabotage campaign. Vorster was to claim that the African Resistance Movement was "a Communist organisation founded by Bram Fischer", leader of the Communist Party in South Africa, but, whatever its source of funds, it was clearly nothing of the kind, consisting rather of disillusioned members of the Liberal Party who had lost their faith in reason, persuasion and the inspiring example of Gandhi. Communist involvement in *Umkhonto*, probably the least ineffective of the three bodies, was important, but it was never a Communist organisation, nor was it controlled by them. But Vorster was not the first strong man to label his opponents as Communists. It was after all an obvious stratagem. A government fighting off the onslaughts of Communist revolutionaries appears in a better light than one ruthlessly suppressing blacks driven to desperation by the brutal apartheid regime, the alternative myth propagated by enemies of the Nationalists.

The safety of the State was hardly endangered. If the strategy was to unnerve the whites and frighten them into sweeping concessions, then it was a lamentable miscalculation. The sporadic acts of sabotage, and even the few killings, were not enough to instil panic into the white ruling class. At the time they were recognised for what they were: exercises in futility. What was so astounding was that the revolutionaries could have believed that actions such as theirs could have led to the overthrow of a regime so powerful and so determined as that of the Nationalists. After the Rivonia arrests, the threat, such as it was, was effectively past. In spite of Vorster's continued scaremongering, Verwoerd saw this clearly enough. On 31 August 1963 he told *The Cape Argus*: "I see no sign of any major upheaval coming in South Africa ... internally this country, I believe, is more stable than it has been for years." He had no illusions about the revolutionaries: "We have our instigators and saboteurs but they are, in fact, relatively few in numbers." Verwoerd added, accurately enough, in words which go far to explain his own preoccupation with foreign policy after 1961: "Our real trouble comes from outside."

The attempts to end apartheid by violence had confirmed one of the best established generalisations about revolutions in the modern world, namely, that a successful internal revolt in any country is all but impossible without substantial support from the armed forces. In South Africa, for reasons only too transparent, this could not happen. Verwoerd was right when he said that South Africa's real troubles came from outside.

If the internal threat was not nearly as frightening as Vorster had tried to make everyone believe, was the Government reaction simply a case of overkill? Did it incur the opprobrium for ruthlessness and persecution for no good reason? Could it have stamped out the revolt with less severity?

No doubt gentler methods would have availed, but these would have involved real costs as well. Suppression of the revolt would not have been so swift. Acts of sabotage, and murder too, would have continued. By no flight of the imagination could they have shaken the Government, but any successful act of defiance would have helped to keep black expectations at an unrealistically high pitch. In the townships immense enthusiasm was generated by *Umkhonto*'s initial successes. The prospect of freedom was suddenly less remote. The Government had no doubt that there was only one course. Blacks had to be informed in the most emphatic way possible that freedom would not be theirs soon. Otherwise, unrest and disturbances would continue; hope and encouragement would never quite disappear. It was essential that the political expectations of the blacks should not be allowed to rise as they did during the previous decade. Exemplary harshness was necessary for black hopes to die.

Quite fortuitously, the rapid economic growth of the 1960s, and the higher black incomes to which it gave rise, strengthened this imperative for a resort to the big stick. Heightened black expectations, induced by a combination of growing prosperity and never quite suppressed political ambitions, could have led to an explosive situation. The violent Government reaction in the post-Sharpeville years left no doubt that white supremacy would still be around for quite a while. Blacks would be free to enjoy their higher incomes, but they were to have no illusions about the prospects for political change.

The political quiescence of the 1960s was an essential condition for a high rate of growth. Continuing unrest would have been a fatal deterrent to the willingness of capitalists, domestic and foreign, to invest. The favourable economic climate was only made possible by a display of power unique in South Africa's history. From the Government's point of view, and presumably that of the white population as a whole, it was an eminently sensible decision. In the nature of things it could not prevent future, larger-scale Sharpevilles. They could be predicted at the time and eventually of course the first outbreak came, in 1976, when a new generation of blacks had arisen, forgetful of the repression of the previous decade, and more aware than ever of their own disabilities and of world condemnation of the Republic's system of government. Black political docility, in short, could not be expected to be a permanent feature of the South African scene.

12 Bantustans and Capitalism

There was another reason for giving short shrift to the fundamental political demands of blacks. If they were frustrated convincingly enough more Africans could be expected to turn to Bantustans, very much a second best, but preferable to nothing at all.

Formally, a new era began in 1959 when Verwoerd accepted the principle of autonomous states for South Africa's blacks. It had been largely a response to foreign reactions to apartheid; its roots in Nationalist theory and practice were shallow. After Sharpeville Verwoerd became more aware than ever of the overriding urgency of providing the outside world with a rationale for apartheid that could be made to appear morally defensible. This required the translation of theory into at least superficially convincing practice.

Of the homelands, the Transkei was by far the most eligible candidate for the benefits of positive apartheid. It already had a tradition of local government before the system of Bantu Authorities was extended to it in 1956. Territorially, it was a single entity, unlike some of the other homelands, which were so widely scattered into separate areas that they could not conceivably become autonomous states in their existing form. The Transkei was extremely backward economically, but in this respect it was no different from any of the other homelands.

The Bantu Authorities system developed rapidly in the Transkei, building as it did upon the previously established council system. But its introduction was no smooth process. Unrest in the eastern part of the Transkei had been endemic since 1959. In revolt against Bantu Authorities and other official policies, the Pondo tribesmen of this area attacked and even murdered chiefs and councillors whom they suspected of being Government "stooges", refused to pay their taxes, rioted and burned huts and kraals. The Government's response had been the usual drastic one. Late in 1960 it issued a proclamation for the whole of the Transkei which placed severe restrictions on meetings of Africans, sealed off certain areas, and gave the police and chiefs extensive powers of arrest and banishment. Thousands of troops were rushed in; by the end of May the revolt had been suppressed. Although most of the troops were then withdrawn, unrest continued and the emergency proclamation remained in force until 1965.

In April 1961 the Government was apparently surprised by the members of the Transkei Territorial Authority when they demanded complete freedom and independence for the territory. A few days later, however, the Government indicated that it would not object to self-government. In December Verwoerd met leading Transkeian politicians in Pretoria and told them that the Government was prepared to cooperate with them in bringing self-rule to the territory. The following month he announced in Parliament that the Transkei would be given a constitution before the end of 1963, which would eventually allow it to have full domestic control. At first the Transkei would be a ward of the Republic, but gradually blacks would supersede whites in the running of affairs. Whites in the territory would still be represented in the South African Parliament, while Transkeian blacks in the white areas could only have political rights in their homeland.[1]

A five-year development plan for the Transkei had been drawn up which provided for aid to agriculture and the extension of roads and water and electricity supplies. A special development corporation would be established which would attempt to co-ordinate and stimulate economic development. Verwoerd made the startling suggestion, further proof of his economic illiteracy, that white entrepreneurs would allow the corporation to utilise their initiative, skills and capital, without the incentive of profit. It would use the services of private firms which "are helpful and obliging but do not expect to acquire private ownership or a business or branch of their own within the Bantu area". Eventually blacks themselves would be allowed to take over these undertakings, as their skills developed and their knowledge grew. "If the Bantu, when they are in full control, wish to invite White firms, that is their affair."

The constitution was jointly drafted by the Government and a recess committee appointed by the Transkei Territorial Authority. It bore the strong imprint of Verwoerd's own ideas. When the committee went to Pretoria in March 1962 for consultation, it was told by Verwoerd that the constitution had to be based on the "traditional form of government of the Bantu", which meant that chiefs, whose positions were of course subject to ultimate Government approval and control, would play a dominant role in the new self-governing Transkei.[2] Verwoerd's instructions were obeyed. In the Legislative Assembly established by the Transkei Constitution Act of 1963 there were 109 members, of whom 64 were chiefs sitting *ex officio*, while only 45 were elected by popular vote. In fairness to Verwoerd it must be pointed out that this closely resembled the official majorities in British and French colonies in the early 1950s; it could reasonably be seen as only the first stage in an inevitably unfolding process of emancipation. Also, the recess committee, not at all averse to Verwoerd's views about the supreme importance of chiefs in the emerging Transkeian democracy, had recommended at the March meeting that there should be 95 *ex officio* members out of a total of 131. This proportion was reduced only after Verwoerd had expressed his opposition.

But it was a minor sacrifice. In December 1963, after elections had been held for the Assembly, the Government's favoured candidate, Chief Kaiser Matanzima, was elected Chief Minister by 54 votes to the 49 gained by Paramount Chief Victor Poto. Matanzima had the support of a majority of the chiefs, while Poto was supported by a majority of the elected members. It was indeed surprising that with the preponderance of chiefs and the very strong pro-Matanzima pressures by the Government behind the scenes, his majority should have been so small.

The overriding feature of the new self-governing Transkei was that the Government intended to remain in control for at least the foreseeable future. The Transkei was to be a guided democracy, with the emphasis on the adjective. The emergency proclamation of 1960 was still in force when the election was held in 1963 and was only to be repealed two years later. The form of government was dyarchical. The Transkei cabinet, elected by the Legislative Assembly, would have control in a number of fields of which some of the most important were direct taxation of Transkeian citizens, agriculture, education, the maintenance of law and order, and public works. Carefully excluded, and still under the control of the South African Government were, *inter alia*, defence, foreign affairs, internal security, customs and excise, postal services, banking and currency, railways and harbours.

The constitution itself had been very much what Verwoerd wanted it to be. He and his Ministers emphasised the role of Transkeians in the drafting, but there is no doubt that the Government had been intimately involved in the whole procedure. Attempts to find what Transkeians, within and outside the territory, thought of the constitution were minimal. When the Transkei Territorial Assembly met in May 1962 to discuss the draft constitution it was told by the Secretary for Bantu Administration and Development, C.B. Young: "It rests in the hands for the Government of South Africa to decide what it will concede to the Transkei in the form of self-government. The committee has been consulting with the Government for a long time and the basis of agreement, you might say, has already been reached." Young advised the members to "accept what has been offered to you and be thankful for this great step forward in the historical and constitutional development of the Transkei Territories".[3] When some members tried to oppose the constitution they found themselves hampered by the ban on public meetings, as well as by relentless pressure from Government officials. In any event, all laws passed by the Legislative Assembly were subject to the approval of the South African Parliament, and had to have the assent of the State President.

Initially therefore the South African Government's control over the Transkei on its road to independence was unashamedly conspicuous. Initially too opponents of the Government persisted in calling Matanzima and his colleagues "stooges" of the Nationalists, hirelings of Pretoria whose self-interest lay in carrying out their masters' commands to the final letter. But the South African Government's control steadily diminished after 1963, and so did the habit of describing Matanzima as the tool of the Nationalists. It is easier now than it was then to realise that this was a dynamic situation which could not be controlled as completely as the Government would have wished. In the interests of its own credibility it had to allow the homeland leaders some room for manoeuvre, a certain amount of leverage. If Matanzima were not to appear a stooge after all, he had to be seen putting a certain amount of successful pressure on the South African Government. His most considerable achievements in this direction probably came after Verwoerd's death, as when he managed to persuade the Government that white capital should be allowed into the Transkei. But the general point holds, that it was a fluid situation which the Government was inherently incapable of shaping entirely according to its own desires.

In one respect the harsh post-Sharpeville strategy had shown the hoped-for dividends. The suppression of the A.N.C. and the P.A.C., with the disappearance from public view of their leaders, had done much to divert the political consciousness of blacks into ethnic channels. Edwin Munger wrote a year after Verwoerd's death: "With the old methods to establishing a power base denied to African nationalists as such, the stage in South Africa is being taken over, as planned by key figures within the Afrikaners' National Party, by essentially tribally based Africans. The Matanzimas, as well as the various successors to the Victor Potos of the Transkei have their counterparts in other tribal areas. This infant nationalism is not really African nationalism in the sense of the last three decades ... What is developing in the rural areas is a Xhosa, Zulu, and a Sotho nationalism."[4] Matanzima was the first of the Bantustan leaders to have his stature enhanced by this largely Government-determined trend. Whereas before politically conscious blacks had looked to men like Luthuli and Sobukwe for leadership and inspiration, now, increasingly, for Transkeians at least, it was to Matanzima. His new prestige was reflected in the Transkei elections of 1968, which reversed the result of five years before, and gave him a popular majority. Over this short period the voters of the Transkei had apparently shifted from being opponents to being supporters of separate development. Had Verwoerd been alive, he certainly would have said, "I told you so."

Politically, Bantustans could never be a solution to South Africa's problems. Of all the black areas, the Transkei had the best prospects for becoming an independent state. Judged by the not very exacting standards of post-colonial Africa these were undeniably good. The objections of the Government's opponents were only valid if Western criteria were accepted. They were irrelevant in the context of Africa where states as economically backward and politically immature, in short, as "non-viable" as the Transkei, if not more so, were becoming independent every year. For a long time still the economic reality of Africa would be dependence on more advanced economic powers. In this respect the Transkei was only typical and not the exception. Nevertheless, it remained true that of all the homelands the Transkei had much the best chance of becoming a characteristically backward and possibly brutal African state. But even by the standards of Africa there was little prospect of most of the other homelands, scattered and fragmented as they were, of ever becoming so. The Government's policy could at most only be a partial answer to the political question in South Africa. It was a positive development in so far as it undermined the traditional status quo of masters and servants and gave black leaders a limited but real basis for exerting effective political pressures. But, in the final analysis, the policy of separate development could merely postpone, but not evade, the choice confronting South Africans of all colours, namely, what kind of multiracial state they wanted to live in.

Perhaps Verwoerd's extreme right-wing critics had a better intuitive grasp of the genuine dangers of the new situation. They sensed that Bantu homelands could not really guarantee white survival as Verwoerd so confidently promised. Their own answer, *baasskap* for ever, was even less likely to do so, but it had the attraction of all short-run solutions. As Harold Laski once asked: "What has posterity ever done for me?"

272

Verwoerd thus had to face heavy pressure within his own party. He had to convince the traditionalists, quite inaccurately, that policies had really changed very little, that he was simply pouring old wine into new bottles. He stressed the continued control of the South African Government over the process of independence. It was merely an "adjustment" within the old policy, not at all a departure from it. It was an unfortunate necessity, dictated by world events. He himself would have much preferred the traditional policies, hallowed as they were by Voortrekker practice, but it was no longer possible in the modern world. It had become necessary "to seek a solution in a continuation of what was actually the old course, namely, of separation".[5] Perhaps Verwoerd did really believe all this but, if so, he misunderstood his own policies. It was important to him to see Bantustans as in the direct line of descent from the hallowed ways of Paul Kruger, but the truth was of course that Verwoerd was no old-time conservative. His policies were a decisive break with the Afrikaner past. He, least of all, super-Afrikaner as he was, could never admit to this, but such was what it amounted to.

In addition to their fragmentation, the great obstacle to the homelands ever becoming a feasible solution to South Africa's race problem was their extreme economic backwardness and indeed stagnation. They were dependent for their survival on the employment of most of their able-bodied men in the white areas. In 1966/67 the total product of the homelands was 1.9 per cent that of the Republic. Average output per head was R34, compared with R611 for the remainder of South Africa. Black family incomes in the larger towns were on an average three to four times the average homeland income, even when the latter was supplemented by the remittances of migrant workers, which were estimated at one-fifth of their earnings. With remittances included the average per capita income in the homelands came to R75.[6]

Migrant labour was an essential condition for the survival and increase of the population of the black areas. For enterprising Africans employment in the white urban areas therefore had far more attractions than trying to live precariously in the overpopulated homelands. But this gave rise to apartheid's most intractable problem: the presence of a large and growing number of black workers in town, indispensable for white prosperity and impossible to send back to stagnant areas unable to support them.

The Government's answer had been the promotion of border industries rather than the black areas themselves, where, between 1960 and 1966, only 35 new "industries" were established, providing employment for 945 blacks. This was scarcely "separate development", nor was it conspicuously successful in providing jobs for Africans. On the contrary, in manufacturing, of which only about 12 per cent was in the border areas, the non-white proportion of the labour force increased from 70 per cent in 1961 to 75 per cent in 1966. The Government's initial policy was to provide incentives for businessmen to establish themselves in border areas. There were inducements in the form of subsidised power and water, tax concessions, reduced railway rates, loans at low interest rates, exemptions from minimum wage provisions, and preference in the award of government contracts. Not many businessmen considered these inducements good enough to transfer their undertakings to such remote parts of the country. During the period June 1960 to December 1966 industrial employment for blacks in the border areas and the homelands increased by 44,600. As the South African economy was growing rapidly during this period, it is not unlikely that most of the increase would have occurred even without official incentives. It has been estimated that the latter were only responsible for about 18,500 of the new jobs for Africans.[7] The Permanent Committee established to deal with industrial decentralisation was decidedly unhappy with the results. In its report for the period June 1960 to December 1965 it concluded: "As indicated, border industries succeeded in employing 8,200 Bantu per year over the past five years. When compared with the average annual entry of 41,000 Bantu into secondary industry for the years 1961–2 to 1963–4, this figure is still too low."[8]

The Government had itself diverted few resources to the development of the black areas. Between 1956 and 1961 less than R16 million had been spent on the development of the reserves. In the 1960s considerably more was spent. Under the first five-year plan for the homelands, ending in 1965, expenditure came to R114 million. It was probably no coincidence that the annual growth in the black areas during this period was just over 5 per cent, compared with 3.5 per cent on average for the previous fourteen years. This higher growth rate was still less than that of the economy as a whole; it was indeed such general growth, rather than official expenditure, which was probably the main explanation for the improved economic performance of the homelands. Yet, in spite of increased spending, agriculture, which still employed the overwhelming majority of blacks in the homelands, continued to stagnate. As population growth was high, of the order of three per cent a year, it is unlikely that black per capita income in the homelands grew very significantly after 1960. In the showpiece Transkei agricultural output per head actually seems to have decreased during the late 1950s and the early 1960s.[9]

An obvious answer, in part, to the development problems of the homelands was the admission of white capital. But on this point Verwoerd was completely adamant. If white entrepreneurs wished to invest in the homelands they had to make funds available to the Bantu Investment Corporation, which in its paternalistic way would decide what to do with them. Verwoerd was to justify his policy in terms that would have done credit to any left-winger, old or new (one economist indeed refers to his "curious stylized communist vocabulary"[10]): "The South African Government would not allow interference in the Transkei, nor would it allow, as had recently been suggested, White investors to invest money in the Transkei and take profits from the territory in the period that the Bantu were still unable fully to do so themselves. South Africa helped the Transkei as a guardian. If industrialists were allowed to exploit the Bantu areas, the Bantu would resent it all the more when they realised what had been taken from them.

"Opposed to this South African policy was the Oppenheimer Capitalist Policy. Mr. Oppenheimer mixes his Progressive Party political policies with his financial policies and advocates what amounts to international colonial capitalism, when he says that White capital should be allowed to operate in the Bantu areas ..."[11]

Of course, this was appallingly crude stuff. No profound knowledge of economics is required to know that foreign investment can make a vital contribution to economic development. That at least seems to be the assumption of those less developed countries which are so eager for foreign capitalist investment. An economist has commented: "Investments are made in order to *build* productive facilities, to expand output capacity and the potential for additional income. In the case of foreign investment, the real issue is whether the facilities thus built represent a *net* addition to the volume of capital in the host country, or simply take the place of existing facilities or of new facilities that might otherwise be built by indigenous enterprise."[12]

In the state of economic backwardness of the black areas, especially with their shortage of homegrown entrepreneurs, there was little reason to believe that investment by white capitalists would be economically harmful. The exclusion of such capital would only help to perpetuate their poverty and deprivation, their role as exporters of labour to the white areas. This has indeed been seen as the basic rationale of the Government's policy towards the homelands. Verwoerd's prohibition on white capital would then simply have been an attempt to provide an ideological camouflage for providing capitalists, especially in the border areas, with adequate supplies of labour from the reserves: "These are to function as reservoirs of cheap labour within easy access to industry rather than to become the economically developed regions pictured in apartheid ideology."[13] Whatever the general merits of typical left-wing pronouncements such as these, and they are not conspicuous, Verwoerd's policy in this respect was no part of any grand Nationalist scheme for keeping the homelands backward, as the lifting of his ban on white capital in these areas after his death shows only too clearly.

This was a rather typical Verwoerd obsession, which he insisted on imposing on everybody else. It was deeply held, virtually to the point of fanaticism. When the prominent Afrikaner businessman, and substantial contributor to National Party funds, Anton Rupert, advocated the opening of the reserves to white capital, Verwoerd did not forgive him and remained hostile to Rupert for the rest of his life. As a member of the cabinet Verwoerd had come to appreciate the contributions that capitalists could make to that economic development which so powerfully increased the State's ability to suppress internal dissent and deter foreign intervention. But he never quite abandoned his pre-Ministerial suspicions of the "British-Jewish capitalism" of which the head of the Anglo American Corporation, Harry Oppenheimer, seemed so prime an exemplar. Capitalists were all right – in their place, and preferably without Jewish antecedents. As long as the Government was in good Afrikaner hands there would be limits on their exploitative propensities. But in an area as backward as the Transkei, political power would not be strong enough to countervail economic power. The way would be open for unchecked capitalist exploitation and the subjection of the hapless Xhosa to an infinitely worse master than they had ever known before. It is some such process of reasoning that best explains Verwoerd's total rigidity in the face of demands for the opening of the reserves to white capital. Whatever the explanation, about his rigidity there can be no doubt. Once Verwoerd got an idea into his head, it was virtually impossible to dislodge it.

His ban on white capital also tells us much about a by now familiar feature of Verwoerd's personality. In politics and economics his approach was the same. His intellectual arrogance was such that, once he had made up his mind, it was inconceivable to him that any other view could be right. If others were not prepared to listen, they must be made to listen. If they would not obey, they must be forced to obey. Whether it was in the announcement of his homelands policy, or in responding "like granite" to demands for Coloured M.Ps, or in banning white capital from the black areas, it was Verwoerd who decided. He meant well by his fellowmen, even those who were not Afrikaners. But his basic assumption was that he knew better than others what was for their own good. At best Verwoerd was a well-meaning paternalist, at worst an unbending autocrat. Whatever he was, Verwoerd never appreciated or understood the basic assumption of any free society, namely, that an individual's right to choose also involves the right to make wrong decisions.

Verwoerd's hostility to white capital in the homelands brings us to the heart of one of the basic issues of South African history. Let us consider some statements which once upon a time, actually not so long ago, were regarded as self-evident.

Verwoerd was perfectly willing to act against the interests of capitalists when he thought it in the larger interest of the nation.

Government racial policies were inimical to business interests.

Till the late 1960s these statements would have seemed blindingly obvious. It was taken for granted by informed observers of all political complexions that there was some conflict between white supremacy and a high rate of economic development. Few were inclined to dispute that policies which discriminated on the basis of colour and not of ability had some adverse implications for growth. The difference lay in the respective responses. Nationalists were inclined to regard it as an unfortunate necessity, the price to be paid for white survival. "I would rather see South Africa poor but white than rich and mixed," in the classic words of Verwoerd. Liberals also saw it as unfortunate but, in their own version of economic determinism, as a temporary phase before the inexorable pressures of a modern industrial economy swept away the antiquated structures of apartheid and presumably, although they were not so clear about this, white supremacy too. But in the 1970s such views came to be rejected with barely concealed contempt by a new generation of self-consciously revisionist historians. Many of these were exiles from South Africa; all of them were Marxists of some variety or other. Particularly influential in Britain, the basic thesis of the revisionists was that the "incompatibility" between growth and apartheid was entirely spurious. Far from any conflict, discrimination and apartheid were in fact both the outcome of the South African version of capitalist development and essential to its survival. The purpose of the State was to make South Africa safe for capitalism. The liberal interpretation of the country's history in terms of racial interaction was the merest conventional wisdom, which actually served "an ideological function in diverting critical attention away from the extensive collaboration of the capitalist system – both in South Africa and internationally – in the economic operation of white supremacy".[14] At long last the truth could be told: the history of South Africa was the history of the class struggle, which only appeared to take the form of racial conflict.

One of the more articulate exponents of this approach, F.A. Johnstone, has summed up the general neo-Marxist thesis in the following terms: "Economic development has thus not been undermining the basic labour structure of white supremacy in South Africa. Access by Africans to the essential means of economic power remains severely restricted and controlled, the distribution of income remains grossly unequal, and the general coercive powers of the Government over African labour have been growing rather than diminishing. The core structure of labour discrimination remains strongly entrenched ... The enormous power and prosperity of the whites in South Africa is (*sic*) based on this systematic exploitation of African labour.

"The strong persistence over time of this discriminatory labour structure testifies to the collaboration of the different white interest groups in perpetuating it. Capitalist business, far from being incompatible with the system, secures high profits through very cheap, unorganised and rightless labour; white nationalists and white workers obtain prosperity and the material strengthening of white supremacy.

"In fact," Johnstone concludes, "far from undermining white supremacy, economic development is constantly reinforcing it."[15]

In the neo-Marxist canon the migrant labour system in particular has been seen as playing a pivotal role in maintaining white supremacy, capitalist profits and black subjection. The massive apparatus of official controls over African workers in the white areas has, so it is argued, kept their wages low by reducing their bargaining power vis-à-vis employers. It was, in effect, a system of forced labour which prevented blacks from advancing through "extra-economic coercion".

The basic difficulty with this thesis, which has become very much the current orthodoxy in certain British and South African academic circles, is that there are no practical means of subjecting it to the test of possible refutation; it is, in other words, unscientific. It starts from the assumption that the South African State's main purpose has been to make life enjoyable for capitalists. Now they are actually an extremely heterogeneous group, including such diverse subdivisions as mine owners and manufacturers, which can again be further subdivided into smaller groups. All this diversity makes any uniformity of interests unlikely except in

278

some highly general, abstract sense, such as a favourable environment for making plenty of money. In South Africa this may well require the maintenance of white rule. But it does not follow that some Government policies may not have been exceedingly inimical to some capitalist interests. This has indeed been so. The gold mines have had the right to recruit migrant workers from territories outside South Africa, a privilege not granted to capitalists in other sectors. But taxation of the mines has traditionally been heavy; discriminatory railway rating has raised the cost of mining machinery and materials, and tariff protection, while undoubtedly beneficial to those capitalists whose industries were being sheltered from foreign competition, has only added to the costs of the manufactured goods purchased by the mines.

Similarly, migrant labour has not been the unvarnished blessing it supposedly has been for capitalists, who always buy in the cheapest market. Controls over black access to the urban areas has limited the supply of workers and raised labour costs higher than they would have been had entry been unrestricted. Rapid turnover of workers has acted directly contrary to the interests of those employers who would benefit from a stabilised labour force which can acquire skills on the job.

In these and other obvious ways there has been a clear conflict of interest between Government policy and the ability of at least some capitalists to make profits. Any Government, at any point in time, is responsive to a diversity of interests. So it has been with the Nationalist Government. Self-evidently, it has been more responsive to the interests of whites than those of blacks. Within the white group it has seen the Afrikaner interest as its own special preserve, while farmers have been among those Afrikaners who have benefited more than most from Government paternalism. It is hardly a coincidence that this can all be related to political power and influence. The whites can vote and the blacks cannot. For years the Nationalist Government consisted exclusively of Afrikaners. The South African political system has given rural voters an influence quite out of proportion to their numbers. All this simply means that political factors have been crucial in explaining the policies of South African governments. They cannot be accounted for in terms of a kind of reductionism which sees South African history as just another case study of the primacy of economic factors as expressed through the class struggle.

It does not follow that the Nationalists have been oblivious to the interests of employers. They have been only too well aware of the importance of a healthy investment climate for the high growth rate and strong economy so vital for the preservation of white privilege. After gaining power they so successfully overcame their anti-capitalist prejudices that no more was heard, at least in public, of avaricious British-Jewish money-grubbers. It became Nationalist policy to promote industrialisation "in every possible way", as Verwoerd put it to the Afrikaanse Handels-instituut in 1961. So it was entirely unsurprising when there proved to be considerable compatibility of interests between white supremacy and capitalist well-being. But the important point is that employers' interests have only been among some of the interests which have weighed heavily with the Government. When it has been considered in the overriding national, i.e. white, interest the Government has not hesitated to adopt policies which have clearly harmed private enterprise, as in its limiting of the supply of black labour to the white areas. There is the sad case of Anton Rupert who, as the leading Afrikaner capitalist and prominent Nationalist supporter, should have been a source of pride and joy to the Government, and perhaps even was, but he and his fellow-capitalists were still not allowed to invest in the homelands, nor did it save him from Verwoerd's permanent enmity for daring to suggest such a course.

Further labouring of the point is unnecessary. The symbiosis between apartheid and capitalism does not exist. South African governments since 1910 have been concerned with maintaining white supremacy. A strong economy has been an essential means to this end, placing as it does more resources at the disposal of the Government. In a market economy this has necessarily entailed an environment which has provided some stimulus to private enterprise. But in a number of ways continued white domination has demanded policies which place severe constraints on profit-maximisation. If capitalists have an interest in white supremacy it is precisely because they have been allowed to make profits in spite of these constraints. It does not follow that they have gained from discrimination as such. In a system of this nature at least some capitalists benefit from official policies, but it is not difficult to find others who do not, or not to the same extent. But the mere fact that some do prosper is enough to convince those who believe as a matter of dogma that Marx was right, that apartheid has simply been a means of making capitalists happy. It is a question of finding those capitalists who do benefit from Government policies and then hastening to the appropriate conclusion. As there will always be some who do thrive and prosper under apartheid there is no way in which this can be refuted. But it is not much of a theory. It cannot explain such differential benefits except by dragging in obvious political factors, which cannot readily be accommodated by this kind of analysis.

What then was the nature of the state over which Verwoerd presided? It was not one in which economic change would inevitably destroy apartheid, as liberals so fondly believed. Nor was it one in which apartheid and discrimination were essential features of the South African variety of capitalism, as radicals so dogmatically asserted. The relations between economic development and political change were considerably more complex than either side was prepared to concede. The South African Government found itself with substantial immunity to the pressures of particular interests. Its overriding commitment to white supremacy meant that it could, with much impunity, confer or withhold favours as it wished. The Government could afford the displeasure of many special interests, knowing that continued white rule was still more important to these interests than their specific grievances. It could be objected that, if it became unpopular enough, many of its supporters would turn to the United Party. The answer is that the unpopularity would have had to be very considerable indeed. After 1953 there was no serious prospect of a change of government in the foreseeable future. The United Party was as committed to white rule as the Nationalists, but its determination and ruthlessness were so manifestly inferior to theirs that "voting Nat" was by far the safest thing to do. Because therefore of its own dedication to white supremacy and the embarrassing uselessness of the official Opposition, there was little chance of the Government being swept out of office by a disgruntled coalition of special interests. This did not mean that the Government was not responsive to the demands of such interests. It certainly was, and in the most realistic way, as its pampering of the white agricultural sector, where so much of its support came from, shows only too convincingly. Also, any obvious interference of the doctrinaire application of ideology with white prosperity could be expected to have disagreeable electoral conse-quences. But within these limits the Government had plenty of scope to do what it pleased. Power was thus highly centralised; under Verwoerd it came close to one-man rule. He had a particular antipathy to being pressurised by special interests. It went against his heroic vision of himself as the disinterested saviour of the Afrikaner people, willing at all times to make the supreme sacrifice for the *volk*.

It was thus a state not primarily concerned with upholding capitalist interests. They were important, but not decisive. If it was required by white domination then capitalists too had to accept policies which restricted their pursuit of self-interest. It was also a state in which economic development would not inevitably lead to greater political democracy. The tremendous boom of the Verwoerd years, 1961–6, was accompanied by unrelenting repression. But it remained true that there was an inherent incompatibility between industrialisation and apartheid which could hardly persist indefinitely. It did not necessarily mean the disintegration of white rule through economic development; it was quite possible that the latter would be the ultimate casualty. Nevertheless, whatever their short-run accommodation, in the long run their continued co-existence was dubious. Finally, it was also a state in which, contrary to all radical predictions, discrimination had proved compatible with a substantial rise in black living standards, in spite of the fast increase in black numbers. Even more surprisingly, although it only came after Verwoerd, apartheid was compatible with a rising black share in national income. Even if black-white income inequalities were still very large, after 1971 black wages in all sectors rose on average more rapidly than those of whites.

In short, events in South Africa after the Second World War have not been of such a kind as to give comfort to the conventional wisdom of either liberals or radicals.

13 Maker of Foreign Policy

Verwoerd's obsessive concern after the coming of the Republic was with foreign policy. He had no apprehensions about domestic disturbances as a threat to white rule. As Minister of Justice, Vorster was eminently satisfactory, the last word in *kragdadigheid*, secure in his conviction that it was better that ten innocent men should suffer rather than that one guilty man should go free. The internal overthrow of the South African Government had never been very likely; Vorster made sure that it was impossible. But externally the pressures on South Africa were becoming more intense. Decolonisation made for a palpably less secure world, reflected every year in the increasingly shrill criticism of apartheid at the United Nations, an organisation whose changing annual composition faithfully portrayed the most recent phase of the end of empire.

For Verwoerd's predecessors, Malan and Strijdom, it had not been a grave problem. Malan had not welcomed African independence and knew little about the continent, but in his day Africa was still almost entirely under colonial rule. Strijdom had been more realistic. He knew that many independent black states would soon be emerging and pleaded for peaceful co-existence between them and South Africa. But it was under Verwoerd that decolonisation happened at a tempo foreseen by no one. As the scramble out of Africa gathered momentum, and as even such pervasively backward colonies as the British High Commission Territories of Basutoland, Bechuanaland and Swaziland were being prepared for their destiny as independent states, it was clear that South Africa's whites had to adapt to a totally new era of history, foreseen by scarcely any of them.

Naturally Verwoerd had no enthusiasm for the new order. He saw the continent as handed over to immature and backward states which for many years still would be incapable of conducting themselves in even a tolerably civilised manner. The colonial powers, Britain, France and Belgium, in their indecent haste to get out, had ditched their responsibilities and handed over Africa to Communist penetration. But, far worse, they, with the British as main culprits, had endangered the position of the white man on the continent, whom they were prepared to sell out in "the auction sale of appeasement".[1] He did not oppose the principle of independence for African colonies; he had after all accepted it for the homelands in South Africa. However, he was quite sure that it was happening too fast. The Congo was the classic example, and was to serve him well in his propaganda both at home and abroad.

Verwoerd always believed that the West's "appeasement" of adolescent states in the hope of winning them as allies against Communism was only a phase of world history. He never lost his faith that South Africa's return to international respectability was merely a matter of time: "I have no doubt in my mind that as we progress with the application of our solution, the world outside and all sections of our own population will realise that our own way, based on justice and goodwill to all, must succeed."[2] In the final analysis, South Africa was simply misunderstood. Eventually, the success of its policy and its undoubted anti-Communism would restore South Africa to its rightful place as a valued member of the Western community.

Time was all-important. While waiting for the West's return to sanity, the Government pursued a foreign policy which made a fetish of forms, of international correctness and legality. The United Nations Charter precluded interference in the domestic affairs of any member state. Smuts had appealed to this provision when he was attacked in 1946 at the United Nations, then still an organisation with very few Afro-Asian members, because of his Government's treatment of South Africa's Indians. It was one respect in which the Nationalists were happy to emulate the celebrated advocate of holism and internationalism. For them the issue of morality was irrelevant. After all, which country was perfect and why single out South Africa? So, after 1948, South African spokesmen at the United Nations took their stand on the principle of non-interference, that the domestic affairs of South Africans concerned only themselves and no one else. This defensive posture was often reinforced by *tu quoque* arguments: many other U.N. members were offenders against human rights; they had no business trying to find the mote in the South African eye when beams were protruding from theirs. It was an approach which became the forté of Verwoerd's first Minister of External Affairs, Eric Louw, who expounded his views at U.N.O. with an unsubtle aggressiveness badly calculated to retain South Africa's diminishing number of friends.

Although Verwoerd's problems in foreign policy were considerably more acute than those of his predecessors, he had advantages denied to them. He could expect a greater measure of support in his conduct of foreign affairs from the white population as a whole than could either Malan or Strijdom. For this there were several reasons. Britain's attempts to ingratiate itself with the new states of Africa and Asia had inevitably alienated a growing number of English-speaking whites. Macmillan on "the wind of change" was for them the symbol of a degenerate Britain which had turned its back on the white man in Africa. Also, after 1960, African membership at U.N.O. grew very rapidly indeed, and with it South Africa's isolation in that organisation. But independence belied the early optimism of Western liberals. The obvious inability of most of these states to be anything but backward dictatorships only made South Africa's whites more determined never to subject themselves to the same kind of regime. Verwoerd was for them the strong man who stood between anarchy and order. His status was vastly enhanced by the failure of the prophecies of the disaster that would surely follow South Africa's departure from the Commonwealth, while the circumstances of its departure proved conclusively that the old white-dominated Commonwealth, to which so many English-speakers were so attached, existed no more. Verwoerd had said that the adverse economic consequences would be minimal; he had been triumphantly right. On the contrary, the first years of the South African Republic were a time of spectacular economic expansion. Not only did it raise his prestige, but South Africa's economic strength also made it invulnerable to external attack.

Verwoerd was thus fortunate in that his foreign policy had strong bi-partisan support. The United Party might carp and cavil and allege with its usual unreal optimism that its own policies would make it possible for the West to support South Africa in international bodies. It was taken no more seriously than it deserved; in any event, the U.P. believed as firmly as the Government in maintaining white rule. Further, as the Republic's foreign policy was so closely related to domestic policies, support for the former could easily merge into support for the latter. In circumstances such as these, criticism of the Government could, with not too much ingenuity, be portrayed as unpatriotic, a conclusion many Nationalists found wholly acceptable.

Verwoerd conducted South Africa's foreign policy, on the whole, with confidence and skill. He had two Ministers of Foreign Affairs, the Oxford-trained and tactful Hilgard Muller succeeding the truculent and abrasive Eric Louw in 1964, but essentially Verwoerd was his own Foreign Minister. Policy-making was his preserve; Louw and Muller were little more than his emissaries. Bi-partisanship and a strong economy justified his confidence; his skill revealed a natural flair for international politics and a flexibility uncharacteristic of his dealings on the home front. This latter aspect was perhaps not so surprising. In domestic policies Verwoerd's authority was virtually unchallenged. He could afford to be hard and uncompromising. In foreign affairs he had to be entirely more circumspect. South Africa was only one state among many, and could not simply do as it wished. Verwoerd gave nothing away, but neither did he merely confine himself to the familiar statements of diehard resolve, although there were plenty of these. He knew when to be conciliatory; it was a valuable asset in his defence of white rule in an unsympathetic world.

Verwoerd's main aim was to prevent international action against South Africa. After Sharpeville anti-apartheid resolutions became an annual ritual at the United Nations. In 1962 the General Assembly passed a resolution calling for economic and diplomatic sanctions against South Africa, although Britain and the United States voted with the minority. In 1963 the Security Council unanimously adopted a resolution calling for an arms embargo. This time Britain and the United States were among those which complied with an anti-South African resolution, although other Western powers such as France and West Germany continued to supply the Republic with arms. In 1964 an international conference was held in London to debate the feasibility of economic sanctions against South Africa, although the results were disappointing to all activists. In 1965 the General Assembly of the United Nations passed a motion recommending mandatory sanctions against the Republic. A sign of the changing times, on this occasion Britain and the United States abstained, compared with their opposition to the similar motion of three years before.

Like its predecessor, the League of Nations, the United Nations had no means of enforcing its resolutions. The countries specially outraged by apartheid, themselves mostly dictatorships whose brutality was only tempered on occasion by administrative incompetence, had little to lose by sanctions. It was the Western countries which did stand to be deprived, and they were understandably not prepared to suffer materially simply because it was demanded of them by United Nations majorities conspicuously versed in hypocrisy and double-talk. Over the years they felt duly compelled to express their own horror at apartheid. After Sharpeville the Western countries would be found voting more and more frequently for anti-apartheid resolutions, but, except for participation in the arms embargo by Britain and the United States, this was as far as they were prepared to go.

Britain especially had much to lose. Its trade with South Africa was substantial, while the return on foreign investment in the country was high enough to overcome the apprehensions of many British capitalists about putting capital into as high a risk area as the Republic was supposed to be. Although British investments in areas like the United States and Australia were larger, earnings from South Africa were higher. Between 1964 and 1966 average earnings on British capital in South Africa was £60 million, compared with £56 million for Australia and £53 million for the United States. American investment was smaller than that of Britain, but it too was particularly profitable. In 1967 United States earning from capital investment in the Republic amounted to 30 per cent of all American earnings from Africa. Trade links with Japan and Western countries, especially West Germany, were strengthened during the 1960s. Between 1960 and 1966 South African exports to Japan grew by more than 300 per cent and to West Germany by more than 400 per cent.[3] The capitalist world had, in short, a stake in South Africa which, while hardly essential to its own survival, was substantial enough to prevent anything as Quixotic as participation in sanctions aimed at ending white minority rule.

Verwoerd of course knew this very well. It was an awareness reflected in the propaganda of the Department of Information, which stressed the economic advantages offered by South Africa to foreign entrepreneurs. It pointed out, tendentiously but irrefutably, that economic development benefited all South Africans, of whichever colour. Effective sanctions would harm both black and white, as well as the Republic's black dependencies, Basutoland, Swaziland and Bechuanaland. Throughout the decade of the 60s the prospect of positive international action to end apartheid remained the special hallucination of Afro-Asians and the left.

Had this been the only threat posed by the United Nations then it could have been safely ignored. But the Republic was far more vulnerable when it came to the Mandated Territory of South West Africa. South Africa had never accepted the United Nations' authority over the area. It maintained that the mandate had lapsed when the League of Nations became defunct. In 1946 Smuts had asked the General Assembly to agree to its annexation by South Africa, but his request was rejected. The Assembly proposed instead that South West Africa become a Trust Territory of the United Nations, but it was a proposal which no South African government was ever prepared to accept. When the International Court of Justice was asked for an advisory opinion by the General Assembly in 1950, it declared that South Africa remained bound by the mandate, but that it was under no legal obligation to place the territory under United Nations Trusteeship. Nevertheless, according to the Court, the United Nations had the right to supervise the administration of South West Africa, as long as it did not go beyond the supervision exercised by the Mandates Commission.

South Africa rejected this interpretation, although it was happy enough with the finding that it was not obliged to make South West Africa a United Nations Trust Territory. From now on conflict between South Africa and the U.N. over the issue never ceased. Resolutions condemning South Africa's administration of the territory far outnumbered those which denounced apartheid. For the Nationalist Government, with its legalistic approach to South Africa's international position, these resolutions could not be as contemptuously ignored as attacks on apartheid. However doubtful the U.N.'s own status vis-à-vis South West Africa, the territory was indubitably not part of South Africa. U.N. resolutions on South West Africa could not simply be rejected on the grounds that they interfered with South Africa's domestic affairs.

Verwoerd's own vision of the future of South West Africa was the same as that for South Africa: it was the way of separate development. He put it unequivocally in the territory's capital city, Windhoek, in September 1962: "I say that the destinies of the Republic and South West Africa are inextricably linked. We shall not be driven away ... There is no difference between the position of South West and that of South Africa."[4] A few weeks before he had appointed the Odendaal Commission to prepare a five-year development plan for the territory. When it reported early in 1964 the Commission recommended the now standard panacea: Bantustan for South West Africa. There was to be a "white" area consisting of about 44 per cent of the territory, as well as ten homelands comprising about 40 per cent. The Commission also proposed a major development programme of more than R114 million for the next five years, but nothing could conceal the fact that here, in a territory as huge and as sparsely populated as South West Africa, was the final *reductio ad absurdum* of apartheid, of ideology which had finally become unhinged from reality. In spite of all the uncertainties about the territory's future, nothing could be more certain than that Verwoerd's way would not be the way for South West Africa. Yet for years the Government clung tenaciously to the make-believe that in essence there was "no difference between the position of South West and that of South Africa". Instead of preparing the white inhabitants of the territory for a future that could not but be different from that of South Africa, Verwoerd encouraged illusions that the whites would never have to join in a common society with the other races. Had he been more far-sighted, less hidebound by doctrinaire obsessions, he would not have left South West

Africa with so little time for changes that were inevitable. The Odendaal Report, in spite of being the white elephant that it so deservedly was, and Verwoerd's own foolish pronouncements made it clear that the territory would continue to be administered as an integral part of South Africa, although the Government would never take the final step of incorporation, for then it would have repudiated its own professed belief in the strict observance of international law. All in all, Verwoerd left South West Africa a legacy that was fraught with disaster.

It was in tactics, in the day-to-day manoeuvering of politics, that Verwoerd's strength lay, not in grand visions of the future, which have a habit of looking absurd and grotesque only a few years after their original formulation. Verwoerd displayed considerable astuteness in his handling of the United Nations. In spite of his poor opinion of its standards of integrity, he preferred, when possible, to conciliate the world body. Thus, he showed rare flexibility when in 1961 he invited its Secretary-General, Dag Hammarskjöld, to visit South Africa. Verwoerd suggested that first-hand knowledge of the country's policies might help to avoid misunderstandings. Hammarskjöld accepted the invitation and came to South Africa on a visit that was apparently so successful that plans were being made for another, when he died in a plane crash. His successor, U Thant, was a Burmese who made it plain that his duties as an international civil servant took a decided second place to his emotional commitment to the Third World. He was not invited to South Africa. But Verwoerd had emerged well from the episode. He had shown a willingness to talk to foreign critics when they themselves came with open minds, not blinded by the standard anti-South African prejudices.

A year before, the dispute over South West Africa entered a new, hazardous phase for South Africa, when Ethiopia and Liberia, as ex-members of the League of Nations, asked the International Court of Justice to rule that the mandate was no longer valid as apartheid was being practised in the territory. It was a clever move, turning the South African Government's own favourite weapon against itself. If the judgement went against South Africa, then rejection would fatally undermine the Government's legalistic stance. But acceptance spelt even worse disaster in terms of Verwoerd's thin-end-of-the-wedge philosophy and his declared belief that the destinies of the Republic and South West Africa were as one. If apartheid were dismantled in the mandated territory it would inevitably happen in South Africa too. Given these alternatives, there was little doubt that Verwoerd would have refused to heed an adverse judgement, with all the international opprobrium that would have brought, as well as the instant destruction of the Government's painfully acquired reputation for international rectitude.

Verwoerd took this development as seriously as it deserved. He sent a formidable legal team to the International Court at The Hague, but from the first the prospects for South Africa appeared bleak. In 1962 the Court gave an interim judgement, by eight votes to seven, that rejected the Government's contention that it had no jurisdiction in the case. The Court subsequently proceeded to examine the merits of the plaintiffs' case, centring around such issues as the restriction of the franchise to whites alone, the pass system and racial segregation in general. Litigation was protracted, but the record of the Court's previous pronouncements on South West Africa suggested clearly enough that the ultimate judgement would go against South Africa.

While the case was still pending, the U.N. Committee on South West Africa was trying, with conspicuous lack of success, to make its way into the territory. The Committee had been the creation of the international body's Trusteeship Council, which had asked South Africa to abolish all apartheid laws in the territory and had then appointed the Committee, with instructions to visit South West Africa. But the South African Government predictably refused to permit the Committee to enter the territory, and Britain would not allow it to enter from Bechuanaland. The Committee returned to New York, a total failure. But the Trusteeship Council now appointed another committee on South West Africa, with similar instructions. Once again South Africa refused entry for the committee as a whole, but this time invited its chairman, Victorio Carpio of the Philippines, and its vice-chairman, Dr. Martínez de Alva of Mexico, to visit South West Africa. They arrived in May 1962 and, after travelling through the territory, came to highly favourable conclusions about South Africa's administration of its mandate. But on leaving the Republic they repudiated the joint communiqué they had issued with the South African Government, producing instead another report which called for sanctions against South Africa. From now on Carpio was to issue ever more incoherent explanations of his own participation in the original communiqué, even claiming that his confinement to bed while the drafting took place had been the result of his coffee having been poisoned. In his individualistic way Carpio was a worthy emissary of the United Nations Organisation. The whole farcical episode did nothing to raise the U.N.'s prestige, while Verwoerd's flexibility had once again showed marked dividends.

In July 1966 the International Court at last came to a decision – and an extraordinary one it was too. By eight votes to seven it found that Ethiopia and Liberia had no *locus standi* in the case. The Court could not pronounce, it held, because the plaintiffs had established no legal right to the claims they had submitted. It seemed, and still seems, an inexplicable decision after the Court's rejection of South Africa's arguments four years earlier. It now refused to make any judgement on South Africa's policies in the territory, on whether apartheid and discrimination were indeed being practised, as of course they were. The Court had said nothing about the merits of South Africa's administration; it had not approved of its policies in South West Africa, but the decision was nonetheless, as Verwoerd put it, "a major victory". The U.N.'s attempt to get at South Africa through its "Achilles heel" had failed. The General Assembly's subsequent setting aside of the Court findings and its "termination" of South Africa's mandate was so obviously the decision of judges in their own case that the Government could ignore it with impunity, aware that its own legalistic approach, by the skin of its teeth, and more by luck than anything else, had once more proved sound.

Verwoerd's handling of the United Nations had been triumphant, even if chance had played a prominent role. There would be no effective international action against apartheid through that futile body. But it did not end the prospect of collective action against South Africa from abroad. One possibility was the threat of joint action against the Republic by the African states themselves.

The Government's attitude to the new states of black Africa had always been ambivalent. Once it became clear that the process of decolonisation could not be reversed or even delayed, the Government tried to make the best of an unfortunate business by stressing the advantages to African countries of economic and technical cooperation with South Africa, so well placed to assist them. But there was no question of diplomatic relations with these states as far as Pretoria was concerned. Verwoerd was to justify this attitude in 1964 in terms of the expense of formal diplomatic representation, favouring instead the idea of a roving ambassador from South Africa who would maintain contact with the black states, which could themselves send ambassadors to the Republic for day visits.[5] It was an elaborately specious argument, designed to conceal the very real strain that would be imposed on traditional South African prejudices by the presence of a black diplomatic community which would have to be treated on the basis of complete equality with the whites. Basically it reflected how little white South Africans were still prepared to accept that the world had changed and that they too were part of Africa, instead of being a fragment of Europe on a continent with which they had hardly anything in common.

As it turned out, there was never any strong prospect of diplomatic relations between South Africa and the independent states of the continent. Egypt's representative in South Africa, a survival from colonial days, was withdrawn in 1961. Two years later the South African Consul-General in Nairobi was recalled, shortly before Kenyan independence. Henceforth the Republic's ties in Africa would be confined to the remaining white-ruled areas: Rhodesia and the Portuguese colonies of Mozambique and Angola.

In May 1963 the Organization of African Unity was formed in Addis Ababa. It was a body which from the first showed unyielding hostility to the South African Government and its policies. Denunciation of apartheid was a powerful unifying force among states which otherwise had little in common except economic backwardness, political instability and, with a few exceptions, a colonial past. But it could hardly go beyond invective and abuse. In 1964 the proposal was made at an O.A.U. meeting that an African High Command be established, with the long-term aim of destroying white supremacy in the south by force. The resolution was not approved, for it was perfectly obvious that a combined military assault on South Africa was out of the question. The O.A.U. decided instead to rely upon a Committee of Liberation, previously established in 1963, which would give aid to "freedom fighters" and resistance movements.

In May the same year, the Algerian Prime Minister, Ahmed Ben Bella, said in a speech that Africans had no right to think of eating while their "brothers" were dying from oppression in South Africa and the Portuguese territories: "So that the peoples still under colonial rule may be liberated, let us all agree to die a little."[6] It was a perfect example of the demagoguism so fashionable on the emotional subject of apartheid, from a ruler whose time of power was short even by African standards. In practice, it proved that African states were reluctant even to spend a little. Material and financial aid to the Committee of Liberation was meagre and, in spite of the guerrilla warfare which later developed in southern Africa, it was never a body which impressed as a spearhead for black revolution in the subcontinent.

While the African states were, for all practical purposes, impotent in their attempts to overthrow white rule, they did have considerable nuisance value. Apart from making life difficult for South Africa in the General Assembly of the United Nations, they succeeded in having it excluded from a growing number of international bodies. In principle the issue of apartheid was of no obvious relevance within technical agencies such as the World Health Organization, the Food and Agriculture Organization and the International Civil Aviation Organization. Their rules, in any event, did not provide for the expulsion of members. This was no deterrent to their Afro-Asian members, who made their normal operations impossible through such well-orchestrated tantrums as frequent walkouts. In many of these bodies South Africa was left with little choice but to withdraw, as it did from the International Labour Organization in 1961 and the World Health Organization in 1965. Particularly unfortunate for the Government, in view of its stress on technical and economic cooperation with the rest of Africa, was the country's forced withdrawal from the Economic Commission for Africa and the Commission for Technical Cooperation in Africa. It was also as a result of Afro-Asian pressure that South Africa was excluded from the Olympic Games after 1960. South African planes and shipping were excluded from the air space and harbours of most independent African states. At the United Nations resolutions were passed by large majorities calling for South Africa's expulsion, but they had no legal basis, and South Africa refused to leave of its own accord. The Afro-Asian states had however very largely succeeded in isolating South Africa in world affairs.

It was an isolation which Verwoerd minimised or made light of. He believed that isolation in race policy could only be an asset in the prevailing climate of world opinion. The price for non-isolation was impossibly high, for it was no less than the abandonment of apartheid. In March 1962, in the House of Assembly, he quoted the Dutch statesman, Kuyper, who had said, "In isolation is your strength." Verwoerd continued: "As far as South Africa is concerned I want to repeat it in respect of our colour policy – in isolation in the sphere of colour policy lies our strength. If we were to agree to the demands of other nations because in that sphere we were afraid of the world isolation then we would go under. But isolation in this one sphere does not mean complete isolation. There is a lot of cooperation gained from states in other spheres." For him the way was clear, as always: "Without any hesitation my choice is to have fewer friends and ensure the survival of my nation."[7]

But in spite of the hostility of the O.A.U. and the substantial isolation it managed to impose on South Africa, black states in the southern part of the continent inevitably had to cooperate with the Republic, however partially and reluctantly. Malawi, Zambia and the High Commission Territories were in no position to participate in any economic boycott of their powerful neighbour. Hastings Banda of Malawi refused to support the O.A.U.'s demand for an economic and political break with South Africa; Zambia openly admitted that it could not afford to cease trading with the Republic. The High Commission Territories, in particular, could never conceivably be anything but economic dependencies of South Africa, to which they exported thousands of migrant workers every year.

It was the dependence on the Republic of these especially backward areas, Basutoland, Bechuanaland and Swaziland, that allowed Verwoerd to project his own brand of internationalism. Britain's refusal to allow South Africa to incorporate the High Commission Territories had been a sore point with Prime Ministers since Hertzog. They were a permanent reminder to the Afrikaner of the imperial factor against which he had struggled so long, and of his incomplete mastery, as he saw it, in his own house. Britain was only prepared to do so with the consent of their inhabitants, who were understandably reluctant to entrust themselves to the mercies of South Africa's white rulers. The issue became still more sensitive as decolonisation gathered momentum throughout Africa and Asia, and as it became apparent that even backwaters such as these would eventually form part of the wave of the future. Independence for the Protectorates, and on the principle of multiracialism so repellent to Nationalists, could have unfortunate repercussions in South Africa itself, where the watchword for black emancipation was still gradualism, on an eternally ethnic basis. Moreover, during the early 60s the territories were becoming havens for political refugees from South Africa, who frequently escaped dramatically across the border in flight from the Republic's police. Britain's willingness to accept them did not improve relations with South Africa.

Against this background Verwoerd made his appeal to Britain in September 1963 that it should entrust the Republic with the task of leading the Protectorates to independence. He too had been an advocate of incorporation, but its obvious impracticability had led him to raise with Harold Macmillan the possibility of a joint trusteeship over the territories by Britain and South Africa. Macmillan had promised to consider Verwoerd's proposal, but South Africa's departure from the Commonwealth was probably the cause of it not being taken any further. Now Verwoerd made a similar proposal, in public: Britain should cooperate with South Africa in planning the orderly development of southern Africa, including the Protectorates, with the aim of consolidating the black and white areas. In particular, the Republic's guardianship would involve a decisive shift from the principle of multiracialism. In effect, the High Commission Territories would be developed as Bantustans, with all the obvious benefits which that policy would confer on their inhabitants. Verwoerd appealed to the British Government to allow him to explain to them just what would be in store for them under separate development. But no one was interested in Verwoerd's explanations. From the people of the Protectorates there were signs of considerable alarm; from Britain there was no response at all.

Now came the ingenious shift in Verwoerd's approach. Later in 1963 Britain announced that the territories would be given independence, making it clear, once and for all, that South Africa would be allowed no role in their constitutional development. Incorporation or formal trusteeship was now finally ruled out. Verwoerd accepted the situation. He announced that South Africa would pursue a policy of friendship with its smaller neighbours. From now on Verwoerd would regard the Protectorates and the Bantu homelands as common participants in a process of decolonisation and emancipation.[8] Independence for the former, he realised, was not necessarily inimical to South Africa's interests, provided they were under reasonably "responsible" governments. Even if they were not they would still be bound by the constraints of their environment, destined for ever to be satellites of the Republic. Once independent they could of course become havens for terrorists and political refugees but unless they wished to incur massive retaliation, they could not play a really significant role in subverting white rule.

Increasingly, therefore, the Government saw the possibility of a multinational state system emerging in southern Africa. Verwoerd spoke about a possible multinational common market "in which none of the member nations would have political control over any of the others, but in which all would cooperate to their mutual benefit".[9] Previously, he had invoked the analogy of the Commonwealth, in which there would be "cooperation between sovereign independent states … for common political interests".[10] Common market or commonwealth, South Africa would inevitably be the dominant partner in any such alliance of states. Once having established its pre-eminence in the south on the basis of a broadly cooperative internationalism, South Africa would feel free to establish firmer ties of cooperation and acceptance with the black states to the north. It was a reflection of South Africa's mood of confidence after the remarkable economic recovery and expansion following Sharpeville. It was relatively quiet on the home front; the threat of international action had, for the time being, proved a mirage. Just then, all things seemed possible.

Rhodesia's unilateral declaration of independence in November 1965 did not destroy the mood, but made the task of African acceptance that much more difficult. The Nationalists had never been enthusiastic about Rhodesia's policy of racial "partnership". *De facto* it enabled the five per cent of the Rhodesian population who were white to rule the country, while allowing them to claim that they did not discriminate as did the Boers down in the south. While the Republic and Rhodesia had in common the practice of white supremacy, the window-dressing was different; in both countries the ruling groups took these differences very seriously indeed. Verwoerd, in particular, was never prepared to accept political union with a country which, even if it was only in theory, accepted multiracialism, "for then two states would come together which maintain opposite principles", and that, as everyone knew, was truly an "impossible situation".[11]

Nevertheless there were all too many advantages from having a white-ruled state to the north, whether founded on erroneous principle or not. Rhodesia had been the dominant partner in the Central African Federation, of which the other members had been Malawi and Zambia (as they later became), countries with even fewer whites than Rhodesia. The Federation had broken up in 1963 because it had by then become clear that the blacks in all three member states wanted no part of it. But while Zambia and Malawi went on to independence, it was impossible to allow Rhodesia to do so except under a black government, euphemistically referred to as "majority rule". Even before the break-up, however, in 1962, the white Rhodesians had finally broken with the past of spurious partnership. They voted into power the Rhodesian Front, committed to independence under white rule.

Before U.D.I. in 1965 Verwoerd had carefully refrained from expressing support for a white government in Rhodesia. There were after all those insuperable ideological differences, nor did South Africa want to be seen as the universal champion of white rule when it was trying to present a more civilised international appearance. Yet when U.D.I. came Verwoerd did not hesitate. He refused to support the sanctions imposed on Rhodesia by Britain, and backed by a United Nations resolution. He immediately issued a statement rejecting boycotts in principle, while criticising Britain for dragging all U.N. members, including South Africa, into what was a "domestic" issue. At the same time he stressed the political differences between South Africa and Rhodesia, which did not preclude friendly relations, but necessarily kept them apart.[12]

In practice, Verwoerd's formula of business as usual meant the indefinite survival of Ian Smith's white regime in Rhodesia. It could hardly have done so without South African support. But it would have been difficult for Verwoerd not to have given his support. It was certainly in South Africa's interests to do so. If sanctions succeeded against Rhodesia, would the U.N. not have seen it as a successful trial run for a boycott of the Republic? In any event, support for the white minority regime, however more unpopular it made South Africa with the black states and the rest of the world, was preferable to the instability which would be bound to follow the violent overthrow of Ian Smith and the imposition of "majority rule".

The emotional identification of white South Africans with their "kith and kin" to the north was intense. Strong pressure was put on Verwoerd to give legal recognition to Rhodesia as an independent state, which he consistently refused to do, although in practice he treated it as such. It was a feeling which Verwoerd recognised, but could not entirely welcome, repugnant as he found the search for cheap popularity. However, careful as he was to explain his policy in terms of tough-minded self-interest, he could not have been immune to such sentiments himself. It must have been a consideration of some weight in his decision not to join the international boycott of Rhodesia.

Verwoerd's studied "neutrality" was astutely maintained. British attempts to persuade him to join the boycott always failed. But it had to be accepted that South Africa's role as sanctions-breaker and *de facto* upholder of U.D.I. did not do the policy of winning friends in Africa any good. The Republic's image of diehard adherence to white rule was sharply accentuated. Still, in the final analysis, this was not of truly vital importance to South Africa's security. What mattered was its ability to fight – and this was formidable. Under Verwoerd defence spending absorbed a steadily rising share of the Government's budget. From 1959/60 to 1966/67 it grew from 7 per cent of the total to 17 per cent. The armed forces were enlarged and military training for all became compulsory. The latest military hardware was purchased from abroad, while in 1964 Verwoerd announced that South Africa would establish its own aircraft industry.

The enemy was actually not too readily identifiable. "International Communism" was usually seen as the great threat, and the posturing of the O.A.U. helped to accentuate white feelings of vulnerability. But it was not easy to imagine just how any onslaught would take place. The military build-up was an insurance policy for the future. Even if the threat from outside was not immediate, it was more likely to grow than to recede. For those who had ideas about liberating the wretched of the South African earth it would be a powerful deterrent. Within the Republic it furthered the mood of optimism and confidence which accompanied the economic boom. Ultimately, it symbolised the will of South Africa's whites to survive, no matter what the cost. As Verwoerd expressed this absolute determination: "We will fight with our economic power against boycotts and with our sons and daughters if there are threats of violence. I give this assurance because for us it is the life or suicide of a nation."[13]

As conductor of foreign policy Verwoerd displayed exceptional abilities. His supreme aim was the same as at home: the preservation of the white man's position in South Africa. In principle he was as little prepared to make concessions in his dealing with the outside world as in the enforcement of apartheid in the Republic itself. The safety of the white man was never negotiable. Large countries like America and Britain, he believed, could make concessions without endangering their existence; South Africa as a small nation could not: "The greater the pressure on us to make concessions, the more emphatic we must be in refusing to do so."[14] Nevertheless, in his conduct of foreign policy he showed a flexibility absent from his handling of internal affairs. Other countries could not be treated with the strong-arm methods reserved for dissidents within South Africa. He had to tread more warily, and did. He had an excellent sense of timing. He knew when to be conciliatory, as in his invitations to Hammarskjöld and to the U.N. Committee on South West Africa. He knew when to accept the inevitable, as in his admission that the Protectorates could no longer be incorporated. Verwoerd's manoeuvering on the international stage was informed by a world view which assured him that eventually apartheid, once proved successful, would be acceptable to the rest of the world, or at least to the West. He could not have been more wrong, but it does not detract from his skill in the conduct of foreign policy. This skill, underpinned by the most powerful economy in Africa, closely linked with those of the West, and formidable armed forces, ensured that in Verwoerd's time there was no serious threat to white supremacy from beyond South Africa's borders.

14 Apotheosis

In 1966 Verwoerd was at the height of his fame. In March he had led the National Party to its greatest ever electoral victory. It won 126 seats out of 166, increasing its share of the vote from the 53.5 per cent of 1961 to 58.6 per cent. For the first time the Nationalists had gained the support of a significant number of English-speaking voters. Verwoerd's attempt to build a broader white nationalism was clearly beginning to bear fruit, however hostile many Nationalists still were to the dilution of cherished and exclusive Afrikaner values and however suspicious many English-speaking still were of Nationalist attitudes and policies.

The Republic was at peace. The prerequisites for a healthy investment climate had returned. Unrest had been suppressed; stability had been restored. The previous year there had been a net capital inflow of R235 million. The economy was buoyant; entrepreneurs throughout the country were being carried away by their exuberant animal spirits. The recovery from Sharpeville had been quite remarkable. The Government's contribution to the revival had been crucial but indirect, through the restoration of political order, irrespective of the cost in human liberty. Inevitably, it redounded to its benefit and, above all, to that of Verwoerd who, more than any other man, was seen as responsible for the return of good times.

He completely dominated his party and his cabinet. No Afrikaner leader in this century had enjoyed such an unchallenged ascendancy among his own people and among the English-speaking. When on 18 July the International Court ruled that it could not pronounce on the South West Africa dispute, his prestige soared to new heights. The decision had little to do with any action of his; it had been taken by a mere majority of one, but somehow it seemed to South Africa's whites as if it had been engineered by Verwoerd himself.

He was one prophet who was honoured in his own country and in his own lifetime. The largest man-made lake in the country was named after him; Stellenbosch University, where he had studied and taught, gave its new Social Science block Verwoerd's name. There were many Hendrik

Verwoerd schools and streets all over the Republic. After the attempt on his life in 1960 some of his worshippers founded a Hendrik Verwoerd Trust Fund. The Trust created a Hendrik Verwoerd Award, consisting of R10,000 and a gold medal, to be given annually to a white South African who had performed important services to the nation. In 1966, the year of the fifth anniversary of the Republic, Verwoerd himself was regarded as the worthiest recipient of the prize; the money was immediately returned by him for the establishment of a scholarship for advanced medical research. Even in a country known for its addiction to "strong leaders", the Verwoerd personality cult seemed to know few limits. Was he not the man who had brought the republic and taken South Africa through its time of troubles to a new era of boundless hope and optimism?

He showed no sign of mellowing with success. The previous year he had gone out of his way to affront the United States in a series of embarrassing and unpleasant incidents. There had been the episode of the American aircraft carrier, *Independence*, which was only given permission to refuel at Cape Town on condition that blacks were not included in the aircrews which could land on local military airfields. The *Independence* did refuel – but in mid-ocean, and at considerable expense to the American Navy, for it was of course unthinkable that such a demand could be complied with. Then there were the multiracial functions given by the American embassy which were boycotted by members of the South African Government, while black scientists were refused permission to man American satellite tracking stations in South Africa. Verwoerd was prepared to be flexible in his relations with foreign states, within limits; those limits were reached when it concerned exemptions from official race policy within the Republic itself. This was "integration" and the familiar thin end of the wedge; Verwoerd was prepared to affront even the United States in his passion to avert evils such as these.

Probably the most conspicuous example of the unchanging Verwoerd hard line came late in 1965, when his intervention brought an end, as long as he was in power, to the traditional rugby tours between South Africa and New Zealand. In the past New Zealand touring sides in South Africa had, in deference to white prejudices, never included Maori players. By now there was widespread resistance in New Zealand to such a tame acceptance of racist attitudes. It had become generally agreed that only a fully representative All Black side would ever be allowed to tour South Africa again. From South Africa the early indications were favourable till Verwoerd spoke. Addressing a Nationalist meeting at the appropriately named Loskop Dam in the Transvaal, his attitude was one of total intransigence. This too was integration and could never be permitted. South Africans overseas, he said, respected the customs of others and expected them to respect theirs when visiting the Republic. It mattered little to Verwoerd that rugby was the national sport of the Afrikaner, or that his rejection came at the worst possible time, when a Springbok side was touring New Zealand. National survival was more important than sport and that was simply that.

But the most absurd instance of this amazing stubbornness over trifles came when Verwoerd had only a few weeks of life remaining to him. He had been invited in August 1966 to a private showing of the film version of *Othello*, with Laurence Olivier in the leading role. No one, including Verwoerd, disputed the excellence of the acting, but when the screening was over Verwoerd immediately expressed his "outspoken" opposition to the film being shown to South African audiences; in the racial set-up of the Republic, its showing was unthinkable.[1] And that, too, was that. Like All Black touring sides with Maoris in them, Olivier's *Othello* had to wait till after Verwoerd's death before South Africans could savour its subversive potential.

His cabinet colleague, Ben Schoeman, has rightly observed that colour was Verwoerd's Achilles heel. Throughout his premiership he had rigidly insisted that all professional associations be segregated on a racial basis, even when the limited number of non-whites in certain professions had made this plainly impractical. "Verwoerd, with all his exceptional ability, was in many respects unbelievably shortsighted, especially when issues of race were concerned."[2]

Of course, Verwoerd could not change. He was a maker of systems; his system was that of racial separation as the pervasive feature of the ordering of human relations in South Africa. Any departure from that system, however trivial, would ineluctably endanger the system as a whole. To him there was no such thing as "small apartheid", the term commonly used by the Opposition to describe those aspects of discrimination which it thought could easily be dispensed with. In the Verwoerdian system the exclusion of Maoris from All Black touring teams in South Africa was as important to white survival as the creation of politically separate states for blacks. "Flexibility" on vital issues such as these he despised, regarding it as a mere synonym for opportunism. Dogma, and consistency in adhering to it, were not to him the unfortunate ideological encumbrances which more pragmatic politicians are so eager to jettison; they gave purpose and direction to Verwoerd's whole political career. This was why he could in 1959 propose a race policy which was in fact a radical break with the past. Verwoerd did not see it as such: was it not simply a logical extension of the principle of racial separation? And this was also why Laurence Olivier's blackened face on South African screens could never be tolerated. Verwoerd, in short, brought to politics the mentality of a natural ideologue. In the final analysis, what he chose to regard as principles was of infinitely more importance to him than human beings.

It seems unlikely therefore that, when Parliament met in Cape Town on 29 July after the general election, any drastic changes in policy or relaxation of discrimination could be expected. Certainly, Verwoerd disclosed no such intentions, or indeed anything at all. He seemed to be resting on his laurels. For the first time since he became Prime Minister, he did not participate in the no-confidence debate. During the first five weeks he spoke only twice, short, formal speeches in which he moved motions of condolence on the death of an M.P. and of a former Speaker. But on 6 September he was due to speak. The Prime Minister's budget vote was up for discussion and Verwoerd was expected to make a major policy speech. A few days before he had met Chief Leabua Jonathan, Prime Minister of the soon to be independent Lesotho. It had been a historic meeting, for it was the first time a South African Prime Minister had met the leader of a black state in South Africa itself. It had also been, to all appearances, an amicable meeting, and Verwoerd was expected to report to the House of Assembly on their discussions. He was also expected to talk about South Africa's international position and the future of the Coloureds in South African society.

Verwoerd and his wife had flown down from the Transvaal early that morning. The previous day had been a public holiday, which he had spent with members of his family at Stokkiesdraai, his farm on the Vaal River. Here he had gone for long walks and showed all that vigour which had been so typical of him all his life. He was indeed looking remarkably fit, ready still for years of public life. In Cape Town he addressed the Nationalist caucus in the morning. Both leader and followers were in a buoyant mood, confident that they were at the beginning of a new era which would see the triumphant implementation of the Government's scheme of race relations for all South Africans.

The public galleries of the House of Assembly were packed after lunchtime, reflecting the accuracy of *The Cape Argus*'s headline the previous day: Verwoerd – Keen Interest. He entered the House at about 2.15 p.m., as the bells were ringing to summon M.Ps for the afternoon's debate. He looked cheerful and confident and sat down in the Prime

Minister's seat to the right of the Speaker. The House was still filling up and members taking their seats when a uniformed Parliamentary messenger entered, walking in a great hurry. At first he went to the right, in the direction of the Opposition benches, but then suddenly changed course and moved towards Verwoerd. The messenger entered the aisle next to Verwoerd's seat, swiftly pulled out a knife and threw himself upon the Prime Minister. In quick succession he stabbed his victim four times in the neck and the chest. At first Verwoerd smiled, as if thinking that the messenger had stumbled upon him by accident, and trying to indicate by his smile that it did not matter. Then his expression changed as he saw the blood which had suddenly appeared on his chest. He pulled the lapels of his jacket together, perhaps to shut out the sight. But it was already far too late for anything to be done. He was virtually a dead man as he gave a sigh and slumped forward in his seat.

By then members had thrown themselves on Verwoerd's assailant who fought back with immense strength, slashing away with his knife. Eventually he was overpowered and then taken away by the police who had appeared on the scene. He had seemed half-unconscious when pinned down on the floor, but had by now regained his senses and when dragged out was shouting, "Where's that bastard? I'll get that bastard!"

M.Ps who were medical doctors tried to restore Verwoerd, but it was quite futile. Five minutes after the attack his heart had stopped beating, but to all intents and purposes he had been dead one minute after the attack. Meanwhile Mrs. Verwoerd had arrived in the gallery of the House for the afternoon's debate, in the company of Mrs. Vorster, wife of the Minister of Justice. It was after the attack and she only saw the members bending over her husband. At once she realised that something was wrong and, at Mrs. Vorster's urging, left the gallery. When she heard what had happened she went into the House and sat behind her husband's desk. It was suggested to her that it would probably be better if she left, upon which she went to Verwoerd, who was still lying there, and kissed his forehead. She was then escorted away. Less than an hour later, at 3.05 p.m., it was announced that Verwoerd had been dead on arrival at the hospital. Two days later he would have been 65 years old.

Verwoerd's murderer was a man named Demetrio Tsafendas, who turned out to be a lunatic, acting entirely on his own. He had been born in Lourenço Marques in 1918, the illegitimate son of a Greek father and a half-breed Portuguese-African mother. He had attended a school for white children in Middelburg in the Transvaal for some years before returning to Mozambique. As youth and adult he had led a wandering and unstable existence. He came to South Africa in 1965, moving from one job to another. It later appeared that Tsafendas had only been allowed into South Africa by the oversight of some minor official, as he was on the list of prohibited entrants to the country; it was a similar oversight which led to the delay in the execution of an order for his deportation. During this delay Tsafendas obtained his final job as temporary messenger in Parliament. By a supreme irony the appointment was largely due to the colour bar. Only whites can be messengers in Parliament, however menial it may be as an occupation. The predictable result has been frequent difficulty in finding suitable applicants for such posts. Tsafendas would have been classified as Coloured had he been born in South Africa. As it was, he managed to pass as white, although of that swarthy variety popularly associated in South Africa with persons of Portuguese descent. Being "white" therefore he was given a temporary job as Parliamentary messenger, in spite of the severe misgiving of his employers from the very beginning.

At his trial Tsafendas was found mentally disordered and was committed to jail for as long as it pleased the State President. The court had indeed little choice. His record revealed that he had been in eight mental institutions in four different countries. As explanation for his attack on Verwoerd, Tsafendas could only blame a huge tapeworm within his body, which tormented him and compelled him to act as he did.

Verwoerd was buried on 10 September 1966. The State funeral service in the amphitheatre of the Union Buildings in Pretoria was attended by a quarter of a million people. Afterwards he was laid to rest in Heroes' Acre, the cemetery in the centre of Pretoria where some of the Afrikaners' most outstanding leaders are buried.

In the subsequent struggle for power it soon became apparent that only one man could become Prime Minister. In spite of being even more junior in the cabinet than Verwoerd had been when he was elected in 1958, B.J. Vorster was unanimously chosen by the Nationalist caucus as its new leader, and thus also as Prime Minister of the Republic of South Africa. Vorster owed his victory to his fearsome reputation as Minister of Justice; one "strong man" had truly succeeded another. He made a point of stressing the unbroken chain of continuity after he had been elected: "My role is to walk further along the road set by Hendrik Verwoerd."

Had he been alive today Verwoerd would have reacted violently, rejecting totally any claims as to Vorster's worthiness as his successor, for the latter managed to scrap some of the more absurd manifestations of apartheid – without any of the feared consequences to white supremacy. Multiracial New Zealand rugby teams have toured South

Africa, *Othello* has been shown on the screens of the Republic. Vorster's accession was the beginning of a more flexible and pragmatic age. But in a more basic sense he did not deviate from the course of Verwoerd at all, or indeed that of Malan and Strijdom. His "concessions" did not shake the structure of white supremacy in the slightest. When Vorster left office in 1978, South Africa was just as much under the control of the white man, or rather of the Afrikaner, as it had ever been before. In this absolutely crucial respect Vorster had made no idle promise when he proclaimed his determination "to walk further along the road set by Hendrik Verwoerd".

References

Introduction to the 2016 edition

1   Gerrit Olivier, *Praat met die ANC* (Taurus, Emmarentia, 1980), p. 26.
2   Biographical information taken from G.D. Scholtz, *Dr Hendrik Frensch Verwoerd: 1901–1966* (Perskor, Johannesburg, 1974, two vols), vol. 1, pp. 1–15.
3   Piet Meiring, *Inside Information* (Howard Timmins, Cape Town, 1973), p. 29.
4   Scholtz, *op. cit.*, p. 19.
5   *The Report of the Carnegie Commission: The Poor White Problem in South Africa* (Pro Ecclesia Drukkery, Stellenbosch, 1932), paras 9, 68.
6   Quoted in Hermann Giliomee: *The Afrikaners: Biography of a People* (Tafelberg Publishers, Cape Town, 2003), p. 351.
7   Scholtz, *op. cit.*, p. 35.
8   For details of Verwoerd's appointment, see *Piet Meiring, Die Transvaler: 50 jaar* (Perskor, Johannesburg, 1987), pp. 84–6.
9   Meiring, *Die Transvaler*, p. 9–10.
10 Dioné Prinsloo, *Die Johannesburg-Periode in Dr HF Verwoerd se Loopbaan* (unpublished PhD thesis, Rand Afrikaans University, 1979), p. 53.
11 For details see Michael Roberts and A.E.G. Trollip, *The South African Opposition 1939–1945* (Longmans, London, 1947).
12 George Cloete Visser, *OB: Traitors or Patriots?* (Macmillan South Africa, Johannesburg, 1976), pp. 146–7.
13 Prinsloo, *op. cit.*, p. 238.
14 Scholtz, *op. cit.*, p. 124.
15 *Ibid*, p. 187.
16 E.L.P. Stals, *Die Geskiedenis van die Afrikaner Broederbond: 1918–1994* (Afrikanerbond, Johannesburg, 1998).
17 E.G. Malherbe, *Education in South Africa* (Juta, Cape Town, 1977), volume II: 1923–75, p. 674.
18 Stals, *op. cit.*, p. 116.
19 Ben Schoeman, *My Lewe in die Politiek* (Perskor, Johannesburg, 1978).
20 P.J. Meyer, *Nog nie ver genoeg nie* (Perskor, Johannesburg, 1984).
21 Prinsloo, *op. cit.*, pp. 201–2.
22 O. Geyser (ed.), *Dr HF Verwoerd die Republikein* (Tafelberg, Cape Town, 1972), p. 88.
23 Prinsloo, *op. cit.*, p. 308.
24 *Ibid*, pp. 456, 516–7.
25 Richard Steyn, *Jan Smuts: Unafraid of Greatness* (Jonathan Ball, Cape Town, 2015), p. 245.
26 Scholtz, *op. cit.*, p. 178.
27 For details see Schoeman, *op. cit.*, pp. 134–40.
28 *Ibid*, pp. 147–8.
29 Beaumont M. Schoeman, *Van Malan tot Verwoerd* (Human & Rousseau, Cape Town, 1973), pp. 35–6.

30   Ben Schoeman, *op. cit.*, p.178.

31   Beaumont Schoeman, *op. cit.*, pp. 44–5.

32   See the bibliography in W.D. Hammond-Tooke, *Imperfect Interpreters: South Africa's Anthropologists 1920–1990* (Witwatersrand University Press, Johannesburg, 1997), p. 221.

33   T. Dunbar Moodie, *The Rise of Afrikanerdom: power, apartheid, and the Afrikaner civil religion* (University of California Press, Berkeley, 1975), p. 273.

34   Fred Barnard, *13 Jaar in die skadu van Dr H.F. Verwoerd* (Voortrekkerpers, Johannesburg, 1967), p. 49.

35   A.N. Pelzer (ed.), *Verwoerd Speaks: Speeches 1948–1966* (APB Publishers, Johannesburg, 1966), p. 40.

36   *Native Laws Commission (Fagan) 1946–1948* (Government Printer, Pretoria, 1948), pp. 6, 9.

37   Pelzer, *op. cit.*, pp. 26, 40.

38   Robert Menzies, *Afternoon Light: some memories of men and events* (Cassell, London, 1967), p. 203.

39   For elaboration of these points see David Welsh, *The Rise and Fall of Apartheid* (Jonathan Ball, Cape Town, 2009), pp. 58–63.

40   Ben Schoeman, *op. cit.*, p. 198–9.

41   *Ibid*, p. 224.

42   *Ibid*, p. 198.

43   *Ibid*, p. 241.

44   For a balanced account of Verwoerd's educational aims – and his overall policy – see Hermann Giliomee, *The Last Afrikaner Leaders: a supreme test of power* (Tafelberg, Cape Town, 2012), pp. 68–73.

45   Welsh, *op. cit.*, pp. 59–60.

46   Giliomee, *The Last Afrikaner Leaders*, pp. 58–9.

47   Ebbe Dommisse, *Anton Rupert: a biography* (Tafelberg, Cape Town, 2005), p. 159.

48   Schalk Pienaar, *Getuie van groot tye* (Tafelberg, Cape Town, 1979), p. 73.

49   Ben Schoeman, *op. cit.*, p. 231.

50   Meiring, *Ons Eerste Ses Premiers* (Tafelberg, Cape Town, 1972), p. 118.

51   Ben Schoeman, *op. cit.*, pp. 239–40.

52   Anton Bekker, *Eben Dönges: Balansstaat* (San Press, Stellenbosch, 2005), p. 133.

53   Ben Schoeman, *op. cit.*, p. 244.

54   Bekker, *op. cit.*, p. 138.

55   Japie Basson, *Politieke Kaarte Op die Tafel* (Politika Kaapstad, Cape Town, 2006), p. 106.

56   Margaret Ballinger, *From Union to Apartheid: a trek to isolation* (Juta, Cape Town, 1969), p. 385.

57   Pelzer, *op. cit.*, p. 283.

58   Helen Suzman, *In No Uncertain Terms* (Jonathan Ball, Johannesburg, 1993), p. 65.

59   Johan Mills, 'Meesterbouer eerder as argitek', in Wilhelm J. Verwoerd (ed.), *Verwoerd: So Onthou Ons Hom* (Protea, Pretoria, 2001), p. 161.

60   Quoted in W.H. Vatcher, Jr., *White Laager: the rise of Afrikaner Nationalism* (Pall Mall Press, London, 1965), p. 110.

61   Welsh, *op. cit.*, pp. 73–4.

62   Pelzer, *op. cit.*, p. 375.

63   Basson, *op. cit.*, p. 106.

64 W.A. Dyason, "Meer as 'n werkgewer", in Wilhelm J. Verwoerd, *op. cit.*, p. 230.

65 A.H. Lückhoff, *Cottesloe* (Tafelberg, Cape Town, 1978).

66 Pierre Hugo, "A Journey Away from Apartheid", in Pierre Hugo (ed.), *South African Perspectives: essays in honour of Nic Olivier* (Sigma Press, Pretoria, 1989), p. 22.

67 *Ibid*, pp. 24–25.

68 J.C. Steyn, *Penvegter: Piet Cillie van Die Burger* (Tafelberg, Cape Town, 2002), pp. 144–8.

69 Pienaar, *op. cit.*, pp. 61–2.

70 Alex Mouton, *Voorloper: Die Lewe van Schalk Pienaar* (Tafelberg, Cape Town, 2002), p. 50.

71 *Ibid*, p.62.

72 See André du Toit, *Die Sondes van die Vaders* (Rubicon, Cape Town, 1982).

73 See J.C. Steyn, *Van Wyk Louw: 'n Lewensverhaal* (Tafelberg, Cape Town, 1998), two vols, vol. 2, pp. 1034–57.

74 Pelzer, *op. cit.*, p. 723.

75 For this and the following discussion see H.F. Verwoerd, "Herinneringe op die Republikeinse pad", in F.A. van Jaarsveld and G.D. Scholtz (eds), *Die Republiek van Suid-Afrika: Agtergrond, Onstaan en Toekoms* (Voortrekker Press, Johannesburg, 1966).

76 Quoted in P.J. Meyer, *Nog nie ver genoeg nie* (Perskor, Johannesburg, 1984), pp. 73–4.

77 Ben Schoeman, *op. cit.*, pp. 250, 266.

78 Pelzer, *op. cit.*, p. 407.

79 *Ibid*, p. 411.

80 J.J.J. Scholtz, *Die Moord op Dr Verwoerd* (Nasionale Boekhandel, Cape Town, 1967).

81 Dommisse, *op. cit.*, p. 169.

82 Mouton, *op. cit.*, p. 66.

83 Pienaar, *op. cit.*, p. 65.

84 *Report of the Commission on Native Education 1949–1951* (UG 53/1951, Government Printer, Pretoria), para. 60.

85 Giliomee, *The Last Afrikaner Leaders*, p. 26.

86 Gilles van der Walt, "Verwoerd, Die Hervormer:, in Wilhelm J. Verwoerd (ed.), *op. cit.*, p. 85.

87 *Ibid*, p. 53.

88 Milton Shain, *The Roots of Antisemitism in South Africa* (University Press of Virginia, Charlottesville, 1994), p. 147.

89 Prinsloo, *op. cit.*, p. 17.

90 Scholtz, *op. cit.*, p. 117.

91 Prinsloo, *op. cit.*, p. 560.

92 *Ibid*, p. 513.

Other sources consulted

D.P. Botha, *Die Opkoms van Ons Derde Stand* (Human & Rousseau, Cape Town, 1960).

H.F. Verwoerd, *Die Afstomping van Gemoedsaandoeninge* (Annale van die Uniwersiteit van Stellenbosch, December 1925).

Chapter 1

1. P. Meiring, *Ons Eerste Ses Premiers* (Cape Town, 1972), p. 125.
2. E. Kedourie, *Nationalism* (London, 1960), p. 80.
3. G.D. Scholtz, *Dr. Hendrik Frensch Verwoerd,1901–60*, 2 vols., (Johannesburg, 1974), vol. 1, p. 12.
4. *Ibid.*, p. 28.
5. *Report of the Carnegie Commission: The Poor White Problem in South Africa* (Stellenbosch, 1932), vol. 1, p. xx.
6. E. Theron, *H.F. Verwoerd as Welsynsbeplanner* (Stellenbosch, 1970), p. 83.
7. *Ibid.*
8. *Ibid.*, pp. 83–4.
9. *Ibid.*, pp. 84–5.
10. Quoted by G.D. Scholtz, vol. 1, p. 38.
11. *Ibid.*, p. 39.
12. *Die Burger*, 4 September 1936.
13. *Die Burger*, 5 November 1936.
14. *Die Burger*, 2 November 1936.
15. *Die Transvaler*, 3 November 1937.
16. Meiring, p. 119.
17. J.M. Keynes, *The Economic Consequences of the Peace* (London, 1920), pp. 29–30.

Chapter 2

1. N.M. Stultz, *Afrikaner Politics in South Africa, 1934–48* (California, 1974), p. 12.
2. M. Roberts and A.E.G. Trollip, *The South African Opposition, 1939–45* (Cape Town, 1947), p. 11.
3. Quoted by Roberts and Trollip, p. 11.
4. Quoted by D. Worrall in D. Worrall (ed.), *South African Government and Politics* (Pretoria, 1975), p. 207.
5. G.D. Scholtz, vol. 1, pp. 180–81.
6. *Die Transvaler*, 10 February 1943.
7. F.A. van Jaarsveld and G.D. Scholtz (eds.), *Die Republiek van Suid-Afrika* (Johannesburg, 1965), p. 5.
8. *Die Burger*, 3 September 1958.
9. Meiring, p. 120.
10. *Die Burger*, 3 September 1958.
11. Stultz, pp. 57–8.
12. *Die Transvaler*, 20 May 1938.
13. *House of Assembly Debates*, 958, col. 4066.
14. *Die Transvaler*, 23 January 1942.
15. *Ibid.*
16. Meiring, p. 122.
17. *Die Transvaler*, 12 May 1941.
18. *Die Transvaler*, 3 November 1937.
19. *The Star*, 31 October 1941.
20. *The Star*, 14 July 1943.
21. G.D. Scholtz, vol. 1, p. 123.
22. Meiring, p. 124.
23. *Ibid.*, p. 125.

24. *Ibid.*, p. 160.
25. *Ibid.*, p. 161.
26. *Die Transvaler*, 3 March 1943.
27. *Ibid.*, p. 157.
28. *Ibid.*, p. 156.
29. *Die Transvaler*, 12 March 1945.
30. *Die Transvaler*, 13 August 1946.
31. *Die Transvaler*, 10 September 1943.
32. *Die Transvaler*, 22 March 1947.
33. Roberts and Trollip, p. 215.

Chapter 3
1.   Quoted by M. Ballinger, *From Union to Apartheid* (Cape Town, 1969), p. 233.
2.   *Senate Debates* 1948, col. 242.
3.   *Ibid*, cols. 243–4.
4.   *Ibid*, cols. 245–6.
5.   *Ibid*, col. 246.
6.   *Ibid*, col. 249.
7.   *Ibid*, cols. 250–2.
8.   *Ibid*, col. 255.
9.   A.N. Pelzer (ed.), *Verwoerd Speaks* (Johannesburg, 1968), p. 31.
10. C.W. de Kiewiet, *A History of South Africa, Social and Economic* (OUP, 1941), p. 79.
11. W.K. Hancock, *Smuts: The Fields of Force, 1919–1950* (Cambridge, 1968), pp. 146–47.
12. Quoted by N.J Rhoodie, *Apartheid and Racial Partnership in Southern Africa* (Pretoria/Cape Town, 1969), p. 53.
13. Quoted by Rhoodie, pp. 54–5.
14. *Senate Debates*, 1948, col. 232.
15. *Ibid.*, col. 242.
16. Quoted by D.W. Krüger, *The Making of a Nation* (Johannesburg, 1969), p. 243.
17. F. Barnard, *13 Years with Dr. H.F. Verwoerd* (Johannesburg, 1967), p. 17.
18. Personal communication from Eiselen, July 1972.
19. W.M.M. Eiselen, *Die Narurellevraagstuk* (Cape Town, 1929), p. 5.
20. *Ibid.*, p. 10.
21. W.M.M. Eiselen, "Harmonious Multi-Community Development", *Optima*, March 1959, p. 14.
22. Pelzer, p. 40.
23. *House of Assembly Debates*, 1956, col. 6969.
24. G.D. Scholtz, vol. 1, p. 213.
25. *Senate Debates*, 1948, col. 246.
26. Quoted by Ballinger, p. 196.
27. G.D. Scholtz, vol.1, p. 215.
28. Quoted by Ballinger, p. 209.
29. *Ibid.*, p. 210.
30. *House of Assembly Debates*, 1952, col. 7816.
31. *Ibid.*, col. 9811.
32. Ballinger, p. 344.

33. *House of Assembly Debates*, 1951, col. 9807 *et seq.*
34. Quoted by Eiselen, *Optima*, March 1959, p. 6.
35. U.G. 28/1948, p. 19.
36. *House of Assembly Debates*, 1958, col. 4066.
37. *House of Assembly Debates*, 1952, col. 551.
38. *House of Assembly Debates*, 1952, cols. 587–98.
39. *Senate Debates*, 1952, col. 3611.
40. G.D. Scholtz, vol. 1, p. 258.

Chapter 4
1. U.G.61/1955 (hereafter Tomlinson), p. xviii.
2. *Ibid.*, p. 194.
3. *Ibid.*, p. 49.
4. T. Bell, *Industrial Decentralisation in South Africa* (OUP, 1973) p. 12.
5. Tomlinson, p. 48.
6. Bell, p. l6.
7. Tomlinson, p. 86.
8. *Ibid.*, p. 99.
9. Bell, pp. 13–4
10. Tomlinson, p. 114.
11. *Ibid.*, p. 184.
12. *Ibid.*, p. 49.
13. *Ibid.*, pp. 140–41.
14. *Ibid.*, p. 141.
15. Bell, p. 7.
16. Tomlinson, p. 138.
17. *Ibid.*, p. 184.
18. W.P.F/1956, p. 3.
19. Ballinger, p. 324.
20. Pelzer, p. 92.
21. *Ibid.*, pp. 99–100.
22. *House of Assembly Debates*, 1956, cols. 5306–7.
23. Personal communication.
24. *House of Assembly Debates*, 1956, cols. 5307–8.
25. *Ibid.*, col. 5300.
26. Tomlinson, p. 192.
27. Pelzer, p. 37.
28. *House of Assembly Debates*, 1956, cols. 5308–9.
29. J.P. Nieuwenhuyzen, "Prospects and Issues in the Development of the Reserves", *South African Journal of Economics*, June 1964, p. 144.
30. *House of Assembly Debates*, 1956, col. 5311.
31. *House of Assembly Debates*, 1958, col. 4164
32. *Ibid.*
33. *House of Assembly Debates*, 1956, cols. 5311–2.
34. *Senate Debates*, 1951, col. 2894.
35. *Senate Debates*, 1952, col. 3588.
36. Quoted by M. Horrell, *A Decade of Bantu Education* (Johannesburg, 1964), p. 4.
37. *House of Assembly Debates*, 1953, col. 2894.

38. *Senate Debates*, 1954, col. 2599.
39. *Ibid.*, col. 2611.
40. A. Hepple, *Verwoerd* (Penguin, 1967), pp. 127–28.
41. E. Hoffer, *The True Believer* (New York, 1951), pp. 27–8.

Chapter 5
1. T.P.1/1922.
2. Rhoodie, p. 96.
3. *Ibid.*, p. 99.
4. *Ibid.*, p. 102.
5. Pelzer, p. 42.
6. *Ibid.*, pp. 46–7.
7. *Ibid.*, p. 48.
8. Cited by Bell, p. 18.
9. *Ibid.*
10. J. Robertson, *Liberalism in South Africa, 1948–1963* (OUP, 1971), pp. 148–9.
11. *House of Assembly Debates*, 1953, col. 202.
12. E. Munger, *Afrikaner and African Nationalism* (OUP, 1967), p. 89.

Chapter 6
1. *Cape Times*, 17 September 1958.
2. Quoted by J. Botha, *Verwoerd is Dead* (Cape Town, 1967), p. 22.
3. *Ibid.*
4. T.R.H. Davenport, *South Africa: A Modern History* (Johannesburg, 1977), p. 273.
5. Quoted by Barnard, p. 46.
6. *Ibid.* pp. 46–7.
7. Quoted by Botha, p. 28.
8. *Ibid.* p. 30.
9. Ben Schoeman, *My Lewe in die Politiek* (Johannesburg, 1978), p. 231.
10. *Die Transvaler*, 28 October 1958.
11. Pelzer, p. 161.
12. *Die Transvaler*, 7 November 1958.
13. *Cape Times*, 2 September 1958.
14. *Dagbreek en Sondagnuus*, 3 September 1958.
15. *Die Burger*, 3 September 1958.
16. *House of Assembly Debates*, 1958, col. 4172.
17. Botha, p. 44.
18. Barnard, p. 25.
19. Personal communication.
20. Quoted by Botha, p. 122.
21. D. and J. de Villiers, *Paul Sauer* (Cape Town, 1977), p. 140.
22. Ben Schoeman, pp. 241, 245–47.
23. Munger, p. 59.
24. J. Barber, *South Africa's Foreign Policy, 1945–70* (OUP, 1973), p. 131.

Chapter 7
1. Eiselen, *Optima*, March 1959, p. 8.
2. *House of Assembly Debates*, 1959, col. 62.

3. *Ibid.*, cols. 63–4.
4. *Ibid.*, col. 6221.
5. *Ibid.*, col. 6241.
6. *Ibid.*, col. 62.
7. *House of Assembly Debates*, 1962, col. 3940.
8. *House of Assembly Debates*, 1963, cols. 226–27.
9. Quoted by Robertson, p. 189.
10. B.M. Schoeman, *Van Malan tot Verwoerd* (Cape Town, 1973), p. 228.
11. Munger, p. 80.
12. *House of Assembly. Debates*, 1959, col. 3490 *et seq.*

Chapter 8
1. G.D. Scholtz, vol. 2, p. 60.
2. Van Jaarsveld and Scholtz, p. 6.
3. B.M. Schoeman, pp. 185–86.
4. *Ibid.*, p. 186.
5. G.D Scholtz, vol. 2, p. 61.
6. Pelzer, p. 323.
7. Van Jaarsveld and Scholtz, p. 6.
8. *House of Assembly Debates*, 1960, cols. 109–113.
9. *The Cape Argus*, 10 March 1960.
10. *Cape Times*, 3 February 1960.
11. *Idem.*
12. *Cape Times*, 12 February 1960.
13. Pelzer, p. 367.

Chapter 9
1. *House of Assembly Debates*, 1960, col. 3759.
2. *Ibid.*, col. 3857 *et seq.*
3. *Cape Times*, 23 March 1960.
4. *House of Assembly Debates*, 1960, col. 4360 *et seq.*
5. Quoted by G.D. Scholtz, vol. 2, p. 153.
6. B.M. Schoeman, pp. 201–02.
7. Pelzer, p. 375.
8. *Die Burger*, 20 April 1960.
9. *House of Assembly Debates*, 1960, col. 8337 *et seq.*
10. pp. 27–28
11. Hoffer, p. 29.
12. Barber, p. l24.

Chapter 10
1. Quoted by G.D. Scholtz, vol. 2, p. 153.
2. Personal communication.
3. Ben Schoeman, p. 288.
4. Botha, p. 67.
5. J.J.J. Scholtz, *Die Moord op Dr. Verwoerd* (Cape Town, 1967), p. 81.
6. *Die Burger*, 11 April 1960.
7. Pelzer, p. 397.

8. *Ibid.*, p. 395.
9. *Cape Times*, 1 June 1960.
10. *Die Burger*, 16 March 1960.
11. *House of Assembly Debates*, 1960, col. 3769.
12. Pelzer, p. 408.
13. 9 September 1960.
14. 10 September 1960.
15. Quoted by Hepple, p. 178.
16. B.M. Schoeman, p. 196.
17. Pelzer, pp. 410–12.
18. *Ibid.*, p. 419.
19. *Sunday Times*, 9 October 1960.
20. Pelzer, p. 431.
21. Quoted by G.D. Scholtz, vol. 2, p. 107.
22. 16 March 1961.
23. 17 March 1961.
24. *Cape Times*, 22 March 1961.
25. *Cape Times*, 21 March 1961.
26. Pelzer, p. 604.
27. *The Cape Argus*, 12 August 1961.
28. *Cape Times*, 17 August 1961.

Chapter 11
1. D.H. Houghton, *The South African Economy* (OUP, 1967), p. 199.
2. *Cape Times*, 21 September 1961.
3. *House of Assembly Debates*, 1951, col. 3797.
4. Cf., e.g., *House of Assembly Debates*, 1964, col. 68.
5. Munger, p. 67.
6. *Die Burger*, 23 July 1960.
7. *Die Burger*, 24 November 1960.
8. *Die Burger*, 1 December 1960.
9. Quoted by Botha, p. 77.
10. Quoted by G.D. Scholtz, vol. 2, p. 171.
11. *The Cape Argus*, 12 September 1962.
12. P. Harris, "Interest Groups in the South African Political Process", in Worrall, pp. 264–66.
13. Quoted by J. D'Oliveira, *Vorster – the Man* (Johannesburg, 1977), p. 215.
14. *House of Assembly Debates*, 1965, cols. 252–67.
15. M. Horrel, *Survey of Race Relations 1964* (Johannesburg, 1965), pp. 84–5.
16. Quoted by D'Oliveira, p. 135.
17. Quoted by D'Oliveira, p. 147.

Chapter 12
1. *House of Assembly Debates*, 1962, cols. 75–91.
2. G.D. Scholtz, vol. 2, p. 158.
3. Quoted by G.M. Carter *et al.*, *South Africa's Transkei: The Politics of Domestic Colonialism* (London, 1967), p. 186.
4. pp. 111–12.

5. *Senate Debates*, 1964, col. 4691.
6. Cited by S. van der Horst, "The Economic Problems of the Homelands", in N.J. Rhoodie (ed.), *South African Dialogue* (Johannesburg, 1972), p. 186.
7. Bell, p. 212.
8. *Ibid.*, p. 213.
9. *Ibid.*, p. 15.
10. R. Horwitz, *The Political Economy of South Africa* (London, 1967), p. 389.
11. Quoted by Horwitz, p. 389.
12. B.J. Cohen, *The Question of Imperialism* (London, 1974), p. 175.
13. F.A. Johnstone, "White Prosperity and White Supremacy in Africa Today". *African Affairs*, vol. 69, 1970, p. 128.
14. *Ibid.*, p. 140.
15. *Ibid.*, p. 136.

Chapter 13
1. *House of Assembly Debates*, 1962, col. 3761.
2. *The Cape Argus*, 31 August 1963.
3. Cited by Barber, p. 207.
4. *Die Burger*, 26 September 1962.
5. *House of Assembly Debates*, 1964, col. 4901.
6. Quoted by J.E. Spence. "South Africa and the Modern World", in L. Thompson and M. Wilson (eds.) *The Oxford History of South Africa* (OUP, 1971), vol. 2, p. 511.
7. *House of Assembly Debates*, 1962, cols. 3452, 3457.
8. M. Horrel, *Survey of Race Relations 1963* (Johannesburg, 1964), p. 126.
9. Quoted by Spence, p. 501.
10. *House of Assembly Debates*, 1963, col. 4599.
11. *Die Transvaler*, 5 September 1962.
12. *Die Burger*, 2 November 1965.
13. *Die Burger*, 27 April 1964.
14. *Die Burger*, 23 November 1964.

Chapter 14
1. A. Boshoff, *Sekretaresse vir die Verwoerds* (Cape Town, 1974), p. 228.
2. Ben Schoeman, pp. 278, 308.

Selected Index

316

319